Advance praise for

Teaching Green: The Elementary Years

"*Teaching Green: The Elementary Years* brings multiple voices and experiences to our practice as teachers, nature interpreters, museum educators, and youth leaders. It's like sitting down with colleagues to share new approaches, discuss current issues, and reflect on what we do. The wide range of topics and activities, the engaging descriptions, and the wealth of references are what we've come to expect from Green Teacher."

— CATHERINE DUMOUCHEL, Project Coordinator,
Canadian Centre for Biodiversity, Canadian Museum of Nature

"*Teaching Green: The Elementary Years* offers educators a wealth of background information and activities to enhance learning about the environment. For those who are just embarking upon their teaching careers as well as those with decades of experience, this resource provides creative and inspiring tips and techniques to help instill passion for the environment in elementary students."

— KAREN SCHEDLER, Program Manager, Heritage Environmental
Education, Arizona Game and Fish Department

"Wow! (And I don't use exclamations points loosely.) *Teaching Green: The Elementary Years* is like a greatest hits collection from the last ten years of *Green Teacher* magazine. Many of my favorite articles are all here in one place, along with many others that I wish I had seen the first time around. I know this resource will become a highly valued text in my Place-based Education course and I envision it dog-eared and well loved on my shelf a decade from now. It's the handbook that the environmental education movement has been looking for."

— DAVID SOBEL, Director of Teacher Certification Programs,
Antioch New England Graduate School,
and Co-Director of the Center for Place-based Education

Teaching Green
The Elementary Years

Hands-on Learning
in Grades K-5

Edited by Tim Grant and Gail Littlejohn

NEW SOCIETY PUBLISHERS

Cataloging in Publication Data:
A catalog record for this publication is available from the National Library of Canada.

Edited by Tim Grant and Gail Littlejohn

Cover design by Diane McIntosh.

Printed in Canada. First printing April 2005.

Green Teacher magazine acknowledges the support of The Ontario Trillium Foundation, an agency of the Ontario Ministry of Culture.

THE ONTARIO TRILLIUM FOUNDATION / LA FONDATION TRILLIUM DE L'ONTARIO

New Society Publishers acknowledges the support of the Government of Canada through the Book Publishing Industry Development Program (BPIDP) for our publishing activities.

Paperback ISBN: 0-86571-534-3

To order directly from the publishers, please contact:

GREEN TEACHER
95 Robert Street, Toronto, ON M5S 2K5, Canada
P.O. Box 452, Niagara Falls, NY 14304-0452, USA
Toll-free (North America): 1-888-804-1486
Outside North America: 1-416-960-1244
www.greenteacher.com

or

NEW SOCIETY PUBLISHERS
P.O. Box 189, Gabriola Island, BC V0R 1X0, Canada
Toll-free (North America): 1-800-567-6772
Outside North America: 1-250-247-9737
www.newsociety.com

New Society Publishers' mission is to publish books that contribute in fundamental ways to building an ecologically sustainable and just society, and to do so with the least possible impact on the environment, in a manner that models this vision. Green Teacher's mission is to publish resources that help educators to foster young people's appreciation of the natural environment, understanding of the Earth's systems, and desire and ability to apply their knowledge in solving environmental problems. Both organizations are acting on their environmental commitments by phasing out paper supplies from ancient forests worldwide. This book is one step towards ending global deforestation and climate change. It is printed on acid-free paper that is **100% old growth forest-free** (100% post-consumer recycled), processed chlorine free, and printed with vegetable based, low VOC inks.

Table of Contents

Environmental Issues

Building Community

Global Awareness

Imagination and Celebration

Index

Acknowledgments

More than 250 individuals have contributed their time and expertise to the publication of this second "best of *Green Teacher*" book in our *Teaching Green* series. In particular, we thank the dozens of contributing authors who have shared their wide-ranging knowledge, their diverse experience, and their passion for a new model of education. During the past year, all of them have volunteered their time to revise articles they had previously contributed to *Green Teacher* magazine, in most cases updating teaching strategies and activities to reflect current practices and further developing their ideas in response to the comments of reviewers.

We also owe an enormous debt to a group of educators who gave their time to review and critique the proposed contents of the book. Their detailed and thoughtful comments showed us where improvements were needed and helped to guide authors in their revisions. They also suggested many additional topics, some of which we incorporated in order to make the book a more complete and helpful resource. We thank the following reviewers:

AUSTRALIA
Tasmania – Nel Smit

CANADA
Alberta – Robert Hodgins, Julia Millen, Elizabeth Surridge

British Columbia – Marnie Cockburn, Liza Ireland, Teresa Kisilevich, Del Morgan, Laurelei Primeau

Manitoba – Sheila Bates, Natalie Bays, Kara Dennis, Barbara McMillan

New Brunswick – Margo Emrich, Katherine Hildebrand, Julie MacDonald, Rachel Malone, Victoria Mosely, Corinne Snider

Nova Scotia – Sandra Chauvin, David Ferns, Susan Kelley, Marion Leier, Sylvia Moore

Ontario – Velos Christou, Melanie Climenhage, Ian Crawford, Barb Imrie, Richard Johnstone, Diane Lawrence, Liz Lundy, Stana Luxford, David J. Ma, Helen Bajorek MacDonald, Sandee Sharpe, Merebeth Switzer

Québec – Tina Jory

Saskatchewan – Judith Benson

Yukon – Terry Markley, Sarah Tillett

UNITED STATES
Alabama – Shirley Farrell, Karni Perez

Alaska – Janet Hoppe

Arizona – Monica Pastor

California – Diana Baker, Deidre Cavazzi, Cheryl Connolly, Dave Ficke, Betsy Leonard, Jill Mulligan, Esther Railton-Rice

Colorado – Holly Hannaway, Sue Kenney, Terra Malmstrom, Tracee Vickery

Florida – Dolly Cummings, Sabiha Daudi, Mary LaLane, Mickey Santerre

Georgia – Chris Robie, Vanessa Freeman

Illinois – Tim Benedict, Theresa Greinig, Dasha Heinemann, Amy Jacobi, Cliff Knapp, Mark Spreyer

Indiana – Krista Bailey, Sam Carman, Bryant Orem

Iowa – John Ehn, Mary Gillaspey

Kentucky – Christie Cook

Maine – Brian Doyle

Maryland – Jeanne Olsen, Geri Schlenoff

Michigan – Tara Egnatuk, Cheryl Lykowski

Minnesota – Teresa Root

Mississippi – John Guyton

Missouri – Donna Dupske, Richard Frazier

Nebraska – Marian Langan, Harley Winfrey, Sarah Winfrey

Nevada – Liz Moore

New Hampshire – Peter Berg

New Jersey – Rosemary L. Beales, Katherine Butler, Patricia Camp, Loris Chen, Lori Garth, Dave Grant, Susan MacDougall, Theresa Santiago

New Mexico – Deb Novak, Cheri Vogel

New York – Margo DiLella, Beth Shiner Klein, Jessica Kratz, Kym Libman, Christina Siry, Barry Weinbrom, Catherine Westerberg

North Carolina – Liz Baird, Kristin Bennett, Denise Dutcher Bolebruch, Kim Harman, Beth Howard

Ohio – Debbie Brill, Danielle Heape

Oregon – Jesica Haxel, Merrill Watrous

Pennsylvania – Theresa Alberici, Jack Marine, Jean Wallace

South Carolina – Pamela Shucker

Tennessee – Kim Cleary Sadler, Dan Edmisten, Karen Hargrove, Patricia Hewitt, Julia Sherman

Texas – Steve Spurger, Adah Stock

Vermont – Bridget Butler

Virginia – Sol Anshien, Jaime Ceruti-Stacy, Adair Collins, Virginia Ewing, Brenda Hypes, Jennifer Landry, Dottie Salvatierra

Washington – Karen Matsumoto, Michele Mohamed

Wisconsin – Joy Conway, Tracy Day, Dawn Sammons, Stacy Smith

Wyoming – Wendy Esponda, Peter Moran

Finally, we offer our heartfelt appreciation for those who worked behind the scenes to make this book a reality: a group of Ontario educators whose letters of support helped us obtain funding from a competitive grants program; the editorial staff at New Society Publishers; Tracy Kett of Green Living Communications, who produced the attractive layout; and, last but not least, our editorial assistant, Lisa Newman, whose months of patient fact-checking, research, and assembly work were critical to the creation of this book.

Tim Grant and Gail Littlejohn
Toronto

Introduction

by Tim Grant and Gail Littlejohn

Since 1991, we have had the pleasure of working with a great many inspired educators who have shared their innovative environmental education programs, strategies, and activities in the pages of *Green Teacher* magazine. This book is a selection of some of the best of those "green" teaching ideas for educators working with children of elementary school age. Virtually all of the more than 60 contributors to the book have updated and revised their articles in response to comments and suggestions made by peer reviewers. The result is a wide variety of up-to-date activities and teaching strategies designed to engage children in learning the fundamentals of environmental citizenship in the 21st century. Some are strategies for nurturing children's sense of wonder and curiosity as they learn about the natural world. Others are hands-on activities for learning about ecosystems, exploring environmental issues, and engaging in local environmental stewardship projects. Still others help students to recognize the ways in which they are dependent on and connected to other people around the world. Perhaps most important, many of the activities help children to form and clarify their environmental values and to participate in decision making and problem solving.

Children learn best through active exploration of the world around them, and for this reason the hands-on, multi-sensory, multidisciplinary nature of environmental education is particularly well suited to meeting the developmental needs of students in the elementary years. But what exactly does it mean to "teach green"? While definitions and frameworks abound among environmental, global, and outdoor educators, most agree on a few fundamental principles:

Students should have opportunities to develop a personal connection with nature.

We protect what we care about, and we care about what we know well. If students are encouraged to explore the natural world — to learn about local plants and animals, to observe and anticipate seasonal patterns, to get their feet wet in local rivers — they are more likely to develop a lifelong love of nature that will translate into a lifelong commitment to environmental stewardship.

Education should emphasize our connections with other people and other species, and between human activities and planetary systems.

We are connected to other people, other species, and other lands through the foods we eat, the clothes we wear, the items and materials we use every day, and our common reliance on a healthy environment. By gaining an understanding of this global interdependence, children become better equipped to make everyday choices that respect the rights of others and lessen their impact on the Earth's life support systems.

Education should help students move from awareness to knowledge to action.

Even young children should have opportunities to take action to improve local environments. When students act on environmental problems, they begin to understand their complexity, to learn the critical thinking and negotiating skills needed to solve them, and to develop the practical competence that democratic societies require of their citizens. At the same time, educators have a responsibility not to burden children with catastrophic and complex environmental problems that are beyond their ability to help remedy — or, as environmental educator David Sobel has expressed it, there should be "no tragedies before fourth grade."

Learning should extend into the community.

Community projects provide authentic "real-world" reference points for classroom studies and help students develop a sense of place and identity while learning the values and skills of responsible citizenship.

Learning should be hands-on.

The benefits of hands-on learning are widely acknowledged among educators and supported by findings in brain research. Learning is a function of experience, and the best education is one that is sensory-rich, emotionally engaging, and linked to the real world.

Education should integrate subject disciplines.

Environmental issues are complex and cannot be separated from social and economic issues. Addressing them requires knowledge and skills from all disciplines. Integrated learning programs, in which several subjects are taught simultaneously, often through field studies and community projects, help students develop a big-picture understanding and provide opportunities for authentic learning.

Education should be future oriented.

Students should have opportunities to envision the kind of world they would like to live in and to think realistically about incremental steps that might be taken to achieve it.

Education should include media literacy.

With constant exposure to mass media, our mental environments can become just as polluted as the natural environment. Media studies can help students learn to distinguish between fact and fiction in advertising, to recognize racial and gender stereotypes, and to consider the difference between needs and wants.

Education should include traditional knowledge.

Students should have opportunities to learn about traditional ways of life that are based on respect for nature and the sustainable use of resources. Across North America, many educators invite Native elders to share aboriginal perspectives on nature and ecology, exposing students to a worldview that recognizes the intrinsic value and interdependence of all living things.

Teachers should be facilitators and co-learners.

The teacher's role is to facilitate inquiry and provide opportunities for learning, not to provide the "answers." Teachers do not need to be experts to teach about the environment. The natural world is an open book that invites endless discovery by all. As co-learners alongside their students, teachers both model and share in the joy of learning.

Whether you are just beginning or are an old hand at environmental education, we hope you will find many ideas in this book to help you to enrich your teaching. The Table of Contents suggests grade levels, but many of the teaching strategies and activities are easily adapted for younger or older students. On the first page of each article is a handy summary that indicates the subject connections, key concepts, skills to be developed, and, if appropriate, the time and materials needed to carry out activities. With more than 60 individual contributors, the book includes a diverse mix of approaches and styles and a wide spectrum of environmental topics. It does not, however, directly address two topics that are central in many environmental education programs: the greening of school grounds and climate change. In response to the current interest in creating outdoor classrooms and the anticipated impact of climate change in the coming decades, we have published two separate books, *Greening School Grounds* (2001), and *Teaching About Climate Change* (2001), each one a collection of the best articles and activities on those topics from *Green Teacher* magazine.

The environmental and social problems bedeviling humankind will not be solved by the same kind of education that helped create these problems. It is our hope that this book — and the companion books for the middle school and secondary school levels — will inspire educators to take a leading role in helping the next generation to develop knowledge, skills, and values that will enable them to enjoy and share the Earth's bounty while living within its means.

Margaret Pennock

Approaches to Learning

Getting An Early Start: Environmental Education for Young Children

Environmental education in the early years focuses on exploring and enjoying the world of nature under the guidance and with the companionship of caring adults

by Ruth A. Wilson

Grade levels: K

Subject areas: science, nature education

Key concepts: awareness and appreciation of nature

Skills: observation, exploration

Location: indoors and outdoors

Photographs by Ruth Wilson

When should we begin educating children about the environment? As early as preschool and kindergarten? The answer is certainly "yes," as many attitudes and values are shaped during the first few years of life. Young children who develop respect and caring for nature, and a sensitivity to its beauty and mystery, are more likely to behave in ways that are protective rather than destructive of the natural environment.

During the earliest years of a child's life, environmental education should be based on positive experiences in the outdoors under the guidance and with the companionship of caring adults. Such experiences enhance learning and play a critical role in shaping lifelong attitudes and behavior toward the natural world. We know that young children learn primarily through their senses and through hands-on manipulation and exploration. The elements of the natural world not only offer the raw materials for manipulation but also inspire the motivation to experiment and explore. The natural environment, then, provides an invaluable avenue for learning because it offers experiences that match so well a young child's way of learning.

In designing environmental education programs for young children, an important consideration is that of developmental appropriateness. Young children learn differently than older children, and education programs need to recognize and reflect these differences. They must also recognize that young children who are close to nature relate to it as a source of wonder, joy, and awe. And it is this wonder — rather than books, words, or facts — that provides the direction and impetus for environmental education during the early years.

The following are a few guidelines for developing and implementing an environmental education program for young children.

Begin with simple experiences

In introducing young children to the world of nature, the best place to start is in their most immediate and familiar environment. It is important that children feel comfortable and unafraid while exploring the natural world. Because many young children have limited experience of natural environments, they may fear certain aspects of nature. They may fear the darkness of a wooded area, for example, or small things that move, such as bugs and spiders. Such children need a gradual and gentle exposure to the world of nature. They need to become familiar with the trees, bushes, and wildlife in the schoolyard before they will feel comfortable hiking in unfamiliar woods. They need to observe and care for classroom pets before they will be ready to accept a caterpillar crawling across their hand.

Provide frequent positive experiences outdoors

Young children tend to develop emotional attachments to what is familiar and comfortable to them, and frequent positive experiences in the outdoors will help them to develop a sense of connectedness with the natural world. Optimally, the exposure should be almost daily. A one-time trip to a park or nature preserve will have a very limited impact on young children. It is better to provide ongoing, simple experiences with the grass, trees, and insects in environments close to school than to spend time and energy arranging field trips to unfamiliar places. You can enrich children's outdoor experiences by transforming their playground into an environmental yard. Start by adding bird feeders, windsocks, flower and vegetable plants, rock piles, and logs. Then, to encourage closer observation and hands-on interaction, add tools for experimenting and investigating, such as magnifying glasses, a water hose and bucket, hoe, rake, and wheelbarrow.

Focus on "experiencing" rather than "teaching"

Because young children learn best through direct, concrete experiences, being immersed in the outdoor environment is the best way for them to learn about it. The aim of environmental education for young children is not to learn facts. Rather, it is to learn respect and appreciation, and to develop a sense of wonder. Young children will learn better by actually experiencing the sights, sounds, feels, smells, and tastes of nature than by talking about it. Therefore, they should not be expected to "watch and listen" for any length of time, but should be given many opportunities for discovery, self-initiated exploration, and immersion in nature. Such immersion involves engaging all of the senses as much as possible. Having students remove articles of clothing, such as shoes and socks, to increase physical contact is one way to enhance their experience of the outdoors. Another is to block one of the senses, such as sight or hearing, in order to heighten the experience of stimuli through the other senses.

Demonstrate enjoyment of and respect for the natural world

A teacher's expression of interest in and enjoyment of the natural world is critical to the success of an early childhood environmental education program. It is the teacher's own sense of wonder, more than his or her scientific knowledge, that will ignite and sustain a child's love of nature. Therefore, even teachers with a minimal background in science need not be intimidated by the thought of implementing an environmental education program for young children. Just keep in

mind that feelings are more important than facts and modeling is more effective than talking when it comes to introducing young children to the world of nature. Care and respect can be modeled through the gentle handling of plants and animals in the classroom, establishing and maintaining outdoor habitats for wildlife, attending to the proper disposal of trash, and recycling or reusing as many materials as possible.

Ruth A. Wilson is Professor Emeritus of Special Education at Bowling Green State University in Ohio and a consultant in early childhood special education and environmental education.

Adapted from Ruth A. Wilson, "Starting Early: Environmental Education during the Early Childhood Years," *ERIC Digest* ED402147, Educational Resources Information Center Clearinghouse for Science, Mathematics, and Environmental Education, 1996.

Resources

Books for teachers

Chalufour, Ingrid, and Karen Worth. *Discovering Nature with Young Children.* Redleaf Press, 2003.

Grant, Tim, and Gail Littlejohn, eds. *Greening School Grounds: Creating Habitats for Learning.* Green Teacher and New Society Publishers, 2001.

Grollman, Sharon, and Karen Worth. *Worms, Shadows and Whirlpools: Science in the Early Childhood Classroom.* Heinemann Press, 2003.

Starbuck, Sara, Marla Olthof, and Karen Midden. *Hollyhocks and Honeybees: Garden Projects for Young Children.* Redleaf Press, 2002.

Books for children

Jenkins, Steve, and Robin Page. *What Do You Do With A Tail Like This?* Houghton Mifflin Children's Books, 2003.

Kuwahara, Ryuichi, and Satoshi Kuribayashi. *In Front of the Ant: Walking with Beetles and Other Insects.* Kane/Miller Book Publishers, 2004.

Posada, Mia. *Ladybugs: Red, Fiery, and Bright.* Carolrhoda Books, 2002.

Young Children as Environmental Citizens

Laying a foundation for environmental literacy

by Carole Basile and Cameron White

Grade levels: K-2

Subject areas: science, social studies

Key concepts: environmental citizenship

Skills: awareness, problem solving, citizenship

Location: schoolyard or other local outdoor environment

Dylana Nering

 raditionally, environmental education for young children has consisted of activities such as nature walks focusing on observation and appreciation of nature. There is no question that young children need to experience nature and to build a foundation of ecological knowledge before being asked to consider complex environmental issues. Thus it is easy to see why exploration and discovery are perceived by practitioners as the precursors to environmental literacy. However, as a key component of environmental literacy is environmental citizenship, environmental education should also lay a foundation for lifelong learning, balanced decision making, and moving towards investigating and taking action on environmental problems.

We believe that environmental citizenship needs to begin at a young age. But where do kids develop the knowledge, skills, and attitudes they need to become responsible environmental citizens? What kinds of issues can young children discuss? How do we provide children with good models of environmental stewardship? We propose that teachers begin to lay the foundations of environmental citizenship in four ways: (1) teaching the basic science concepts that children

need to understand how natural systems work; (2) nurturing children's respect for all living things; (3) facilitating problem solving, decision making, and critical thinking; and (4) modeling environmental stewardship.

Teaching basic science concepts

In teaching how natural systems work, we must begin by providing a context for environmental learning that is meaningful and relevant to children. Rather than creating a "rainforest" or an "ocean" in the classroom, focus on the places that are most familiar to children, such as their backyards, schoolyards, neighborhoods, and local parks. At first glance, it may appear that these environments are not conducive to teaching much of anything; but taking another look with a bug box and a shovel can open many doors for learning. Even a "vacant" lot can reveal many species of plants and

4

Approaches to Learning

animals and provide opportunities to explore basic concepts of biology and ecology. One advantage of teaching about the environment in your schoolyard or local park is that it does not require a great deal of money or materials. But the most wonderful aspect of it is that it helps students to attune to the natural world in their own neighborhood. Nearby settings, visited frequently, provide the backdrop for beginning to focus not just on the names and parts of animals and plants, but on processes and behavior in the natural world. Children become curious about what an animal is doing, how a plant looks at different times of the day, or what is living in the grass; and this curiosity leads to observation of seasonal cycles, food webs, and other ecological relationships.

A second critical part of teaching about the environment is to make connections between science and other subjects such as mathematics, social studies, and language arts. For young children, all disciplines naturally fit together. Both mathematics and science help the child describe the world, solve problems, and gather information; and both require children to learn such skills as graphing, classifying, sorting, counting, ordering, estimating, and problem solving. Social studies provide opportunities for children to apply the knowledge they gain from studying the environment to civic action for the common good. Even very young children can undertake projects that promote sound environmental stewardship in their neighborhood. Experiences that pique children's interest in the world around them often motivate them to read more, to listen with more interest, and to write with more expression. Use these experiences to enhance language skills. And don't be afraid of big words. Science is full of three- and four-syllable words, and the more you use them, the more you will increase children's vocabulary. Support students' learning with both fiction and nonfiction that teaches great environmental lessons and is scientifically accurate and unbiased. (See list of suggested titles, page 8.)

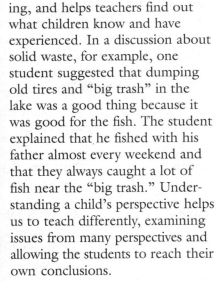

Connie McClain

Lydia Olsen

The last component of environmental education is communication. Communication needs to be two-way. Teachers need to communicate "with" children, not "to" children. Our schools are dominated by teacher talk. Encouraging dialogue and allowing for students' voices helps children to become more engaged in learning, and helps teachers find out what children know and have experienced. In a discussion about solid waste, for example, one student suggested that dumping old tires and "big trash" in the lake was a good thing because it was good for the fish. The student explained that he fished with his father almost every weekend and that they always caught a lot of fish near the "big trash." Understanding a child's perspective helps us to teach differently, examining issues from many perspectives and allowing the students to reach their own conclusions.

Nurturing respect for living things

We need to model respect for living things by teaching children to "catch and release," to use their eyes to observe instead of using their hands to touch or their feet to step on, or, simply, by using the word "gently" with every action. These simple things should be basic ground rules for working with children in the environment and will go a long way toward fostering a respectful relationship with other creatures.

Discussing issues with young children

It is not necessarily the content of education, but what children do with the content, that facilitates learning. Thus students begin to understand issues when they are involved in issues. Young children do have their own issues. They are not global ones like acid rain, climate change, or habitat loss, but little-kid issues such as: Should I take this lizard or frog home for a pet? Should I feed the animals I see in the park? Why do I need to stay on the trails at the nature center? Why should I turn off the lights when I leave the room or turn off the water after

I get a drink? Why can't I throw trash down the storm sewer or out in the schoolyard? Young children cannot be expected to think globally; rather, they need to "think locally, act locally" right in their own neighborhood and school community. When children are encouraged to discuss issues that arise in their daily lives, they begin to build the foundation for environmental citizenship and to practice the skills they will need to examine larger issues later in life.

Betty Blade

Modeling environmental stewardship

Teaching environmental stewardship means practicing what you preach, and then allowing children to take stewardship actions that are meaningful to them. If you tell children to be gentle with animals, then you must be careful not to step on the spider or cockroach in your classroom. Instead, use the insect's appearance in the classroom as a teachable moment and later

Education for Environmental Citizenship: A Sampler

Topic	Building Science Knowledge	Respecting Living Things	Decision Making	Citizenship
Habitat Loss	What is a habitat? What animals live in our habitat? How do they use our habitat?	How can we take care of our habitat?	How can we make our habitat better for animals?	Plant a habitat for butterflies; build nesting boxes or bat houses.
Water Conservation	Where does our water come from? How much water do we use?	Who uses water?	How can we help to make sure there is enough water for all living things?	Design a brochure with tips for water conservation; present ideas to students in another grade or to the PTA.
Trash	What's in our trash? What happens to our trash?	How does trash affect wildlife?	What happens if we throw trash around?	Design a process for reusing or recycling in the classroom.
Interacting with Wild Animals	What do animals in our environment eat? How do they protect themselves?	How can we use our eyes instead of our hands or feet?	What can happen if we feed the animals? Do wild animals make good pets?	Make signs for the schoolyard that inform others on how to handle wildlife.
Alternative Fuels	What kinds of transportation do we use?	What kinds of transportation are better for living things?	Can we find other ways to go places?	Take a walking field trip.
Rehabilitation of Wildlife	How can animals get hurt?	What do you do when you find a hurt animal?	Should we take care of animals that are hurt?	Develop a brochure or poster telling other kids what to do when they find a hurt animal.
Nonpoint Source Pollution	What is a storm sewer? Why do we have them? When something goes down a storm sewer, where does it end up?	What's living at the other end of the drain?	Should we put our waste into storm sewers?	Stencil the storm sewers around the school to remind the community of where their waste is going.

release it outside. If you teach children about recycling, then you need to recycle at home and in your classroom. If you teach children about how littering affects the environment, then be careful not to litter or to have things falling all over the floor in your classroom. Outside of the classroom, if you spend your weekend birdwatching, helping with a beach cleanup, or going to your local park, let your students know.

Teaching from your passions is critical to developing those same passions in students. However, it is also important to examine your own biases as you practice what you preach in the classroom. Teachers are human: they come to the classroom with a variety of prejudices, from fears of snakes and spiders to personal feelings about the destruction of a rainforest or the construction of a new chemical or nuclear power plant. Make decisions about what to teach or share based on its appropriateness and not on emotion. You may feel strongly about the loss of biodiversity resulting from the destruction of tropical rainforests, and so you may talk about it and engage students in raising funds for the cause, creating rainforest projects, and reading books about the rainforest. But your students likely have no experience that enables them to understand and relate to the concept of a rainforest. Perhaps a more appropriate approach is to study biodiversity in the natural habitat around your schoolyard so that children can begin to develop a more personalized understanding of biodiversity.

While modeling is a vital component of teaching environmental stewardship, we cannot stop there. The necessary next step is to allow students to decide the direction of their own stewardship. This is one of the primary reasons that we need to begin with what the students know best, be it the schoolyard, the neighborhood, or the community. Local stewardship is the scaffolding necessary for internalizing a concept of environmental responsibility that can later be applied in the context of the wider world.

Dylana Nering

Finding time for environmental education

It is important to remember that environmental education is not about fitting something into a curriculum; it is about fostering environmental literacy and helping children become global citizens who can make thoughtful decisions about human interactions with the environment. It should not be a contrived curriculum. It should not consist of trying to find 15 or 20 minutes in a day to do an episodic activity from a book, but rather taking advantage of teachable moments that come from the children or the immediate environment. These moments are often not earth-shattering, but they are important to the child: finding a baby bird out of its nest, noticing that the creek behind the school looks yucky, or finding a venomous snake or spider that school policy demands must be destroyed. These are situations in which teachers and students can have meaningful discussion about varying points of view, and which can lead to activities that broaden children's knowledge, incorporate decision making, and, in some cases, allow them to take action on an issue of significance to them.

What does education for environmental citizenship look like?

The accompanying table provides a sample of activities on a variety of topics that teachers have used to take students from awareness to citizenship. These are not the only topics, but they are ones that come up frequently with young children. Questions are used to promote thinking about the process we are proposing. Curriculum that supports these topics is abundant but should be chosen wisely so that it is meaningful to students and appropriate for their age and environment.

To be a "green" teacher is to facilitate the acquisition of knowledge and the development of skills and values that will encourage students to become green kids. There may be no better way for us to model democratic values that promote an active and engaged citizenry than through problem-based investigation of real-world environmental issues. Students become excited about learning when it is meaningful, integrative, challenging, active, and value-based. By moving students beyond simple awareness toward active citizenship, environmental education can lay a new foundation and provide a richer culture for environmental literacy. ✒

Carole Basile is Associate Dean at the University of Colorado at Denver in the Initial Teacher Education program and has been involved with K-12 environmental education for over 20 years. Cameron White is an Associate Professor at the University of Houston and teaches social studies education. His work has included the integration of environmental education with social studies education.

Suggested Children's Literature

The questions following each reference reflect possible discussion topics.

Baker, Jeannie. **Window**. Greenwillow, 1991.
- *How has our neighborhood changed?*
- *If you could live anywhere, would it be in the country or city? Why?*

Bash, Barbara. **Urban Roosts**. Sierra Club, 1990.
- *What are the animals in our neighborhood?*
- *How have they adapted to being around people?*

Bunting, Eve. **Night Tree**. Harcourt Brace, 1991.
- *What are ways we can appreciate nature?*

Cooney, Barbara. **Miss Rumphius**. Viking-Penguin, 1982.
- *What kinds of things can we do to make the world more beautiful?*

Fleming, Denise. **Where Once Was a Wood**. Henry Holt, 1996.
- *How are things in our neighborhood changing?*
- *How do you think the changes are affecting the wildlife?*

French, Vivian. **Caterpillar, Caterpillar**. Candlewick Press, 1993.
- *Why is it important to preserve different plant species?*
- *What can happen if we don't preserve them?*

Hoose, Phillip, and Hoose, Hannah. **Hey, Little Ant**. Scholastic, 1998.
- *Should we kill insects or other living things just for fun?*
- *Is it ever acceptable to kill living things?*

James, Simon. **Sally and the Limpet**. McElderry, 1990.
- *Should we touch or catch animals in the wild?*

James, S. **Dear Mr. Blueberry**. McElderry Books, 1991.
- *How do we find out about things we don't know or understand?*

Larson, Gary. **There's a Hair in My Dirt! A Worm's Story**. HarperPerennial, 1998.
- *What can we do to find out about the real stories of how nature works?*

Lasky, Kathryn. **She's Wearing a Dead Bird on Her Head!** Hyperion, 1995.
- *How can we let others know about things we care about?*
- *Is there anything we care about that we would like others to know about?*

London, Jonathan. **Voices of the Wild**. Crown, 1993.
- *What is our relationship with other living things?*

Mazer, Anne. **The Salamander Room**. Alfred A. Knopf, 1991.
- *Is it okay to take animals out of the wild?*
- *When we take animals from the wild, how can we take care of them?*

Peet, Bill. **Farewell to Shady Glade**. Houghton-Mifflin, 1966.
- *What things do we see changing in our neighborhood?*

Ryder, Joanne. **Earthdance.** Henry Holt, 1996.
- *How can we learn more about our community and our world?*

Schimmel, Schim. **Dear Children of the Earth**. NorthWord Press, 1994.
- *What are humans' responsibilities to other animals and living things?*
- *How can we respect living things?*

Stewart, Sarah. **The Gardener**. Farrar, Starus, and Giroux, 1997.
- *How can we create natural habitats in the city?*

Ward, Lorraine, and Jacques, Laura. **A Walk in the Wild: Exploring a Wildlife Refuge**. Charlesbridge, 1993.
- *Why is some land protected for refuges or parks?*

Wood, Douglas. **Old Turtle**. Pfeifer-Hamilton, 1992.
- *What is our relationship to other animals and living things?*

Source: Basile, Carole, Cameron White, and Stacey Robinson, *Awareness to Citizenship: Environmental Literacy for the Elementary Child.* University Press of America, 2000.

Green Empowerment in Kindergarten

*Giving children opportunities to take action
on environmental concerns is to plant seeds of hope and power*

by Chris Wright

Grade levels: K-1

Subject areas: science, ecology

Key concepts: Four Rs, decomposition, dehydration, composting

Skills: scientific method, vermicomposting

Location: indoors

Photographs by Chris Wright

The young daughter of a friend of mine came home one day from a school discussion about the environment and was so worried about global warming and the ozone layer that she was unable to sleep. It made me wonder how the children in my kindergarten class responded to similar discussions.

I consider myself a "nouveau environmentalist." In class we do various activities that I feel are on the right green path. Our classroom is inviting and lively. A rabbit roams around and a dove flies freely, occasionally laying eggs in odd corners of the room. The children are encouraged to feel comfortable holding guinea pigs, rats, and gerbils. Mealworms, insects, snails, and earthworms live in terraria and wormeries. Simplified models of ecosystems have been set up so that children can observe natural processes. Much time is spent on environmental projects, from collecting news stories to creating art and writing books. Yet the experience of my friend's daughter prompted certain questions. What more could I do to plant seeds of hope and power that would grow with the children through their school lives? Informing without empowering is a recipe for anxiety and paralysis. I didn't want to burden them with the weight of environmental problems: I wanted the children to feel that they could move mountains and were powerful enough to teach their own adults a thing or two.

Blue box beginnings

With this in mind, I sat down with my class to decide together what we — 22 very bright young people and three adults — could do to effect change. At about this time, our municipality was beginning curbside collection of recyclable metal and glass; but recycling boxes has been distributed only to private homes, not to schools. In a class discussion, we decided to provide each classroom in the school with a recycling box and ensure that these boxes were emptied each week with the city's regular pickup. It was an exciting project for the kids. They had to figure out how many boxes were needed, construct the boxes, paint them the familiar bright blue used on municipal boxes, print "We Recycle" on them, and, finally, distribute them. It was a wonderful project to start with: it was concrete, it was do-able, and it produced rapid results, which the kids could see and measure and which provided them with empowering feedback.

Subsequently, recycling became integrated into the curriculum and the life of the school. For example, we did sophisticated graphing of the quantities of cans and bottles that went through our system weekly, tabulating the results by class. We made a nine-minute video called "We Recycle," in which the children explained how they had gotten the whole school to recycle. The blue boxes were augmented by green boxes for paper recycling (only after both sides of the paper were used!). Finally, we decided to have recycling representatives appointed in each classroom, from Junior Kindergarten to Grade 6. This expansion of our recycling team provided lessons in organizational skills and in interacting with others to achieve a common goal. We were on our way to empowerment.

What is garbage?

Recycling naturally led to discussions of waste and garbage. What makes something garbage? Can a garbage item become a useful item? We built a "garbage giant" in the classroom, using a variety of materials that had been discarded around the school or put out for garbage pickup on residential streets. Our giant had a computer for a brain, shreds of paper and old gloves as hair, and old gears and other scrap machinery for lungs, heart, and other internal organs, so that as he took shape he became a lesson in both creative reuse and human anatomy. The children began to re-evaluate their definition of garbage as they discovered that a great many items that people throw away

Top: Students share the classroom with a menagerie of "holdable" creatures. Bottom: Through Wetland and Dryland experiments, children learn what's biodegradable and get to observe the fascinating process of decomposition.

still have a use. Later, it became apparent to us that reducing was really the king of the four Rs (reduce, reuse, recycle, rethink).

Investigations in biodegradables

Garbage opened the door to science in a way that was immediate and powerful. To investigate what happens to garbage when it is dumped, we created two simplified models of ecosystems, which we called Wetland and Dryland. Wetland was a plastic tub filled with about 20 centimeters (8 inches) of soil and leaves that the children collected in the fall. It was "rained on" daily, so that the soil was always moist. Dryland was a similar tub containing leaves and earth, but left dry to simulate a semi-arid system such as a dry prairie. We added worms to Wetland, but decided they would be too thirsty in Dryland and would likely die. Each week we stirred the contents of the two tubs and then laid them out on garbage bags to see what was happening. As the leaves started to break down, we began to add left-over food scraps and animal droppings. We maintained a list of everything that went in: droppings from rat, dove, rabbit, gerbil, and hamster; fruit and vegetables; flowers; and so on. We found that all of these items decomposed in Wetland, whereas Dryland was not quite as interesting: everything there disintegrated to dust. Watching things rot is uniquely and endlessly fascinating to small children, and many of the students started experiments in biodegrading at home (to the disgruntled mutterings of a few parents!).

By this point, the children had learned to observe things closely and were at ease with such words as dehydration, evaporation, biodegradable, and composting. They were being equipped with knowledge and were ready to take the next step in their investigation of garbage. We buried a plastic bag, a small can, and a polystyrene cup into the Wetland tub to see what would happen, and after a few weeks we emptied the tub. The children were shocked to see that the plastic, metal, and polystyrene had not changed. (Some things did not decompose!) This led to discussions of the consequences of this kind of garbage, and the children became committed to reducing or eliminating their use of plastic materials.

One offshoot was a garbageless lunch program. The children decided which items in their daily lunches were garbage and which items could be reused or recycled. Any items with throwaway wrappers and any unnecessary plastic utensils were no longer welcome in the lunch buckets.

A "garbage giant" made of materials discarded at school and around the neighborhood.

Parents spoke of their children terrorizing them about using plastic; but as they realized how serious the children were about eliminating garbage from their lunches, they listened and joined the effort. The kids had gained knowledge, they had set a goal, and they had found ways of reaching that goal.

Our green program continues to expand and diversify. For example, worms of all kinds are very popular in our class, and I recently introduced vermicomposting (worm composting with red wrigglers). We initially named many of our small number of worms, but as time went on, the children realized that this was just too big a job: the reproduction rate of red wrigglers is truly impressive. Another kind of worm we have studied is the mealworm. Each child has a small clear container of mealworms living comfortably in a cupful of oatmeal. As the mealworms go through their life cycle from worm to pupa to beetle, we watch the magic of life unfold. The scientific principles of observation, measurement, and notation are followed by discussions that not only sharpen logic but also stimulate a love of all things that make our planet work. These children hold the worms with something near to affection. They know that worms aerate the soil and make plants and trees possible. The knowledge they have gained from their experience has given them the power to care and nurture life, and to take steps, even at their young age, to help preserve our delicate environment. ❧

*At the time of writing, **Chris Wright** taught kindergarten at Alternative Primary School in Toronto, Ontario. She now teaches at The Mabin School in Toronto.*

Environmental Project Learning

In this integrated "nature immersion" program, students meet all curriculum outcomes through environmental projects that restore school ground habitats and local ecosystems

Photographs by Hollywood Elementary School

by Julie Tracy with Kathleen Glaser

Grade levels: K-5

Subject areas: science, language arts, math, social studies, art

Key concepts: environmental awareness and action projects

Skills: observing, investigating, reading, writing, measuring, problem solving

Location: indoors and outdoors

Observing praying mantises laying eggs in the meadow, investigating a rotting log, monitoring bird feeding and nesting, studying dragonfly nymphs and adults, restoring a meadow — these are but a few of the inquiry-based environmental projects that students conduct as part of the "nature immersion"

curriculum at Hollywood Elementary School in Hollywood, Maryland. Situated in the Chesapeake Bay watershed, the school's 72-acre site encompasses a meadow, woodland, stream, and wetland — habitats that provide for first-hand observations and stimulating discoveries of how natural systems operate. The school's 620 students take an active role in the conservation, restoration, and celebration of this rich natural environment by assuming responsibility for planning and implementing projects that improve both the ecological and educational value of the school site. As a vehicle for curriculum in Grades K to 5, these environmental projects integrate subject areas; develop scientific skills of inquiry, observation, and experimentation; and demonstrate to students that their knowledge and skills can be applied in a meaningful context.

Hollywood Elementary School's use of the environment in integrated learning projects began more than a decade ago when teachers discovered the connection between the mastery of basic skills and students' natural interest in the outdoors. Early curriculum projects included assessing the water quality in the stream by analyzing ratios of aquatic insect populations, and initiating a community recycling program before local government officials had even recognized the need to organize such a program for citizens. Over time, integrated environmental projects have grown organically, nourished by teachers' ideas, by students' motivation to engage in project learning, and by the increasing need to take measures to preserve the wonderful resources of the Chesapeake Bay.

Other key factors in the evolution of the program have been the administration's support for integrated curriculum, and regular opportunities for teachers to increase their knowledge of primary sources and methodology through such workshops as Project Wet, Project Learning Tree, and summer sessions with education professor Dr. Sylvia Chard, author of *The Project Approach*. Community support has also contributed immensely to the program's success. Parent and community volunteers, naturalists from local nature parks, a biologist from U.S. Fish and Wildlife, experts from the Department of Natural Resources and Soil Conservation, as well as county and state environmental educators and organizations, have been essential sources of information and support for teachers and students.

Getting students outside to engage in integrated studies in the environment has enhanced learning significantly. In the 1990s, Hollywood Elementary

---

Keys to Success: Starting Integrated Environmental Project-Based Programs

Taking children outdoors to engage in purposeful learning is the first step in initiating a program that uses the environment as a vehicle for integrated project learning. Beyond that, our experience has shown there to be four major components that contribute to the successful development of an integrated environmental project-based program: starting small, curriculum planning, cultivation of a school climate, and outreach to the community.

Starting small: Because each school is unique, there is no one-size-fits-all model for moving from a traditional curriculum to one that uses the environment as a vehicle for integrated project-based learning. Most programs start out small, teacher by teacher, project by project. All it takes is a supportive principal and one or two teachers who are willing to venture outside with their students. By attending environmental education workshops and conferences, teachers can obtain resource materials and network with other educators. The program grows incrementally as more and more teachers get involved, collaborate, and team up on various projects. Pairing older students with younger students often enhances the learning experience for both groups. As the number and scope of the school's projects increase, it is important to establish an environmental advisory committee to coordinate and seek resources to support the variety of environmental projects on the school site.

Curriculum planning: The interdisciplinary nature of environmental project work enables teachers to meet curriculum outcomes in several subject areas, thereby maximizing instructional time. When planning environmental projects, teachers match curriculum objectives with the activities students will be engaged in throughout the project. Collaboration among teachers, school administration, and school volunteers provides the support for project planning and curriculum mapping.

Cultivating school climate: It is important to cultivate a school climate or culture that reflects and supports environmental project work, reinforcing the message that students' learning is valued and respected. At Hollywood Elementary School, hallways are galleries of student project work, bulletin boards report on ongoing projects and animal sightings, and aquaria in the front lobby are temporary homes for Chesapeake Bay organisms collected for observation, identification, and monitoring.

Community outreach: Community outreach expands the audience for students' work and provides opportunities for forming community partnerships. Through school-hosted events, performances, and science fairs with a focus on the environment, members of the community can share and celebrate the learning. Visitors to Hollywood Elementary School can take a gallery walk or go on a tour hosted by student guides who explain outdoor habitat areas and student project work. Students feel a sense of pride and ownership when sharing their work with others. In addition, partnerships with members of the community or with local, state/provincial, or national organizations enable students, teachers, and parents to benefit from others' knowledge and expertise. It is also beneficial to seek volunteers among parents and/or education students from a local college, assigning each volunteer to work with a small group of students throughout the stages of the project.

School participated in a study that compared the achievement of students in schools with traditional curricula with that of students in 40 schools in the U.S. that were successfully integrating subject areas through environmental education. The report, published in 1998 by the State Education and Environment Round Table (SEER), noted higher achievement in schools that were "using the environment as an integrating context for learning" — which SEER defined as "using a school's surroundings and community as a framework within which students can construct their own learning, guided by teachers and administrators using proven educational practices."[1] The study found that students in these programs perform better on standardized tests in reading, writing, math, science, and social studies;

have fewer discipline problems; are more engaged in learning; and have a greater sense of ownership in their accomplishments.

Environmental project overview

In general, the various stages of an integrated environmental project can be classified into six broad categories of learning: observation, investigation, restoration, monitoring, celebration, and education (see "Stages and Types of Learning" chart, below). As each project evolves, it encompasses most, if not all, of these types of learning. At the beginning of a project, students are encouraged to make their own observations and to ask questions about their surroundings on the school grounds. These observations then lead to investigations

Stages and Types of Learning in Integrated Environmental Projects

1. Observation
Students use magnifying lenses and microscopes to observe components of various habitats. Observations are recorded and shared through field notes, drawings, and discussion of:
- plant and animal structures
- seed dispersal and seasonal changes in leaves twigs and buds
- life cycles and adaptations
- predator/prey relationships
- animal homes
- animal signs (tracks, scat, bones, chewed stems, egg masses, owl pellets, sounds)
- rotting logs, soil, and erosion

2. Investigation
Inquiry-based investigations are conducted in habitat study areas. These often develop from questions that arise during observation, and include:
- using field guides to identify plants and animals
- surveying and comparing the biodiversity of different habitats
- comparing the habitat value of different sites
- measuring the water quality of the stream, pond, and vernal pools
- mapping sections of outdoor sites and piecing the maps together like a jigsaw puzzle

3. Restoration
After studying the wildlife value of a site, students may initiate restoration projects. These have included:
- creating a wetland in the school's stormwater management pond
- converting a mowed lawn to a wildflower meadow
- planting a new forest
- planting berry-producing shrubs to benefit migratory birds
- researching, building, and mounting birdhouses
- planting a butterfly garden and a colonial herb garden
- composting school wastes

4. Monitoring
Many projects require maintenance and monitoring. Examples are:
- enhancing wildlife habitat through plantings
- constructing bird houses and feeders
- watching for spotted salamander egg masses
- collecting, marking, and releasing green darner dragonflies and box turtles
- monitoring weather
- monitoring water quality of the stream, pond and vernal pools
- tracking animal migration as part of the Journey North program

5. Celebration
Students engage in activities that celebrate their experiences in the natural environment. For example:
- reading and writing stories and poetry outdoors
- developing projects through the creative arts of drawing, drama, and music
- using the trails on the school site for physical education
- exchanging drawings, letters, and information about neotropical migratory birds with a partner class in Costa Rica

6. Education
Students educate others about their projects and the environment by:
- presenting information about ongoing projects during the annual Earth Day celebration
- designing and constructing tile murals that depict and describe different habitats
- performing musicals such as *Every Day is Earth Day* to inform others about the need to respect the environment
- giving presentations to visiting educators about the school's environmental program

— by Julie Tracy

to determine how well the schoolyard provides habitat for wildlife and how it affects the water quality of the Chesapeake Bay. Next, students identify an area where wildlife habitat could be enhanced or where erosion needs to be controlled in order to prevent runoff into the bay. Once they have identified a problem area, they design an environmental restoration project. The project

The Bay Grasses in Classes project has students growing, monitoring, and planting grasses in Chesapeake Bay.

often involves measuring and mapping the area, conducting soil tests and other investigations, selecting native plants from nursery catalogs, applying for grant funding, and planting the plants. Afterwards, the students care for and monitor the growth of the plants. They are also involved in celebrating and educating others about their project and the natural world.

Throughout a project, all of the subject areas are naturally integrated. Reading and writing are incorporated as students read and write about their topic of study, use resources such as field guides and nursery catalogs, write about their investigations, and apply for grants. Mathematics is used in taking measurements and recording data. Connections are drawn between social studies and science so that students understand how the geography, culture, history, and economics of a place are closely tied to its living and nonliving components. The visual arts are included as students make observational drawings. Through meaningful learning activities that integrate subject areas, students better understand the importance and application of each subject area in real life.

Project examples

The following is a brief description of three sets of projects conducted by students in Grade 3 at Hollywood Elementary School. They illustrate four key elements of the success of the environmental project approach: the interdisciplinary nature of project learning; the relationships that form between projects; the connections to the local and global community that are promoted by project learning; and the empowerment that students feel as they take on new projects and educate others. Although a few of the projects described are specific to the Chesapeake Bay region,

most can be adapted for use in other regions or watersheds and can be done in any schoolyard or local park.

Bay habitat projects
Grass shrimp investigation

During the fall, a group of third grade students went on a field trip to a marsh as part of their study of the Chesapeake Bay. Prior to the trip, the students had studied maps and a model of the Chesapeake Bay watershed, as well as a map of the peninsula where the marsh is situated. At the marsh, the students used dip nets to find out what kinds of organisms live there. They collected small fish, blue crabs, and grass shrimp. They released most of what they caught, but they were so interested in the grass shrimp that they brought some of them back to school to observe under a microscope.

In the classroom, the students began to discuss whether the best place for catching grass shrimp would be in marsh grasses or in the open water. They then designed an experiment to test which habitat the shrimp prefer. They put a sample of grass shrimp into an aquarium that had marsh grass on one side and open water on the other. For each of three trials, the students counted the grass shrimp on each side of the aquarium every 5 minutes for 30 minutes. Because the grass grows in dense clusters, it was difficult to count the shrimp on the grassy side of the tank; but the students reasoned that if they counted the shrimp on the open-water side, they could subtract to determine the number of shrimp hidden in the grassy side. Organizing the data into a graph, they observed that at first the shrimp explored their new environment, but then spent most of their time in the grasses.

The results of the experiment raised a new question: What might be the reason that grass shrimp prefer marsh grass to open water? While observing the shrimp, the students had noticed them eating algae on the grass blades, and they hypothesized that the shrimp prefer the marsh grass because it provides food. However, they wondered if the shrimp prefer the grasses because they also provide protection from predators. To find out, the students recreated the aquarium experiment, except that this time they used plastic plants that would not have any algae on them. Into the center of the tank the students placed, first, the shrimp, and then two predator fish. The students observed that immediately after the fish were introduced, the shrimp moved to the side containing the plastic plants and hid behind them. If a fish swam to the plant side of the tank, the shrimp would move to a different area of the plant side. Occasionally, one or two shrimp would wander over to the open-water side, but when they came near a fish, they would back up into the plant side while keeping their eyes on the fish. During each of three trials, the students recorded the number of shrimp in the plant side and the number of shrimp in the open-water side every 5 minutes for 30 minutes. The data showed that the grasses provide both food and protection for the grass shrimp. The students made

Glass shrimp investigations designed by students.

observational drawings of the shrimp and enhanced the drawings with watercolors. Their experiments and drawings were published in the March/April 1999 issue of *Dragonfly* magazine.

Several curriculum outcomes were addressed through this project. The students met science curriculum outcomes by conducting a well-designed investigation and by identifying the relationship between organisms, populations, communities, and habitats. They met math curriculum outcomes by brainstorming and implementing a problem-solving strategy, using estimation and computational skills, and by collecting, organizing, and displaying data. The social studies outcome of interpreting maps was met through study of watershed and peninsula maps. Reading and writing were incorporated as students researched marshes and recorded their scientific investigation for publication. In addition, the students met art curriculum outcomes through their observational drawings and use of watercolors.

Tile mural project

Third grade classes worked on a year-long project to design and construct large tile murals that depict different habitats in the Chesapeake Bay watershed. The tile murals were made in art class, where students brainstormed possible designs and then voted on the layout of their habitat scene. Beginning with an actual-size drawing of the entire habitat scene, they made each of the clay tiles to depict a section of the scene. Those who had studied marshes in the grass shrimp project made tiles that depicted a salt marsh, while each of the other classes selected a habitat they had been studying. All students researched their chosen habitat and composed a written description that would educate others about the plants and animals shown in the murals and the importance of that habitat to the Chesapeake Bay ecosystem. The murals hang in the school courtyard with the students' descriptions mounted on adjacent plaques.

This project demonstrates the interdisciplinary nature of environmental projects. What the students learned about their habitat through research and scientific investigation was presented through the visual arts to educate others in the school community.

Bay Grasses in Classes project

Much of the bay grass, or submerged aquatic vegetation, in the Chesapeake Bay and its tributaries has been lost. This vegetation is important to the bay ecosystem for a number of reasons: it slows water movement, thereby helping to remove suspended particles and stabilize sediments; it absorbs nutrients from the water and produces oxygen; and it provides food and habitat for many aquatic species. However, too many sediments and nutrients going into the Chesapeake Bay have overwhelmed the bay grasses, causing them to die off.

Third grade students participated in Bay Grasses in Classes, a restoration project developed by the Chesapeake Bay Foundation (CBF) and the Maryland Department of Natural Resources (DNR) with funding from the Chesapeake Bay Trust. The students grew the aquatic grass known as wild celery (*Vallisneria americana*) in the school's science lab, monitored the growth of the grass and the water quality in the growth chambers, and reported their data to DNR scientists.

They also used the Internet to compare their data with data collected by students at other schools involved in the project. In May, a group of students assisted the CBF and DNR scientists in planting the grasses in the Chesapeake Bay.

In this project, the students engaged in problem solving and measuring to figure out how to plant tiny seeds in a tray with one-inch spacing. Knowing that their data would be reported to DNR scientists, they understood the need to take accurate measurements.

The learning that Grade 3 students gained from such projects went beyond the application of skills in the various subject areas; it took the students into the real world of scientific inquiry that leads to taking action. In the grass shrimp investigation and the tile mural project, students learned the importance of grass beds in keeping the Chesapeake Bay healthy. Through the Bay Grasses in Classes project, they were able to take action by helping to restore healthy bay grass habitat in local waterways.

Planting projects

As the students progress through the primary and upper elementary grades, a web of interconnections begins to form between environmental projects. The following examples demonstrate how projects build on one another and are revisited over the years.

Planting a meadow

Students in Grade 3 conducted a study to compare a mowed lawn and a meadow as habitats for wildlife. Then, in a schoolwide project, students in Grades K to 5 converted one-third of an acre of lawn to a wildflower meadow. They researched which kinds of birds, butterflies, and other animals would be attracted to the plants listed in the seed mixes. They tested the soil to determine its compaction and drainage. They observed the sun's movement across the planting area, and made drawings at regular times throughout the day to record the amount of sunlight and shade reaching different parts of the site. They used trundle wheels to measure the planting site, and calculated the area and the amount of seed needed. After planting the meadow, the students wrote letters to students in another school who had expressed interest in such a project to inform them of the importance of meadow habitat and describe the technique they had used. They continue to monitor plant growth and record sightings of animals in the meadow.

Ball fields versus meadow debate

The year after planting the meadow, the students learned about a plan to convert a mature meadow on the school site to six grassy ball fields. Several students expressed concern about the destruction of the mature

---

Tips for Environmental Project Work

◐ Establish expectations for outdoor excursions, just as you establish classroom expectations. Encourage students to think and behave as scientists when they are conducting field observations and investigations. Provide opportunities for students to share their discoveries.

◐ Set a focus question for every outdoor field study, breaking down big questions into supporting questions. Focus questions might include the following: In what ways does our schoolyard affect local water bodies? How well does our schoolyard provide habitat (food, water, shelter, and space) for migratory birds?

◐ Begin a project with careful observation. Encourage students to use their senses to become more aware of their surroundings. Provide clipboards and have students take field notes, make observational drawings, and/or complete data sheets. Collect natural objects and have students observe them under a dissection microscope, taking measurements and making observational drawings. (Return these items when the students are finished with them.)

◐ Follow up outdoor observations with classroom discussion. Encourage students to ask questions that may lead to investigations and project ideas.

◐ Empower your students to take on the projects that flow from the class discussion. When students help to initiate projects and play a key role in planning and decision making, their sense of ownership increases.

◐ Team up with another teacher in order to share resources and divide the responsibility of helping students plan and carry out projects. Pairing older students with younger students can enhance the learning experience for both groups.

◐ Seek community resources. Have students write to experts in forestry, soil conservation, or gardening to ask for advice or assistance in the project.

◐ Seek parent volunteers and assign each to work with a small group of students throughout the stages of the project.

◐ Educate yourself. Attend educators' workshops provided by environmental education organizations.

— *by Julie Tracy and Kathleen Glaser*

---

meadow. They developed and conducted a survey of students in Grades 4 and 5, who would be the primary users of the new ball fields. The survey asked respondents whether they played on a soccer or lacrosse team, how far they had to travel to get to a field, how long they usually waited for the field to become available, and whether they thought it was more important to protect the meadow habitat or to build more ball fields. Students of all ages engaged in debates both at school and at home and wrote letters to persuade others to take their side on the issue. In the end, much of the mature meadow at Hollywood Elementary was lost to ball fields. However, situating the ball fields at the school may have protected a nearby nature park from a proposed plan to construct several ball fields there. In addition, students converted another area of the school-yard to meadow habitat.

Planting a butterfly garden: Students take responsibility for improving the ecological value of the school site.

Replanting a wetland

In the construction of the ball fields, the dense vegetation of the meadow was replaced by grass turf, a surface that absorbed less rainwater. Therefore, the stormwater management pond at the school had to be expanded. This affected another environmental project of recent years, the planting of upland and obligate wetland plants to create a wetland habitat in the pond. With the help of a DNR forester and other community and parent volunteers, the students removed the wetland plants, stored them until the pond expansion was complete, and then transplanted them back into the pond.

In these projects, students learned that, as citizens, they have a responsibility to voice their opinions and make informed decisions about land use and natural resource management.

Bird projects

As the following examples illustrate, students discover many connections to the global community through their environmental projects. They begin to recognize the commonalties between themselves and people of other cultures. The environment builds bridges between diverse groups of people and promotes an exchange between them. Technology greatly enhances the ease and speed of communication through the Internet.

Building bird boxes and feeders

Students researched the habitat requirements, territory size, and nesting box specifications for several species of birds. Then they measured, built, and mounted nesting boxes according to the specifications. Bird feeders were also mounted on the school site. The students use binoculars to observe and record activity at the bird feeders and nesting boxes.

Bridging the Americas project

The students participated in Bridging the Americas/ Unidos por las Aves!, a cross-cultural environmental education program coordinated by the Smithsonian Migratory Bird Center and the Education Committee of the Maryland Partners in Flight. Hollywood Elementary students were partnered with a class in Costa Rica, and they used field guides to make drawings and habitat maps of neotropical migratory birds that are common to both Costa Rica and eastern North America. A native of Costa Rica visited the school to share pictures of indigenous plant and animal species. Students' drawings, maps, letters, and other cultural items were mailed to their Costa Rican friends who, in return, sent similar items that were put on display at the school.

Planting shrubs for neotropical migratory birds

The students listened to *Flute's Journey: The Life of a Wood Thrush*, a story by Lynne Cherry about the challenges that a wood thrush faces during migration. Learning that the populations of migratory birds are declining due to habitat loss and that the birds' primary plant food is berries, students became interested in planting berry-producing shrubs. They explored the school grounds to locate the most suitable planting areas. They chose areas of compacted soil in the ecotone between the newly planted meadow and woodland because planting in this area would have the additional benefit of reducing erosion near the stream. Given a budget of $1,000, the students selected shrubs from nursery catalogs, explained the reasons for their selections, and calculated the total cost. The plans were finalized and submitted as a grant proposal to the Chesapeake Bay Trust who approved the funding. The students planted the shrubs with help from parent and community volunteers. They continue to care for and monitor the growth of the shrubs.

The "living" curriculum at Hollywood Elementary maintains its momentum and creative energy through the will and imagination of teachers leading exciting yet focused projects such as those described here. In the school's lobby and hallways, students' artwork, murals, and displays tell the story of their immersion in learning about the natural surroundings in the Chesapeake Bay Watershed. A floor-to-ceiling map of the entire watershed is featured on the cafeteria wall; and during recess children play on a circular map of the watershed that is painted on the school playground. Since statewide testing began in 1993, Hollywood students have consistently scored above local and state averages. Numerous parents and visitors to the school have commented on students' high level of engagement and their ability to ask questions, make decisions, and use basic skills in real world contexts.

Through these integrated environmental projects, the school community has experienced that each person can make a difference: one teacher's enthusiasm and commitment to a project engenders students' learning and interest, and this circle of success ripples out to an ever-widening community of learners and leaders who, together, are making vital connections with the natural world. ✒

Julie Tracy taught third grade at Hollywood Elementary School in Hollywood, Maryland, from 1990 to 2000 and was the 1996 recipient of The Presidential Award for Excellence in Science Teaching. **Kathleen Glaser** *was the principal of Hollywood Elementary School from 1982 to 2001 and currently teaches and supervises student teachers at St. Mary's College of Maryland.*

Note

[1] G.A. Lieberman and L.L. Hoody, *Closing the Achievement Gap: Using the Environment as an Integrating Context for Learning*, State Education and Environment Roundtable, 1998, p. 1.

References

American Association for the Advancement of Science. *Benchmarks for Science Literacy: Project 2061.* Oxford University Press, 1993.

American Forest Foundation. *Project Learning Tree: Pre K-8 Environmental Education Activity Guide.* American Forest Foundation, 1993.

Chard, Sylvia C. *The Project Approach: A Practical Guide for Teachers.* Scholastic, 1992.

Chard, Sylvia C. *The Project Approach: A Second Practical Guide for Teachers.* Scholastic, 1994.

Cherry, Lynne. *Flute's Journey: The Life of a Wood Thrush.* Harcourt Brace & Company, 1997.

Hollywood Elementary School students. "Shrimp Survival!" *Dragonfly: A Magazine for Young Investigators.* National Science Teachers' Association, March/April 1999.

Kesselheim, Alan S., Britt Eckhardt Slattery, Susan H. Higgins, and Mark R. Schilling. *WOW! The Wonders of Wetlands.* Environmental Concern and The Watercourse, 1995.

Lieberman, G. A., and L. L. Hoody. *Closing the Achievement Gap: Using the Environment as an Integrating Context for Learning.* State Education and Environment Roundtable, 1998.

Lingelbach, Jenepher, ed. *Hands-On Nature: Information and Activities for Exploring the Environment with Children.* Vermont Institute of Natural Science, 1986.

Maryland State Department of Education. *Conserving and Enhancing the Natural Environment.* Maryland State Department of Education, 1999.

National Science Education Standards. The National Academies Press, 1996.

North American Association for Environmental Education (NAAEE). *Excellence in EE — Guidelines for Learning (Pre K-12).* NAAEE, 1999.

Project WET Curriculum and Activity Guide. The Watercourse and Council for Environmental Education, 1995.

Project WILD K-12 Curriculum and Activity Guide. Council for Environmental Education, 1992.

U.S. Fish & Wildlife Service. *Schoolyard Habitat Project Guide.* U.S. Fish & Wildlife Service, 1999.

Websites

Chesapeake Bay Foundation

<www.learner.org/jnorth/index.html> Journey North

National Wildlife Federation

Project WILD and Project WET

Project Learning Tree

<http://nationalzoo.si.edu/ConservationAndScience/MigratoryBirds/Education/Teacher_Resources/Bridging_the_americas/default.cfm> Smithsonian Migratory Bird Center, Bridging the Americas Project

<www.seer.org> State Education and Environment Roundtable

Democratic Education for Environmental Stewardship

Practicing authentic democracy at school is one of the best means of preparing students for environmental citizenship

Kay Hyatt-McKenny

by Peter Blaze Corcoran and Margaret Pennock

Grade levels: 3-5

Subject areas: multidisciplinary

Key concepts: democracy in school as the basis for environmental citizenship

Skills: decision making, problem solving, citizenship skills

I f we are to exercise effective stewardship of the planet's natural resources, if we are to be able, through democracy, to reduce consumption and make the changes in lifestyle that are necessary to sustain the Earth's growing population, then we need citizens who are both knowledgeable about environ-

mental issues and skilled in participatory governance. If schools can improve society, it is by preparing children to fulfill these adult responsibilities in democratic and progressive ways.

Over several years from 1974 to 1994, we taught at a unique public elementary school in Freeport, Maine, in which the multi-sensory power of the arts and nature was used to drive learning, and where environmental education and participatory democracy were central concerns in the life of the school. Since we left, the Soule School has merged with two other Freeport Public Schools and its program is now offered as one of three program options for children in Grades 3 to 5. Despite these changes, the Soule School philosophy remains intact; indeed, Soule School's progressive example appears to have had an important influence on the philosophies of the other programs.

In the following, we describe the program and philosophy of the George C. Soule School as an example of how environmental education can be fused with democracy to prepare students for environmental citizenship. The classic definition of environmental education is education in, about, and for the environment. While Soule School provides extraordinary opportunities for learning in and about the natural and cultural environments, our emphasis here is on education *for* the environment, which results from the school's unusual democratic structure and from class and extracurricular activities related to environmental citizenship.

The Soule School program and philosophy

Soule School operates by a vital philosophy written by students, parents, and teachers many years ago but reiteratively interpreted by succeeding "generations" of stakeholders. The school's philosophy holds that children, even at the youngest ages, "should be encouraged to be self-directing, to make decisions and accept the consequences."[1] Thus students are allowed to take responsibility for their own education by choosing their teachers, their classes, and what they do at recess. Students also take part in building and maintaining the quality of life in their school environment by helping to develop school rules, running for and serving on student council, voting in school elections, serving as conflict managers on the playground,[2] meeting to resolve problems that arise at the school, and interviewing adults applying for teaching positions at the school.

Over the years, Soule School has usually had four or five teachers and an enrolment of 90 to 140 students. The important decisions in the life of the school are made by a participatory body of the whole. Each stu-

Kay Hyatt-McKenny

> "Democracy is learned behavior. We are not born with it …. It is only when young people in school experience over and over again, in thousands of individual incidents, the ways in which democracy works and feels that they are going to be able to act democratically."
>
> – G. Grambs and L. Carr, Modern Methods in Secondary Education *(Holt, 1979), p. 111.*

dent (regardless of age), each teacher, each teacher's aide, each cook — everyone — has a vote. The "Big Meeting in the Hall" establishes, and amends as necessary, all school rules. It gives policy direction and advice to the elected student council, which is ultimately responsible to it. In past years, it could be called into session at any time by any single member of the community who felt a meeting was necessary. This extraordinary authority to convene the ultimate legislative body was often tested by the youngest children, who learned early on that their definition of an urgent matter can differ from that of the commonweal.[3]

In the Soule School, listening and speaking skills are considered important outcomes of education because both are needed for action and change. Listening permits new information and ideas to be integrated into decisions. Speaking involves moving out of silence to naming that which is problematic, a necessary step for change. In daily half-hour meetings, students discuss difficulties on the playground, ideas about how to combat stealing, or other pertinent issues that affect the life of the school. They learn to express opinions and listen to all sides of issues, discuss alternatives and the repercussions of those alternatives, make decisions, and later evaluate the effectiveness of those decisions and revise them if necessary.

These small-meeting discussions build thoughtful decision-making skills by encouraging students to anticipate the consequences of their decisions. They develop social responsibility by providing students with feedback on how their actions affect others. They encourage the development of values by immersing students in ethical and moral issues that directly affect their environment. And they often necessitate thinking about complex circumstances, thus preparing children for the intricacies of social and environmental issues. Most importantly, students' participation in all aspects of school life allows them to take authentic action on issues relevant to them and to become the creators of their world at school.

Environment as curriculum

Environmental education is a valued and central aspect of the curriculum and educational experience in the school. It is not uncommon for a visitor to find students in math class studying environmental issues; or students, teachers, and parents heading out on a field trip to a local landfill or a logging site, or going to muck through a salt marsh, or taking a boat to an island they have studied. Soule School lives its philosophy that "children should have the total community as their learning environment and should be taken to every possible place of their interest."[4]

Margaret Pennock

Margaret Pennock

ing and finding joy in nature. Value is also placed on studying issues and their causes, solving problems, and taking action. Thus the Soule School program not only abundantly provides the content of environmental education, but also fosters the integrated thinking and interdisciplinary problem solving central to the comprehension and resolution of environmental problems.

During the years that we were at the school, several three-week units provided in-depth opportunities for students to practice decision making and take action. A unit entitled "Become an Environmental Expert" focused on issues of ozone depletion, smog, and global warming — concerns that were raised by students. Early in the unit, the class learned of a pending bill in the Maine Legislature that would set higher emission-control standards for automobiles sold in the state of Maine. The class considered whether this was an issue they

Class periods are fewer but longer than in traditional schools, reflecting the importance placed on the integration of and relationships among disciplines. Most mornings are divided between classes in mathematics and language arts, while afternoons are devoted to interdisciplinary units that integrate literature, history, geography, social and cultural studies, and the arts. These units are of three weeks' duration and are offered on every imaginable environmental topic: forests, seashores, coral reefs, mammals, ponds, migration, environmental issues, birds, beavers, rivers, acid rain, and rainforests, to name a few. The emphasis is on understanding ecology; on direct observation, experience, and immersion in the outdoors; and on appreciat-

wanted to study, and whether they wished to commit the time that would be needed to prepare testimonies to present at the upcoming hearing in the Legislature. In order to study the issue and prepare materials, the class would need to meet all day for the following two days of school. This would require them to get permission to miss their morning math and language arts classes. Further, the students considered whether they were willing to forego physical education and recess, if necessary, to complete their work. After much deliberation, the class came to the conclusion that this was a unique opportunity that was not to be missed. Thus they dedicated two solid days to researching the issues, considering their opinions, and preparing statements to present before the Legislature. The Legislature

22

acknowledged their eloquent presentation and clear understanding of the issue, and local legislators later informed students that their testimony influenced the final decision to pass the bill.

Students initiated a school environmental club, which they called CAKE (Concerns About Kids' Environment). The group was run democratically, with students making all of the decisions affecting the group. Each year they selected an issue to study and developed a related project. For example, they educated the local community about deforestation of tropical rainforests and raised money to purchase rainforest land in Costa Rica. Their efforts were responsible for a local ordinance to ban the use of polystyrene products, and they supported a bill in the Maine Legislature to ban the use of chlorofluorocarbons in refrigerators.

Education for empowerment

Direct action projects raise the legitimate concern among some adults that young people are being indoctrinated. But this is the antithesis of the Soule School philosophy, which stresses that the role of adults is not to indoctrinate but to attend to concerns expressed by children and to facilitate remedial action. Should students have worries, these worries are acknowledged, and students are given opportunities to take action that in some way improves the situation, whether it affects the life of the school or the life of the broader community. Students not only learn that they can make a difference, they experience making a difference in their communities. Thus their education involves knowledge as well as praxis, both in the school and the community. In this way, Soule School embraces a "pedagogy of empowerment."[5]

An example of this empowerment at work is reflected in the handling of a crisis that was brought on by CAKE's unexpected celebrity. Media coverage of the group's activities had reached local and national levels, but the media consistently chose to portray only the work of the three girls who had initiated the group. Jealousy and resentment erupted, and the group seemed on the verge of breaking up. At the same time, a letter arrived announcing that one of the group's three founders had received an award from the Giraffe Project[6] and would be flown to the former Soviet Union to meet with other young people involved in community action. Up to this point, every decision regarding the group had been made by the students; but the Giraffe Project award raised concerns among the adults working with CAKE students. Should the adults tell the young people about the award, and, if so, how should it be dealt with? Would the award spark the breakup of the group? They reminded themselves of the school's commitment to trusting young people to make the best decision they could.

School Democracy Checklist

Classroom level

✓ Do students share decision making about the curriculum? (Do students have an opportunity to discuss what they want to gain from a course and to shape the direction of a course? Do they have input into how fast the class covers material and the nature of the assignments?)

✓ Do students share decision making about how the class operates? (Do students discuss how they will be evaluated? Do they write self-evaluations of their work? Are they given opportunities to facilitate discussions and teach each other?)

✓ Do the teaching methodologies support democratic skills? (Are students engaged in cooperative learning and collaborative problem-solving activities? Do classroom activities encourage dialogue, active listening, analysis, negotiation, reflection, and evaluation?)

Schoolwide level

✓ Is the school organized in such a way that students and teachers know each other? (For example, are there houses or programs within a large school?)

✓ Is the school or student council involved in policy making about issues that affect the life of the school, such as cheating, attendance, and the use of alcohol and drugs?

✓ Do students, teachers, and staff engage in discussion to determine school rules beyond those required by the state, province, or district?

✓ Is there a community process, such as a judiciary committee, for dealing with infractions of school rules?

✓ Does the school have a school service-learning program? (Is there a process for engaging students, teachers, staff, administrators, and parents in decisions affecting the school? Is there a process for them to be involved in actively creating and improving their school community?)

Community level

✓ Does the school curriculum bridge the classroom experience and the local community?

✓ Are students given opportunities to be of service to their community through courses or service learning programs?

✓ Does the school draw upon the resources of the community, providing opportunities for students to interact with a wide variety of people who have a range of perspectives, values, and experiences?

— *by Margaret Pennock*

23

The CAKE group met 30 minutes a day for a week. The first meeting was fraught with feelings of anger and resentment, but each day the students listened to one another and were asked to think about what they heard in the group that day. After three or four meetings, they agreed that it was important to work through their difficulties because they did not want to miss this opportunity to share their work with others in the world. But they insisted that the Giraffe Project allow them to select a representative since it was their combined efforts that enabled them to accomplish what they did. The Project agreed to accept their choice. Over the next few days the group discussed criteria for selecting their representative and decided how they would vote. They didn't want to know how many votes each person received; they just wanted to know the result, and then celebrate with ice cream. Interestingly, the girl who had been selected by the Giraffe Project was not chosen by the group, yet it was evident that she was genuinely pleased that the choice was a group decision.

The children of Soule School learn to work, to struggle, and to celebrate together, and to care for and respect one another. We have rarely seen adults do as well. They have moved us deeply with their ability to be compassionate, thoughtful, and intelligent. They are testimony to what is possible in education. We believe that this vital spirit of community, democracy, and empowerment can survive childhood and make a difference in the lives of these students and in the communi-

Margaret Pennock

ties and institutions of which they become a part. We believe that democratic education, which includes empowerment, social responsibility, and caring, can prepare students for environmental citizenship. ✍

Peter Blaze Corcoran is a Professor of Environmental Studies and Environmental Education at Florida Gulf Coast University, and the Director of the Center for Environmental and Sustainability Education. He began his teaching career as a mathematics teacher at George C. Soule School and served as teaching principal from 1976 to 1979. Margaret Tatnall Pennock teaches middle school science at Sidwell Friends School in Washington, D.C. She went to George C. Soule School as an intern during her high school senior year and later returned as a mathematics teacher from 1986 to 1990 and from 1992 to 1994.

Notes

1. From the George C. Soule School Program Philosophy; see <www.freeportpublicschools.org/mls/choices/soule.html>.

2. Interested students are trained as mediators to attend to conflicts between students both in school and on the playground.

3. Many students, years later, have remarked on the exhilarating and empowering nature of this practice.

4. From the George C. Soule School Program Philosophy; see <www.freeportpublicschools.org/mls/choices/soule.html>.

5. Seth Kreisberg, *Transforming Power: Domination, Empowerment, and Education,* State University of New York Press, 1992.

6. The Giraffe Project is a nonprofit initiative to recognize young people who "stick their necks out for the common good"; see <www.giraffe.org>.

Guiding Your School Toward Environmental Literacy

Photographs by Calgary Board of Education

by Jeff Reading

Grade levels: K-6

Subject areas: multidisciplinary

Key concepts: environmental literacy

Professional skills: collaborative curriculum planning using an environmental literacy model

Time: 6 days of staff time over the course of a school year

An environmentally literate citizenry — one with the capacity to perceive, interpret, and take appropriate action to improve the health of natural systems — is the ultimate goal of environmental education. Yet environmental education often stops short of achieving this goal because it aims no further than to increase students' knowledge of natural systems and awareness of environmental issues. While these are important aims, we know that knowledge and awareness alone do not necessarily lead people to change their lifestyles and behavior or to take action on environmental issues. Education for environmental literacy must also help students to make personal connections to issues, and it must include a lifestyle-modification and action phase that is a conscious application of their new understanding.

Guiding a school community toward environmentally literacy is not difficult. It does, however, require a subtle, yet profound, shift in teaching strategies and a dedication to long-term change. The following is an overview of a five-step process that has been employed and honed over the past ten years by many schools in Calgary, Alberta. The objective of the process is to develop a three- to five-year school plan for leading teachers, students, and their families to become knowledgeable, concerned, and empowered individuals who understand their personal impact on the Earth and actively seek ways to maintain or improve the health of the planet.

Environmental literacy model

At the center of this process is an environmental literacy model that serves as a framework for developing a program that supports environmental literacy across all grades and curricular areas. (See Environmental and

Outdoor Education Model, below.) Within this framework, action is supported by awareness, understanding, and examination of personal values, and it is coupled with decision making, communication, and leadership. In program planning, teachers work to achieve the outcomes described in each cell of the model through a carefully crafted sequence of activities that provide opportunities to build knowledge (Foundation level) through interactive experiences (Exploration level) that ultimately lead to responsible action (Empowerment).

Adopting an environmental literacy model that fosters both environmental understanding and stewardship requires no more time than any school typically allocates to fostering culture and academic excellence. Further, it can be done within the existing program of studies (regardless of regional variations), and hence does not add to an already crowded curriculum. It requires no extra money and does not depend on teachers being well informed about science or the environment. All it requires is that everyone approach change with a positive and open attitude and be willing to take a fresh look at how their curriculum is being

delivered. The use of this model has been particularly successful at the elementary and middle school levels where there tends to be an integrated approach to curriculum delivery and a school climate that is flexible and tolerant of change. Within schools that have adopted it, the environmental literacy model has been shown to enhance achievement test results, community and family involvement in schools, and students' interest in learning.

A collaborative and long-term approach

This path to programming for environmental literacy is a collaborative and cooperative adventure that affords participants the opportunity to clarify what is important to them and articulate a common vision of a preferred future. It begins with teachers examining what they are presently doing to address environmental topics and issues across the curriculum. Efforts are then refocused, using the environment as a vehicle, toward a curriculum that will foster healthier connections with the Earth and its life-supporting systems. The challenge is to step beyond the present paradigm that usually finds

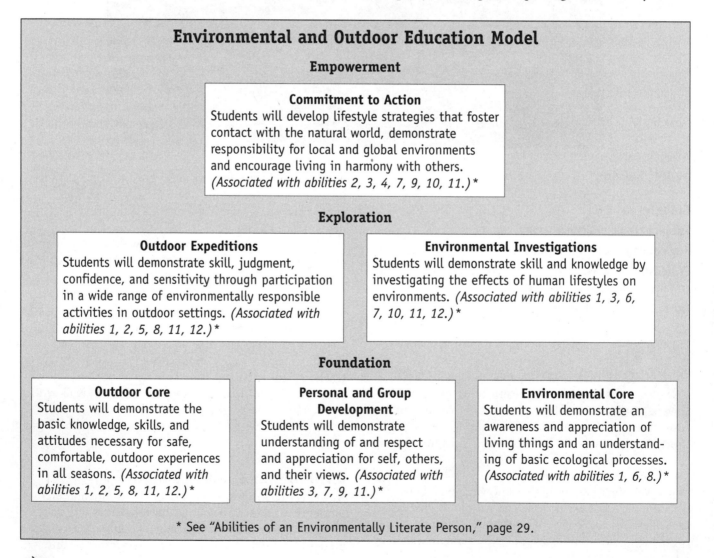

Environmental and Outdoor Education Model

Empowerment

Commitment to Action
Students will develop lifestyle strategies that foster contact with the natural world, demonstrate responsibility for local and global environments and encourage living in harmony with others. *(Associated with abilities 2, 3, 4, 7, 9, 10, 11.)* *

Exploration

Outdoor Expeditions
Students will demonstrate skill, judgment, confidence, and sensitivity through participation in a wide range of environmentally responsible activities in outdoor settings. *(Associated with abilities 1, 2, 5, 8, 11, 12.)* *

Environmental Investigations
Students will demonstrate skill and knowledge by investigating the effects of human lifestyles on environments. *(Associated with abilities 1, 3, 6, 7, 10, 11, 12.)* *

Foundation

Outdoor Core
Students will demonstrate the basic knowledge, skills, and attitudes necessary for safe, comfortable, outdoor experiences in all seasons. *(Associated with abilities 1, 2, 5, 8, 11, 12.)* *

Personal and Group Development
Students will demonstrate understanding of and respect and appreciation for self, others, and their views. *(Associated with abilities 3, 7, 9, 11.)* *

Environmental Core
Students will demonstrate an awareness and appreciation of living things and an understanding of basic ecological processes. *(Associated with abilities 1, 6, 8.)* *

* See "Abilities of an Environmentally Literate Person," page 29.

26

individual teachers doing their own thing for the environment, to create a sequential program in which each teacher's efforts support and build upon the efforts of others.

Central to the process is the notion that the new plan that emerges will be a long-term commitment; hence is not a process that can be rushed. Ideally, a school will devote a full year to developing a vision, piloting activities, and eventually articulating a three- to five-year school improvement plan. After that, the plan is regularly revisited and revised to reflect new learning and changes in school and community dynamics. Becoming environmentally literate does not have an end point, but is rather a process in which we are constantly challenged to increase our knowledge and improve our skills of stewardship. The plan that the school develops is therefore a "living tool" of sorts, a model that guides a process of continually reflecting on teaching practices.

The process

Developing a program that fosters environmental literacy throughout a school community is a five-step process that includes teachers, administration, maintenance staff, parents, and community members. It usually requires five or six full days of meetings and discussions over the course of the school year. Establishing a relaxed and comfortable atmosphere is important for making the most of this process. Consider holding these deliberations somewhere other than at school. An outdoor center, away from the day-to-day distractions of school and with access to the natural world, is optimal, so that the discussion can be broken up with outdoor activities. This also provides an opportunity for participants who have limited background in outdoor activities to see local facilities and experience first hand how environment-focused activities can integrate learning.

Keep in mind that not everyone will engage enthusiastically in these new directions. Therefore, at each phase of the process sufficient time must be allocated to allow complete review, debate, and exploration of whatever issues unfold. Opportunities to clarify personal values and to examine differences in culture,

pedagogy — and even workload — are essential. It will be helpful if the process is facilitated by someone who has experience in navigating groups through a thought-provoking process such as this. This could be a school staff person, district consultant, community member, professional facilitator, or school administrator.

1. Establish a school council

Developing a model for environmental literacy requires that the school community rethink how the school operates — not just in the classrooms, but also in the front office and behind the scenes. It is important for teachers to model positive environmental habits, but equally important to use energy and resources efficiently throughout the school and to consider the types of materials used by custodians. To facilitate the changes that will be needed throughout the school, a school council should be assembled that consists of teachers, administrators, support staff, students, parents, and community members. The more familiar that parents and community are with the new direction the school is considering, the more successful the overall results will be. Businesses will be more supportive and encouraging, parents will be more tolerant and involved, and, most importantly, students are less likely to be caught up in a quagmire of conflicting values and habits as they try to adopt a new environmental ethic in their personal lives.

The school council serves as an advisory board in all decisions and phases of the process. The council's first challenges are to create awareness of the need for change and to develop grassroots support. This is done through classroom conversations with students; through presentations and discussions at staff meetings, school council meetings, and community functions; and through the school newsletter, website, and other communication vehicles. As the process unfolds, the council facilitates meetings, collates and distributes the documents produced, and keeps everyone informed of developments and progress. From the outset it is important that members of the school council "walk the talk" and act as role models for environmental literacy.

Simple things such as reducing paper consumption or serving healthy, locally produced snacks on non-disposable dishes at meetings send important informal messages about the school's dedication to a new way of thinking.

2. Identify and evaluate the environmental education presently being done in the school and community (1 day)

The goal of the first day-long meeting is to produce a snapshot of what is currently being done in the school and community to foster learning about the environment. The following steps are offered as a guideline for proceedings.

Materials: Copies of the Environmental and Outdoor Education Model (see page 26), blank planning charts (see "Preparation" below), materials to conduct outdoor activities.

Preparation: Create a planning chart on 11-by-17-inch paper. Place headings for all of the subject areas of the curriculum across the top, and headings for all areas (cells) in the Environmental and Outdoor Education Model down the left side. What results is a chart of boxes that can be filled in to reflect the current state of affairs and/or to plan for the future. Make a supply of these charts, as they will be used throughout the process.

Procedure:

1. Organize participants into planning teams comprised of teachers from every grade in the school, together with representatives of the school council.

2. Provide each group with blank planning charts (one for each grade level) and a copy of the Environmental and Outdoor Education Model (see page 26).

3. Using the Environmental and Outdoor Education Model as a guide, ask groups to work together to answer the question, "What is currently being taught or done at each grade level to enhance environmental awareness in students?" For each component of the model (three Foundation components, two Exploration components, and one Empowerment component) and for each subject taught, they are to list the activities

that help to enhance environmental awareness. The result is a series of charts, one for each grade level, showing individual efforts in each subject and indicating which areas of the environmental literacy model those activities fit into.

4. Conclude with a sharing session during which each multi-grade group presents their charts to the entire group. Collectively, the charts form a snapshot of the current practice across all grades at the school.

5. Copy and collate the completed charts from each group and distribute them to all. These can be reviewed in preparation for the next step in the process.

The importance of this part of the process is threefold. First, it fosters greater understanding and appreciation for what is happening in other classrooms at all grade levels. (One teacher remarked how surprised he was at how little he knew about what other people were teaching, and how creatively the required curriculum was being interpreted and taught.) Second, it requires that everyone discuss what environmental issues are important and relevant to them and at the grade level they teach, as well as to the school and community. And third, it identifies the "holes" in the present approach to addressing environmental concerns across the curriculum. This stage in the process cannot be rushed. The opportunity to share ideas, compare philosophies, and gain common ground is essential. Break up the day with a selection of outdoor activities that provide opportunities for team building and interaction with the natural world.

3. Establish a vision and mission (1-2 days)

In the second session, participants gain an understanding of environmental literacy and begin to develop a collective vision of how it could be articulated across all grades, curricula, and school operations.

Materials: List of abilities associated with environmental literacy (see sidebar), copies of the Environmental and Outdoor Education Model, blank planning charts, materials for a few outdoor activities, and a selection of books and other resources to stimulate thought and provide ideas.

Procedure:

1. Begin this part of the process with an in-depth look at environmental literacy. Discuss the differences between environmental awareness and environmental literacy. Environmental literacy is defined as "the capacity to perceive and interpret the relative health of environmental systems and to take appropriate action to maintain, restore or improve the relative health of those systems."[1] In essence, environmental awareness is a state of *knowing*, while environmental literacy is a state of *being*. Education for environmental awareness is often about describing or identifying. Education for environmental literacy, on the other hand, weaves knowledge and

experience into action. It takes students beyond knowing to a new understanding that they are part of the environment, and an intrinsic motivation to make responsible day-to-day lifestyle choices and take actions that contribute to a healthy planet.

2. Next, discuss the 12 abilities that characterize an environmentally literate person (see sidebar). If possible, introduce each ability in conjunction with an activity that illustrates it. For example, to facilitate discussion of the ability to communicate, set up a "minefield" of obstacles (natural and otherwise) within a designated natural area. Ask each person to select a partner. One partner is then blind-

Abilities of an Environmentally Literate Person

The following 12 abilities of an environmentally literate person are distilled from research on environmental literacy and systems thinking. They are intended only to provide direction. Environmentally literacy is a constant state of becoming. It is not an end unto itself. These abilities are not intended as a checklist or as measures of success. Instead, they represent characteristics or capabilities that individuals and systems, like schools, constantly aspire to achieve.

1. Ability to understand how natural systems work and to recognize that human health is connected to the health of these systems

2. Ability to think ahead, to forecast, and to plan

3. Ability to think critically about issues that involve personal values and cultural or societal beliefs

4. Ability to move from awareness, to understanding, to appropriate action

5. Ability to distinguish reality from projected views
The ability to recognize that visual images of beautiful and seemingly healthy environments do not necessarily represent reality.

6. Ability to learn new concepts, to challenge current thinking, and to relinquish old ideas

7. Ability to communicate ideas and to offer persuasive and informed arguments, both orally and in writing

8. Ability to value the aesthetic as well as the conceptual
The ability to grasp scientific concepts related to the environment, but at the same time to recognize the value of such aesthetic characteristics as beauty, harmony, and balance, and to include these in decision making.

9. Ability to make a long-term commitment to work cooperatively on issues of concern
The ability to recognize that problems are solved incrementally over time; and that most environmental concerns are very complex and require a cooperative effort both to identify the problem and to chart and implement an effective course of action.

10. Ability to evaluate the effects of change critically before influencing change
The ability to consider the consequences of action and change and to avoid quick-fix solutions in favor of solutions that are long term and sustainable.

11. Ability to offer leadership that supports meaningful change
The ability to demonstrate personal conviction and dedication to environmental stewardship, despite a plethora of media, consumer, and social pressures to do otherwise.

12. Ability to attain a balanced lifestyle that includes experiences outdoors in the natural world

— based on research on environmental literacy and systems thinking by Carey Booth, Skid Crease, John Disinger, Milton McLaren, David Orr, Charles Roth, David Selby, Peter Senge, Ian Waugh, Edward Wilson, and others.

folded and must walk through the minefield (barefoot if possible) guided only by the voice of the partner, who gives directions from outside the designated area.

After each activity, discuss the insights that emerge about the ability being discussed. For example, the minefield activity may reveal cultural differences in the interpretation of words or phrases, or the difficulty of discriminating a single voice amidst the "white noise" of several people talking at once. Such communication challenges parallel those encountered in discussing environmental issues and underscore the importance of articulating opinions in a thoughtful, respectful manner.

3. Have participants form teams consisting of teachers from the same grade level and members of the school council. With a fresh understanding of environmental literacy and an awareness of how environmental topics are currently being addressed at school (charts from previous session), teams can begin to develop a collective vision and mission. The question during this phase is "How can we integrate environmental literacy across the grades, disciplines, and the school community to create environmentally literate citizens?"

4. Re-introduce the Environmental and Outdoor Education Model, this time emphasizing the environmental literacy abilities that are associated with each cell of the model.

5. Provide each group with a blank planning chart (the same template that was used in the first session). Ask them to refer to the charts developed during the first session, and begin the process of filling in gaps, redefining their learning and teaching practices, and injecting into the curriculum a sequence of lessons, activities, and experiences that support the Empowerment actions they select. The key is not to add to the curriculum, but to use the environment as a vehicle to teach what is already being taught. This often means integrating the subject areas and moving away from a compartmentalized approach to curriculum delivery. Special attention should be given to how Foundation and Exploration activities will develop environmental literacy while still addressing the program of studies. Consider that, to become environmentally literate, students need to understand basic natural processes; explore, through environmental investigation, the effects that lifestyles have on the environment; and recognize how individual actions can maintain or improve the health of the planet.

As an example, Cecil Swanson Elementary School in northeast Calgary had a problem with lunchtime garbage and food waste. Through science, language arts, and social studies, the *foundations* of waste management were discussed. To build on this base on knowledge, a variety of *explorations* were planned: students visited landfill sites; toured the community to determine the sources of local litter and garbage; invited waste management experts into the classroom; and buried a variety of typical lunch garbage in the school field, creating their own mini-landfill site to be dug up periodically over the years to see how the contents decomposed. Their efforts culminated in *empowerment* activities through which they translated what they had learned into responsible action. A recycling center was built to collect lunchtime recyclables (it also served as a fundraiser). The students initiated a garbage-free lunch campaign and began composting the remains of lunches brought to school. The compost was used in large planter boxes in which students grew vegetables, flowers, and herbs in each classroom. Local businesses were encouraged to adopt practices that reduced litter. To complete the empowerment phase, multi-grade student groups made presentations on waste reduction at neighboring schools.

6. The final goal of this phase is for the groups to explore how school practices could better reflect environmental literacy, such as through reducing the consumption of energy and materials, creating a natural area on school grounds, and using more environment-friendly cleaning materials in the school. Many schools have achieved significant energy conservation and sizable financial savings by doing simple things such as turning off lights, computers, and unnecessary appliances at night; recycling materials for which deposits are offered; and working with after-hours user groups to ensure that they support the school's efforts to reduce their environmental impact.

In essence, during this phase of the process, school communities create a common vision and establish the framework to realize it. They re-examine what they are presently doing and discuss what aspects of the current curriculum and school operations could be addressed using environmental issues, concepts, and approaches. When this phase is finished, the completed charts from each group are shared, collated, and circulated to everyone. These charts are grade-specific curriculum maps that indicate how the program of studies is integrated, bridged, and addressed as they pursue educational activities that reflect environmental literacy.

4. Explore opportunities for out-of-classroom activities (1 day)

Any classroom teaching is more effective if students perceive it to be relevant outside of school. For this reason, it is important to include out-of-classroom learning activities in the plan. In this session, participants create a field trip chart and a list of potential partnerships to support the new educational objectives.

Materials: All materials developed to date.

Procedure:

1. Have participants reconvene in multi-grade teams to review and edit the curriculum charts. After they review the future plans for each grade level, have them complete a chart to outline potential field study opportunities. The aim is to share ideas to ensure that the best venues are being used, and that there is a logical sequence of off-site activities, and minimal repetition, from one grade to the next.

As an example, Grade 5 students at Deer Run Elementary School in Calgary spend at least 25 percent of their instructional time in the following out-of-classroom activities:

Wilderness: Five-day residential outdoor school experience in the autumn to enhance class dynamics and lay the foundation for the year ahead; three day-trips to an urban protected area for ecology studies; three day-trips to the mountains to explore wilderness environments.

Rural: Visit to a local heritage park to explore the historical connections of people with the land; trip to a local Hutterite colony to learn a different cultural perspective on the environment; visits to a local produce and dairy farm to learn about food production issues.

Urban: Raft trip down a river through the city to explore influences on the river (stormwater and water treatment center outflows, flora, fauna, recreation, etc.); a public transit "scavenger hunt"

leading to unique natural areas within the city; visits to landfill sites, water treatment facilities, utility plants, and engineered wetlands; urban contrast program to compare land uses in different areas of the city; walking and cycling trips to explore ways to apply learning in the local community.

Schoolyard: Regular walks through a local natural area to augment all curriculum areas; work on restoring a portion of the schoolyard to a natural state.

2. Have each multi-grade team assemble a list of potential partners that could support this new educational objective. These could include granting organizations, local businesses that offer educational venues, organizations that could provide in-class expertise on designated environmental topics, government organizations that have educational materials already developed, and so on.

3. Copy, collate, and distribute all of the revised curriculum charts, lists of off-site activities from each group, and the lists of potential partnerships.

5. Develop a strategic plan (1 day)

The final phase of the process is to develop a strategic plan or grade-specific road map that consolidates, prioritizes, and charts these new curricular opportunities and directions. The advisory council synthesizes all the planning charts, information about environmental literacy, resource lists, off-site activity charts, and lists of potential partners and community supporters. These, along with pertinent ideas and insights that have emerged from the process are woven into a comprehensive three- to five-year strategic plan. (There is no template for this, as expectations and documentation requirements vary from school to school and district to district.) This strategic plan is the blueprint for future curriculum implementation and the guide for revising teaching strategies, directing school purchasing, and designing professional development programs for teachers and the school community as a whole. The plan should continue to grow through regular revision as expertise increases and educational successes add new insights into how to teach for environmental literacy.

Communicating the plan

Every effort should be made to communicate the new plan widely and to celebrate the successes that come from it. Host an information night at the school to profile the school's new direction. Publicize plans and successes in a school newsletter, post them on a school website, and circulate then to local businesses and potential partners. Also consider the development of a "How to" booklet for parents that describes what it means to be environmentally literate and how families can support their children and the school.

This process of guiding a school toward environmental literacy is effective because it is simple and it accommodates local educational goals and topical environmental concerns. It involves all of the educational stakeholders and consciously channels their creative talents towards building a common vision for the future. The strategic plan that emerges involves many disciplines, incorporates the community, gets students out of the classroom, and, most important, provides experiences and learning that is relevant to `the students.

As adults, we can best prepare students to solve environmental problems by providing them with experiences now that will enable them to make informed decisions about their lifestyle and impact on the Earth. When individuals are aware of their personal connection to the natural world and understand natural processes, when they take responsibility for their own impact, when they make efforts to optimize this impact and assist others with similar goals, then they are well along the path to becoming environmentally literate citizens. ✍

Jeff Reading is a Specialist in Off-site Activities in Environmental and Outdoor Education with the Calgary Board of Education in Calgary, Alberta.

Note

1 John F. Disinger and Charles E. Roth, "Environmental Literacy," *ERIC/CSMEE Digest,* ERIC Clearinghouse for Science, Mathematics and Environmental Education, November 1992, ED 351201.

Chris Earley

Exploring Nature Around Us

The Single Concept Field Trip

A collection of quick single-topic outings focusing on nature and ecology

by Clarke Birchard and Alan Crook

Grade levels: K-5

Subject areas: multidisciplinary

Key concepts: natural cycles and patterns, seed dispersal, adaptation, classification

Skills: observation, inference, analysis, synthesis, problem solving, creative writing, drawing

Location: outdoors

Time: 10 minutes or more per activity

 an ten minutes outside make a difference? You bet it can. There is good evidence that immediate contact with the outdoor environment leads to effective learning and makes school more engaging and relevant to students. An easy, quick, and fun way to make that contact is by taking short single-concept field trips to the school-yard or a nearby park. Such trips can be used to stimulate sensory awareness, introduce key concepts, or provide concrete examples of textbook lessons. They can also overcome many of the logistical problems that often keep classes indoors. As Helen Ross Russell states in her classic book *Ten-Minute Field Trips*, "There are many important advantages to using the school grounds as the main base of operations. There is no scheduling problem; no waiting for a date; no need to hurry or interrupt a classroom topic; you can go for ten minutes several times a day if it suits the topic; and the number of field trips is limitless."

Following is a selection of "single topic" outings that may be completed in 10 to 30 minutes on or near the school grounds. Some outings could be extended for longer periods, or they could be joined in various sequences to form the "script" of longer, themed trips taken near the school or as part of an outing to a park or conservation area. Some of the suggestions are very simple and concrete, while others involve higher-level thinking or more abstract concepts. Just remember that these outings should be connected to larger learning goals rather than undertaken in isolation. Always look for ways to reinforce the experience and link it to the curriculum through discussion or some method of physical record keeping.

Relationships

Look for evidence of things that need other things. After listing and discussing a number of examples, have students find examples that fit the following categories:

- two things that cannot get along without each other (two-way relationships)

- one thing that cannot get along without the other (a one-way relationship)

- one thing, process, or event that is the direct cause of another

  - one thing, process, or event that is the result of another

    Classroom link: In the classroom, have students create a web or a mobile that shows examples of these relationships. Illustrate it with students' drawings, digital images from the trip, or with physical representations such as leaves, twigs, stones, and feathers.

    Note: When collecting natural objects, ensure that taking them will not have a negative impact on the surrounding area. Return the items where they were found when the class has finished using them.

Changes

Find evidence of changes taking place. Students may not be able to see the changes and so will have to infer them from the observable evidence. Ask students to find changes that fit the following categories:

- something that is getting bigger

- something that is getting smaller

- something that is getting more complex (e.g., a sprouting seed or an insect egg, cocoon, or pupa)

- something that is getting simpler (e.g., parts of plants or animals that are decaying)

- something that is harming something else (a value judgment, of course)

- something that is benefiting something else
- changes that follow predictable patterns and repeat regularly (cycles)

Extension: Provide students with pencils, index cards, and string. Have them make tags on which to record their predictions of change (e.g., "4 cm at widest point on April 7; will get bigger" or "Will turn yellow in September"). Students can attach the tags to the items and check later to see if their predictions were correct.

Classifying

Classify natural objects in a variety of ways:

1. Give students bags and have them gather many different kinds of leaves, pebbles, or other natural objects.

2. Spread the objects on a table or on sheets of plastic for sorting. It is best to sort natural objects on site so that they can be returned to their source immediately afterward.

3. Ask students to suggest categories into which the items could be sorted. Initially, allow them to come up with their own criteria. Then, through discussion, move them toward an understanding of the usefulness of observable physical characteristics (e.g., big, small) and the difficulty of qualitative characteristics (e.g., pretty, ugly).

4. Have students sort the objects into the categories that have been agreed on. For example, leaves could be sorted according to whether they are smooth-edged or jagged, simple (one part) or compound (more than one part); pebbles could be sorted according to whether they are rounded or angular, colored or plain, harder than a nail or softer than a nail.

Extension: In a diverse, deciduous woodlot, have students collect as many leaves as they can in a specified period of time (30 seconds to three minutes, depending on ease of collecting). Then ask them to sort this random sample into as many different categories as they can. Count the number of leaves in each category and rank the categories accordingly. Which type of leaf is the most common? Which is the least common? What does this say about the relative dominance of various tree species in the woodlot? *Caution:* Inspect the area for poison ivy/oak before beginning this exercise.

Classroom link: In the classroom, have students graph the results of their leaf classification and find the percentage that each type represents.

Seed travelers

Provide each student or group of students with an egg carton for collecting seeds. Challenge them to collect a seed that hitchhikes, a seed that blows in the wind, a seed that travels by tummy (has "fruit" around it), a seed that spins like a helicopter rotor, a seed case that explodes, and any other kinds of seeds that you can think of. Alternatively, have students make seed "magnets" by stuffing old tube socks with newspaper. Tie a long string to the end of each sock, and drag it through a field or along the edge of a woodland. Use magnifying lenses to study the seeds that adhere to the socks.

Classroom link: Have students try to sprout some of the seeds they have collected on a piece of moist filter paper. If the students have used sock collectors, have them pull out the newspaper, place the ends of the socks in a dish of water, and watch their socks sprout![1]

Signs of the seasons

Have students find signs of the seasons and either collect objects or make drawings to represent them. Seasonal signs might include the following:

Fall: colored leaves, cricket songs, flocking birds, cool air, drifting seeds
Winter: snow, ice, leafless trees, animal tracks in snow, empty bird nests, icicles
Spring: warm air, melting snow, growing buds, spring flowers, singing birds
Summer: hot sun, leafed-out trees, busy insects, young birds, animal tracks in mud

Classroom link: In class, create a collage of collected items and images for each season, and compare. What's similar? different? Why?

Nature sounds

Have students create sound maps:

1. Ask students to stop, close their eyes, and listen to all the sounds they can hear, such as wind, rain, crickets, frogs, birds, and footfalls. If it is windy and trees are nearby, have students put one ear against the trunk of a tree, plug the other ear with a finger, and listen to the creaks and taps as the tree is tossed and bent by the breeze.

2. Have students mark a dot in the center of a piece of paper to represent themselves. Then ask them locate each sound they hear on the map and draw the sound using symbols or combinations of vowels and consonants that approximate the sounds.[2]

Classroom link: In class, compare the sound maps. Ask students to recreate some of the sounds on their maps and find out if others heard it, or heard it the same way. Relate the sounds of nature to the sounds of various instruments.

Untimely ends ... new beginnings

Look for signs of destruction or death in nature, such as a fly caught in a spider web, a rock or sidewalk cracked by a tree root, a tree cut or blown down, something burned by fire, an animal killed by a car, a leaf eaten by an insect, or a flower stepped on by a human. Many examples may be found of human activities and the built environment bumping up against the natural environment, but some of the interactions may be entirely natural. Ask students whether they think these "untimely ends" are good or bad, and have them explain why. What ends may lead to new beginnings? Photograph or sketch any evidence of these new beginnings, and create a class display. Go back to visit the site later to see what changes have taken place.

Movements

Have students focus on movement in nature. Look for moving clouds; things blowing in the wind; flowers that open and close; things that fly, walk, run, hop, jump, or gallop; things that grow larger or get smaller; things that flow, and so on. Ask students to work either individually or in small groups to imitate or interpret some of these natural motions, and have others try to guess what is being represented.

Discards

Look for things that have been left behind, such as droppings, litter, tracks, the crumbs left after a meal by birds or mammals (including humans), cocoons, snakeskins, insect molts, egg cases, etc. Have students become detectives, asking questions such as: What animal might have left the item behind? What is the evidence? What happened here? Discuss the similarities and differences between nature's discards and humans' discards. Collect any litter that is found and take it back to the classroom.

Classroom link: In the classroom, analyze the litter by classifying, counting, and graphing each type. What is the most common type of litter? Where did it come from? Who might have left it there? Is there any way to reduce littering (more waste cans, less packaging, educating litterbugs, etc.)? Try to do it!

Patterns and shapes

Have students look for shapes in nature, such as circles, stars, lines, and triangles, and for patterns, such as waves and radiations. Record as many as possible through sketches, rubbings, or photos. To help students focus on the shapes and patterns, provide frames made from index cards, or "telescopes" made from toilet paper tubes.

Classroom link: In class, have students sort the shapes into major groups and count the number in each group. Order and graph the groups by total number or percentage. Combine the items in each group, or the items from several groups, into larger works of art.

Coverings and textures

Have students sensitize their fingers by rubbing them lightly over fine sandpaper. Then have them gently touch a variety of natural objects with only their fingertips. Objects to touch might include rocks, trees, feathers, leaves, seeds, nuts, fruit, and small animals (e.g., insects, frogs, salamanders, worms, and small fish that can be caught with a dip net and carefully touched with wet fingers). In pairs, have one partner  touch something while blindfolded, and then, with the blindfold removed, attempt to find the item by sight and then by touch. Collect textures by making rubbings that can be brought back to class.

Adaptations

Look for evidence of the ways in which animals and plants have adapted to their environment. Focus on diggers, climbers, jumpers, flyers, swimmers, runners; and on plants that climb, spread, grow tall, like sun, like shade. What physical characteristics do many or most members of a group have in common? How do some members differ from others in their group? Do they do some things differently? If so, are their adaptations different? For example, all frogs and toads leap about on strong hind legs, but frogs are moist and toads are dry; tree frogs use suction cups on their fingers and toes to stick to and climb vertical surfaces. All flying creatures have wings, but the variations in number, size, material, and structure are almost infinite.

Classroom link: In class, look up other members of a group that you saw on your trip, and see how they solve the challenges of living as they do.

Remnants of yesterday

Look for old nests, leaf skeletons, trails, footprints, naturally dried flowers, tree stumps, old fences and foundations, driftwood, etc. What stories might they tell?

Classroom link: In class, have students create stories that link several of the remnants observed on the field trip.

Miniatures

Go on a hike to find things that can be best observed with a magnifying glass, such as spider webs, flies' wings, grass blades, and the insides of flowers. Sketch some of these items. Find a log or boulder and take a visual "hike" along it with a magnifying glass held to one eye. Create an interpretive trail by marking interesting things with flags that are attached to round toothpicks (use modeling clay to hold toothpicks to rocks). Invite others to go on your trail.[3]

Classroom link: In class, have students use their sketches to create an illustrated story of their hike.

Cycles

Find something that is part of a natural cycle such as plant–bud–flower–seed–plant, egg–larva–pupa–adult–egg, or egg–tadpole–frog–egg. Have students draw or tag the object so that they can find it later. Go back several times during the year and identify as many parts of the cycle as possible.

Homes and habitat

Look for the homes of animals, such as nests, burrows, dens, hiding places, and tree holes, and check for any signs of activity. Have students speculate on what animal might live there. Look for places nearby that might provide food, water, and other shelter that the animal might use. Mark these spots with surveyor's tape in order to help students get a visual sense of the whole area, or habitat, that the animal lives in.

Ten minutes *can* make a difference. Just stepping out the door can change perceptions and perspectives and awaken the senses. All it takes is a bit of planning, some simple tools, and a little time. ✿

The Ten-minute Toolbox

Simple field-study tools for focusing attention, shifting perspective, enhancing the senses, and collecting objects and information that will extend the learning back in the classroom. Add your own tools to the following basic set:

Bandanas: use as blindfolds or carry-alls

Toilet paper tubes, note card frames: focus on small objects; frame landscape elements

Magnifying lenses, bug boxes: observe objects close up

Paper, pencils, chalk, crayons: take field notes; make maps, drawings, and rubbings

Tape recorder, camera: bring information back to the classroom

Surveyor's tape: use as a quick identifier; mark borders or boundaries

Egg cartons: collect and organize objects

Clarke Birchard is the former Supervisor of Outdoor Education and Science for the Bruce County Board of Education in Ontario. He is retired and lives in Chesley, Ontario. Alan Crook has worked in environmental, outdoor, and resource education for over 25 years, and is currently an educator with the Ontario Ministry of Natural Resources in Peterborough, Ontario.

Adapted from *Pathways* 7:4, June 1994.

Notes

1 Kathryn Sheehan and Mary Waidner, *Earth Child, Games, Stories, Activities, Experiments & Ideas About Living Lightly on Planet Earth*, Council Oak Books, 1994, p. 98.

2 Van Matre, Steve, *Acclimatizing: A Personal and Reflective Approach to a Natural Relationship*, American Camping Association, 1974, p. 64.

3 Van Matre, p. 80.

References

Blakey, Nancy. *Go Outside: Over 130 Activities for Outdoor Adventures.* Ten Speed Press, 2002.

Burnie, David. *101 Nature Experiments.* DK Publishing, 2001. (Ages 9-12.)

Institute of Ecosystem Studies, "Annotated Resource Directory of Schoolyard/Backyard Ecology Activities," on-line at <http://www.ecostudies.org/syefest/ap3res2.htm>.

Roberts, Allene. *The Curiosity Club: Kids' Nature Activity Book.* John Wiley & Sons, 1992.

Rockwell, Robert. *Hug a Tree and Other Things to Do Outdoors With Young Children.* Gryphon House, 1983.

Roth, Chas. E., Cleti Cervoni, Thomas Wellnitz, and Elizabeth Arms. *Beyond the Classroom: Exploration of Schoolground and Backyard.* University of Massachusetts Press, 1991. (K-6 activities.)

Rothschild, Cynthia. "Walking into Wonder." *Green Teacher* 74, Fall 2004, pp. 24-26.

Russell, H.R. *Ten Minute Field Trips.* National Science Teachers Association, 1990.

Sheehan, Kathryn, and Mary Waidner. *Earth Child, Games, Stories, Activities, Experiments & Ideas About Living Lightly on Planet Earth.* Council Oak Books, 1994.

Silver, Donald. *One Small Square: Backyard* (interactive multimedia CD). Virgin Sound and Vision, 1995. (Ages 6-10.)

Van Matre, Steve. *Acclimatizing: A Personal and Reflective Approach to a Natural Relationship.* American Camping Association, 1974.

From Pattern to Principle:
Discovering Science Through Observing Patterns in Nature

Illustrations by Sandy Orris

by Robert Barkman

Grade levels: 3-6
Subject areas: science, biology, ecology
Key concepts: adaptation, diversity, energy distribution
Skills: observation, pattern recognition, measurement
Location: outdoors

Lichens growing in circles, the sun's changing position at sunrise, Earth's warming trend, the "Morse code" of firefly flashes — all are patterns of nature. These and other natural patterns have inspired great questions leading to historical discoveries in science. In fact, one way to define science is as the human attempt to account for patterns in nature. When Alfred Wegener noticed that the continents seem to fit together like pieces of a puzzle, he speculated that they were once part of the same landmass; later, evidence from fossil, rock, and plant patterns supported his theory of continental drift. When Charles Darwin synthesized his theory of evolution, he drew upon repeating patterns that he had observed in living organisms during his long sea voyage on the Beagle. Our laws of heredity are a product of Gregor Mendel's careful recording of patterns of inheritance in pea plants.

Howard Gardner's theory of multiple intelligences recognizes the special gifts of these pattern-seekers as the "naturalist intelligence." Along with sensitivity to the natural world and the talent to discriminate among living things, those with a strong naturalist intelligence quickly see patterns in the natural world and grasp relationships in ecosystems. Whether studying the classification of wetlands or an organism's coloration, the recognition of patterns at all levels is critical to the science of ecology.

The power of patterns can be put to work in education. A good graphic, for example, can show at a glance both the key parts of a whole and the relationships between those parts, thereby providing a holistic view that words cannot convey. The brain is designed to perceive and derive meaning from patterns, and it resists having meaningless information imposed on it. Therefore, educators should consider beginning lessons by giving students a pattern to discover rather than a principle to memorize. Patterns inspire questions, reveal connections, and prompt predictions about what's next, leading to a deep understanding of the principles behind the patterns. By beginning with a pattern to discover, students are able to construct the big ideas of science on their own. Moreover, pattern recognition comes naturally to even the youngest child.

The following activities take students into the field and lead them from observation to pattern to principle. By studying the nest-building behavior of squirrels, the "Morse code" of fireflies, and the patterns of energy and life on north- and south-facing slopes, children can discover important ecological concepts for themselves. This active seeking fosters the need to know, persistence, respect for evidence, and the sense of stewardship and care that characterize good science.

Note that the activities refer to species that may not be present year-round or in all regions. The bioluminescent species of the firefly family, for example, are

38

nocturnal and found only east of the Rocky Mountains. And not all squirrels are arboreal; those that do make their nests in trees are easier to spot in the winter when the leaf cover is gone.

Patterns of adaptation: Observing squirrels at home

The principle of adaptation can be constructed from studying patterns in the nest-building behavior of squirrels. Tree squirrels, like monkeys, porcupines, and sloths, belong to a large group of animals that call the tree canopy home. Trees provide a place to nest, reproduce, raise young, and find food; and the complex networks of tree branches serve as transportation and escape routes high above the forest floor.

Squirrels choose their nest sites very carefully to ensure strong structural support, protection from predators, and access to food and sunlight. They do not build nests close to the ground or near the tops of trees unless the nests are well protected in some way. This is because the nests have to withstand high winds and other inclement weather, and must offer security from predators. Nests are often situated in the fork of large branches, close to the main trunk, for support, and they usually face south or east to benefit from the sunlight during winter months and on chilly mornings. Squirrels do not build nests in isolated trees because they need to be able to jump from tree to tree to escape threats; sometimes they will even build multiple nests in adjoining trees to avoid predators. Having other trees nearby also ensures a more abundant food supply.

In the following activity, students discover many of the adaptive factors in squirrels' choices of nest sites by identifying patterns in nest building. Note that squirrels' winter nests tend to be larger and more elaborate than their summer nests, and nests are more easily discerned against the sky when there is no foliage to hide them. Therefore, it is best to conduct this activity in winter, if possible.

Materials: paper, pencils, compass

Procedure:
1. Begin by challenging students to think like a squirrel. Ask them, "If you were squirrels, where and how would you build your nests?" Encourage them to consider such factors as the kind of tree they would select,

how high in the tree they would build their nest, and in which direction they would want their nest to face.

2. Out in the field, have students test their nest-building logic against the logic of the squirrels. Explain that patterns are shapes or events that repeat three or more times. They will be observing and recording information about the location of at least three squirrel nests to determine if there are patterns.

3. Ask students to look for squirrels' nests in trees. Squirrels' nests are often confused with birds' nests, but if students look closely, they should be able to tell the difference. Squirrels' nests are usually much larger (30 to 40 centimeters in diameter) and made of twigs and leaves.

4. Stop at each tree that has a nest, and have students:

- identify the type of tree, either broadleafed or coniferous
- use a compass to determine the direction the nest faces, i.e., whether the nest is positioned on the north, south, east, or west side of the tree
- estimate the distance between the ground and the nest, and from the nest to the top of the canopy
- note the configuration of branches where the nest is secured to the tree
- note the distance between the nesting tree and any other trees in the immediate vicinity

5. After surveying several nesting sites, ask students if they can detect any patterns in the data they have collected. Through observation and reflection, they should be able to discover patterns of nest building and the adaptive logic behind these patterns. Following are some questions that may help students determine the reasons for squirrels' nesting decisions:

- Do squirrels choose conifers (e.g., pines, spruces) or broadleafed (e.g., maple, oak) trees more often? What advantages and disadvantages does each offer?
- What are the pros and cons of nesting at the bottom, middle, and the top of the trees?
- What advantages could trees whose branches overlap with those of other trees have over isolated trees?
- What kinds of branch configuration (think about geometric shapes) provide a stable support for the nest?

What are the advantages and disadvantages of a nest that faces south? north? east? west?

Patterns of diversity: Observing fireflies on a warm night

The childhood fascination with observing fireflies on a warm summer evening can be the starting point for teaching about biodiversity. The cold light, or bioluminescence, that is produced by many species of the beetle family *Lampyridae* is the result of a chemical reaction that takes place in special cells of the firefly's abdomen. A substance called *luciferin* is acted upon by the enzyme *luciferinase*, creating a rhythm of short and long intervals of light, much like the Morse code of dots and dashes. This flashing pattern is encoded so that males and females of the same species can recognize each other. A male in the air signals "hello" to females, and when a female on the ground recognizes a male of her kind, she signals back. Because there are more than 100 species of bioluminescent fireflies in North America, there are more than 100 different codes. These distinct codes keep species separate and thus maintain species diversity.

Having students observe the light patterns of fireflies inspires questions such as the following:

- Why do fireflies flash lights at night?

- Why do some fireflies flash light from the air, and others from the ground?

- What is the purpose of the pattern of flashing?

- Do fireflies all use the same flashing pattern?

- What makes the firefly light work?

- If fireflies did not recognize their own codes, what impact would it have on their individual species and on the diversity within the firefly family?

Materials: pencils, paper, penlights or flashlights, colored cellophane

Procedure:
The best time to observe fireflies is during their mating season, from late summer to early fall, when the nights are still warm. A good place to observe them is over a grassy area or marsh. Alternatively, students can collect fireflies in jars and bring them to class for study.

1. Have students use dots and dashes to record the "Morse codes" of the flashing lights they observe (for example, · · · or · – ·). It is not unusual for two or more species of fireflies to occupy the same area, so students should look for two or more patterns to compare.

2. Ask students to watch and record the flash pattern of one firefly for a minute or longer to determine if the firefly repeats the same pattern.

3. Challenge students to try to duplicate one of the observed light patterns with a penlight or flashlight.

4. Have students work in pairs to create their own codes for saying "hello" based on their observations. Just as each firefly species encodes a greeting that is recognized only by members of the same species, students may vary the frequency of flashes or the intensity or color of the light.

Extension: The female firefly of one species has learned how break the rules. Nicknamed "femme fatale," she imitates the codes of other species. When she flashes their code instead of her own, the males interpret this as an invitation to land. And when a male lands nearby, she invites him to dinner — but he soon finds out that he's the dinner. She is a voracious predator, known to eat four or five males daily. Ask students to mimic the behavior of "femme fatale" by observing a male firefly signal and then making "conversation" by flashing the same pattern with a flashlight. When students signal, does a firefly fly toward their light?

Patterns of energy: Observing sides, north and south

An activity that leads to an appreciation of how patterns of energy create diversity can be done right outside the classroom doors. Solar heat is not distributed equally over the Earth's surface. Because of the motion of the planet and because Earth is a sphere, the intensity of the solar energy that strikes Earth's surface varies with latitude. The level of radiation is highest at the equator and decreases toward the poles. As a result, south-facing slopes in the Northern Hemisphere receive more energy than north-facing slopes. The north-facing slope of a mountain, for example, may be covered with snow while the south-facing slope is snow-free. Even in winter, the organisms living in or on the south-facing side may enjoy spring-like warmth.

Any school grounds can be used to compare north- and south-facing slopes. By comparing the temperature, light intensity, and soil moisture between the north- and south-facing sides of buildings, students discover that solar radiation is not distributed equally in the environment. The unequal distribution of energy creates, in turn, different patterns of plant and animal diversity. This understanding can be applied to explaining the difference between north- and south-facing sides of natural systems such as mountains and valleys.

Materials: paper, pencils, compass

Procedure:

1. Sketch a map of the outside perimeter of the school building. Using a compass, identify the north- and south-facing sides and label them on the map.

2. Have students make predictions about different patterns they will find on the north- and south-facing sides of the building, such as differences in temperature, light, soil moisture, and vegetation.

3. On a sunny day, go outside and have students touch the north- and south-facing walls with their hands. Does the south-facing wall feel warmer? Confirm the difference by measuring and recording the temperatures of the two sides. Ask students which wall is likely to give off more heat at night.

4. Have students take soil samples from the north- and south-facing sides and compare them by crumbling the soil with their fingers. Does the soil of the south-facing side feel drier? Students can measure soil moisture by weighing scoops of soil before and after drying them overnight in an oven. The difference between the two weights represents the moisture lost.

5. Have students compare the plant diversity on the two sides of the building. Are there differences? If the same species lives on both sides, compare the stature and development of individual plants on the two sides. Which are larger? Which bloom first?

6. Have students note any differences in the number and diversity of animals on the two sides of the building. Cold-blooded animals, such as insects, choose warm habitats over cold ones. They take advantage of the sun's warmth, which enables them to crawl, run, and fly faster. Even in winter, insects such as snow fleas will darken the snow on the south-facing sides of trees. Looking like tiny black dots, they leap about much like actual fleas, appearing to celebrate the warmth of the sun. ✒

Robert Barkman is a Professor of Education and Biology at Springfield College in Springfield, Massachusetts, a recipient of the Sears Roebuck Foundation Award for Teaching Excellence, and the author of Science Through Multiple Intelligences: Patterns That Inspire Inquiry *(Zephyr Press, 1999), from which these activities are adapted.*

References

Barkman, Robert C. *Science Through Multiple Intelligences.* Zephyr Press, 1999.

Barkman, Robert C. "Patterns, the Brain, and Learning." *Classroom Leadership* 4:3, November 2000, pp. 1, 4-5.

Brooks, Jacqueline Grennon, and Marin G. Brooks. *The Case for Constuctivist Classrooms.* Association for Supervision and Classroom Development, 1993.

Caine, Renate Nummela, and Geoffrey Caine. *Making Connections.* Addison-Wesley, 1994.

Cale, William, Geoffrey Henebry, and J. Alan Yeakley. "Inferring Process from Pattern in Natural Communities." *Bioscience* 39:9, 1989, pp. 600-604.

Durie, Veronica. "Multiple Intelligences: And Now There Are 8." *Mindshift,* April 1997, pp.1-2.

Gardner, Howard. *Frames of Mind: The Theory of Multiple Intelligences.* Basic Books, 1993.

Jones, Beau Fly, Jean Pierce, and Barbara Hunter. "Teaching Graphics to Construct Graphic Representations." *Educational Leadership,* December 1988/January 1989, pp. 20-25.

Judson, Horace F. *The Search for Solutions.* The John Hopkins University Press, 1987.

Roth, Karen. *The Naturalist Intelligence.* Skylight Training and Publishing, 1998.

Studying Pond Creatures

Getting the most out of class excursion to a nearby pond

by Chris Earley

Grade levels: 2-5

Subject areas: science

Key concepts: adaptations, food webs, pond ecosystems

Skills: observation, classification, exploration

Location: outdoors and indoors

Materials: hand nets, magnifying glasses, white plastic basins, laminated identification sheets or field guides

Photographs by Chris Earley

There's something about a pond that intrigues almost every child — a combination of water, frogs, mud, nets, and buckets that seems to be a kind of kid magnet. And because ponds are found nearly everywhere, often nearby, they are great destinations for field trips. A freshwater aquatic environment is often teeming with life that is easily observed, even by very small children. Even a prairie farm dugout or flooded roadside ditch will harbor creatures such as chorus frogs, mosquito larvae, snails, and larval salamanders. Such places provide living examples of food webs, life cycles, and animal and plant adaptations. In learning about pond creatures first hand, your students will develop an appreciation for the outdoors and its inhabitants.

Field trip objectives

Three main objectives of a field trip to a pond, or to any natural area, are that children should:

- be comfortable in and familiar with natural habitats

- ask questions about the natural world and discuss the validity of the answers

- understand that their behavior and actions affect the environment and that they can take an active part in preserving resources

Preparing for the trip

Going to a new environment is one of the most exciting experiences children can have, but the new and unknown can be scary. Help to ease any apprehensions students may have by talking about the pond before they go so that they will develop a familiarity and link the pond visit to their classroom experience. To ensure their physical comfort on the trip, provide students and their parents with a list of items to wear or to bring. The list should include rubber boots, raincoat, sun hat and sun screen, long-sleeved shirt, long pants, and insect repellent if it is mosquito season.

To make sure that *you* are comfortable, visit the pond ahead of time to ensure that it is a safe environment for children and suitable for the activities you are planning. Avoid ponds with steep drop-offs or slippery banks, and check that there is sufficient clearance around the water's edge to accommodate your class and their equipment. Take a net and bucket and do some sampling so that you can find the best sampling spots and become familiar with the pond creatures. Finally, decide where to set boundaries along the pond's edge to contain the students' activity. If you go to the pond more than two weeks ahead of the class's visit, try to visit again a couple of days before your trip to check the water level. Ponds can change rapidly due to recent rain or drought, so be ready to modify your boundaries if necessary.

Protecting the pond environment and your students

Certain rules should be followed to ensure the safety of the students as well as the protection of the pond habitat.

⚭ Recruit parents and other adult volunteers so that you have at least one adult on the trip for every five students.

⚭ Be sure that each student has a partner.

⚭ Remind students that they are expected to follow the same rules of behavior that are used in the classroom: pushing and shoving will not be tolerated.

⚭ Do not allow students to step into the pond. Explain that their rubber boots are for walking in the mud around the edge of the pond. Let students know that if they step into the pond they will be stepping on living creatures that dwell on the bottom; and if they walk in the pond they will stir up mud and make it difficult to see what is to be caught. The fact that staying out of the water lessens the chance that someone will fall into it is a bonus safety feature.

⚭ Have the students wash their hands after their pond exploration and before eating snacks or lunch.

Using nets and basins

Small nets such as those used for netting fish in an aquarium are great for a pond visit because they are sturdy and cannot get too heavy with of mud. You will also need to set up several basins, half-filled with pond water, into which students can place pond creatures for observation. If available, use shallow white plastic basins rather than buckets for observing pond organisms. The creatures show up well against the white background; and because the basins are wide and shallow, more students can see into them, making observation of a single creature much easier. The water in a basin can get quite murky as students add their catches to it, so you may wish to give each group two basins. Have students empty their nets into the first one and then use a clean net or a white plastic spoon to transfer a creature from the first basin into the "clean" basin.

Encourage the students first to look into the water and try to scoop out what they can see. When they catch something, have them gently turn their nets inside out and dip the contents into the basin. After a few of these scoops, have them do some "blind scoops;" that is, have them scoop through the water among pond plants even though they may not see any creatures there. When they look closely into their nets they will likely see damselfly and dragonfly nymphs or water mites. Even if they see only algae and debris in their nets, they should still empty the nets into basins because many creatures that are not visible in the net will be easily spotted once they are swimming in the basin. Because they jump and may get stepped on before they escape, frogs and toads should not be caught, only pointed out and watched.

When the creatures in the basins are to be released, have two students, one on each side, gently dump the

Common Pond Organisms

The following are common pond animals and aquatic plants that you might expect to see on a field trip with your students. If they are unfamiliar to you, look them up in a book before the trip to see what they look like. Better yet, have your students study them in the library as a pre-visit activity.

water mite	giant water bug
spider	caddisfly larva
water strider	diving beetle
dragonfly nymph and adult	leech
newt	snail
damselfly nymph and adult	water scorpion
crayfish	duck weed
mosquito larva and pupa	cattail
water boatman	pond lily
backswimmer	algae

whole basin into the pond and then rinse it. Some creatures such as snails may be stuck to the basin and should be carefully removed and released.

Answering questions

Be prepared for lots of questions...

What is this?

Ponds are full of creatures that look so bizarre that your students are bound to ask you what they are. If you do not know what a creature is, try to focus on one of its adaptations instead of its name. You could say, "I don't know what it is, but look at those paddle-like legs that it uses for swimming." Then encourage students to think of a descriptive name for the creature based on their observation of its special features (such as "pale green pond paddler"). Use this name as other similar creatures are found.

It is not essential to identify every creature, as the purpose of the field trip is to see the diversity of life and how creatures adapt to their habitat. For students who

wish to identify the creatures they catch, it is useful to have on hand some laminated identification sheets showing common pond creatures. Alternatively, provide pocket-sized field guides such as the Golden Guide *Pond Life* by George Reid. This is an excellent resource that covers the little creatures; has pictures of larger organisms that you may see on your pond visit, such as muskrats, cattails, ducks, and herons; and discusses such concepts as food webs, characteristics of water, habitat types, and habitat succession. And do not forget another useful resource that you will have brought with you: your students. When I was in Grade 5, my teacher took our class to the local conservation area to study ponds. Because I lived right beside the area and had spent a lot of time there on my own with nets, buckets, books, and binoculars, my teacher used me as a resource. This worked out well for everyone: the teacher has a "pond biologist" on her field trip, the other students got answers to many of their questions, and I went on to a career as an interpretive naturalist! You probably have students who have visited ponds already and will love to share their knowledge.

Pre-visit Activity

Amazing adaptations: Creating a pond creature
Materials: books about pond organisms, drawing materials
Procedure:

1. Read about aquatic organisms with the class and then discuss the following:

☙ In what ways are aquatic and terrestrial animals the same? *(Both need oxygen; both need to move around in their environment; both need food.)*

☙ How might an aquatic organism breathe? *(Go to the surface for air; swim just below the surface using a "snorkel" to breathe; use gills to breathe underwater.)*

☙ How might an aquatic animal move? *(Swim using paddle-like legs and/or a long tail; crawl along the bottom; skate on the surface.)*

2. After these discussions, have students make a drawing of an imaginary pond creature. Ask them to decide what the creature eats, how it breathes, how it moves, and where in a pond it would live (surface, edge, bottom, in pond weeds). Because you are trying to make the students comfortable before their visit to a pond, let them have fun with their creations. They will usually design creatures wonderfully adapted to the pond, even though some may move with underwater rockets and eat "pond pizza."

3. Ask students to present their creature to the class. You may wish to repeat this activity after the pond visit, thereby giving students an opportunity to incorporate real adaptations that they have observed.

Post-visit activity

Making a pond field guide
Following the visit to the pond, have students create a pond field guide that can be used on future visits or by other classes. Each student could be in charge of researching and completing the entry for a particular organism.

Field guides made by students in Grades K-1 could consist simply of drawings of each pond creature they have seen. For older students, make a template page that has a box for a drawing, and several headings followed by space for information to be entered. Headings could include: Size and shape, Number of legs, Means of locomotion (float, swim, crawl), Food, Predators, Number of eggs, and Descriptive name (e.g., "pale green pond paddler"). Finding information for some of these categories will likely require library research.

If you have a digital camera, be sure to take it with you on your pond visit. Many digital cameras have a super-macro mode for photographing small things close up. Practice with this feature before you go. Back in the classroom, students can refer to these photos as they make their drawings (but do not allow the photos to replace the valuable experience of drawing a newly found creature!). Once the book is bound, take it on future pond field trips and let other classes borrow it. It could even be added to the school's library.

Does it bite?

The majority of pond creatures that will be caught are harmless to humans, but some can inflict a painful bite. As a precaution, tell your students not to touch the animals with their bare hands and to leave them alone once they are in a bucket or basin. Backswimmers, diving beetles, spiders, giant water bugs, turtles, and leeches are some of the creatures that bite. Snails, on the other hand, do not, and are great to touch and good for learning patience. Have the students put a small amount of water and a small snail in their palm, and wait. Eventually, the snail will come out of its shell and crawl across their hand. Of course, they have to be sure they have a live snail and not just a snail shell, or it could be a very long wait!

Can I keep it?

This question often comes up as soon as a frog is spotted or a turtle caught. Communicating the point that an animal should be left in its own environment can be difficult. Point out that everything that lives in the pond depends on everything else, that each is an important strand in a web of life, and that to remove a creature is not fair to it or to the other organisms in its environment.

Nature tidbits

Be prepared with some nature tidbits in case a certain creature is caught. Some examples are:

◈ The eyes of a whirligig beetle are divided into two parts: the upper part sees above the water and the bottom part sees below the surface.

◈ Some water spiders catch minnows for their dinner.

◈ Diving beetles and backswimmers take air with them when they dive.

◈ A male stickleback (a small fish) builds a nest and, after a female has laid her eggs in it, guards the eggs.

◈ Caddisfly larvae build their own "shells" out of pebbles, sticks, or leaves and carry it along with them. If they are disturbed, they will hide inside their moveable home.

◈ Frogs and dragonflies have a three-stage life cycle: egg → frog tadpole or dragonfly nymph → adult.

◈ Mosquitoes have a four-stage life cycle, just as butterflies do: egg → larva → pupa → adult.

Becoming pond stewards

Remember that the focus of the trip is not only to catch and observe small aquatic animals, but also to encourage students to think about how they can help the pond. For instance, they could collect any litter that they find around the pond and carry it back with them for recycling or disposal. They could keep a record of all the creatures they observe and publish it in a school newsletter to let others know about the diversity of life in the pond. Classes could create and present skits about pond creatures to encourage other classes to visit and learn about the pond. Older students could monitor water quality and publish their results; this might include making interpretive signs to place around the pond to inform visitors about the organisms that live there and about human activities that threaten the health of the pond environment.

If you still feel uncomfortable about taking your class to a pond by yourself, local nature centers usually offer pond-study programs. Try attending one of these with your class and pick up ideas for your own future field trip. Once you are comfortable with ponds, try other habitats such as forests, meadows, and rivers. There is no limit to what the outdoor classroom has to offer. ↵

Chris Earley is an interpretive biologist and the Education Coordinator at The Arboretum at the University of Guelph in Guelph, Ontario.

Resources

Dawe, Karen, and Neil Dawe. *The Pond Book.* Somerville House Publishing, 1990.

Hickman, Pamela. *A New Frog: My First Look at the Life Cycle of an Amphibian.* Kids Can Press, 1999.

Reid, George. *Pond Life: A Guide to Common Plants and Animals of North American Ponds and Lakes* (Golden Nature Guide). St. Martin's Press, 2001.

Rockwell, Anne. *Ducklings and Pollywogs.* Macmillan Publishing Company, 1994.

Stokes, Donald. *Observing Insect Lives.* Little, Brown and Company, 1983.

The Numbered Forest

Numbering trees in the schoolyard or in a nearby woodland opens the door to a variety of activities

Charles Pearce

Emily Kissner

by Emily Kissner

Grade levels: 4-5

Subject areas: science, language arts, math

Skills: writing, reading, mapping, observing

Location: outdoors

Time: 1 hour or more

Although it may sound like an exotic locale, the Forest of Fractions is an ordinary stretch of forest. Walking into it, you would likely find your attention drawn, as in any other forest, to the deep shadows of the trees and to the twitter of birds overhead or the crunch of a pine cone underfoot. But venture a little further and you begin to notice what makes this ordinary stretch of forest something extraordinary. Here and there, on this tree and that, are wooden plaques with numbers carved into them.

"Hey, what is that number doing there?" a student asks, pulling at the teacher's sleeve. "Why would someone put numbers on the trees?"

"And strange numbers, too," another student adds. "I think I saw 16.25 back there."

The idea of assigning numbers to trees is not new. Trees along nature trails often display numbers that are keyed to information on interpretative signs or trail guides. But the numbered trees on the grounds of the environmental learning center at Biglerville Elementary School in Pennsylvania have a wider purpose. They encourage students to look beyond their feet as they walk through the forest, and they open the door to a variety of mapping, mathematics, language arts, and environmental monitoring activities. They also make the schoolyard a more friendly, accessible place.

Whether you have an entire forest in your outdoor classroom or just a few trees scattered in your schoolyard, you can do some pretty neat things with numbered trees. The following are tips on numbering your trees and suggestions for activities and investigations that can be done using the numbered trees as a focal point.

Numbering the trees

The first step in numbering trees is to make a list of the numbers you want to include. For example, to facilitate math activities, you may wish to select a wide range of prime numbers, factors, fractions, and decimals. If you teach younger children, limit your list to numbers that the students will recognize.

If you intend to use the numbers for only a few seasonal activities, laminated index cards tied around the trunks of trees with string work well. This method allows your students to help with the work of numbering. (My students take it very seriously!) Cards that are double-laminated should survive a season or two of soaking rains; but for more permanent numbers, use stencils and exterior paint to paint the numbers directly on the trees. Painted numbers will last several years and are resistant to vandalism. Alternatively, permanent placards can be made by using a router to inscribe numbers on 10-centimeter-square (4-inch-square) boards. Drill holes in the corners of the placards and use weather-resistant rope or clothesline wire to attach them to the tree. Affixing the numbers high enough to be out of reach will encourage the children to look up in the trees and will also minimize vandalism.

Charles Pearce

Which trees do you number? In a schoolyard that has only a few trees, you may want to number them all. If you are fortunate enough to have a wooded area nearby, you can number trees at random throughout the forest, or assign different kinds of numbers to different areas. A deciduous forest, for example, might become a Forest of Integers, while a pine forest might become a deep, dark Forest of Fractions.

Quick and simple activities

Charles Pearce

When you have only a short period of time for an outdoor lesson, numbered trees provide a focus for simple activities such as the following. Related concepts and skills are noted for each activity.

Number searches

๏ Challenge students to find as many numbered trees as they can and record the numbers in a journal or keep track orally. (Number recognition, counting, recording)

๏ Ask students to look for numbers that meet certain criteria. Depending on how you numbered the trees, you can have students look for multiples of three, prime numbers, even numbers, and so forth. Younger students may look for numbers with one, two, or three digits. (Number recognition, mathematical concepts)

Attribute scavenger hunt

Build vocabulary skills by taking students on attribute scavenger hunts. Create a list of words that signify tree attributes such as "crimson," "enormous," and "gnarled," and ask the students to find numbered trees that have these attributes. (Building vocabulary)

Tree ID

Have students use field guides to identify numbered trees. Then ask them to defend their identifications to the group, referring both to the details noted in the field guide and to the observable features of the trees. Heated debates can arise over whether a tree is a sugar maple or a red maple! (Observation, language arts, plant studies)

Mapping the forest

Give students maps of the area and ask them to find and mark the locations of all of the numbered trees. (Mapping skills)

Tree food webs

Ask students to sit beside a tree and draw the food chains that they can deduce from their observations. Remind them to look carefully for evidence of decomposers. As a class, discuss factors that might influence the types of wildlife and interactions that students see, such as the species and forms of the trees or their locations. (Observation, drawing, ecological relationships)

Tree house tales

Have students select a tree to observe every day over a period of time. Ask them to make a list of the various organisms that inhabit or visit the tree, using it for shelter, food, escape from predators, structural support, or for some other purpose. Have students write and illustrate stories or create skits about the creatures that use the tree or call it their home. (Observation, identification, drawing, creative writing, dramatic arts)

Giving directions

In the outdoor classroom, ask students to choose a point of interest (something other than a numbered tree). Then have them write clear directions for getting to their site, using a nearby numbered tree as a starting point; for example, "From Tree 23, walk four paces toward the path and then turn left." Have students test the clarity of their directions, as well as their ability to read and follow others' directions, by trading with one another. This activity works well in helping students get acquainted with an outdoor site. (Writing skills)

Extended investigations

The following are more detailed activities and longer-term projects for those who have more time or are able to take students outdoors frequently through the year.

Trees in all seasons

Read the book *Sky Tree: Seeing Science Through Art* by Thomas Locker (HarperCollins, 1995) and discuss how trees change through the seasons. Then ask each student to choose a tree to observe, describe, and draw as it changes through the year. (With younger students, you may wish to choose one tree to monitor as a class.) This activity could take the form of an "adopt-a-tree" project in which students complete a tree-adoption form and then make drawings, write poems or songs, and jot down observations and facts about their tree throughout the year. Many students feel an immense sense of ownership for their trees and even return to visit them after they have moved on to other schools. (Observation, drawing, language arts)

Numbered tree tours

Have students use numbered trees as focal points in creating an illustrated trail guide to the natural features of the outdoor classroom. The guide could be in the form of a pamphlet, booklet, or large map, which members of the school community can use for self-guided tours of the grounds. (Science, writing, drawing)

Charles Pearce

Emily Kissner

Growing concern

Students can practice the skills of estimation and measurement by tracking the growth of numbered trees. Have students measure the circumference of trees and then calculate the "dbh," or diameter at breast height, a standard height measurement taken at a point 1.37 meters (4 feet) from the ground. This information, recorded in a journal from year to year, will allow students to track the annual growth of individual trees and to compare the growth rates of different species of trees. (Measurement, math, recordkeeping)

Signs of discovery

Have students use the numbered trees as reference points in recording where they make observations and discoveries throughout the year. Finding "a rotten stump next to Tree 106" is far easier than finding "a rotten stump halfway down the path, over the ditch, a bit to the left of a big bush." If classes record observations each year, students can monitor changes in many different sites of interest, such as a nesting site, a patch of spring ephemerals around the base of a tree, the encroachment of invasive species, or the natural succession that occurs after a disruption. (Data collection, environmental monitoring)

Emily Kissner teaches elementary school in Maryland and lives in Gettysburg, Pennsylvania. She credits the idea of using numbered trees to Charles Pearce, a former Grade 5 teacher at Manchester Elementary School in Manchester, Maryland, and author of Nurturing Inquiry: Real Science for the Elementary Classroom *(Heinemann, 1999).*

An Overnight Trip with First-graders

Camp staff staged a costumed dramatization of The Lorax *by Dr. Suess.*

Photographs by Liz Kornelsen

by Liz Kornelsen

Grade level: 1

Subject areas: science, language arts, art, physical education

Key concepts: nature awareness, outdoor adventure

Skills: observation, oral and written communication, variety of motor skills

Location: outdoor center

"I want to stay here a hundred million years!"

his wish, expressed by a student named Cody, reflected the feelings of my first-graders in the middle of a two-day adventure at a residential camp. The idea of an overnight trip with my Grade 1 class had started back in September when I was perusing a teachers' guide that suggested a pretend camp-out as a culminating activity for a nighttime theme. Immediately I envisioned an overnight campout in the

school gym, my little students snugly rolled up in their sleeping bags on gym mats, their arms clutching teddy bears. The last sparkles of excitement would fade from their eyes as they fell asleep in a pretend forest complete with glow-in-the-dark constellations and mobiles of night animals with glowing eyes.

It was the children themselves who inspired me to make the transition from the pretend campout to the real thing. They arrived on the first day of school with eager minds, open hearts, and great curiosity. Many came with strong emotional needs, but soon proved themselves to be resilient and self-reliant. As the year progressed, the children affirmed my confidence in their ability to handle the challenge of an overnight campout: on our numerous trips to the neighborhood park, they demonstrated exemplary behavior as well an affinity for nature and sensitivity to the environment. It was these qualities in the children that prompted me to initiate plans for an overnight trip.

The purpose of the overnight excursion was three-fold: to provide the children with a socially enriching experience; to help them grow in awareness and appreciation of the natural environment; and to extend the curriculum into the outdoors where they could be actively engaged in hands-on learning.

Making plans

To begin, I enlisted help and made plans to ensure that safety issues would be addressed and that each child's needs could be adequately met on the trip. One factor that posed both challenges and advantages in the planning and implementing of the trip was that there were three special education students in the class. Two of the children were in wheelchairs, posing some physical challenges, and there were social and academic issues that needed to be considered as well. On the upside, the special education teacher who worked in my classroom on a half-time basis shared my passion for outdoor learning and became an enthusiastic partner in the planning and implementation of the overnight excursion. I also had two teaching assistants assigned to my class to support the special education students. In addition, a resource teacher and parent volunteer joined us on the trip, giving us an adult-to-child ratio of about one adult to every four children.

We chose for our site a camp situated just outside of the city of Winnipeg on the banks of the Assiniboine River. The camp offered sleeping and dining quarters under one roof, as well as excellent program possibilities led by staff who were well trained in outdoor and environmental education. With the site selected and a brief plan written, we got the approval of our principal and funding from the school division. (Parents were asked to contribute a small amount towards the funding as well.)

At the beginning of November I announced the plan to my class. Excitement flashed in their eyes — along with hints of nervousness. The questions began. Will there be any bears? snakes? Will our moms and dads be there? Can we take a teddy bear? How long till we go? I pulled out a calendar and we counted the months before the trip (which was scheduled for mid-May). From then on, the countdown was a ritual at the beginning of each month.

Students showing off their solar prints.

A few weeks later, parents and students attended an informational meeting to which the camp director was invited to present a slide show. The children were captivated, exclaiming with delight at the activities and natural scenes depicted in the slides and bombarding the director with questions after the presentation. To my surprise, very few parents voiced concerns, either initially or as the trip drew near. The parents of a special education student were reluctant to allow their son to go, but were won over by the persistent encouragement of the special education teacher. In another case, I made a hurried trip to a student's home the morning of the trip and persuaded the mother to let her child go by inviting her to join us.

Pre-trip "nighttime" explorations

About four weeks prior to the trip we immersed ourselves in a thematic exploration of "nighttime." We learned songs and poems about nighttime. We read stories about nighttime fears and dreams. We visited the planetarium and made glow-in-the-dark Big Dippers. We made owl masks and recited poems about owls. We dramatized the activities of nocturnal animals. Bulletin boards displayed writing and artwork about nighttime. Countdowns were scaled from months to weeks, then days.

The excursion

The day of the excursion dawned with clear sky and bright sun. The children arrived early, escorted by parents toting bedrolls and all manner of fuzzy bedtime toys. Soon the bus was loaded and we started the half-hour bus ride to Camp Manitou.

Upon arrival, children and gear tumbled out of the big yellow bus and the children were whisked off on orientation tours conducted by camp staff. The boys came back with enthusiastic reports of an owl sighting. Meanwhile, the girls were caught in a rain shower and, with an abundance of giggles, gathered single file underneath a large blue tarp and maneuvered caterpillar-style across the campground.

After a light snack, one group of children headed for the dock. Following safety instruction, they boarded a stable voyageur canoe and started paddling downstream. A fairly strong wind was blowing, which was later reflected in several journals as: "We almost tipped over!" While one group paddled on the river, a second group of students went on a "nature detectives" hike. We asked the children to use all of their senses to gather clues about the natural world around them, and led them through a series of activities that helped them observe and explore their new learning environment. They were given toilet paper rolls and asked them to examine small natural objects by looking at them through their "monoculars." As they focused in on everything from a small red bug to yellow lichen growing on the bark of a fallen tree, one student remarked, "It really does make things look bigger!"

Five more activity sessions were planned over the two days, including rock-climbing techniques, group initiative tasks, predator/prey games, and making solar tea and solargraphic prints. After each activity session, we had a brief sharing time. This, along with journal writing, drew everyone together and helped the children reflect on their experience and extract meaning from it. It was also important in helping them develop the language with which to give expression to their experience. The children attached themselves to this great new classroom with growing fondness. During one journaling session, my eyes scanned the room. Children sat in small groups, drawing, writing, and sharing tales of the day. Adults mingled with the children, chatting and helping them with their writing. A pleasant hum of voices and laughter filled the air. "Why can't we go to school here all the time?" mused one student aloud.

In the evening, the camp staff staged a costumed dramatization of Dr. Suess' *The Lorax* and sent the

Top: "Climbing the wall" took on new meaning at Camp Manitou as children learned basic rock climbing techniques. Bottom: Solar tea for two.

children on a natural treasure hunt. The reward was a small box containing a white spruce seedling, which they planted with great care and pride. Later, everyone gathered in the warm glow of the evening campfire. As rowdy action songs gave way to quiet singing and reflective stories, heads started nodding and several children snuggled up beside a nearby adult.

By the end of the campfire, some of the children opted for bedtime, but 12 adventurous campers gathered at the back entrance of the lodge for a night hike. We ushered them into the cool night air. The fading sun was painting a crimson glow across the west and a few stars were faintly visible in the evening sky. We made our way along the river trail, nervous giggles subsiding to soft whispers as the night cast its magic spell on the children. Every once in a while a child stumbled on the path, distracted by a bright star piercing the dark sky through a canopy of trees.

We stopped in a clearing. Mallard ducks called to each other from across the river. We sat down, and one of the camp leaders told us a legend of how the sun, moon, and stars came to be. We continued the hike, following the trail all the way around the perimeter of the camp, a 45-minute hike in all. What an accomplishment for first-graders!

As we arrived back at the campground, the open sky was revealed above us, now lit by myriad stars — to the utter astonishment of the children. Amid exclamations of delight, they found the Big Dipper. It was a moment they had anticipated for a long time. On the way back to the lodge, one student, still scanning the night sky, walked full-speed into a picnic table. Despite this unfortunate ending to our stargazing, the night-hikers returned, exhausted but thoroughly happy.

Reflections

The next morning brought more sunshine, and the campers were up, bright and eager, ready for a hearty breakfast and another day of adventure. The morning slipped away quickly, and halfway through it I stood back and reflected on the many factors that had made our camping trip such a huge success. I had support from the principal, school division, colleagues, and parents; extra support for special education students; and an ideal camp location with accompanying resources. Add to that children's natural enthusiasm for adventure, their love of the outdoors, and a teacher's willingness to take a risk, and you have a recipe for success.

Would I encourage other primary teachers to consider an overnight excursion with their classes? Given sufficient support and resources, my answer would be a resounding yes. Set up your objectives and plan around them. Plan for pre- and post- activities to help children get the most out of the experience. Recruit parent volunteers to help reduce the adult-to-child ratio. Make your outing part of a larger theme. Try to integrate as many subject areas as you can. Plan a culminating activity for children to showcase their learning, such as a "gallery" exhibit of photographs, poetry, writing, solargraphics, and other artwork inspired by the event. Invite parents to the exhibit, and have the children share some of the campfire songs they learned or orally present poems, stories, or dramatizations of their experiences.

Before we boarded the bus to return home, we sat down in a circle on the grass. As we passed around a dreamcatcher made by one the children, each person

shared one significant memory from camp. But I was certain that each child was taking home much more than one happy memory. Throughout our time at Camp Manitou I was acutely of aware the great affinity children have for nature. Guide them along a path through the forest or along the course of a river. Set their imaginations free on a vast expanse of sky. Let them examine insects crawling in the bark of dead trees. Let them smell spring flowers in bloom. Give them an experience of nature and a sense of their place in it, and they are hooked. My hope is that these young nature lovers of today will become the protectors of the environment tomorrow. ✺

Liz Kornelsen teaches Grades 2/3 at George V School in Winnipeg, Manitoba. At the time of writing, she taught Grade 1 at Norquay Community School in Winnipeg.

Resources

Caduto, Michael J., and Joseph Bruchac. *Keepers of the Earth.* Fifth House Publishers, 1989.

Caduto, Michael J., and Joseph Bruchac. *Keepers of the Night.* Fulcrum Publishing, 1994.

Canadian Wildlife Federation. *Project WILD Activity Guide.* Canadian Wildlife Federation, 1990.

Cornell, Joseph. *Sharing Nature with Children.* Ananda Publications, 1979.

Cornell, Joseph. *Sharing the Joy of Nature.* Dawn Publications, 1989.

Geisel, Theodor Seuss (Dr. Seuss). *The Lorax.* Random House, 1976.

Van Matre, Steve. *Acclimatizing: A Personal and Reflective Approach to Nature.* American Camping Association, 1972.

Enjoying Winter with Your Class

Outdoor activities for learning about animals' adaptations to the snowy season

by Gareth Thomson

Grade levels: 4-5

Subject areas: science, physical education

Key concepts: behavioral and physical adaptations to survive winter

Skills: nature interpretation, winter survival

Location: outdoors in a park or natural area

Time: 1-2 hours, depending on weather

Illustrations by Tom Goldsmith

If you live in a northern region where much of the teaching year takes place during the winter, shouldn't you be prepared to help your students learn to appreciate the winter wonderland? Experiencing the beauty of winter can foster a closer connection with nature year round and give students a sense of stewardship for a local natural area. Taking your class on a winter hike also provides an excellent opportunity for students to marvel at the behavioral and structural adaptations that animals — including humans — have evolved to cope with extreme weather conditions. How better to understand the concept of energy loss and the value of insulation than to succeed at staying warm on a cold winter day?

As Education Director of an environmental organization, part of my job is to prepare outdoor experiences for school groups. The following describes an afternoon that I spent in a provincial park examining animals' adaptations to winter with students from a local school. These activities could be done in any outdoor area close to your school.

Trip preparation

The word "warmth" can attain almost mystical proportions during a winter hike — and rightly so, for no student who is cold or uncomfortable can learn. Before our trip, the teacher had prepared the class by reviewing the insulating properties of different types of materials and how to dress warmly for a successful outdoor experience: dressing in layers and wearing proper headwear and footwear. The teacher had also ensured that there would be a heated place — in this case, a cabin in a provincial park campground — where students could warm up after the hike. Every winter hike needs a warm place as a base, whether it is a heated building or a school bus.

Mouse microhabits

After I met the school group at the cabin in the park campground, we began our first activity, Mouse Micro-habitats. We handed each student an empty film canister and then filled the canisters with water. The students carried these down the trail about 100 meters

(30 yards), at which point they were told that each canister represented the body of a deer mouse. Their task was to find a well-insulated place in the forest where the mouse could "sleep" for the next hour without becoming too cold. If the water in the canister froze, that would mean that their mouse had frozen! (At the end of the hike, students retrieved their canisters and measured the temperature of the water, if it had not frozen. We then discussed what natural materials best insulated the "mice." Everyone agreed that little mouse-fur jackets would be ideal, as the activity had demonstrated that any material that traps air, an excellent insulator in itself, will help animals stay warm.)

Warming up

Did I mention that it was cold? The temperature was minus 15 degrees Celsius (4 degrees Fahrenheit) and the wind was blowing, so we took time out to warm up. We taught the students how to swing their arms like helicopter rotors, using centrifugal force to send warm blood to numb fingertips, and how to wear their hats, scarves, hoods, and mittens to maximize their insulation values. As we walked, we noted the variation in the air temperature (using our thermometer) and the change in the wind chill factor (using our exposed skin!) as the path rose to the crests of hills and fell into low hollows filled with cold air.

We also played Migration Headache, an active game that illustrates what happens to migrating birds when their flyways and habitats are disturbed by human activities (see sidebar). Our student "birds" raced from their winter to their summer habitats and back again, striving to avoid being tagged by a bevy of students who played the role of hazards — from bulldozed swamps to lighted office towers. Amidst the squawking and the bedlam of wildly flapping arms, our cold extremities mysteriously warmed up.

Chickadee huddle and legend

We continued down the trail, pausing to examine recent tree blowdowns and some interesting ice formations around an open stream. We were thrilled when a blizzard of chickadees that we "pssshed" in (that is, we attracted them by making sibilant squeaking noises) turned out to be habituated to humans: they swirled around us and perched on our fingers as they searched for handouts. Although the park rules forbid the feeding of wildlife — with good reason — my environmental educator's heart was gladdened by the look in the students' eyes as they felt the touch of those tiny, wild claws.

Migration Headache Game

Migration Headache is a lively game that illustrates the various threats to the survival of migrating birds as their habitats are destroyed or altered by human activities

1. In an open outdoor area, create a playing area resembling a tiny football field with two "end zones." Clearly delineate the goal lines by telling students that they are imaginary lines between two objects, such as branches or knapsacks, placed on the ground.

2. Tell students that they will play the role of migrating birds as they travel between their summer and winter habitats (the two end zones). Have them begin by standing in the summer habitat, and ask students to name the kind of bird they have chosen to play.

3. Tell students that in order to succeed they must avoid being caught by players who will represent bird-killing hazards.

4. Ask for a volunteer to be a catcher. Tell students that this catcher represents an early winter storm that kills late migrants.

5. Shout "Go!" and let the students "fly" from the summer to the winter habitat.

6. Gather the students who got caught during that round and tell them that, in the next round, they are to become hazards such as lighted high-rise buildings (which kill many night-migrating birds), a pollution spill in a pond, a human-caused or natural drought, etc.

7. Ask students to migrate from the winter to the summer habitat. You can either continue the game until all birds are tagged or you can replenish the ranks of the successful migrants by moving some birds from the hazards group to the bird group (this move represents reproduction).

8. Conclude by asking the students to suggest ways in which we can help migrating birds.

This activity was adapted from the Project WILD activity of the same name in *Project WILD Activity Guide* (Canadian Wildlife Federation, 1990).

Exploring Nature Around Us

Serendipitously, a large spruce near us on the trail offered the opportunity for a story and a "chickadee huddle." The students began by holding hands in a circle. Then one student let go with one hand and started to spin, wrapping the whole class around him in a tightly packed, laughing cluster that resembled a cinnamon roll. (Chickadees have been observed "huddling" in nature by jointly occupying a nesting cavity in order to share body heat.) The students stayed in their huddle for a few minutes, getting warm, while they listened to a Native legend of a chickadee that flitted from tree to tree asking for shelter. At last, the chickadee was offered shelter by the spruce, and the spruce was rewarded for its kindness by being allowed to keep its needles through the winter from then on. Students always appreciate the whimsical nature of legends; and in ascribing human thoughts to trees, birds, and other animals, such stories help students to relate to these other beings.

Observing adaptations

We went on, pausing to examine the tracks and paths of snowshoe hares, squirrels, elk, and deer that frequent the area. Near the freshly gnawed stumps of some aspens, we stopped and examined a beaver skull that we had brought with us. Winter offers a superb opportunity to discuss both physical and behavioral adaptations, and we found some prime examples of both as we walked on the frozen surface of the beaver pond: an American dipper, an unusual aquatic songbird that is a veritable triumph of adaptation, lollygagged beside a patch of open water, providing the sort of teachable moment that outdoor educators dream about.

Indoors again …

By this time, we had been outdoors for over an hour, and it was time to get back for some indoor fun. Pausing only for some jumping jacks and running on the spot, we hastened back to the cabin, where we made hot drinks and looked at some animal skins that we had brought to show the students.

We then declared it game time and brought out a white bed sheet for playing The One-Second Hunt. The students — playing hungry goshawks — surrounded the sheet, put thumb and forefinger together as pincers, and closed their eyes. We scattered different-colored cutouts of snowshoe hares onto the sheet and then gave the goshawks precisely one second to open their eyes and pounce on a hare. Every goshawk was successful — but not a single white cutout form was captured, a dramatic illustration of the advantage of camouflage.

Next we sat down for a fireside chat, showing pictures of animals and discussing how each deals with winter, from the migrating robin to the hibernating ground squirrel to the color-changing weasel. We finished with another Native legend, the story of how the bear stole the chinook to keep his cave warm, and of the brave girl and her animal friends who conspired to steal the chinook back. As an informal evaluation, I asked the students to tell me the most interesting thing they had learned that day.

Is a winter hike worth all the trouble? Sitting in the cabin with the fire crackling and the low winter sun streaming obliquely through the window and lighting the children's faces as they wait in anticipation to hear whether the coyote succeeds in stealing the chinook, I'd have to say, yes, a winter experience is certainly worth it! ✍

Gareth Thomson is Education Director of the Canadian Parks and Wilderness Society, Calgary Banff Chapter in Canmore, Alberta.

This article is adapted, with permission of the Alberta Environmental and Outdoor Education Council, from *Connections* 17:2, Spring 1993.

References

Caduto, Michael J., and Joseph Bruchac. *Keepers of the Earth: Native Stories and Environmental Activities for Children.* Fifth House Publishers, 1989.

Canadian Wildlife Federation. *Project WILD Activity Guide.* Canadian Wildlife Federation, 1990.

Hayley, Diane, and Pat Wishart. *Knee High Nature: Winter in Alberta.* Jasper Printing Group, 1990.

The Art of Science

Realistic nature drawing integrates art and science and brings challenging new dimensions to both

Photographs by Tina Jory

by Tina Jory

Grade levels: K-3

Subject areas: science, art

Key concepts: understanding and rendering the detailed outer structure of a small animal

Skills: observation, fine motor skills, realistic drawing

Location: indoors

Time: 1-2 hours over 2 lessons

he beauty, complexity, and functionality of nature have the power to startle and amaze us. Yet our compartmentalized curriculum does not often provide opportunities to appreciate at once both the art and the science of nature. Teachers may encourage young artists in their whimsical, impressionistic renditions of tree or flower, but when it comes to the nuts and bolts — the phloem and the xylem — away go the paints and out come the science lessons. Introducing young students to realistic nature drawing is one way to integrate art and science while bringing challenging new dimensions to both subjects.

Realistic, true-to-life drawing can lead students to know a subject in a way that is not possible by any other means. The tracing of form leads to questions about function, and knowledge of the biology of a plant or animal leads the eye to details that might otherwise be missed. Students are often amazed by what they see. Such lessons broaden children's appreciation of nature, lead them to look at the world more attentively, and help them to develop the patience and ability to observe closely — a rewarding habit of mind and an essential skill for a naturalist.

Choosing a subject

Almost any subject will do for realistic drawing. For the classroom, it is best to choose natural objects or creatures that are small, easy to find and to keep temporarily, and safe to handle. Insects are exciting subjects for most children to study and draw. While live insects are difficult to observe because they move around, many have short life spans and can easily be found on the ground after they have died. When placed in a petri dish, safe from handling, they can be kept for a long time. If your class is fortunate enough to have a computer-linked microscope, a live insect can be quickly photographed, projected on a large screen for all to see, and then released. Another interesting subject for observation and drawing is a leaf in the process of decomposition. This project needs to be done in stages, and may be expanded into a comparative study by using leaves from trees or other plants of different species. Finally, I have found that earthworms fascinate very young students and provide a wonderful focus for art and science lessons. The following lesson, which uses earthworms as the topic, can be adapted for use with many other topics of study.

Caution: Natural items, even those that are non-toxic, may contain substances that are allergenic to some students. Therefore, it is best not to encourage children to touch natural items with their bare hands. Explain that, if they do touch, they must be careful not to put their hands near their eyes, ears, nose, or mouth, and they must wash well afterwards. Every lesson should begin with a safety lesson: nature can be fun and beautiful, but it must be respected.

Earthworm art project

In this project, students make a salt-dough model and a drawing of an earthworm. Scientific drawing is an exciting new art form for most young children, but it can also be challenging. You may therefore wish to have your students sculpt the worm from modeling clay before attempting to draw it, as modeling in three dimensions reinforces the concept of realistic representation. Throughout the activity, provide a wide variety

Earthworms are picked up carefully on a stick, not touched with bare hands.

of books and magazines for reading and research on the topic (see Resources listing). This generates discussion and gives the children some necessary background information to which they can refer when working on their art project.

Objectives:

- To read about and closely observe earthworms.
- To identify the body parts of a worm and describe the function of each part.
- To render realistic two- and three-dimensional models.
- To learn to treat living creatures with care and respect.

Background: Earthworms are members of a group called *annelids*, which are worms that have segmented bodies. An earthworm has no eyes, ears, or nose, but its body is extremely sensitive to light and touch. It breathes by absorbing oxygen through its moist, slimy skin. It has a thick band around its body, called a *clitellum*, where breeding takes place. Each segment of the earthworm's body has eight retractable bristles, called *setae*, which give the worm traction and enable it to cling to the soil when looking for food or trying to save itself from becoming food. Earthworms are one group of the Earth's decomposers. They eat dead and decaying matter, such as leaves, grass, and microbes in or on the soil. Their wastes, or castings, are rich in nutrients that fertilize and revitalize the soil. Their tunneling way of life keeps the soil loose and fine, allowing air to penetrate and providing for good drainage.

Materials: Most of the materials for this project can be found around the home. If salt dough is used for modeling, the total cost is around two dollars for a class of 30 students; if purchasing clay, the cost will be somewhat higher. You will need:

- 8 live earthworms (collected in the backyard or schoolyard, or obtained from fishing stores that sell small containers of live worms)
- 2 or 3 cups of fresh garden soil
- 1 large clear glass or plastic container with holes in

the lid (to keep soil and worms)

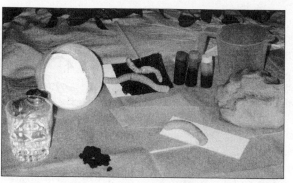

- 1 piece of dark paper (to wrap around the large worm container when the worms are not being observed, as they are very sensitive to light)

- 1 large polystyrene meat tray or a small cookie sheet (for displaying worms during group discussion)

- 1 small twig or wooden stick (for gently picking up worms when transferring them to other containers)

- 7 or 8 small clear plastic containers (for viewing worms)

- salt dough ingredients (flour, salt, water, food coloring; see recipe below); or non-toxic red earth clay, which may be purchased at art stores

As a temporary home, a clear glass jar filled with fresh soil and covered in black paper protects the worms from exposure to light.

- 1 small piece of cardboard, 7 x 13 cm (3 x 5 in.), per student (for holding a dough worm)

- 1 piece of drawing paper per student

- pencils, erasers, pencil crayons

- toothpicks for making features in dough

- (optional) magnifying glass (to inspect worms)

- books about worms

Note: As live worms are taken out of their natural habitat for this project, it is important that they be protected until they are returned to the area where they were collected. Keep them in a darkened container with moist soil, and do not expose them to air or light for more than two or three minutes at a time.

Preparation: If using commercially prepared clay for modeling, ensure that it is non-toxic and follow the manufacturer's instructions for use and cleanup. Otherwise, prepare a quantity of salt dough, as follows. This recipe makes enough dough for 30 students to make one life-sized worm each (approximately 17 centimeters long and 1 centimeter in diameter/7 inches long and ½ inch in diameter).

2 cups (500 mL) of all-purpose flour
½ cup (125 mL) of salt

1 cup (250 mL) of water
20 drops of red food coloring
6 drops of yellow food coloring
3 drops of green food coloring

Mix together the salt, water, and food coloring. Pour the water mixture into the flour and blend. Knead the mixture on a lightly floured board for 10 minutes until it is smooth and elastic. If the dough seems too dry, add a little more water; if too wet, add a little more flour.

Introducing the worms

1. Invite the students to sit in a circle around the teacher for a small discussion and learning session prior to the activities. Start by asking the students what they know about worms: e.g., where worms live, how they got there, what they do to improve the soil, how they look, and how they live.

2. Next, read a book about worms to the children. (See Resources list, page 60, for recommendations.)

3. Before bringing out the large container of worms, explain to the students that worms are very sensitive to light and air. Therefore, the worm container is kept covered with dark paper most of the time, and the worms must not be taken out for more than a few minutes. Also explain that worms' skin is tender and so worms must be picked up gently with a twig or wooden stick and never dropped. (Only the teacher should pick up the worms to ensure the worms' safety.)

4. Remove the paper from around the large container of worms and allow the students to observe the environment the worms are in and to ask questions. When everyone has had a look, gently pour out some of the soil and worms onto the large meat tray or cookie sheet so the students may observe the worms more closely. Remind them that the worms cannot stay out of the container for long and that they should not touch them.

5. When all discussion, questions, and information sharing are over, put the worms back into the large container and cover the container with the dark paper.

Earthworm models

1. Organize the children into groups of four or five so they may work together and share creative ideas.

2. Place a worm and a small amount of soil in each of the small clear containers (one or two per group).

3. Place one or two worm containers in the center of each group of students. The containers allow children to observe and refer to the worms while completing their art projects, and protect the worms from too much handling. Have books and pictures available for those who want more information. (See Resources listing, next page.)

3. Give each child one small piece of dough about the size of a ping-pong ball, and one small piece of cardboard.

4. Ask the students to roll their pieces of dough carefully and gently into worm-like shapes that resemble, as closely as possible, the real worms in the containers.

5. Show the children how to press slightly with the point of a pencil or a toothpick to make the rings on the dough worm. Have them refer to the real worms to determine how many rings to make and how closely the rings should be spaced.

6. Have the children place their completed dough worms on the pieces of cardboard.

7. When everyone is finished, clean up the work area and set the dough worms aside to dry, perhaps on a window ledge in the classroom near the heaters. It takes about a week for them to dry thoroughly.

Earthworm drawings

1. Provide each child with a piece of drawing paper and an ordinary pencil (no colors).

2. Explain that this is not an ordinary art lesson, but a scientific art lesson. This means they must draw a picture of a real worm and carefully label the various parts of the worm on their drawing. Remind them that books are available for finding the information they require.

3. When students have finished drawing the worms, have them identify and label the parts of the drawing in A, B, C order. Under the drawing, they are to write a brief description of each part drawn (see example below). With younger students, omit labeling and allow for more creativity by asking them to draw a surrounding environment for their worm.

4. When everyone is finished, gently return the worms to the big container. Wash and dry all items for reuse. Take the worms to the garden and release them in the area they came from, or in an area where the soil is soft and rich in organic matter.

Extensions:

⌀ The biology of earthworms is unique and interesting. Using books as references, have students make colored-pencil drawings of the insides of a worm, showing the hearts, brain, intestine, crop, gizzard, etc. These drawings can be quite simple but are a good extension of scientific drawings.

⌀ The decomposing and soil-processing services of native earthworms are beneficial to the environment. However, in some parts of North America, non-native earthworms have invaded forests and become a destructive force rather than a beneficial one. Have students research this environmental problem and report on its causes and possible solutions. For reference, see Peter Friederici, "Earthwormed Over," *Audubon Magazine*, January-March 2004, online at <www.magazine.audubon.org/content/content.html>.

More interesting realistic art subjects

⌀ Seashells: draw both interior and exterior surfaces; compare and contrast the shells of freshwater and saltwater organisms.

a) Mouth: opening used for eating
b) Clitellum: swollen band around body, which plays a part in breeding
c) Segments: rings around the worm's body that have muscles and 4 pairs of setae
d) Egg sack or cocoon: develops from clitellum after mating and usually contains 3 or 4 baby worms
e) Setae or retractable bristles: like a cat's claws, the bristles can come in or out of the worm and are used for moving and gripping the soil.

6 Rocks: the different minerals in rocks provide a great variety of shape, size, and color.

6 Fruits and vegetables: after drawing the whole fruit or vegetable, slice it in half and draw the interior view.

6 Seeds: sunflower, corn, and squash seeds are large enough to cut in half so that children can examine and draw the insides.

6 Flowers: draw flowers from many positions — the top, side, and bottom; then slowly take the flower apart and draw each part, or slice the flower in half to do cross-section drawings.

6 Roots: draw roots; compare and contrast the roots of different plants. ✒

Tina Jory has taught as an art specialist and reading specialist in Grades 1 to 6, and currently teaches for the Lester B. Pearson School Board in Dorval, Québec, which serves the Montreal West Island communities.

Resources

Books on art

Brooks, Mona. *Drawing With Children*. G.P. Putnam's Sons, 1986.

Schecter, Deborah. *Science Art*. Scholastic Professional Books, 1997.

Books on worms

Appelhof, Mary. *Worms Eat My Garbage: How to set up and maintain a worm composting system*. Flower Press, 1997.

Appelhof, Mary, Fenton, Mary Frances and Harris, Barbara Loss. *Worms Eat Our Garbage: Classroom Activities for a Better Environment*. Flower Press, 1993.

Coldrey, Jennifer. *Discovering Worms*. Bookwright Press, 1986.

Dell'Oro, Suzanne P. *Tunneling Earthworms*. Lerner Publications, 2001.

Himmelman, John. *An Earthworm's Life*. Children's Press, 2001.

Kalman, Bobbie. *The Life Cycle of an Earthworm*. Crabtree Publishing Company, 2004.

Llewellyn, Claire and Watts, Barrie. *Earthworms*. Franklin Watts, 2002.

Nancarrow, Loren, and Taylor, Janet Hogan. *The Worm Book*. Ten Speed Press, 1998.

Websites on worms

<http://yucky.kids.discovery.com/noflash/worm/> Worm World (Discovery Communications): Great information and pictures of worms and many science-related craft activities, games, and experiments.

<www.wormwoman.com> WormWomanCom (Mary Apelhof's site for worm composting resources): Excellent information on worms and worm composting and a resource section where books and other items may be purchased.

<www.urbanext.uiuc.edu/worms/index.html> The Adventures of Herman (Urban Programs Resource Network, University of Illinois Extension): A fabulous site for young children to explore and learn about the history, biology, anatomy, etc. of worms. It also provides teacher resources.

<www.attentionnature.ca/english/wormwatch/about/guide/intro.html> WormWatch (part of Environment Canada's NatureWatch program): Geared to Grade 3 and up, this site has detailed drawings of the inside and outside of worms and explains how to identify the various parts.

<www.thegreencommunity.org/giant_worms.html> Giant Gippsland Earthworms (The Green Community, Australia): A great site to learn about an unusual species of worm that can measure up to four meters (13 feet) long.

<www.wormwrld.com> Worm World!: Here you can buy everything you need for worm composting.

Teaming with Nature

Turning a square kilometer around your school into an outdoor classroom

Students calculate the velocity of water in a stream that flows through their square-kilometer study area.

by Mark Baldwin

Grade levels: 4-8

Subject areas: multidisciplinary

Key concepts: natural and human history of community; other concepts depending on curriculum links developed

Skills: observation, writing, drawing, measuring, graphing, using maps, gathering oral histories, research, analysis

Location: indoors and outdoors

Time: flexible

ilbert White was an 18th century cleric who spent most of his life in the tiny English village of Selborne. His name would probably have vanished quickly from memory were it not for three other facts about him. He was intensely curious about the natural world, he kept detailed records and corresponded vigorously with scientists about what he saw, and his records and letters were published. In fact, White's *The Natural History of Selborne* has been in continuous publication for more than 200 years. His humble, childlike questioning about everything, especially the commonplace close to home, has inspired generations of naturalists — including Henry David Thoreau, who is said to have kept a copy of White's book with him during his sojourn at Walden Pond. At the Roger Tory Peterson Institute of Natural History, we were inspired by White's legacy to develop a place-based professional development program for teachers called the Selborne Project. The program is now called Teaming with Nature and offered as a graduate course in partnership with the State University of New York at Fredonia. Although the name of the program has changed, we still ask our teacher participants to imagine their students as young, inquisitive Gilbert Whites who want to learn more and more about their own communities.

Teachers who participate in the Teaming with Nature program learn how a one-square-kilometer area can be used as an open-air, real-life laboratory for the study of natural and human systems in their communities. A square kilometer was chosen because it is a unit that we can comprehend. It is community sized. Any part of it is reachable in a 20-minute walk, and yet it encompasses one million square meters. To learn everything there is to know about one square meter would be daunting. Multiply that by a million and you have a lifetime's occupation — and many links to your curriculum.

The Teaming with Nature program enables teachers to use the nature and culture of their local community as a meaningful context for learning, and to make good use of elementary and middle school constructs such as common planning time for teachers, heterogeneous grouping of students, and block scheduling. Recent education reforms highlight the importance of an inquiry approach and tasks that require higher-order thinking skills such as evaluation and analysis. Such tasks can naturally be incorporated into local outdoor nature investigations.

The following steps introduce the Teaming with Nature idea and suggest how you can use it to create a rigorous, place-based unit of study rooted in the environment of your own school and community.

Teaming with Nature step by step
Observe your school's surroundings

Many teachers know little about their school's immediate surroundings because they simply drive there to work each day. Therefore, the first step is to sketch or jot down what you see of interest within walking distance of your school. As you become acquainted with the area, start to consider how the school's environment could spark learning. It may help to make two lists:

1. *What do I know about my school's surroundings?* (e.g., "The school is on Maple Street. Highway 380 is nearby. There is a bridge over a stream about half a kilometer from the school, but I'm not sure if the stream has a name. There is a cemetery three blocks from the school.")

2. *What questions do I have?* Productive inquiry is propelled by good questions that stem from careful observation. Some of your questions may be very broad (e.g., "What is the human history of this area?") and could be the focus of an entire unit. Others may be

Topic	Sample Questions to Stimulate Inquiry
Geology	What kind of bedrock underlies the area? How old is it? What formed the soil? Is the soil derived from forces that acted on the bedrock, or have glaciers or other forces brought the soil to the area from elsewhere?
Paleontology	If the soil or bedrock contains fossils, what do they reveal about what lived here before. When did those organisms live here? How can we find out more about the ancient history of this area?
Hydrology	Where does water that enters this area come from? What watershed is it part of? Where does our school's drinking water come from? Once water is used and goes down the drain, where does it go? Are surface water (streams, lakes, ponds, vernal pools) or wetlands present?
Meteorology	From what direction does air usually flow over this area? What difference does this make to our weather? How much annual precipitation does the area receive?
Biology	What are the dominant life forms of this area? Which are native or indigenous and which are non-native or alien? How has the biology here changed over time, and in response to what forces? What types of ecosystems are present? How can we investigate them?
Patterns of energy flow	Where do stored forms of sunlight, such as carbohydrates and hydrocarbons, come from in this area? How are they used? Are any crops, trees, natural gas, or other stored forms of solar energy harvested or mined here? If so, where do they go and how do they get there? What other energy transformations, such as mechanical to electrical or electrical to heat, take place here?
Patterns of matter cycling	Where do various organisms obtain the materials they need to live and grow? Are commercial fertilizers used in this area? What materials are recycled here? How could recycling be made more efficient?
Demography	Where do people tend to live (e.g., up on the hillside, down by the river) and why do they live where they do? What are the ages and ethnic backgrounds of the people who live here? What else can we learn about them?
Human history	What is the history of human habitation of this area? What is the archaeological evidence for it? If villages, towns, or cities have occupied this site over time, why was this site chosen?
Economy	What kinds of economic activities do people engage in here? Does the area have stores, restaurants, factories, or other places where people work besides our school?

Exploring Nature Around Us

quite specific and easily answered with a little research, but nevertheless have broad implications (e.g., the answer to a question such as "How much precipitation does the area receive annually?" may be closely linked to questions about dominant vegetation or economic activity). Some sample questions are shown here to help guide you (see chart on previous page).

Map your study area

First, gather several maps or aerial photographs that show the area. Topographic maps, street maps, soil maps, tax maps, and aerial photographs are all useful for gathering facts and seeing your plot in new ways. While ordinary paper maps are adequate, you may be able to obtain digital information about your plot from a local business or government agency that uses a geographic information system (GIS) for land-use planning.

Next, determine the boundaries of your study area. Refer to the map scale and draw onto a transparency a square that represents one square kilometer on the map. Place this template over the map so that your school is inside the square (but not necessarily in the middle of it), and move the template around to determine what features a square kilometer around your school might include. Position your study area so that it encompasses certain human-made boundaries such as streets, roads, or property lines. (One Teaming with Nature school in Washington, D.C., settled on a triangular study site because of the way the streets of that city are laid out.) Also consider both the unique and the commonplace features in the environment of your school. No other place has the same latitude and longitude or the same combination of soil, ecosystems, watersheds, topography, or history of human presence. But the particularity of your area is balanced by the fact that it is connected to and has much in common with other places.

Once you have decided where your study area will be, you will need a large-scale map of your square kilometer. An ordinary map can be enlarged using a scanner or digital camera and graphics software. You may also find aerial photographs and other images on the Internet that can be used for making large working maps of your site. (See Resources, page 65.)

At Nashoba Brooks School in Concord, Massachusetts, students adopted small plots within their square-kilometer study area and kept detailed notes on plants, animals, and seasonal changes.

A map that is poster sized or even bigger will be very useful as you plan and implement your unit.

Consider these points as you map your study area:

◉ *Interest.* Identify features that make your plot special. These might include a stream, grove of old trees, or historic home. Wetlands are wildlife magnets; if one is within walking distance of your school, you are lucky. Cemeteries are not only open-air museums of local history; they are often rich in natural history as well.

◉ *Safety.* Make the safety of your students your top priority. As you plan fieldwork for your class, assess the risks that may be involved. Avoid busy highways, cliffs, electric fences, or other hazards, as well as neighborhoods that may be unsafe even during the day.

◉ *Curriculum.* Pinpoint (literally, with colored pushpins, if you like) places that link to various areas of your curriculum. A door-to-door survey in a residential neighborhood could tie in to a unit on graphing and statistics. The biodiversity of a park could be studied in a unit on ecology, a cemetery in a unit on history, a business in a unit on economics, and so on. Think creatively about how to use your locality to achieve your curricular goals.

◉ *Accessibility.* Use a highlighter pen to color in all the walking routes and places in your study area that are accessible to the public. Think about the requirements of students who have disabilities or special needs. Do not neglect points of interest that are on private property; ask the owner of a beautiful specimen tree, for example, if your students may study it up close.

◉ *People.* As well as places, think about local resource people, volunteers who can help you interpret your community's natural and cultural history. Perhaps someone with a special interest in local architecture would be willing to take your students on an architectural tour of the neighborhood. Elderly residents of a housing facility could share their oral histories and give your students an invaluable opportunity to bond with senior citizens.

The next steps make the connection between "your" square kilometer and your curriculum.

Create a curriculum grid

Make a curriculum grid that lists all the concepts or topics you normally teach. Organize these by subject area along the Y-axis, and by time frame (e.g., month or marking period) along the X-axis. Once you have completed the grid, look for potential areas of curriculum alignment, where one topic could be taught in conjunction with others. New ideas for instructional efficiency will emerge as you refer to your grid during the development of your unit. For example, exercises in classification and comparison/contrast in both language arts and science could be covered during a tree survey in a local cemetery. At the same time, you might have students gather data from headstones in the cemetery for a study of mortality due to an influenza epidemic or other event in your community's past. In this way, you could cover graphing in math and topics of local history and time lines in social studies. Creating the curriculum grid will help ensure that the unit you develop is rooted in your curriculum.

Draw a concept map

A concept map will help in identifying the concepts or topics you teach that relate to your square kilometer. To make the concept map, write the organizing concept ("The Square Kilometer") in the center of a sheet of paper. Draw spokes, which represent the subject areas, radiating from the organizing concept. At the end of each spoke, list concepts in that discipline and indicate how they relate to the organizing concept. For example, concepts listed under math might be "averaging" and "graphing." Under these might be listed "tree survey" and "daily weather observations." The concept map reveals how place-based studies connect to specific areas of the curriculum, as well as areas of overlap among different disciplines.

Identify focusing questions

The focusing questions that will drive your students' learning are of two kinds: Unit Focusing Questions and Daily Focusing Questions. Unit Focusing Questions identify the main themes of your place-based studies throughout the unit. Each question is worded so that students: (1) can understand the question, (2) cannot answer the question with a simple yes or no, (3) cannot

A Teaming with Nature teacher examines a goldenrod gall with one of his students.

answer the question using skills or concepts from only one discipline, and (4) cannot answer the question in one day's learning. An example of a Unit Focusing Question is *"What are the relationships between humans and the natural world in our square kilometer?"* The Daily Focusing Questions, which students may help generate, maintain a sense of discipline and purpose in the creation and implementation of learning activities. Examples are *"What have you learned about the history of our plot today?"* and *"What are the characteristics of trees that help us identify them?"*

List and plan activities

List potential activities for the unit, and evaluate them on the basis of how well they provide information or develop skills that are needed to answer the focusing questions. Activities that pass muster will compose the syllabus for your unit.

Once you have carefully considered the learning possibilities in the community around your school and have completed the steps described above, you will have a plan that meets the requirements of your curriculum and forges strong links between your curriculum and your place. At the same time, you will find that the unit of study addresses the growing demand for curriculum integration — learning that links writing, reading, speaking, and listening with critical thinking, mathematical reasoning, and scientific inquiry.

Implement the plan

Now consider how to implement your plan. Teaming with Nature veterans have reported that ingredients for success include the following:

⚬ *Principal's and parents' support.* Leaving the school building to pursue first-hand learning seems reasonable, but is a nontraditional approach in many communities. Discuss your plan with your principal and make sure before you proceed that he or she supports it. Write letters to parents informing them of your plans and inviting their comments and participation.

⚬ *Parent volunteers or other community members.* A volunteer coordinator and a team of volunteers to help organize and supervise field trips will make your life easier and provide the child–adult ratio necessary for safe learning experiences outdoors.

Safety. Consider outfitting your students with highly visible, brightly colored T-shirts, perhaps with a logo that they help to create. Keep first aid supplies, students' asthma inhalers, and bee sting kits where you can get to them quickly in an emergency. Have a cell phone with you at all times, and make sure that school personnel know how to reach you.

Student comfort. Make sure students dress for the weather. A well-timed snack can make a big difference in the energy levels and attitudes of your students. A tarp or sheet of plastic can make dew-covered ground a more inviting place to sit.

A culminating event. Plan a public gathering to give your students an opportunity to share what they have learned. Invite the local media to cover the event. Community members will appreciate what your students are discovering about the community you share.

Gilbert White professed to be "an outdoor naturalist, one that takes his observations from the subject itself, and not from the writings of others." Like White, today's students can be inspired to discover first hand the richness, beauty, and complexity of their local community. The Teaming with Nature model provides enough structure and yet enough room for creativity to enable teachers to do just that. ✿

Teachers identify a fish they have netted from a stream as part of their work at the Teaming with Nature summer institute.

Mark Baldwin is the Director of Education at the Roger Tory Peterson Institute of Natural History in Jamestown, New York.

Resources

Aerial photographs

To obtain aerial photographs and maps of the U.S., visit TerraServer USA at <terraserver.microsoft.com> or see the "Publications" section of the U.S. Geological Survey website at <www.usgs.gov>. For aerial photographs of Canada, visit the Natural Resources Canada National Air Photo Library website at <airphotos.nrcan.gc.ca>.

Topographic maps

For U.S. sites, topographic maps on a scale of 1:24,000 are available from the U.S. Geological Survey at <http://topomaps.usgs.gov>.You can find 1:50,000-scale topographic maps of Canada at the Natural Resources Canada Centre for Topographic Information website at <maps.nrcan.gc.ca>.

Teaming with Nature program

Teaming with Nature is a professional development program for teachers offered by the Roger Tory Peterson Institute of Natural History in partnership with State University of New York at Fredonia. Teachers participate in a two-year cycle of implementation that starts with a five-day summer institute in Jamestown, New York. For more information, visit the Institute's website at <www.rtpi.org>.

The Creative Journal: A Power Tool for Learning

More than a place for recording observations and data, an environmental education journal can be a springboard to fresh insights and new discoveries about the natural world

Tom Goldsmith

by William F. Hammond

Grade levels: 1-5

Subject areas: multidisciplinary

Skills: observation, writing, drawing, creative thinking, pattern recognition

Location: indoors and outdoors

any environmental educators have students keep journals because they recognize them as valuable tools that support the aims of education in general and of environmental education in particular. When students are given the opportunity to stretch their creativity, journaling can be fun to do and a terrific stimulus to learning about the natural world. Keeping a journal can help students to improve their writing and observation skills, and encourages them to

think and express themselves in new ways — visually, poetically, and scientifically. In an environmental education journal, these skills are developed in the context of experience in the environment. The journal thus becomes a personal record of the growth of learners' powers of critical observation of the world that surrounds them.

Journals in environmental education

The use of creative journals in environmental education is consistent with brain research, which has shown that drawing and writing about what we experience fixes that experience in long-term memory and stimulates relational thought. In this way, journals can help students to develop a personal and lifelong connection to their local environment. They will never forget the snake they saw, the swamp they waded, the turtle they held, or the thunderstorm they encountered while out in the canoe. Once translated into words and illustrations, these experiences are archived in memory for future reinforcement.

But more than a place for recording observations and data, the creative journal is a springboard to fresh insights and new discoveries. It helps learners to recognize and compare patterns and relationships in the environment, and to discern discrepant events and pattern changes. It is a place to reflect upon these discoveries, to hypothesize how they happen, and to critique and revise ideas. Finally, a terrific sense of accomplishment comes to students when they complete a journal and think, "I am the author of this book." Students often claim that keeping a creative journal is one of their most enriching experiences in school.

The creative approach

The creative journal is not exclusively a nature, scientific, or personal journal, but one that blends all of these forms. It is a style of journaling modeled after a variety of work by creative journal keepers of the past. Leonardo da Vinci, Thomas Edison, Charles Darwin, Margaret Mead, Jonas Salk, Charles Russell, and Aldo Leopold are but a few who provide rich examples. All wrote and drew in their journals, yet each had a unique style, so that their journal entries range from very elaborate drawings and polished prose to very primitive sketches and informal notes. Their journals were not logs or diaries, but rather places for reflection, for metacognition (thinking about how one thinks and learns), and for free-ranging exploration and insight into the events, activities, observations, and possibilities of the day.

The creative approach to journaling is an open one that often requires teachers to rethink why and how they use journals in the classroom. Why have students create journals? Do I want students to write more? draw more? think and express themselves more deeply? Do I want to provide open-ended, student-directed learning opportunities? Do I want to give students freedom to respond creatively to assignments? Do I wish them to reflect on their work patterns, learning strategies, or creative expression? How often should assignments be given? Should I evaluate journal work? If so, how? Where can I find ideas for creative assignments? These are but a few questions that deserve consideration.

The creative approach to journaling also requires that both teachers and students free themselves from the notion that journals are written-only documentation tools. To help students become creative and enthusiastic journal keepers, consider the following:

⚲ Gather a diverse collection of tools. Keep a class art box or backpack that can travel easily outdoors, and invite students and parents to contribute to this creative tool kit. Rescue usable paper from recycling bins and ask print shops in the community if they will donate trim ends of colored paper and card stock. I try to have many different tools with me in my pencil bag and backpack: pens, pencils, watercolors, water-based color pens, colored pencils, markers, highlighters, scissors (the small fold-up type), kneaded eraser, watercolor paper, many different paint brushes, film canisters for storing water, glue sticks, and precut pieces of clear plastic contact paper to cover leaves, sand, and other objects I want to seal in my journal.

⚲ Have students construct their own journals. Use cardboard or heavy cloth for covers and recycled paper for the pages. Bind the books with old shoelaces, string, rope, leather strips, or binder rings. Students can save paper bags and bind them into their journals for use as pockets into which they can slip important artifacts.

⚲ Invite students to develop some of their own rules for journal keeping. The rules themselves are not as important as the fact that students will have thought through their reasons for keeping a journal and the manner in which they will do it. For example, one of my own goals is to use my journal to become a more inventive and creative person. I therefore need to learn

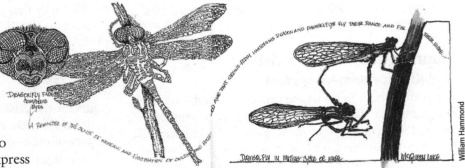

to think more flexibly and to try many different possibilities. To encourage myself to do this, I have made a rule that I can't use my favorite pen or art materials for more than three pages in a row. I have found that if I change the tools I work with, I often change the way I think! I must also learn to be more fluent, and so I have a rule that I must attempt many creative works rather than stopping at the first one that pleases me. Fluency also requires that I feel motivated to work in my journal regularly. Therefore, I have a rule that I must do things that are positive and fun in my journal; the only negative entries allowed are responses to the question "What did I learn from the dumb thing I just did?"

⑥ Encourage creative approaches to filling the pages. For example, I use the transcontinental railroad approach to a journal: I make some journal entries at the front of the book and others at the back, and the book is finished when the two sets of entries meet near the middle. Everyday stuff — notes, undigested observations, facts, and so on — is recorded from the back to the front. Big ideas, creative thinking, unique insights, and major entries go from front to back. I also start each journal with a "bonding page" on which I put an image (sketch or glued-in picture) and a written reflection on who and where I am as I begin this segment of my life's journey. In this way, I ensure that each journal is unique and starts fresh. This technique also helps with fluency, in that I feel a sense of accomplishment at finishing one book and anticipation at starting a new record of my work, play, travel experiences, and creative thinking.

⑥ Model what you want students to do. Keep a journal and use it for completing some of the students' assignments as well as your own work. Be willing to share your work with the students. Your modeling will speak much louder than any instructions you can provide.

William Hammond

Lake County, Arkansas November 8–12, 1989 ≈ A predawn solo canoe paddle.........

Planning journaling activities
Activities for primary students

For young children up to the primary school level, the main goal and focus of journal activity is experimentation with a wide range of tools. Encourage children to have fun, experiment with new media, and celebrate each creative activity. For example, have them create wet-on-wet color-blending watercolor images on index cards that can be glued onto journal pages. Children might make five or six such cards and then choose the one or two they like best, mount them in their journals, and sign them with their signature marks. Other types of images that young children enjoy making are rubbings, rubber-stamp images, pencil-and-pen scribbles, tracings of objects, and stencil patterns. These activities provide children with opportunities to experiment, to choose among various options, to value the work they have produced, and to learn to judge their own work by selecting which of their images will go into their journal and which ones will not.

I prefer to give young children watercolor sets that contain only the primary colors (red, blue, yellow) and

black, along with large, high-quality paintbrushes. In this way the children must learn to find the other colors that are "hiding" in their paint boxes. It is amazing how quickly students find the secondary colors (orange, green, purple) and become confident at mixing and experimenting. If you have students who tend to use only one favorite color, put a set of water-based marking pens in a paper bag and ask each student to reach in, without peeking, and select a pen. Then provide brushes and film canisters full of water, and invite the students to create a special journal page using only the new color.

Activities for upper elementary students

The key to journal assignments for older students is open-endedness combined with just enough specificity to help them bring closure to the task. For example: "Choose your favorite color. Put a swatch of that color on your journal page. Find the color in at least three places in nature. Write two or more sentences to explain how that color became the favorite color of one of the objects you observed. Finally, describe why that color is your favorite."

Many journaling activity books provide ideas for writing and drawing assignments (see Resources list, page 70), and local art teachers may be able to offer starter ideas. Another strategy is to ask individual students or teams of students to create journal assignments for the class. If this task is rotated each week, all students will have the opportunity to become the inventors of exciting and productive journaling activities. When using this approach, it is helpful to determine collaboratively what the characteristics of a good journal assignment would be. For example, students may suggest that assignments be fun or exciting; have no one right answer or way of doing them; require both writing and drawing; and encourage them to do things they have not done before, such as using new materials, going to new places, and trying new ways of doing things. The class may also decide whether it is acceptable to repeat a successful activity if it is given a new twist or changed in some way.

Like many adults, some students are intimidated by a blank page. A strategy for overcoming this blockage is to give a starter assignment that enables students to put something on the page quickly and serves as the foundation for the more complex next task. The following are a couple of assignments that I use often. Both start with a quick and easy graphic that helps to reduce initial anxiety, develop momentum, and stimulate decision-making, creativity, and productivity.

⊚   Cover at least half of the page with a blending of your favorite two colors. Now write three sentences over the color pattern.

⊚   Trace the outlines of any five coins you choose. Now do your math assignment inside the outlines the coins.

More journal ideas

Journal activities should stimulate exploration of the outdoor environment, encourage observation and pattern recognition, and, indeed, elicit deep personal feelings about life and living in the environment. Try to provide a balance between open-ended assignments and those with high levels of specificity. The follow ideas can be adapted in a variety of ways:

⊚   Glue objects into your journal, such as postcards, pictures, picture and object collages, soil, beach sand, leaves, insects, hair locks, and flowers. Next to the object, write something about it and its context, and then cover it with clear contact paper.

⊚   Create watercolor images using water from a local creek or from puddles on the playground. Then the image actually has that place in it!

⊚   Look carefully at the school grounds and record what you find living there. Next, choose one living thing you observed and draw it, or (without harming it) make a real-life impression such as a gentle rubbing, a track print, or other representation. Taking the perspective of the plant or animal, write about how it experiences the schoolyard from day to day through a year of its life. Then write what action(s) you could take to enhance the life of your chosen plant or animal.

⊚   Complete a journal page that gives an example of something that is changing, something beautiful, something ugly, something scary.

⊚   Complete your science assignment within the outline of a leaf from a tree near your home. Outside of the leaf's outline, write how you feel about the tree whose leaf you chose and about the science assignment you just completed.

⊚   Find an example of thoughtfulness or kindness and then copy it! Record in your journal how it feels to multiply kindness or thoughtfulness.

⊚   Find an animal or plant outside. Watch it and study it over several days or at different times of the day.

Then put yourself in the place of your chosen plant or animal. Write and draw its response to your presence.

⊚   Create a three-dimensional, pop-up page that depicts an animal, plant, or natural setting you have observed. (Check the children's section of the library for pop-up examples and, with students' help, determine how such pages are constructed.)

⊚   Use the largest paintbrush you can find to paint a picture of the smallest living thing you can find.

⊚   Write all of your observations of a plant or animal within an outline of the shape of that animal or plant.

⊚   Study an object or event and then imagine how it got to be the way it is right now. Tell its story in words and pictures.

William Hammond

Easy to see how water is the wonder and liquid of life..."

Sharing journals

The act of sharing journals is very important in affirming students' work and reinforcing the thoughts and feelings reflected in it. Sharing also provides a platform for metacognition: seeing how others think and create can lead students to consider strategies, media, and solutions that they have never previously considered.

The basic process is simple. Create an assignment that has both open-endedness and specificity, and give students a reasonable time to complete it. Then form a journal-sharing circle and invite (not require) students to share how they responded to the assignment. Be prepared, if needed, to wait patiently in silence for one or two minutes before asking, "Is someone else willing to share?" Typically, when you are first starting journal experiences, there will be a first rush of sharing and then a lull. This cycle may repeat itself two or three times. If there is a third lull, ask again if anyone else is willing to share. Pause for about 30 seconds and, if no one volunteers, thank the group and remind them that the next journal assignment will be shared the same way tomorrow.

I have never met a child who would not share his or her journal work with the group within the first two weeks of journaling. When you encounter shy or insecure students, make an extra effort to keep an eye on their journal work. Praise them with specific feedback on what you observe when you notice them doing good work, and in this manner help them become more confident and recognize the quality of the work they are doing. Invite (but do not require) them to share their work with the class or group at the next sharing session.

Evaluating journals

Research into the creative process strongly suggests that evaluation can dampen or stifle creative risk-taking. Since this is the antithesis of the purpose of the keeping a creative journal, external evaluation must be used carefully, if at all (see also "Evaluating Nature Journals," page 71). Frequent journal-sharing sessions provide an opportunity to check that students are doing the assigned work, to assess a student's performance and level of engagement, and to give positive encouragement and individual attention to those who may not be fully engaged or comfortable with the journaling process.

Another low-threat but helpful strategy is to provide a self-assessment tool so that students can evaluate their own work and growth. An assignment to respond to the following questions provides a good base for discussion once trust is built in the classroom:

🕭 Has your journal work helped you become a better observer of objects and events around you? If yes, give some examples of how it has improved your observation skills. If no, why do you think this is the case?

🕭 Has your journal helped you become a more flexible and fluent thinker? How so?

🕭 Has your journal helped you improve the way you express what you see and feel? How so?

🕭 Has your journal been a place in which you have done things and used tools that you have never tried before? What was the most difficult thing you tried?

🕭 Has your journal helped you become more aware of and connected to the environment around you and helped you learn more about the environment? How so?

William Hammond

🕭 What is the thing you like most about your journal? The thing you like least?

Regardless of how, or whether, you choose to evaluate journals, remember that journal keeping is a journey rather than a destination. It is a stimulus to touch, smell, listen, and observe. It encourages the student to stop and linger, to explore connections, and to look deeper than the surface of the pond or the life events of each day. Processed on the pages of a journal, these experiences and reflections become fixed and internalized — steps on a personal journey into the magic of the natural world. 🍃

William F. Hammond teaches ecology, interdisciplinary studies, and marine systems at Florida Gulf Coast University and conducts workshops internationally in creative journaling.

Resources

Dvorak, Robert Regis. *Drawing Without Fear*. Inkwell Press, 1987.

Hinchman, Hannah. *A Life in Hand: Creating the Illuminated Journal*. Peregrine Smith Books, 1991.

Johnson, Cathy. *The Sierra Club Guide To Sketching in Nature*. Sierra Club Books, 1990.

Leslie, Clare Walker, and Charles E. Roth. *Nature Journaling: Learning to Observe and Connect the World Around You*. Storey Books, 1998.

Narale, Arvind. *For the Love of Simple Linework: A Diary of an Artist*. Creative Group 2, 1994

Nice, Claudia. *Creating Textures in Pen and Ink with Watercolor*. North Light Books, 1999.

Rico, Gabrielle. *Writing the Natural Way*. Jeremy P. Tarcher/Putnam, 1983.

Evaluating Nature Journals

*Measuring growth without squelching creativity requires
a special kind of yardstick*

by Mike Moutoux

Grade levels: K-5
Subject areas: nature studies, language arts
Key concepts: holistic evaluation
Professional skills: evaluating students' journals

Ideally, nature journals are cherished records of the wild places and things we have encountered and our personal reactions to them. The freedom to explore what is all around me and what's inside me is exactly what I wish for as a writer, and it's exactly the kind of freedom I want to give to everyone else either inclined or assigned to write. Our challenge as teachers and mentors is to give students some idea of the scope of their freedom and encourage them to explore and express using all the skills and gifts they have.

First, let's consider the difference between a diary and a journal. They look the same, and each has an air of privacy about it, but they are different. A diary is often a chronicle of a love life; a journal is a chronicle of a life we love. In my journals, I hope you see the results of that love all laid out in a big mess. Sometimes there is a drawing, other times pages and pages of free writing. Here and there is a quote I've found and written down. You will also find lists, poems, and ideas for future projects all bound together in just the happiest mess you can imagine. Neatness, grammar, and most other rules of writing don't apply in journal writing, because they take away the best freedom of all: freedom to think. My journals are where my ideas begin to take shape.

Nature inspires writing, and I believe a pen will get us further in the wilderness than a compass. And whether we are talking about nature or the wilderness

Photographs by Mike Moutoux

of the mind, getting in can be harder than getting out. I can't imagine asking someone to take a close look at their surroundings without arming them with a blank book and a pencil. What if they see something unusual or beautiful? What if they have a question or an idea? What if they feel the beginning of a poem, as Robert Frost described it, as a lump in their throat? Keeping a nature journal helps me to pay attention to the natural world and increases the pleasure I find in the outdoors. I don't know if it's possible to evaluate that joy, but I do believe it's possible to measure a writer's thinking if you study a journal carefully. Evaluating students' nature journals can give teachers an exciting look at the young minds they are working with and also give feedback about the general atmosphere of a classroom. Once in a while, writers will want to take a risk, but they need to feel safe before they will take a chance and your classroom should be that safe place.

Nature journals have great potential as learning tools, but much of that potential may be missed if we don't have some way of grading them. No grade spells "relief" for many students, the very ones that need more from us as teachers. But how do we measure growth and provide feedback when one child creates a drawing, one produces a list of terse observations, and another writes an essay? Measuring growth while allowing individual response to an experience requires an unusual yardstick, a device that gives credit for all kinds of seeing and thinking.

Following are some ideas that can help in evaluating the odd collection of observations, notes, lists, drawings, and essays that are often found in nature journals. We want to give our students a lot of room to discover, think, and take creative risks, while encouraging them to fill those blank pages. The challenge for us as teachers is to make sense of and, somehow, compare all those apples and oranges.

Evaluative critera

1. Does the writer express curiosity?

- Asks questions
- Describes discoveries

2. Is there evidence of metacognition?

- Comparisons to previous entries
- Additions to lists, observations
- Validations for or arguments against previous statements
- Reflecting on someone else's thinking

3. Is there evidence of right-brained thinking?

- Use of metaphors or similes
- Discoveries of relationships or connections
- Intuitive understandings or conclusions
- Use of artwork to document or decorate

4. Is there evidence of left-brained thinking?

- Sequential or linear entries (lists, organization of information)
- Conclusions based on facts or direct observations

5. Is the student sharing personal reactions to events or observations?

- Expressed emotions
- Vows to take action
- Resolutions

6. Is the student processing information?

- Using previously learned information to draw new conclusions
- Using newly learned words or concepts
- Connecting information (current events to history, seasons to cycles, etc.)
- Validating or challenging information

There are certainly other ways to grade student journals; the main thing is that your students understand what it is you will be looking for in their pages. You may wish to use these criteria to create a rubric

with a scoring system that reflects the specific outcomes you are working toward. Remember to keep it simple so that you don't get bogged down with work and so that students themselves can understand what is expected and even judge their own efforts as their journal pages get filled. One idea for lower elementary grades is a scoring system using smiley faces instead of a numerical score; the more effort shown, the more smiley faces given.

You'll see that journals must be looked at holistically: a single day's work or a single journal page is simply not enough to evaluate all six of the criteria I suggest. This means you might be collecting journals only once in awhile, so I suggest that you not grab them all up at once. Once a week, collect a portion of them to grade so that you see every journal at least twice in a grading period.

Use sticky notes to provide feedback instead of writing on the pages. Encourage students to expand on their ideas, and give lots of positive feedback as you evaluate their thinking. As writers, they should be looking for "The Truth," that elusive knowledge that gives meaning to everything. And they should look for this truth with both sides of their brains, because when they do that they are really giving it all they've got. Randal Marlin, a professor of philosophy, put this quite nicely when he said, "The pursuit of truth is like picking raspberries. You miss a lot if you approach it from only one angle." Encourage your students to use all of their talents, not just the few they feel best about. Now and then, suggest that they revise or rewrite something and this time use all their research, grammar, and usage skills so it is ready to share with the rest of the world. And let them share.

Finally, allow students to see your work as well. You are keeping a journal for your own growth and enjoyment, I hope! Letting them see your work builds trust and shows them that paying attention to their surroundings is not simply a requirement for a passing grade: it's a way of life. That's a very powerful message. ✍

Mike Moutoux is a retired non-formal educator in Dalton, Ohio. He leads sessions on nature writing at workshops and conferences, and performs cowboy poetry for students through his "Cowboys in the Classroom" program.

Karen Oberhauser

Plants and Animals

Forest Studies With Children

*Through this integrated unit, children sharpen
their sensory awareness of trees, examine tree anatomy and biology,
and consider the importance of forests in our daily lives*

Toronto Hydro

by Susan Argast and Cheryl Macdonald

Grade levels: 2-4

Subject areas: science, ecology, language arts, social studies, art, mathematics

Key concepts: collaborative learning, geometric shapes, interdependence

Skills: classifying, listening, observing, drawing, problem solving

Location: indoors and outdoors

orestry is a prominent part of our community life here on the west coast, and our students are naturally curious about it. But no matter where students live, they depend upon forests in their everyday lives and enjoy learning about trees. This integrated unit is one that we use to promote young children's awareness and appreciation of forest ecosystems. Throughout the unit, students work in cooperative groups. The main goal is to provide many opportunities for children to explore trees with their senses; sharpen their knowledge of tree biology; learn about

the impact of the forest on daily life; explore the interdependence of plants, animals (including humans), soil, water, air, and light; and solve problems that involve conflicting values and needs.

Preparatory activities

Before beginning the unit, organize the students into collaborative groups. Consider placing the children in groups of three, with one member who is a good thinker, another who is a good facilitator, and a third who will work well with the other two and benefit from their skills. Brainstorm with the class the conditions that would help their groups work well together (e.g., say kind things to one another, listen to each other's ideas, stay with the group, talk quietly but clearly). Decide which of these criteria are most important and use them in evaluation.

Brainstorm and categorize the knowledge of trees and forests that children already have. First, ask students what they know about trees and forests, and record the key words of their responses on index cards. Then distribute at least one card to every student. Put four or five strips of masking tape on the chalkboard, sticky side out, and invite the children to place their cards on the strips. Have one student start by placing a card on a strip and giving the category a name. The other children add their cards, one at a time. As they do, they explain why their card belongs in that particular category, or they create and name a new category. For example:

> *Parts of trees:* bark, leaves, stem, branches, roots
> *Types of trees:* coniferous (keeps needles all year), deciduous (sheds leaves)
> *Tree products:* paper, lumber, house, furniture
> *Forest animals:* birds, deer, bears, slugs
> *Recreation:* camping, snowshoeing, wilderness hiking

🍎 Select as a study area a woodlot or forested site that is free of water hazards, logging roads, and other potential hazards. (Since the unit requires many field studies, we selected a forested area within walking distance of the school.) Use surveyor's tape to mark activity areas clearly. Recruit parent helpers or older buddies to go along on field trips.

🍎 Discuss the rules of the forest: You are invited to enter and discover the secrets of the forest. You must remember that you are a visitor. This forest is a home for many different plants and animals. As a visitor, you must respect the following rules: stay on the trail, and leave it only when given permission; do not take or touch anything without permission; do not damage or destroy anything; try to make as little noise as possible — you never know what you might see or hear if you are quiet.

Sensory activities

For the following sensory activities, have students create a blank "Forest Sounds, Textures, and Sights" booklet, or designate pages of their field journals for this purpose.

Sound

Have each group find a spot within a defined area of the forest. Ask them to sit silently for ten minutes,

Cheryl Macdonald

A "blindfold walk" helps students focus on the textures of the forest.

listening to sounds and noting what they hear in their "Forest Sounds, Textures, and Sights" booklets or journals. If possible, make an audio recording of the sounds of the forest during this ten-minute period. At the end of the time, have them compile a group list of sounds and classify them (e.g., school sounds, city sounds, tree sounds, bird sounds). Back in the classroom, have each group report what they heard, and compare. Discuss the feelings the children had while sitting silently in the forest. If you recorded the forest sounds, listen to the recording and try to identify each sound on the students' lists. Repeat this activity to compare the sounds in different weather conditions (e.g., during a rainfall, snowfall, light breeze; on a sunny day).

Touch

Within a clearly defined area of the forest, have the trios take each other on a blindfold walk:

1. Have each group select one member to be blindfolded; the other two are the leaders.

2. Ask the two leaders to choose a tree and then carefully lead the blindfolded partner to that tree.

3. Allow a few minutes for the blindfolded partner to feel such things as the tree's leaves or needles, its bark, and any plants that grow on or around it.

4. Have the leaders take the blindfolded partner back to the starting place, remove the blindfold, and ask the partner to try to find the tree.

5. As a class, brainstorm words that describe the textures of things (e.g., rough, smooth, soft). Then have the groups move through an area of the forest feeling objects and noting the texture categories they belong in. For example:

> *Rough:* soil, bark
> *Smooth:* rocks, leaves
> *Furry:* moss
> *Prickly:* needles, fern fronds, cones

6. Back in the classroom, put forest objects in a "touchy-feely" box. Pass the box around, and have the

Leslie Harting, BBEMA

children feel, describe, and try to identify the objects. Classify the objects into living and non-living categories. As a follow-up activity, have children make their own boxes to share objects with one another through touch.

Sight

☙ Make "binoculars" by taping together two paper rolls. In the forest, have students select a tree and use the binoculars to focus on such things as its bark, leaves or needles, cones, branches, lichens, and moss. Have them explore these things close up and far away. In groups, have one child use the binoculars to describe something in detail while the others try to identify what it is.

☙ Have the students lie down on the forest floor to see the forest from a new perspective. If dry leaves are on the ground, have them cover each other with leaves so that they feel as if they are a part of the ground. Then ask them to remain still and quiet for a short time, observing the tree trunks, branches, leaves and needles, sunlight through the canopy, birds, etc. Afterwards, have the groups share and record their observations and discuss their experiences. As a follow-up activity in the classroom, the children could draw and paint pictures of the forest as seen from the ground and/or write about the forest from the perspective of something on ground: e.g., "I am a speck of dirt in the forest. It is nice to feel the warmth coming through the green canopy of the tall trees. I gaze up at tall, brown, scaly tree trunks and see a robin sitting on her nest in a branch above me."

☙ In the classroom, have the children make a charcoal drawing of a schoolyard tree from memory. Then go outside to observe the tree, noting markings on the bark, the color and shape of the needles or leaves, and the shapes and directions of the branches. Have students make a second sketch of the tree based on these fresh observations.

☙ Review basic geometric shapes and have the groups search for these shapes in nature, recording their findings in sketches and/or words. While on outings in the forest, search for repeating patterns in design or color (e.g., branching patterns on trees, leaf patterns on branches, circular patterns in flowers, colors in flowers).

☙ Collect ten common natural objects from the forest (e.g., cone, twig, dead bark, leaf, seeds, fern frond, berry). Show the children the collection for 25 seconds, and then ask the groups to collect a duplicate set of objects from memory. Remind the children that nothing is to be picked from a tree or a plant; the items must be found lying on the ground.

Smell

☙ Collect small blocks of aromatic woods, such as cedar and pine, and have the children try to identify them by smell.

☙ Show photographs and paintings of trees and forests. Ask the following questions: If you were in this painting, what might you smell? (hear? see? feel?)

Adopt a Tree

Once the children have explored trees with their senses, have each group identify a favorite tree to "adopt." Adopted trees can be the focus of a variety of activities through the year; for example:

☙ Have each group create an "Our Adopted Tree" booklet in which they record such things as what the tree looks like (size, leaf shape and color, bark color and markings); whether it is alive or dead, and the evidence; the sounds it makes; what the tree smells like (do different parts of the tree smell different?); what depends upon the tree; and what the tree needs for survival.

☙ Have the groups measure the circumference of their trees and record this in their booklets.

☙ With help from parent volunteers or older buddies, have students measure the height of their tree using its shadow. First, measure the shadow of a student and the shadow of the tree. Then calculate the ratio of height to shadow. For example, if a 1.5-meter person casts a shadow of 2.5 meters, the height-to-shadow ratio is 1.5

Plants and Animals

to 2.5, or 0.6 to 1. A tree that casts a shadow of 20 meters would therefore be 12 meters tall.

⊚ Have students eat lunch under their adopted trees, observing any animals that come to visit and recording what it is like to sit under the tree.

⊚ Have the groups visit their trees at different times of the year to observe how the trees have changed and in what ways they have remained the same. Follow-up activities could include making sequencing charts showing the trees and their surroundings throughout the year, or making flipbooks illustrating the how the trees change through the seasons.

The parts of a tree
Roots

⊚ Plant two seedlings, one in a container of water and the other well rooted in a pot of soil. Have the children observe how well the two seedlings stand and hypothesize about one of the functions of roots and soil.

⊚ Have the children observe the size of the stem and branches of a bush and predict how big its roots are. Carefully dig up a small shrub so that the children may observe its roots. Discuss the functions of the roots.

Stems

⊚ Place a stalk of celery in a solution of water and food coloring to illustrate one of the functions of stems. Alternatively, put small pieces of cedar in food coloring for a day, and then split them open and observe.

⊚ Observe the bark of a tree and notice the direction, length, and pattern of the cracks. A tree's bark or "skin" does not stretch as the tree grows, so it must crack and widen. Have the groups sketch and compare the bark of different trees, and try to identify the trees by their bark (using a tree identification book).

⊚ Explain to the class that a tree grows quickly during the spring when there is usually abundant moisture; during this time, a light-colored ring of wood forms. In the summer, when less water is available, the growth

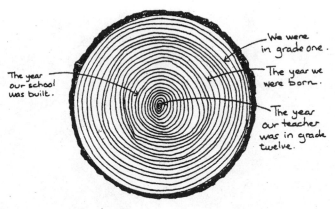

The year our school was built.

We were in grade one.

The year we were born.

The year our teacher was in grade twelve.

of the tree slows; during this season, a dark ring of wood forms beside the light-colored ring. Thus, each year, a light and a dark ring of wood forms. The age of a tree can be determined by counting either the light rings or the dark rings.

⊚ Bring a "tree cookie" (cross-section of a tree trunk) to class, and count the number of rings to determine how old the tree was. Attach a string to each year's growth ring, date it, and list important community events that may have occurred during that year of its life.

Leaves

⊚ Cover a branch of a broadleafed seedling or plant with a plastic bag. Holding the bag closed, use a straw to draw the air out of it and then quickly seal the bag with tape. Observe the branch each day for several days, and hypothesize about one of the functions of leaves. (The bag will fill with air as the plant produces oxygen.)

⊚ Cover a leaf of a broad-leaved tree with aluminum foil. Remove the foil after several days and observe the changes. (The leaf will turn yellow and eventually die.) Hypothesize what caused the changes. Discuss the importance of light in producing the green color of leaves and as the "food" of plants.

⊚ Place one seedling in a dark cupboard, leaving the cupboard door open by a crack. Put another seedling in full sunlight. Compare the two seedlings after several days.

⊚ Put leaves and needle clusters on an overhead projector and observe leaf edges, veins, and patterns. Ask the students to create a system of classifying leaves and needle clusters, based on their observations. Later have them try to identify the leaves and needle clusters using an identification guide.

⊚ Collect fallen leaves and branches of needles; have the children classify them according to their color, shape, texture, and twig patterns.

Henry Kock

⚮ Collect leaves and needle clusters from several species of trees that are common in your forest study site or schoolyard. Have the groups match the leaves with the trees and then use field guides to identify the trees.

⚮ Have students use leaves in art projects. These might include crayon rubbings; spatter-paint prints; ink prints; mobiles made of leaves that have been pressed between waxed paper with an iron; leaf casts made from plaster of Paris; and tiles made from leaves imprinted into square slabs of salt dough, which is then baked, painted, and varnished.

Students learning to use wedge prisms to estimate the basal area of trees on a site.

Nova Scotia Forestry Association

⚮ Have the groups rehearse and act out scenes that demonstrate interactions between living organisms and such environmental factors as water, air, sunlight, and soil (e.g., a thirsty animal or a dry plant receiving water, a plant being moved from darkness into sunlight). Have the spectators describe how each scene shows the importance of water, air, sun, and soil.

Seeds

⚮ Collect seeds by dragging a piece of rough-textured wool (such as an old sock) through the forest. Also collect cones and bring them into the classroom to dry; when the scales have separated, tap the cones to release the seeds.

⚮ Try germinating the seeds you have collected. Place them on damp paper towels on a cookie sheet, cover the cookie sheet with plastic wrap, and place the sheet in a bright, warm spot. Have the children predict, and then observe, how long it will take the seeds to germinate. Hypothesize as to why some seeds will not germinate in classroom conditions. Plant the germinated seeds in potting soil, and observe and try to identify what grows.

The concept of interdependence

⚮ Have each cooperative group plant a garden in a large pot or aluminum roasting pan, or, if possible, in a real garden plot on the school grounds. Have the students monitor and graph the growth of their plants.

⚮ Plant seeds under different conditions, isolating the variables in order to observe what plants need in order to grow well (e.g., compare seeds planted in soil, watered, and kept in sunlight to seeds planted in soil, watered, and kept in the dark; compare seeds planted in soil, kept in sunlight, and watered with seeds planted in soil, kept in sunlight, and not watered).

⚮ Classify common foods according to whether they come from plants or animals. Pose the questions: What do the animals eat? Where do the plants get their food? As the discussion proceeds, draw a web illustrating the interdependence of animals, plants, air, sunlight, water, and soil.

⚮ As a class, brainstorm the answer to the question "What is soil?" Have each group measure a 30-centimeter-square (one square foot) area of soil, and use a small trowel to collect a soil sample. Have the students observe and record the smell, feel, and color of the soil. Then have them use a hand lens to examine the top layer of the soil collected, and, if possible, classify their findings into such categories as animal, plant, mineral, synthetic, and so on. There are from 1,000 to 10,000 nematodes in every cubic centimeter of soil, so students are likely to have some live specimens in their samples. Most of these "monsters" can be seen only with a strong magnifying lens. Putting a heat lamp on top of the sample and a tray of ice below the sample may bring an interesting hoard of creatures to the surface. Have the students research such questions as: How have these creatures adapted to their life underground? What do they do there? What role do they play in the forest?

⚮ Ask the class what they think happens to the leaves, berries, and insects that die and remain on the ground. In the autumn, have the children collect fallen leaves, put them into a plastic mesh bag (such as an onion bag), and bury the bag. After six or seven months, dig up the bag and observe what has happened. Discuss what might have caused the leaves to break down.

Plants and Animals

⑥ Have the children play the role of trees under a variety of conditions (e.g., in a gentle breeze, during a windstorm, during a gentle rain, in a thunderstorm, during a forest fire, with squirrels running up and down branches, with a bird building a nest, with a person climbing up into the branches, being planted, being harvested).

The impact of forests on our lives

⑥ Have collaborative groups brainstorm things that are made of wood (e.g., paper, houses, toys, furniture, tree houses) and services that trees provide (e.g., shade, beauty, homes for animals). Then have each group share its ideas with the class, making a large, combined list.

⑥ Arrange to visit a house construction site to interview the house builder about the materials used, the importance of trees in the construction, and the steps in building a house. Back in the classroom, have the children recall construction materials needed to build a house, categorizing them into wood and non-wood products. Have the groups make a sequencing chart of the steps in building a house (clearing the lot, digging the hole, pouring the foundation, constructing on the floor, putting up the walls, framing the roof).

⑥ Sawmills do not generally allow young children to tour, but it may be possible to observe how a tree is milled into lumber by visiting a community member who operates a small portable mill. Standing well back, have the children observe the milling process. They can also interview the mill operator about the work and his/her views on harvesting the forest. Back in the classroom, have each group prepare a small mural depicting the milling process, writing captions to explain each step.

⑥ Visit a tree nursery to observe how seedlings are cultivated for reforestation. (September or late June is the best time for such a field trip; foresters at the nursery are often too busy at other times of the year.) While there, interview a forester about the job, and about the life cycle of a seedling from sowing, to growing, to

Cheryl Macdonald
Visiting a tree nursery.

harvesting. Back in the classroom, have each group prepare a short report about what they saw and learned and a pictorial representation of the life cycle of a seedling.

⑥ Have each group invent a game using sticks, stones, and other natural objects. Once the rules are clear and the games have been "field tested," have the groups teach each other their games.

⑥ Have students make colored drawings by rubbing natural objects from the forest onto paper (e.g., charcoal for black, grass for green, rotting wood for shades of red and brown, soil for brown shades).

Problem solving and forest conservation

⑥ Discuss with the class what a healthy forest would look like compared to an unhealthy one. Then discuss some of the causes of poor forest health (e.g., acid rain, disease, insect infestation, logging without reforestation, damage to trees by wind or by humans, litter left by campers). Have each group make a small mural that contrasts a healthy forest with an unhealthy forest.

⑥ Have the groups brainstorm ways to protect a forest. From their lists of ideas, have them make a poster or booklet to publish and illustrate "rules" that people should follow to keep forests beautiful and healthy.

⑥ Pose problems such as those listed below and have students discuss them in their groups and as a class. (If possible, also discuss a real problem that exists in the community.)

1. Last year, your class planted small fir trees along the border of the school playground. You have been watering them when it is dry, and watching out for pests that might harm them. Last week, you noticed that most of them had already grown by three and four inches. When you came to school this morning, you found that many of the trees had been kicked over and trampled. You aren't sure who is responsible. You decide it is time to take some action to prevent disaster. What are you going to do?

Leslie Hartling, BBEMA

2. There are few parks in the city. When the city was first formed, there were so many trees everywhere that no one really worried about preserving wilderness or creating parks. You and your friends enjoy playing in the wooded area in the park down the street. Your dad told you last night that the park is going to be used for a big new construction yard. He was excited because your uncle might be able to get a job there when it opens. You can't imagine not being able to play there any more. After you have thought things over, you go to your dad and tell him how you feel.

3. When you were in kindergarten, you went on a field trip to a tree nursery. You received a seedling, and you brought it home and planted it in a very good location in your backyard. It has grown well, and you feel proud of it. Your parents have decided to build a shed in the backyard to make room for the garden tools and bicycles. They plan to build it where the tree is growing. What do you think should be done?

4. For as long as you can remember, an eagle has used the tall tree in your neighbor's yard as a look-out tree when hunting. Your neighbors have decided that the tree shades their home too much, and they worry that it might fall down in a severe storm. They want to cut the tree down. What do you think they should do?

5. The vacant lot on the corner of your street sold a few months ago. The family that bought it is going to build a house on it. You heard them say that they are going to remove all the mature trees because it will be easier for them to start with a cleared lot, but that they will plant new trees afterwards. Do you think they should save any of the trees? What advice would you give to them? Why?

6. Your family belongs to a nature club whose members canoe and hike all year round. The club has volunteered to help create a hiking trail in the state/provincial park just outside of town. What is the best way for the club to decide which trees to remove to make way for the trail? Should they try to save any special kind of tree? If so, which ones? What about the animals that might live along the new trail?

7. On your way across the school playground, you have seen four older kids carving on the trunks of the poplar trees just outside the schoolyard fence. Once you saw them swinging from lower branches until they broke. You know that these kids are not afraid of anything and that they don't always do the right thing. Is there anything you can or should do about the damage they are causing to the trees? ✎

Susan Argast and *Cheryl Macdonald* *teach in the Campbell River School District on Vancouver Island in British Columbia.*

This article was adapted from "Co-operative Learning – Forest Studies," in *Prime Areas*, 31:3, Spring 1989, pp. 61-71.

Resources

Some of the activities in this unit have been adapted from the following sources:

The American Forest Foundation. *Project Learning Tree.* The American Forest Foundation, 1977.

Cornell, Joseph B. *Sharing Nature with Children.* Ananda Publications, 1979.

Edwards, Harry, Stephanie Goulet, Michael Hoebel, and Kip Anastasiou. *Touch a Tree.* Western Development Group, 1983.

A Walk in the Tropical Rainforest

Creating and leading a multi-sensory rainforest tour

by Glenn Gustafson

Grade levels: 4-6

Subject areas: science, social studies, arts

Key concepts: tropical ecology, resource conservation, ethnobotany

Skills: critical and creative thinking, research, communication

Location: indoors in gym, hallway, or large classroom

Time: several weeks for preparation, one day/evening for presentation

Glenn Gustafson

Step off the boat into the blue surf and wade to shore under the watchful eyes and noisy calls of a pair of scarlet macaws feeding in an almond tree. Watch and listen for signs of the deadly fer-de-lance, the most dangerous snake in Central America. It's raining, it's hot, you're dirty, and you feel more alive then you've ever felt before. You have arrived in the rainforest!

It's not easy to convey in the classroom the wealth of sensory impressions that greets visitors to a tropical rainforest. But as it is unlikely that we can take our students on an adventure to the tropics, we must try other ways of bringing the rainforest to life here at home. With a little ingenuity, a teacher can recreate the sights, smells, sounds, tastes, and atmosphere of this unique ecosystem and, in so doing, help children understand its importance and recognize their own connections to it.

A fun way to do this is to work with a group of students to prepare a multi-sensory Walk in the Tropical Rainforest that can be offered as a guided tour to other classes or to the community. In preparing and presenting the walk, students become rainforest experts, absorbing a wealth of information about this ecosystem. The following suggestions for creating a tropical rainforest walk are based on research for an interpretive trail brochure that I developed as a volunteer in a park in Costa Rica in 1999. It is a learning adventure that I want to share with as many people as possible in order that places like these continue to exist.

Learning objectives

The objectives of the rainforest walk are that students will:

- experience aspects of the rainforest in a multi-sensory way

- understand the global importance of rainforests

- understand some of the ecological relationships in rainforests

- learn what they can do to help preserve rainforests

Introductory activity

This activity helps to generate interest in the rainforest by raising students' awareness of the importance of rainforest products in their daily lives.

Procedure:

1. Begin by presenting a variety of everyday items and common foods that originate in tropical rainforests. Do not tell students where they came from; instead challenge students to guess what these items have in common. Items could include potatoes, cinnamon, vanilla, brazil nuts, chewing gum, a rubber bicycle tire, a tropical plant, chocolate, coffee, and bananas.

2. When students have guessed the rainforest origin of the items, show where they come from by pointing out on a map or globe where tropical rainforests are located.

3. Ask students how their lives would be affected if they did not have any of the items provided by rainforests.

4. Show a video such as *Bosque Eterno De Los Niños* or read a book such as Lynne Cherry's *The Great Kapok Tree* (see Resources list, pages 85-86) as a general introduction to rainforests. Discuss the disappearance of rainforests and the consequent loss of many useful and beautiful things.

Preparing the rainforest tour

Over several sessions, have students research and develop the script, props, and other materials necessary to "produce" several interpretive stops on a tropical rainforest walk. Each stop should present a theme or illustrate an important aspect of the ecology of the rainforest (see suggestions in discussion below). Set up the walk in a large area such as a school gym, hallway, or classroom, and invite other classes and/or community members to be guest "explorers." Set the mood by dimming the lights, playing a recording of rainforest sounds, running a humidifier, and, if possible, turning up the heat. To add drama and keep groups together during the walk, link the stops with a guide rope and have the guest explorers wear blindfolds as they follow the rope from stop to stop. Encourage the student guides to dress for the jungle in long sleeves, long pants, rubber boots, and sun hats.

Glenn Gustafson
Cecropia tree.

Stop 1: Light gaps and pioneers

An undisturbed primary rainforest has very sparse growth near the ground because very little light penetrates the canopy. When a tree falls, causing what is called a "light gap," the seeds of many light-loving or pioneer species will germinate and grow quickly. For example, Cecropia trees, often seen in light gaps, can grow up to 2.4 meters (8 feet) per year; but they live for only about 30 years and are eventually replaced by shade-loving species that can grow beneath the forest canopy. Forests are dynamic, constantly undergoing succession in this way. Research shows that the average square meter of forest lies within a light gap every 100 years.

Materials: heat lamp; several tall potted tropical plants; piece of a decomposing log in an airtight container; tape or CD recording of rainforest sounds; and materials for making a model of a Cecropia tree: a cardboard carpet tube mounted upright on wooden base, heavy green construction paper, tempera paint, sponge, wire coat hangers, scissors, tape, Cecropia leaf pattern template.

Procedure:

1. Have students research to learn about rainforest light gaps, rainforest succession, and pioneer species such as the Cecropia tree.

2. Work with students to create a model of a Cecropia tree (or other pioneer tree) based on photos or illustrations they have found during their research. Create a leaf template that can be traced and cut out of construction paper. Use a carpet tube for the trunk of the tree (you might paint it a mottled brown/green using a sponge) and attach the leaves to it with coat hangers inserted into holes punched in the tube.

3. To set up the tour stop, create a forest clearing by surrounding an area with tropical plants. Set the Cecropia tree in the clearing, shine the heat lamp down from above, and dim all other lights in the room.

4. During the tour, lead small groups of guest explorers to the "light gap" while they are blindfolded and holding onto the rope. Ask the explorers to describe what they feel (heat from the sun lamp), what they hear (rainforest sounds from the recording), and what they smell and touch (pass around the container of decomposing wood). Then have them remove their blindfolds while the guides explain how a light gap forms, the concept of succession, and interesting things they have learned about Cecropia trees and other pioneer species.

Stop 2: Things are looking up

A rainforest has diverse and abundant vegetation that provides many places for jungle creatures to live. From the top of the tallest trees down to the forest floor, these habitats are stratified into several identifiable layers:

Emergent Layer: The tallest trees form the emergent layer, which receives the most light, heat, and rain.

Canopy: Beneath the giant trees of the emergent layer is a second, more uniform layer of tall trees called the canopy. Because of the wet conditions, canopy trees support an abundance of plant growth such as mosses, orchids, and bromeliads. These plants are called epiphytes, or air plants, as they obtain nutrients and moisture from the air and rain, not from the trees.

Where dense canopies of rain forest vegetation intercept the force of rainfall, soils are protected from erosion and streams are clear and gently flowing.

Understory: Under the canopy trees are a variety of smaller or younger trees, as well as many vines, lianas, and the infamous strangler fig (*Ficus spp.*). The strangler fig begins life as an epiphyte, but grows downwards from the canopy to take root in the ground, eventually strangling the host tree with its interconnecting tendrils.

Forest Floor: Whenever light is available, an abundance of ferns, palms, and tropical plants cover the ground of the rainforest.

Materials: Rolls of craft paper, scissors, tempera paints, brushes, flashlights, reference books that show rainforest levels and a variety of rainforest plants and animals (e.g., *Destination: Rainforest* or *Up a Rainforest Tree,* see Resources, pages 85-86).

Procedure:

1. Have students work in groups to research the levels in the rainforest, the plants and animals that are found at each, and the ways in which these organisms interact.

2. Use craft paper and tempera paints to create a large diorama that depicts all of the rainforest levels and the plants and animals at each level. Each group can be responsible for depicting the level of the forest that they researched, while the groups can all work together to make the components that pass through several levels (such as canopy trees and emergent trees).

3. Mount the rainforest trees, with the associated vines, animals, and other organisms, on the gym wall. Birds and insects might be made three-dimensional and suspended by fishing line from the ceiling. Be sure to

include some creatures whose camouflage enables them to blend almost invisibly into the background.

4. During the tour, have the guides use flashlights to illuminate different features of the diorama as they explain the various layers and habitats of the forest. Challenge the visitors to find camouflaged creatures in the scene, or invite them to return to discover these creatures after the flashlight tour is over.

Stop 3: Water, water everywhere

Rainforests receive as much as 3,000 millimeters (118 inches) of rainfall per year. This high level of precipitation, in combination with typically nutrient-poor, high-clay soils, means that whenever forest cover is removed serious soil erosion occurs. Under normal conditions, as rain falls in the forest some of the moisture is used by epiphytic plants, but much of it gently percolates through the canopy to the forest floor, where it is absorbed. Even in times of high rainfall, rainforest streams tend to be relatively gently flowing streams of clean, clear water. If the tree cover is removed, however, stream flow increases dramatically and red soil washes away in the water, looking almost like a stream of blood.

Materials: Two clear shallow basins, sand, garden tools, tropical plants, sticks and twigs, two spray misters.

Procedure:

1. Read a book or watch a video that depicts what happens when a tropical rainforests are logged (e.g., *The Great Kapok Tree* or the video *Bosque Eterno De Los Niños*).

2. As a reference, find pictures of healthy, intact rainforests and of rainforests after they have been cleared. Have two groups of students prepare two mini-ecosystems in shallow plastic basins as follows:

Healthy ecosystem: Create a landscape from sand (red sand if possible) that has a river valley in the center and hills on either side. Plant the hillsides with tropical plants right up to the bottom of the valley.

Logged ecosystem: Create the same landscape with sand, but instead of tropical plants, use sticks and twigs to represent the stumps and fallen wood left over after logging.

3. During the tour, have the guides explain what has happened on both sites. Then have volunteers take turns being the "rainstorm," that is, using the spray bottles to heavily mist both ecosystems. Observe and discuss what happens to the soil in both situations as the rains continue.

Stop 4: Rainforest restaurant

The rainforest is an abundant source of food crops, and some its plants could even save our lives! One of the rather unusual plants in the rainforest is a ladder-like vine called a monkey ladder — yes, monkeys do climb it! Indigenous people have traditionally ingested an infusion of the vine to treat diabetes, and research has proven it to be equivalent to insulin. Sap from a somewhat similar vine, the common liana, is used to make an infusion to treat fever in children. So far, only about 5,000 of the world's 250,000 plant species have been investigated for medicinal use. Think what we may be missing!

The common liana has its roots in the ground and its leaves high in the canopy.

Materials: plants, stuffed tropical birds, tropical music, rainforest treats prepared by students, and, if desired, rainforest products displayed in a "corner store" atmosphere.

Procedure:

1. Research the various rainforest items that we use in our lives: for example, food items such as brazil nuts, and medicines such as quinine used to combat malaria. (Suggested resources: *Jungles* and *Earth Child 2000*).

2. Have students set up a "Rainforest Restaurant" that serves treats from the rainforest, such as rainforest cookies made with cashews and brazil nuts. Students may wish to make a menu (and perhaps translate it into Spanish) detailing what is being served and where it comes from.

3. Students can also create a small "corner store" with rainforest products such as rubber tires, medicines, chewing gum, fruit, and Panama hats.

The Rainforest Restaurant is the refreshment stop on the rainforest tour. It can be decorated as elaborately as the class would like, with everything from tropical plants to toy parrots. Music from a tropical country adds a nice touch. As visitors stop on their walk, the student servers can explain what is in the rainforest treats they are serving and the importance of using rainforest products.

Stop 5: Disturbing behavior

When an area of rainforest is cleared, it can regrow relatively quickly if allowed to. For example, at the Campanario Biological Reserve in Costa Rica, a large field that had been cultivated was allowed to regenerate naturally, with some additional planting by staff. After only nine years the field became an area of dense growth, providing an abundance of hiding places and food sources that attract a variety of animals, from hummingbirds to spider monkeys.

Materials: large ball of heavy string or yarn.

Procedure:

1. Have students research the various life forms that can be found in a regenerating rainforest, noting the order in which plants and animals return following a disturbance, as well as "who eats whom" in the food web of the regenerating forest.

2. At this last stop on their walk, have a large rectangle marked on the floor and ask visitors to sit around the edges of it. This represents the edges of an imaginary field that has been cleared in the rainforest. Have the student guides review the life forms that return to the clearing (based on "who eats whom") and have visitors step forward to represent these various plants and animals. Connect them with string as the story unfolds to show "who eats whom." For example, the first plant to start growing many be a Heliconia (the student representing the plant steps forward and takes the end of the string). The Heliconia quickly blooms and is visited by a hummingbird (the student representing the hummingbird now steps forward and picks up the string). The hummingbird is then connected to something else that it may eat or be eaten by. This continues until all the visitors have become part of the web of life in the newly established rainforest.

3. To demonstrate how interconnected this new ecosystem is, have someone leave the web, tugging on the string as they go (perhaps a parrot is captured by a smuggler for resale in North America). Have everyone who feels the tug likewise pull on the string. This ripple effect will eventually pass through the entire web,

demonstrating that harming one part of the ecosystem will affect everything in the rainforest.

Summary activities

☙ As visitors complete the tour, ask them to share what they have learned about the rainforest and talk about things they can do to help preserve it. A before-and-after Jungle Explorer quiz on the plants, animals, products, and ecology of the rainforest will help to focus attention and discussion.

☙ Plan an action stage of the project, such as fundraising for the purchase of rainforest land through organizations such as the Rainforest Action Network or Bosque Eterno de los Niños/Children's Eternal Rainforest. If this is planned beforehand, funds can be raised by charging admission for the rainforest tour and for treats in the rainforest restaurant. As a follow-up, all of the classes involved in the tour may participate in a rainforest bake sale for the community at large.

☙ Have students make a rainforest scrapbook based on the tour they organized, including drawings, research, photos, and any observations they made. These scrapbooks could be constructed from paper that the class makes using rainforest materials such as coconut fibers that are added to the pulp.

Extensions:

☙ Investigate local connections to the rainforest by visiting local grocers and specialty stores to see what tropical products are for sale in your community.

☙ Visit a local natural area and conduct research to find out what migratory birds (or butterflies) either live in or pass through your area. Have students plot on a world map the places to which these colorful visitors migrate in winter. Discuss the importance of maintaining rainforest and local habitat in order to protect these species.

☙ Compare and contrast the ecology of the tropical rainforest and that of forests in your region. Students should find that the same ecological principles (e.g., light gaps and forest succession) are at work in both. Some resources to help with these explorations are *TRFic! A Temperate Rainforest Teacher's Guidebook and Poster Kit* (Sierra Club of Canada, BC Chapter) and *Exploring the Boreal Forest: Understanding an Ecosystem* by Dave Glaze and Kay Wilson (Saskatchewan Environmental Society, 1991).

Through creating and hosting a Walk in the Rainforest, students can develop a sense of the amazingly intricate and complex world of tropical rainforests and help to educate others about it as well. It is only through awareness of this marvelous resource that we can generate the will to preserve it. It is my hope that every child who experiences the rainforest through activities such as these will one day step off a boat along a sandy shore and walk through warm surf under the watchful eye of scarlet macaws to discover first-hand the marvelous world that they once only imagined. ☙

Glenn Gustafson is an environmental educator with Alberta Environment and an enthusiastic traveler to the rainforest regions of South and Central America.

Resources

Books for younger students

Cherry, Lynne. *The Great Kapok Tree: A Tale of the Amazon Rainforest*. Harcourt Brace, 1990. In this beautifully illustrated children's book, many different animals that live in a great kapok tree in the Brazilian rainforest try to convince a man with an ax not to cut down their home.

Green, Jen. *Rainforests*. Gareth Stevens Publishing, 1998. An interesting book of facts and activities for studies of rainforest topics.

Grupper, Jonathan. *Destination Rainforest*. National Geographic Society, 1997. A good scientific look at many aspects of life in the rainforest, with large, high-quality color photographs and minimal text.

Jordan, Martin and Tanis. *Jungle Days — Jungle Nights*. Kingfisher Books, 1993. Beautiful paintings illustrate this story of animals and their activities in the rainforests of South America. A good book to read to a group over several sessions.

Patent, Dorothy Hinshaw. *Children Save the Rainforest*. Cobblehill Books/Dutton, 1996. Documents the work taking place through the Bosque Eterno de los Niños/Children's Eternal Rainforest in Costa Rica.

Telford, Carole, and Rod Teodorou. *Up a Rainforest Tree*. Heinemann Interactive Library, 1998. Looks at the animals and plants found at each level of the forest, from the rainforest floor to the highest emergent trees.

Books for older students and adults

Ayensu, Edward S., ed. *Jungles*. Crown Publishers, 1980. A wonderful encyclopedia of the tropics that is well illustrated and includes a very helpful "Products of the Jungle" section.

Forsyth, Adrian. *Portraits of the Rainforest*. Camden House, 1990. Good information for teachers and great color photographs to share with a class. Organized by interesting categories such as "rarity," "beetlejuice," and "El Tigre."

Forsyth, Adrian, and Kenneth Miyata. *Tropical Nature: Life and Death in the Rainforest of Central and South America*. Charles Scribner's Sons, 1984. Seventeen essays tell of some fascinating and shocking aspects of life in the rainforest. Anyone want a maggot?

continued on next page ➤

Kricher, John. *A Neotropical Companion: An Introduction to the Animals, Plants and Ecosystems of the New World Tropics.* Princeton University Press, 1997. Everything you've ever wanted to know about the rainforest, explained in an easy-to-read, entertaining style.

National Wildlife Federation. *Rainforests: Tropical Treasures.* Chelsea House Publishers, 1997. An excellent resource featuring stories, activities, songs, crafts, and resources that can be the basis of an entire unit of rainforest study. Aimed at Grades K to 8.

Perry, Donald. *Life Above the Jungle Floor: A Biologist Explores a Strange and Hidden Treetop World.* Simon & Schuster, 1986. Find out about the "real" rainforest in an entertaining look at the two-thirds of jungle wildlife that lives in the forest canopy.

Sheehan, Kathryn, and Mary Waidner. *Earth Child 2000: Games, Stories, Activities, Experiments and Ideas About Living Lightly on Planet Earth.* Council Oak Books, 2000. An excellent resource that covers a variety of environmental topics, including rainforests. It has a wide selection of activities, stories, and resource descriptions.

Music

There are many rainforest tapes and CDs available that have either nature sounds alone or combine nature sounds with music. *Simbiosis — Piano and Rainforest*, a CD by Manuel Obregon (1999), is a marvelous mixture of piano and nature sounds recorded live in the tropical cloud forests of Monteverde, Costa Rica.

Videos, DVDs, and CD-ROMS

Bosque Eterno de los Niños (15-minute video). Monteverde Conservation League, Apartado 10581-1000, San Jose, Costa Rica. This short video for younger students provides an excellent introduction to the beauty and wonder of the rainforest, while also examining threats to it.

Magic School Bus Explores the Rainforest (CD-ROM). Microsoft Corporation, 1997. An animated journey in the rainforest with Ms. Fizzle and her class. Looks at seven eco-zones within the three main layers of the forest. Ages 6 to 10.

Really Wild Animals — Totally Tropical Rainforest (40-minute video). National Geographic Video, Columbia Tristar Home Video, 1994. A great video for a younger audience, with excellent footage and music and an animated mascot with the voice of Dudley Moore.

Rainforest for Children: Animals of the Rainforest (25-minute video). Schlessinger Video Productions, 1996. Straightforward, simple narration and footage that is indicative of what one might see on a visit to a rainforest. Also in the series are people and plants of the rainforest. Grades 3 to 6.

Rainforest (60-minute video). National Geographic Video, Columbia Tristar Home Video, 1993. A well filmed and well researched educational video suitable for older students.

Tropical Rainforest (40-minute DVD). Science Museum of Minnesota, SlingShot Entertainment, 1992. Originally presented in IMAX theaters, this production looks at the evolution of the rainforest over 400 million years.

Organizations and websites

<www.tropical-forest.com> Children's Tropical Forests. A non-profit organization in the U.K. that, among many activities, publishes an excellent newsletter summarizing rainforest activities worldwide.

<www.rain-tree.com> Rain Tree. Advocates preservation of the rainforest through the sustainable use of rainforest resources and products. The site includes a section to help with school reports and a gallery of rainforest pictures.

<www.ran.org> Rainforest Action Network. An excellent resource for rainforest information, with a focus on issues and actions. The Protect-An-Acre program supports organizations and communities working to protect rainforests; certificates are given for donations of US$25. Contact: Rainforest Action Network, Protect-An-Acre Program, 221 Pine St., 5th floor, San Francisco, CA 94104, rainforest@ran.org.

<www.savetherest.org> The Rainforest Foundation. A group focused on protecting the rights of rainforest peoples. The site includes a children's section with background information and ideas for assisting this cause.

<www.rainforestweb.org> Rainforest Web. This site is truly the world rainforest information portal with links to articles and other websites dealing with everything from rainforest news to what you can do to protect rainforests from home.

Training and field courses

Rainforest and Reef: A non-profit organization that offers field courses in rainforest and marine ecology. Credits are available through Aquinas College in Grand Rapids, Michigan. Contact: Rainforest and Reef, P.O. Box 141543, Grand Rapids, MI 49514-1543, <www.rainforestandreef.org>.

Campanario Biological Reserve/Proyecto Campanario: A privately owned, education-focused reserve in Costa Rica that can provide first-hand explorations of lowland tropical rainforests to groups of teachers or students. It is located on the Osa Peninsula, a 60-minute walk north of Costa Rica's largest national park. All groups visiting the reserve are accompanied by a qualified tropical biologist. Contact: Proyecto Campanario, Apartado 263-1260, Plaza Colonial, Escazu, 1260, Costa Rica, <www.campanario.org>.

Monteverde Conservation League: Stewards of the Bosque Eterno de los Niños/Children's Eternal Rainforest as well as Monteverde Cloud Forest Preserve. Ecology workshops are offered for teachers and high school students. Contact: Monteverde Conservation League, Apartado 10581-1000, San Jose, Costa Rica.

Plants and Animals

Making Connections With Insect Royalty

Raising monarch butterflies in the classroom helps students develop a personal connection to a remarkable member of the most populous class of animals on Earth

Lonnie Duberstein

by Ann Hobbie

Grade levels: 3-6

Subject areas: science, language arts

Concepts: life cycle, migration, plant and animal adaptations

Skills: systematics, observation, descriptive writing

Location: indoors and outdoors

Time: 3-9 weeks

f you ask ten-year-olds to name as many animals as they can, chances are the list will be made up mostly of mammals. Little mention will be made of insects, the animals most prevalent on our planet in species and number. On the first day of school, I asked my fifth grade students to bring in as many pictures of animals as they could find. The next day, we sorted through the collection of magazine cutouts, postcards, drawings, and dog-eared photographs that they felt represented the animal kingdom. After sorting them several ways, we grouped them by class and discovered that we had 53 mammals, 8 fish, 6 birds, 5 amphibians, 4 reptiles, and 1 insect — which happened to be a butterfly. The students felt pretty sure that our numbers represented the proportions of species, as well as populations, of each animal class. In other words, like most children, they were confident that the animal world is largely mammals and had no awareness of the real numbers: that there are more than one million species of insects, while the number of mammal species is about 4,500 (over half of which are rodents and bats).

Unbeknownst to them, my fifth graders were about to develop a new and profound relationship with the insect world, one that began with a fascinating example: the monarch butterfly. While we had been poring

over pictures of creatures, the students had also been watching small petri dishes that were placed on their tables on the first morning of school. Each dish housed a mysterious package: an egg no larger than a pinhead, secured to a milkweed leaf. With hand lenses and journals, the students began to record what was happening in their dishes. These observations marked the start of an important connection between the students and the monarch butterfly. It was a connection that was at first personal, characterized by great affection and concern for an individual larva, but grew into an interest in the monarch's local habitat and the vast geography of this organism's migration route.

The distinctive yellow, black, and white monarch caterpillar.

Personal connections

Because some of the larvae began hatching immediately on the first day, the students quickly concluded that they were indeed looking at eggs. "It looks like a tiny Cyclops with a black eye," wrote one student. "I think it's some kind of worm," suggested another.

Every morning over the next three days, the students arrived wild with excitement to find out what was happening in their petri dishes. Our monarch larvae proved to be highly cooperative and dramatic subjects. Because they go through a complete life cycle in one month, from egg to larva to pupa to adult butterfly, there is profound growth and change on a daily basis. Students often did not believe that they were looking at the same individuals from one day to the next, and even accused me of exchanging their larvae for larger ones.

To enable the students to make observations, we brainstormed a list of the monarch caterpillar's physical attributes and behaviors. This list served as a descriptor pool from which they could draw while writing. (See lesson "Focus on Features" on page 93.) Students learned new words and metaphors. They also noticed a new level of detail in their insect friends — the tiny holes through which the larva breathes, the head capsules left behind with each molting, the delicate threads that emerge from the spinerette when handled, the distinct mandibles with which the larva voraciously consumes milkweed, and the wrinkled and undulating pattern of black, yellow, and white stripes. Daily, the children recorded in their journals the changes they

beheld, as well as questions that arose. Soon the larvae outgrew their petri dishes and we moved them to clear plastic boxes.

By the time the larvae had molted for the fourth time, students were familiar with the behavior and daily needs of the caterpillars. All 32 larvae had been named, fed, cleaned up after, and even delicately "petted." Over this period we investigated many questions that students raised in their journals. How much do they eat in a day? How much do they weigh? Do they hear us? Do they eat anything besides milkweed? Do they eat each other? What caused the deaths of several larvae in our classroom? How should we care for and handle the larvae to minimize these deaths? All questions were listed and displayed on a piece of butcher paper and, as we found answers, checked off.

After nine days, the caterpillars began the journey to the top of their plastic containers and prepared for their fifth and final molt. I had warned my students that this was a prelude to something marvelous, and many a math and history lesson were put on hold while they watched transfixed by what happened next. In a breathtaking climax, the monarch larvae pushed away their striped coats one last time, presenting with tiny shudders the translucent emerald green bodies of their pupal stage. Within an hour, each pupa rested firm and still, glimmering with tiny gold beads in characteristic patterns. Journals quickly recorded new questions. How long will this stage last? What are the gold dots for? Why are they bright green?

We moved some of the pupae out of their cages, gently tying their silk pads with thread and hanging them from various points in our classroom. I knew that when they emerged in about ten days, they would not fly at first, and I didn't want anyone to miss this next transition.

While our monarchs were pupae, the students needed to gather more information. What will we need to do for the adults when they emerge? What will they eat? Where will we keep them? We made a chart of what we already knew and what we wanted to know. It was during this conversation that a boy named Tim asked a very important question: "Every fall my grandma has tons of monarchs land in a tree at her house. She says they come there every year. Do they drink from trees?"

This led to a conversation about what insects do during winter. I revealed to the students that, besides their exciting life cycle, there is another amazing thing about monarchs. I explained that the monarchs at Tim's grandmother's trees, near the Minnesota-Iowa border, were not nectaring, but instead beginning a 3,200-kilometer (2,000-mile) journey to Mexico. We discussed the magnitude of this flight, and my students were awed by what lay ahead of the still, green forms that hung around our room, silently developing on the ends of strings and the lids of cages. But they also wondered why such a trip was necessary. Why not just go somewhere warmer where there are flowers to drink from and fields to fly in? Won't they die along the way? How do scientists know that the butterflies from Minnesota end up down there? Can you see them migrate?

It was clear that my students had come to care a great deal about these butterflies. I was convinced that this was the crucial connection, for only if they came to know these insects would they become cognizant of the delicate ecosystem that sustains them. The children were starting to see the bigger picture.

Local connections

I asked the students to tell me what they had already learned about what monarchs need to survive. While their larvae were growing, the children had needed to gather milkweed every day. It was not long before they were seeing milkweed everywhere: in backyards, along railroad tracks, in highway ditches, at the edges of ball fields, and in local parks. We also had daily reports of monarch butterfly sightings, and the students were noticing other butterflies as well. One student became quite upset that her milkweed source at a nearby baseball field had been mowed down. After a couple of larvae died, we theorized as a class that maybe some of our milkweed was cleaner than others, and we talked about why this might be. Another teacher in our building had many larvae die one day after eating milkweed that had been sprayed with pesticide. (See lesson "Is

Gail Littlejohn

The common milkweed (Asclepias syriaca) *is one of more than 100 species of milkweed in North America that monarch larvae depend on for food.*

Your Community a Good Home for Monarchs?" on page 92.)

After our larvae had pupated, we turned our attention to the question of what the monarchs would need when they emerged. A walking field trip to a restored prairie revealed a multitude of organisms living in the monarch's ecosystem. At that time of year (autumn), there were not many sources of nectar still blooming except for some goldenrod and blazing star. Aging milkweed plants, which were tall, leathery, and yellowing, had long since gone to seed. Students looked for clues about how plants and animals prepare for the coming winter, and we talked about the driving forces — temperature, food source, humidity, and day length — that compel some organisms to journey elsewhere.

Global connections

With their new understanding of migration, students began to perceive connections beyond our community. They came to realize that these monarchs were related to a much bigger world than first appeared. They were dependent not only on the milkweed and flowers here, but on milkweed and flowers between here and Mexico! The students also saw that the monarchs' survival is dependent on all that happens along this route. I asked the students, "How do scientists know what happens to monarchs during the course of their lives? How do we know that they migrate?" I showed them the wing tags that scientists use to track monarchs during their migration (see Monarch Watch <www.monarchwatch.org>).

The class began to prepare for the adult stage of the monarch's life. We learned how to care for the butterflies and prepared several larger cages for keeping them. We began to chart the temperatures in our town of Roseville, Minnesota, as well as in cities in Iowa, Missouri, Kansas, Oklahoma, Texas, and Mexico. We played a game that simulated some of the limiting factors our butterflies would face while making the migration. We learned about a research project run by monarch biologists at the University of Minnesota in which the public helps gather information about monarchs and milkweed in the wild (see Monarch Resources, page 95). We looked at pictures of the monarchs' overwintering sites in Mexico in which tree branches bowed with millions of butterflies. The children were thrilled that their monarchs could be part of a study of migration and might be recovered along their journey south. They started to see the connection between the well-being of insects in Roseville's fields and those in places far away.

It wasn't long before the first monarch emerged as a butterfly. It was one that we had hung from our ceiling, and it happened in the morning during a break. Students were drawn en masse, clustered around the dangling string to get a glimpse of what was, literally, unfolding. With beads of liquid rolling off crumpled wings, this female (named "Thelma" by the students) clung to the empty shell of her pupal casing, letting gravity and physiology pump up her royal cloak of orange and black. I had never seen such delight and intrigue on my students' faces.

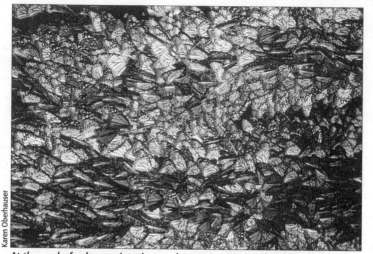

Karen Oberhauser

At the end of a long migration each autumn, monarchs mass by the millions in their winter habitats in Mexico and California.

This elegant drama repeated itself many times in the coming days. We took photos. We weighed and measured. We made observations, offered fresh flowers, and organized a twice-daily feeding regimen of fresh honey water. My students even learned from those monarchs that didn't make it. Using a light brush of clear tape to the abdomen and wings, several students created slides of the monarch scales to examine under the microscope. (See lesson "Observing Butterfly Scales," page 92.)

It was with great anticipation and undeniable melancholy that we arrived at the sunny release day in late September. The students gave the monarchs a final feeding and brought them to our school nature area to let them go. Not all of the monarchs had made it this far, but I had reared some extras so that everyone gingerly held a monarch's folded, velvety wings one last time. There were squeals, claps, and cries when, on the count of three, wings lifted these insect voyagers into the air.

After watching for a while, we convened back in our room. I assured the children that our journey with the monarchs wasn't yet over. We looked at our list of questions. Many of them had been checked off, but many more had not. What route would these butterflies take? What would they see on their way? How do the butterflies know how to get to Mexico? Are there

other insects that make such a trek? As it turned out, many of our questions are the very ones that monarch biologists are still working to understand.

I feared that with the release of the monarchs would come a letdown that would halt our monarch study. But there was so much more to know about the world of monarchs beyond our walls. We watched for our butterflies on the Monarch Watch website, and learned more about the oyamel fir forest ecosystem and the Mexican farmers who own the forest. I was reluctant to focus too much on the complex tension between the poverty of the landowners, who need the forests for lumber and firewood, and the unique climatic needs of migrant monarchs. Instead, I tried to share with the students all the ways that people are cooperating to preserve the monarch's habitat throughout North America. Prairie restorations, the Monarch Butterfly Sanctuary Foundation, and collaborations among the governments of Canada, the United States, and Mexico provided some examples.

Sometime in the days following our monarch release, I put up the chart of the world's animal biodiversity that we had made on the second day of school. I asked them to rethink what we had predicted about the number of species of mammals, reptiles, insects, and other organisms. I used a bar graph to show them how vastly greater were the number of species of insects than of mammals. I asked them why this might be? We discussed how the world might be different for other groups of animals and plants if the numbers and kinds of insects in the world were fewer.

I became convinced of two things as a result of this experience. First, I believe that my students had never thought about the importance of insects because they had never felt any personal connection to them. Second, the experience of observing, caring for, and inquiring about monarchs helped them to understand the connections between the organism and its habitat, thus influencing the way they think about and appreciate the world of organisms around us. ✒

Ann Hobbie formerly taught Grades 5 and 6 in the Roseville Schools in Roseville, Minnesota. She currently teaches enrichment classes for the Minnesota Institute for Talented Youth, and teaches about monarchs through the Monarchs in the Classroom program.

ACTIVITIES

More than Mammals

Many people have the impression that mammals are the most numerous and important animals on Earth. However, mammals are a relatively small group. In this lesson, students sort pictures of animals, compare their groupings with those that scientists use, and then discuss how well their pictures represent the actual proportions of species in animal groups.

Materials: 14 large pieces of paper, each labeled with the name of an animal group (see chart); paper on which to make a large class bar graph; a transparency of a bar graph showing the numbers of species in groups (using data from chart); picture of an animal from each animal group (optional); pictures of animals cut from magazines (5 to 10 per student, optional)

Procedure:

1. Before class, label 14 pages with the names of the 14 animal groups listed on the chart. Place the pages face down where they will not be seen by students.

2. Ask each student to bring 5 to 10 pictures of different animals to class, or provide magazines and have them cut out pictures during class time. Alternatively, have students write down the names of 5 to 10 animals on separate slips of paper.

Animal Groups	Species (approx)
Amphibians	2,800
Sponges	4,200
Mammals	4,500
Starfish, sand dollars, sea urchins	5,000
Centipedes/millipedes	6,800
Reptiles	7,000
Birds	8,600
Jellyfish and corals	9,200
Arachnids	15,000
Fish	20,600
Worms	22,500
Crustaceans	26,000
Mollusks	128,000
Insects	over 1,000,000

3. Divide the class into small groups and have them sort their pictures into categories, using criteria they establish.

4. Show students some of the categories that scientists use (see chart), but do not show them the number of species in each group. Display the list of animal groups while the students do the next steps.

5. Have students sort their pictures into the 14 scientific categories and place them on the labeled pages, or hang the pages on the wall and have students tape their pictures onto them. Make a "Question" pile for any animals they cannot fit into a category.

6. Have students count the number of pictures in each group and graph the categories on a class bar graph. (You may wish to stop here and wait until you are finished rearing monarchs to share the actual number of species with students.) Compare the class graph to the actual proportions of animals in each of these groups by looking first at their graph and then at the actual numbers. Tell students that new animal species are discovered each year, and that these are the approximate number of known species in each group. Note the enormous number of insect species in comparison to the number of other animals.

7. Students will likely bring in many more pictures of mammals and birds than of other animals. Ask them why this happened. Are they surprised at the actual proportions? Remind them that there are many species of animals that we rarely encounter, and that this diversity is very important to the world's ecosystems. Discuss the roles that insects and other invertebrates play in their ecosystems.

What your class can do to help monarchs

◉ Plant a butterfly garden that includes milkweed species native to your area, as well as nectaring plants.

◉ Encourage your city or state/province to preserve and create habitat that monarchs can use and to minimize the spraying of insecticides.

◉ Support conservation organizations working to preserve overwintering habitat in Mexico, such as the Monarch Butterfly Sanctuary Foundation, <www.mbsf.org>.

◉ Raise monarchs in the classroom and release them outdoors in the spring or fall (see Monarch Resources, page 95).

The lessons on pages 91 to 93 have been excerpted, with permission, from curriculum guides produced by the Monarchs in the Classroom program, directed by Dr. Karen Oberhauser at the University of Minnesota.

Observing Butterfly Scales

Scales give butterflies and moths their name, *Lepidoptera*, which means "scaly wings" in Latin. Lepidopteran scales serve many important functions. They increase the mass of the wings and thus their heat-retaining capacity. Because they are filled with air, they also serve to insulate the body. Scales help to generate thrust during flight, which is especially important for a long distance flier such as the monarch.

Scales also give butterflies their amazing color patterns. While each scale is only one color, beautiful patterns result when the wings are covered by a mosaic of many colors and kinds of scales. The colors we see when we look at butterfly scales are of two types. Some are due to pigmentation. In this case, scales emit a particular color because they reflect light of a particular wavelength. Other scale colors are structural. For example, the scales of Morpho butterflies are iridescent blue because they have ridges on them that cause light in a narrow range of color (blue) to be reflected and reinforced. Complex and intense color mixtures result when pigmentation and structural reflection are intermixed.

Karen Oberhauser

In this lesson, students observe and draw scales from many parts of the monarch's body. They should note the different shapes, color patterns, and sizes, thus increasing their observational skills.

Materials:

◈ Several dead butterflies and moths, if available, from which to collect scales. These can often be found in car grills, spider webs, and other places. Try to find different species for comparison.

◈ Drawing paper for each student, folded to create six sections.

◈ Colored pencils, fine-tipped markers, clear tape (not "magic tape"), index cards, glass slides.

◈ Hand lenses or dissecting microscopes.

◈ Optional: compound microscopes, close-up photographs of butterfly wings such as found in *Butterfly Alphabet* by Kjell Sandved.

Procedure:

1. Discuss the function and coloration of butterfly scales, and show close-up photographs of butterfly wings.

2. Have students carefully observe an intact butterfly wing, and draw a section of this wing on one section of their drawing paper.

3. Observe the same part of the wing through a hand lens or magnifying glass, and draw it on another section of paper.

4. Carefully touch a piece of clear tape to part of the butterfly's wing and remove a small patch of scales.

5. Put the tape on a glass slide if you have compound microscopes, or on a piece of white paper or index card if you have dissecting scopes or hand lenses. Observe the scales carefully and draw several individual scales on another section of the paper.

6. Remove scales from other parts of the bodies of butterflies (thorax, abdomen, head, and legs) and observe and draw them in the same way. Be sure to label each piece of tape, telling where on the body the scales were found.

7. Make a classroom display of drawings of different scales. Label each drawing with the part of the butterfly from which the scales were removed. If you use more than one butterfly species, compare sizes, shapes, and colors.

8. As an enrichment activity, students could learn more about the functions and design of Lepidopteran scales.

Is Your Community a Good Home for Monarchs?

Every monarch that winters in Mexico is there because there was milkweed growing in a monarch breeding ground in the United States or Canada. Yet in some Canadian provinces, milkweed is considered a noxious weed and is actively controlled. In the United States, there are no explicit laws to control milkweed, but the plant often grows in or near places subject to mowing and the application of herbicide, such as roadside ditches, agricultural fields, power line right-of-ways and railroad tracks. These practices may kill larvae and destroy plants on which eggs are laid.

In this lesson, students learn whether milkweed is controlled in their city, state, or province; how frequently areas that may contain milkweed are mowed; and whether pest control in their area may harm monarchs or other non-pest insects.

Materials: phone directories with government listings; access to the Internet (optional)

Procedure:

1. Ask students, "What do monarchs need for survival?" and list these needs on the board. Make sure the list includes requirements for breeding (*milkweed and nectar flowers*), migrating (*flyways and nectar flowers*) and overwintering (*oyamel fir forests*). Then ask, "Which of these requirements are found in our area?"

continued next page

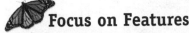 # Focus on Features

In this lesson students develop observation skills that can be transferred to the study of monarch larvae or other organisms.

Materials: paper and pencils; an apple; 6-8 paper bags, each containing a different kitchen gadget or classroom object (e.g., bottle cap, garlic press, juicer, staple remover); monarch larvae and milkweed (or another organism you are studying); hand lenses; thesaurus

Procedure:

1. Divide the class into groups of three or four. Assign the following jobs in each group: Recorder, to record the group's observations; Reporter, to speak for the group; Encourager, to give positive feedback and to ask for input from all members; and Getter, to get and return materials.

2. Ask the students what it means to observe something. Hold up or pass around a familiar object such as an apple, asking students to describe exactly what they observe. For example, students might describe an apple as red, round, smooth, having a woody stem, about the size of a fist, shiny, waxy, streaked with green, spotted, having pin-sized yellow dots, firm. Students might also describe the apple as delicious, gross, crunchy, yucky, yummy. Help them understand the difference between their observations of the apple and their opinions or assumptions about it.

3. Give each group a paper bag containing a familiar object (give a different object to each group). Have students pass their bag around, allowing each group member to observe and touch the object. They may take the object out of the bag, but warn them not to name it aloud or to let other groups see it.

4. Have each group work for three to five minutes to describe their object, using terms related to its color, size, texture, material, and other attributes. Have the Recorder list all of the group's observations.

5. After five minutes, have each Reporter read the list of observed attributes and characteristics. As each object is described, the rest of the class should guess what it is. Discuss which observations were most useful.

6. Students are now ready to transfer these skills to the study of monarchs. Have the Getters bring a container of monarch larvae with milkweed and hand lenses to their table. Instruct the students to examine the larvae closely, using the following questions to direct their initial observation:

- How big is your larva?
- What color(s) is it?
- Describe the body.
- How many legs are there? Where are they? Are they all the same?
- Are the caterpillars eating? How do they eat?
- How does the caterpillar move?
- What do the caterpillars feel like when you touch them?
- Can you tell the front from the back of the caterpillars? How?
- Can you see eyes?

7. Give individual students 5 to 10 minutes to observe a larva, making a list of as many attributes as they can. (You might incorporate a lesson on using the thesaurus during this section.)

8. Instruct group members to share their individual observations, forming one group list.

9. Make a class list of the observations by having the Reporters take turns telling one observation from their group lists. You may want to separate physical from behavioral observations. Post this class list to serve as a descriptor pool from which students may draw as they write in journals or do other work with monarchs.

---

continued from previous page

2. If you have raised monarchs in the classroom, discuss how easy it was to find milkweed to feed the larvae. Where were students most likely to find it? Did they encounter problems such as limited availability and mowing of milkweed sites? Discuss the effects of these problems on wild monarch populations.

3. Sometimes insecticides sprayed onto fields or into ponds for pest control may inadvertently get onto milkweed. Discuss problems that pesticides pose to non-target organisms such as monarchs.

4. Discuss methods of and reasons for the control of certain plants and insects by individuals or governments (e.g., spraying herbicides to eradicate invasive weeds, mowing roadsides

Karen Oberhauser

so they look neater or so that drivers can see more easily, using pesticides to control insects on crops).

5. Have students find out which government agencies control the use of herbicides and pesticides and then call or write letters to ask about the frequency of mowing in public areas. Students could also write letters to public agencies to explain why milkweed habitat should be protected.

6. Discuss actions taken in your area to preserve resources for monarchs and other butterflies, such as restoring prairie habitat or creating parks or gardens that contain milkweed and plants for nectaring. If possible, visit some of these sites. Discuss other organisms that benefit from projects that increase monarch habitat.

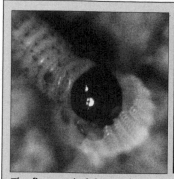

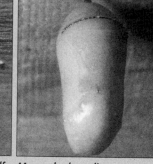

The first meal of the newly hatched larva is its egg casing.

Larvae fatten up dramatically during their five stages of growth.

A pre-pupal larva attaches itself to the silk pad it has spun.

Monarch chrysalis or pupa.

Left to right: Sonia Altizer, D. Alstad, Karen Oberhauser, Karen Oberhauser

Meet the Monarch!

by Karen Oberhauser

In a sense, monarch butterflies undergo two life cycles. Like all butterflies, moths, and other insects that have complete metamorphosis, individual monarchs change from eggs to larvae (caterpillars) to pupae to adults. We refer to this as their "individual life cycle." Monarchs as a group undergo an astonishing "yearly life cycle," which involves several generations and covers thousands of kilometers.

A monarch's life

An individual monarch's life cycle begins when a female lays an egg on a plant in the milkweed family. The most widespread of these is the common milkweed (*Asclepias syriaca*) found in the northern United States and Canada, but there are approximately 110 other milkweed species in North America,

with a diversity of growth habits and habitats. Females generally lay a single egg on the underside of a milkweed leaf and then move to another plant. They appear to be quite picky about the plants on which they lay eggs, often testing several plants before finally choosing one. Three to seven days later, a tiny larva chews its way out of the egg. The newly hatched larva's first food is its egg-casing, but when this is consumed it soon begins eating the plant chosen by its mother. It will go through five larval stadia, or stages called instars, shedding its old skin between instars to allow for growth. The main activity of the larva is eating, and monarchs will eat only plants in the milkweed family. They gain some protection from predators by sequestering toxins that they obtain from these plants. All of this feeding results in rapid growth: during the larval period of about 8 to 14 days, monarchs increase their mass by about 2,000 times!

When the monarch is ready for the pupa instar, it seeks a protected location and spins a white silk pad using a spinneret located just under its mouth. It then attaches itself to this silk pad and dangles head down. About a day later it sheds its skin for the last time, and forms the chrysalis, or pupa. This stage will last for 9 to 15 days, depending on temperature.

The day before the butterfly emerges, its folded wings are visible through the pupa case and it is possible to see the black, orange, and white color pattern that is the monarch's trademark. This pattern is formed by scales, tiny appendages that cover the monarch's wings and body. Scale pigmentation is one of the final steps in adult development. On the day the monarch will emerge, the colors are very distinctive and the pupa no longer has any green coloring. Adults usually emerge in mid-morning, making it likely that students will be able to observe the wondrous procedure that begins with the pupa case splitting and ends as the monarch's abdomen, full of fluid, and then its wings, tiny and crumpled, drop down from the pupa case. The newly emerged adult immediately begins to pump fluid from its body into its tiny wings, and the wings take their final shape over a period of several minutes.

A magical migration

Three to four generations of monarchs complete their life cycles through the spring and summer, reproducing soon after they emerge as adults, and living for two to five weeks. The important jobs of these monarchs are to find flowers from which to nectar, milkweed plants for egg laying, and mates. The monarchs that emerge in late August and September are behaviorally and physiologically different, and they have the more complicated task of finding their winter home, which may be thousands of kilometers from their birthplace. This generation puts reproduction

continued next page

Plants and Animals

Emerging from pupa case.

Adult monarch on milkweed.

Winter sanctuary in the mountains of central Mexico.

Monarchs become active in late winter and begin migration in March.

continued from previous page

on hold and heads south, making an annual migration that is unique among insects. The monarchs west of the Rocky Mountains head to coastal California (although recent evidence suggests that some western monarchs may enter the Mexican state of Sonora from Arizona). The larger eastern population, destined to live up to nine times as long as their spring and summer counterparts, travel the length of southern Canada and the United States to oyamel fir forests high in the Transvolcanic mountains of central Mexico.

As they arrive in Mexico, beginning in early November, monarchs form roosts of mind-boggling density, which cover the trunks and branches of hundreds of trees on steep mountain slopes. They remain in a nearly dormant state until the temperature rises in February, when they become more active, mating and seeking water and nectar. In mid-March, they fly north to look for the milkweed plants they need to produce a new generation that will continue the journey their parents began. Monarchs re-colonize spring and summer breeding grounds in the northern United States and southern Canada soon after their host plants emerge from their own winter rest.

While the monarch butterfly is the best-known insect migrant, other insects migrate. In most species, different individuals make the northward and southward journeys, often stopping to breed along the way, so that journeys are completed by "leapfrogging" generations. Many pest insects migrate, including potato leafhoppers and many aphid species, as do milkweed bugs, many dragonflies and damselflies, and several other butterflies. However, as far as we know, no other species migrates as far or as regularly as monarchs.

Because of their yearly cycle, monarchs depend on a suite of resources in widely dispersed locations. In their breeding habitat, throughout the United States and southern Canada, the larvae need milkweed plants and the adults need nectar sources — resources they find in fields, roadsides, gardens, and prairies, which serve as nurseries for monarchs and many other organisms. During their fall migration monarchs need safe flyways, expanses of land

that contain nectar sources to fuel their long flight. Finally, the migratory generation requires intact wintering sites, oyamel forests in Mexico and coastal forests in California, which protect them from extremes of temperature and humidity during their long winter rest. Preserving the spectacular phenomenon of the monarch's yearly life cycle will require the preservation of these habitats and resources, and the interest, knowledge, and cooperation of citizens throughout North America.

Karen Oberhauser is Assistant Professor in the Fisheries, Wildlife and Conservation Biology Department at the University of Minnesota, and director of Monarchs in the Classroom and the Monarch Larva Monitoring Project.

Monarch Resources

Monarchs in the Classroom is a program of inquiry-based science that encourages K-12 teachers and students to raise monarch butterflies as a means of bringing science, ecology, and conservation issues to life in the classroom. The program promotes research collaboration between students and scientists, conducts workshops for teachers, and provides instructional materials that include books, CDs, videos, field guides, and posters. Contact: Monarchs in the Classroom, University of Minnesota, 1980 Folwell Avenue, 200 Hodson Hall, St. Paul, MN 55108, <www.monarchlab.org>.

Monarch Larva Monitoring Project is a monitoring program for monarch enthusiasts across North America that helps to increase understanding of monarch ecology during the summer portion of their life cycle. The project's website includes directions for participation and summaries of results. Contact: MLMP, University of Minnesota, 1980 Folwell Avenue, 200 Hodson Hall, St. Paul, MN 55108, <www.mlmp.org>.

Monarch Watch is a continent-wide research network of schools involved in monitoring and tagging monarchs. Participants receive tagging kits and monitoring instructions, and enter their observations into a database used by scientists to study migration. Contact: Monarch Watch, Department of Entomology, University of Kansas, Lawrence, KS 66045, <www.monarchwatch.org>.

The Milkweed Farm is a great source of milkweed seeds and books on monarchs and monarch-related activities and investigations, <www.milkweedfarm.com>.

Tracking Migratory Animals On-line

by Bob Coulter

Grade levels: 3-5

Subject areas: science, language arts, social studies

Key concepts: migration, seasonal change

Skills: Internet research; basic reading, writing, and thinking skills

Location: indoors

Over the past decade, nearly all schools have added computer studies to their curricula and Internet access to their classrooms. Parents, teachers, and students routinely e-mail each other, transforming the communication patterns in schools. Websites are instructional resources, and, increasingly, students are creating their own web pages as part of their learning. It is clear that we live in a much more technologically advanced world than we did even ten years ago.

Photographs by Bob Coulter

This expansion of computers into nearly every facet of our lives presents a special challenge to environmental educators, given the emphasis that we place on first-hand experience. Our most meaningful learning experiences have occurred through close investigation of nature, and we want to keep this interest in the natural environment alive in our students. We want to use technology where it is appropriate, but not at the expense of first-hand experience where that is better. Balancing the two is never easy, but when we do this well, the curriculum is transformed and the classroom comes alive as a center of inquiry.

As a relatively early adopter of the Internet in the classroom, I had the good fortune of experiencing this transformation through a project involving migratory animals. My third grade students were given the assignment of working in small groups to learn all they could about an individual species and to develop a portfolio to be shared with peers and parents. This was not intended to be a standard read-and-copy report for which elementary schools are notorious. Instead, project requirements were structured to challenge students to pursue information widely, to think deeply about their animal, and to engage thoughtfully with the world of science. Students used books, magazines, and CD-ROMs, but only as a starting point. Most of the information was gained from using the Internet to track authentic scientific research and through writing letters to organizations working with their group's species. They were required to prepare a short report with a map of the animal's migration pattern and a drawing of the animal in its habitat. They were also required to include copies of electronic and paper correspondence sent and received. In this way, a wide range of science, language, and geography skills were enhanced.

Clearly, these nine-year-old students were not equipped to comprehend, let alone appreciate, all of the nuances of professional scientific research. Fortunately, mediation between the authentic data and the students' level of comprehension was available through the on-line environmental education initiative Journey North (see sidebar). Journey North is an environmental monitoring program through which participants share data on migrating species and the northward progression of spring. Students can contribute data to the Journey North network by reporting local signs of spring, such as first sightings of monarch butterflies and the first blooming of tulips. They can also obtain data, including radio-telemetric data that allow them to track the migration of individual members of such species as eagles and manatees. This real-time data provides a window into the life of an animal in the wild and is supplemented by extensive information on the background of the species. Students can also pose questions on-line to an expert on each species. The use of background readings, authentic research data, and questions to experts was a uniquely valuable learning experience for my students. Each found something to be passionate about as they learned about their species, compared notes with peers, and shared the joy of receiving booklets and posters in the mail from conservation organizations they had read about and corresponded with on-line.

The three components in the students' research — background readings, on-line data, and communication with experts — are discussed separately below, but each was inextricably linked to the others in fostering students' growing empathy with their particular species and with wildlife in general. For a teacher, each provides an example of how computer technology can be integrated into a classroom to support effective environmental education.

Background readings

As they sought information about their species, students made good use of a range of books, magazine articles from publications such as *Ranger Rick* and *Zoobooks*, websites, and CD-ROMs. This process of searching through information from a variety of sources proved valuable for the students. Instead of being content with only one author's presentation, they could see that their understanding deepened as they gathered new information from a variety of sources.

In a couple of cases, this led to those unique teachable moments that we treasure as teachers but can never plan for. For example, a student researching whooping cranes was puzzled by conflicting information on the number of these birds known to exist in the wild. Each source he consulted presented a different number; and while some of these population estimates were close to each other, others varied quite a bit. Most of his sources agreed that the whooping crane was making a comeback, and so we compared the numbers presented with the copyright of the source. Sources that were a decade or more old had much lower population counts, no doubt reflecting the recent successes in conservation of this endangered species. The most up-to-date data were the current counts available on-line through Journey North.

Reading on-line background information about the work of scientists helping the whooping crane made the conservation challenge very real. The provision of up-to-date information about the species' total population — not possible in a book or CD-ROM format — further enhanced the value of the Internet in promoting understanding.

Finding On-line Projects and Resources

On-line projects for students

There are a wide variety of on-line environmental monitoring and data-exchange projects that invite students' participation. Several are listed below, but searching on terms such as "environmental monitoring" and "citizen science," or searching by a particular species or natural phenomenon will also return useful links.

FrogWatch: Participants gather and report data on frogs and toads at local wetlands; see <www.nwf.org/frogwatchUSA/> in the U.S. and <www.frogwatch.ca> in Canada.

Journey North and Journey South: Participants share data on sightings of migrating species and track the progression of seasonal change; see <http://www.learner.org/jnorth>.

Pathfinder Science: A collection of community-based science projects that include data exchanges. Current projects include stream monitoring, phenology, and pollution studies; see <www.pathfinderscience.net>.

Project FeederWatch: A project of the Cornell Lab of Ornithology in which students and others report on their sightings at bird feeders, data that is used to track winter bird populations and long-term trends in bird distribution and abundance; see <www.birds.cornell.edu/pfw/>.

RoadKill Project: An unusual project in which students monitor and report on the animal casualties of vehicular traffic in their communities; see <http://edutel.musenet.org:8042/roadkill/>.

Square of Life: A data exchange project in which students report on life in a square meter of their local community; see <www.k12science.org/curriculum/squareproj/>.

On-line research tip

To guide students in on-line research, you may wish to preview a variety of Internet sites and make "hotlists" of sites and portals that would be particularly useful in students' research projects. Hotlists are simply word-processing documents in which URLs (Uniform Resource Locators, or website addresses) are hyperlinked to the corresponding websites, thereby enabling students to go immediately to an intended site by clicking on the URL.

Authentic data

Authentic data gathered as part of scientific research can do a great deal to illuminate animals' behavior, habits, and population trends. Particularly dramatic migration data can be obtained through The Raptor Center's Highway to the Tropics project,[1] which follows the movements of more than a dozen ospreys as they migrate to the south and then return to their breeding grounds in several northern states. The prodigious course these birds take each year is tracked by the use of telemetric data obtained through satellite transmitters attached to the backs of the birds. The mapping of their course provides a striking display of long distance migration.

The migration of bald eagles is much more modest than that of ospreys in terms of distance traveled, but it is no less interesting. The students who were researching eagles were struck by the apparently meandering path taken by the eagle they were following. Much of the literature on migration that is written for children implies that migration routes are straightforward paths from north to south in the autumn and back north in the spring. Our eagle proved this not to be the case: it wandered from New York to the middle Atlantic region and back again, before heading up to Ontario, presumably to breed. This nuance in flight plans was particularly interesting to us since we are located near major bald eagle wintering grounds. Given what we learned about the eagles being tracked, we wondered what "our" eagles did as they migrated to and from our area.

Ask the expert

Journey North provides a two-week period during which students can submit questions to experts on migrating species. The experience of posing questions helped the students to reflect carefully on what they knew and what they still wanted to know. To make the best use of the experts' time, I encouraged the students to be sure that what they were asking did not have a simple answer that could be found in a book. Great care was put into the phrasing and editing of each question because, as one student put it, "You don't want to look dumb." When this was done, students prepared and submitted their questions through Journey North's web page. Responses, when they were posted, were read eagerly, answering such questions as: What is the record for the largest eagle? and Do manatees allow people to get close to them?

Throughout this project, students were led to think deeply about the species they were studying and to relate the real animals they were tracking to previously learned concepts, such as adaptation, ecosystem, and habitat. By applying these concepts in the broader context offered through the Internet, they considerably extended their perspectives on the natural world. Along the way, they also extended their basic reading, writing, and thinking skills.

Ultimately, the Internet presents both a danger and an opportunity. Used poorly, it can become an electronic substitute for authentic experience. Used well in the service of clear learning goals, it can provide access to many productive resources to deepen and extend students' investigations. My students and I had a glimpse of its power in this project. ✒

Bob Coulter is the Director of the Litzsinger Road Ecology Center, affiliated with the Missouri Botanical Garden. The project described here was undertaken with the assistance of Liz Haspiel and Nancy Mollman while he was a teacher at the Forsyth School in St. Louis, Missouri.

Editor's note

[1] The Highway to the Tropics project began in 1995 and concluded in 2002, but students can still access the data collected during that period. The project tracked the migratory movements of ospreys, Swainson's hawks, and bald eagles. See the Migration Tracking link at <www.raptor.cvm.umn.edu>.

Mouse Roulette

A lively investigation of food chains, competition for resources, and adaptations for survival

by Gareth Thomson

Grade levels: 4-5

Subject area: science, ecology, physical education

Key concepts: adaptation, natural selection, food chains, environmental and genetic factors that influence the survival rate of young animals

Skills: active questioning, kinesthetic learning

Location: indoors

Time: 20 to 40 minutes, plus time for extension activities

Materials: small, different-colored items such as durable candies or buttons; plastic forks (some with missing tines) and a few spoons; reusable cups; large bowl or tray

 very school child knows that owls have baby owls that they have to feed. But surely an investigation of concepts such as food chain structure, the relationship between nestling survival rate and clutch size, distance to feeding ground, injury to hunting adults, and the poisoning of the mouse supply — not to mention Darwinian evolution — is too complex for elementary level students. Don't be too sure ....

Procedure:

1. Place a large bowl or tray of candies (or buttons, or some other colored item) in the center of the playing area.

2. Divide the class into groups of between three and six students.

3. Assign one or two of the students in each group to be the parent. Give each parent a fork to hunt with. Some forks should have their tines broken off or bent out of shape, representing a hunting adult that is injured.

4. The remaining students in each group are owlets. Give each of these students a cup and explain that this represents the owlet's mouth and stomach.

5. Place the nests of owlets at varying distances from the hunting ground, which is represented by the large bowl with the candies in it. Instruct the owlets to stay in their nests, to make as much noise as possible during the game, and to endeavor to get as many candies from an adult as possible — just as a baby owl would.

6. Tell the adults that when you say "Go!" they are to rush to the feeding area and pick up as many candies as possible with their fork. They are not allowed to put their hands over the fork to stabilize their load of candy, and they are not allowed to jostle other owls at the feeding grounds.

7. Say "Go!" and let the game begin. Encourage the owlets to crowd one another out in their efforts to get candy, but don't let them become too physically aggressive. End the game after a minimum of five minutes or when the feeding bowl is empty.

Discussion:

The following questions should lead to discussion that helps students to understand some of the factors that operate in a natural ecosystem.

How many students have three or more candies in their cups?

Ask for a show of hands. Then ask the students to keep their hands up if they have five or more candies, ten or more, and so on. Continue until you reach a number at which only 50 to 70 percent of students still have their hands up. Then tell students that, regrettably, it was this number of candies that they needed in order to

survive. Students who have fewer than this number of candies didn't make it. They died of starvation or malnutrition.

In this game, what factors determine whether an owlet will live or die?

The following factors should be among those that students mention:

🦉 It is harder to feed a large family than a small family.

🦉 The ratio of parents to owlets is important. Families with two adults have twice the feeding power of single-parent families.

🦉 Those owls who had further to fly to the feeding ground will be able to "catch" less food than an adult whose nest is close by.

🦉 Sibling competition (more aggressive nest mates) may crowd out weaker owlets (or at least the ones with the shorter arms!).

🦉 Hunters with damaged forks (an "injury") cannot bring home as many candies. Their hunting efficiency is impaired, as if one of their talons were damaged.

Have students relate the game to real life by asking if these factors exist in the life of a real owl. (They do, although you may want to point out that owl nestlings remain quiet while on the nest so that predators can't find them.) Have students compare human behavior to owl behavior. In our society, we generally have enough food, and we discourage aggressive behavior at the dinner table. Ask the students if they can imagine any instances in their own lives in which lack of food might lead to aggressive behavior.

Tell the students that they were in fact playing "Mouse Roulette" and that some of the mice in the hunting grounds ate grain contaminated with a high dose of pesticide. Ask the students: "Do any of you have two or more red candies in your cups? If you do, you have died of poisoning!" This question can direct discussion towards environmental contamination that can lead to the deaths of animals at the top of the food chain. A good example of this is the use of dichloro-diphenyl-trichloroethane (DDT), an insecticide that caused raptor populations to plummet in the 1970s. This is a particularly good example to use, because banning DDT worked, allowing populations of North American raptors such as the bald eagle and peregrine falcon to recover.

Would it be an advantage in this game to have a wider fork or a cup with a larger diameter opening?

This question introduces the concept of adaptation and natural selection. The answer, of course, is yes. According to the theory of natural selection, owls with these advantages would be more successful at feeding, and therefore more likely to raise offspring, than other owls of the same species. As a result, this trait (wider fork/larger mouth) would become the dominant trait in the species. It is this process that has resulted in the owl's having the superb adaptations that it does (ability to see at night, silent flight, excellent hearing, etc.).

What other traits would be an advantage in this game?

Long arms and loud mouths may be among those traits suggested for the baby owls; fast legs and steady hands may be among those suggested for the parent owls.

Extensions:

🦉 The identification of red candies as poison can be used as a springboard to investigate the concept of food chains, food webs, and bioaccumulation of toxins by animals that occupy a niche towards the top of the food pyramid.

🦉 Have students design an animal wonderfully adapted to living in a particular environment, and present it to the rest of the class in a large, labeled, colored diagram. You may choose to have them "perfect" the owl (giving rise, perhaps, to owls with radar and a superb sense of smell) or simply challenge them to invent an animal that lives in a particular environment (in a dresser drawer, on top of a hockey puck, and so on). ⏎

Gareth Thomson lives and works in Canmore, Alberta, where he is Education Director of the Canadian Parks and Wilderness Society (CPAWS), Calgary Banff Chapter. "Mouse Roulette" is part of a suite of hands-on activities provided by CPAWS at <www.cpawscalgary.org/education/free-resources/lessons.html>.

Plants and Animals

Animals in the Classroom

*Caring for classroom pets can help students
develop empathy and respect for all living creatures*

**by Stephen Huddart
and Craig Naherniak**

Grade levels: K-5

Subject areas:
interdisciplinary

Key concepts: violence
prevention, self-esteem,
cruelty, adoption

Skills: empathy, verbal and
non-verbal communication,
animal care

Location: indoors

O ne of our
favorite
examples
of leverage
is from
Buckminster Fuller:

A trim tab is a small
"rudder on the rudder"
of a ship. It is only a
fraction the size of the
rudder. Its function is
to make it easier to turn
the rudder, which, then,
makes it easier to turn
the ship. The larger the
ship, the more important is the trim tab, because a
large volume of water flowing around the rudder
can make it difficult to turn.[1]

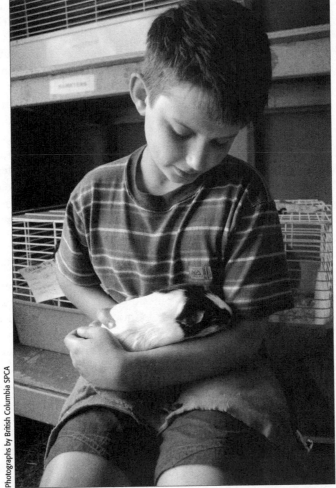

Photographs by British Columbia SPCA

So, a metal plate about the size of a placemat — the
trim tab — enables course changes on a 200,000-ton
bulk carrier travelling at 18 knots! As humane educators, we often observe similarly disproportionate effects
when the care of animals is integrated into the life of a
classroom. Vancouver teacher Alex Angelomatis, who
regularly takes his elderly dog Seymour to school,
commented: "Just by being in the classroom, Seymour
acts as a catalyst for participation. Shy kids get involved,
listening improves, and the class gets along better.
From the changes I've seen, every class should have
an animal for students to relate to and care for."

How animals change us: the research

This is more than an iso-
lated case of an old dog
teaching people new tricks.
In his landmark book
Biophilia,[2] biologist E.O.
Wilson persuasively linked
the evolutionary develop-
ment of human thought,
language, and socialization
to our relationships with
nature, and, especially,
animals. Over the past
decade, researchers work-
ing in educational and
therapeutic settings have
demonstrated that Wil-
son's hypothesis is equally
applicable to learning and
healing today. Caring for
animals has been shown
to improve self-esteem,[3]
to alleviate anxiety[4] and
depression,[5] to improve
social skills,[6] promote
empathy,[7] and foster verbal
and non-verbal communi-
cation[8] — to cite only a
few recent studies in the growing field of animal-
assisted therapy and education.

This is education of the heart, and when hearts
change, the effects are felt nearby and at a distance.
Children who experience looking after animals develop
confidence, cooperative spirit, empathy and respect,
extending to classmates and beyond. The leveling
quality of an animal's gaze gives recognition, irrespec-
tive of race or culture, which is perhaps the reason that
some of the most enthusiastic responses to our classroom animal programs come from schools with large
numbers of immigrant students.[9] With surprising frequency, teachers report that having animals in their
classrooms helps children with problems ranging from
shyness to aggression to difficulty in expressing emotion appropriately.[10] One promising area for researchers

is humane education's potential contribution to the prevention of violence, given the often-cited calming effect of animals' presence[11] and their capacity to teach us understanding of non-verbal cues.[12] There is also intriguing evidence to support the notion that the movements and behavior of animals who are safe and well cared for stimulate brainwave activity conducive to human learning.[13]

The links between childhood cruelty to animals and anti-social behaviour are well documented.[14] Perhaps less well known is animals' potential for healing such pathologies. At the Psychiatric Unit of the British Columbia Children's Hospital, for example, head nurse Sharie Scheske works with victims of abuse to overcome fears, defuse anger, establish appropriate touching boundaries, and build healing narratives — all with the invaluable help of Chimo, an American Eskimo Spitz. According to Scheske, "Chimo helps to create a more relaxed, family-like atmosphere ... just knowing that a big, bureaucratic system is progressive enough to support this program creates a caring environment."[15] In a school setting, classroom animals can foster a caring atmosphere while imparting lessons in practical stewardship. In some respects, this parallels and complements the goals of the school ground greening movement.[16]

Cultural, health, and humane considerations

Important practical and ethical matters must be considered before acquiring a classroom animal. Educators must be attuned to the differing cultural and religious perspectives on animals that students may have. In some cultures dogs are kept for a utilitarian purpose, such as protection, while in others they are considered family members. A pet in one culture could be viewed in another as a food source, guinea pigs being a prime example. Likewise, in some religious traditions animals are revered, in others exploited. This can be an entry point for discussion of how we view animals and why attitudes toward animals differ.

Educators must also consider allergies that their students may have to animals. It is uncommon for children to have severe reactions unless they are in direct contact with an animal. Nevertheless, it may be necessary on occasion to limit the exposure of allergic students by placing the animal in another classroom for a term. Keeping the environment clean and the animal well groomed reduces airborne allergens. There are also dander-reducing products available through veterinarians. Interestingly, emerging research indicates that exposure to animals early in life — particularly in the first two years — reduces the risk of developing allergies later in life,[17] contradicting previously held beliefs that exposure to animals triggers a genetic predisposition to developing allergic sensitivities.

From the animal's perspective, adoption must be a commitment for the animal's lifetime, and the need for teachers to serve as humane role models cannot be overstated. If a teacher extols the importance of showing respect for a classroom animal on the one hand, and then casually kills a spider on the other, children receive mixed messages about how other life forms are to be treated. Likewise, if the cleaning or feeding of the animal is haphazard or delayed because of other commitments, students may learn that responsibility is flexible and animal care not all that important. In addition, should a teacher surrender the classroom animal to a shelter at the end of the year, the underlying message may be that animals are disposable. Reports of such behavior have led some humane societies to recommend that no animals be allowed in schools. Teachers must take it upon themselves to learn how to care for and assess the condition of the animals for whom they are responsible. Where improvement is called for, the resulting process itself can be of lasting educational benefit, not to mention of inestimable value to animals.

The intimate expression of a profound relationship between child and animal is a fundamental part of human development. During 99 percent of human history, we internalized and gained experiential knowledge of a world around us that was not contrived by humans. Today, as we seek to reintegrate human endeavor with the natural world by means both sustainable and humane, we are not alone — the animals are here, too, and, clearly, they have much to teach us.

Classroom animal guidelines

Be aware that having a classroom pet is a full-time responsibility requiring one principal guardian and a major time commitment. While children should be involved in the care of the animal, the ultimate responsibility for the animal's well-being rests with the teacher. Below are points to consider before you get an animal. Some are obvious; some you may not have considered:

๑ Ask yourself, do I really need to have a live animal in my classroom to accomplish the learning objectives in mind? Would a field trip, playground outing, video, guest presentation, picture book, story, computer software, or puppet accomplish the same objectives?

๑ Choose the pet most appropriate for your classroom (see "Choosing the Right Pet" chart, page 104). Note that wild animals, including snakes, lizards, frogs, newts, salamanders, spiders, and snails, should never be kept in a classroom. If they are brought into the classroom, they should be released within 24 hours in the exact location and at the same time of day they were collected. It is illegal in most jurisdictions to keep wild animals in captivity without a permit.

๑ Exotic animals from pet stores should not be kept as pets. This is the same as keeping an indigenous wild animal. Lizards, turtles, hedgehogs and other exotics are difficult to care for, can be vectors for disease, and usually suffer and die prematurely.

Relaxing with Peanut Butter and Jelly
(A guinea for your thoughts)

"Hey Peanut Butter! Hello Jelly! Did you guys enjoy your breakfast? Feel like coming out to play? How about spending some time with Robert or James this morning?"

It's 8:30 a.m., and Vancouver teacher Aaron Espley is apparently speaking to Peanut Butter and Jelly, a couple of guinea pigs. But she's really trying to get through to Robert and James (not their real names) — two students who are looking troubled. Robert has had some bad nights at home lately, and has been taking it out on James, who is new to the class. They're hanging back right now, but she can tell both are listening.

"In the mornings, I usually spend some time with the guinea pigs," explains Espley. "This draws the children over to see them. In fact, we have a routine, and most of the children look forward to seeing Peanut Butter and Jelly when they first arrive. That's when I can suggest that they hold a guinea pig, if I think they're having a hard time coping. It helps them relax for the day." She adds, "Some of the new students are so emotionally traumatized, it helps them adjust to the class to let them sit for a while just holding a guinea pig. They find it comforting because they don't want to face the other children right away."

This morning, James shyly but proudly has accepted the responsibility of holding Jelly, listening carefully as a classmate explains how to handle him. "The children have learned to be very gentle when holding the animals," Espley says. "They are also actively involved in their feeding and care, and a schedule is posted to provide each student with time to interact."

Robert, on the other hand, has declined the offer, and

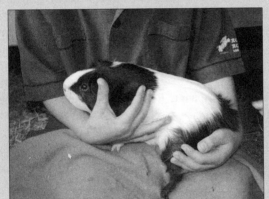

moments later he is disturbing a group of girls over by the coat rack. Espley asks him to sit down to do some work on his own.

After half an hour, James puts Jelly back into the large enclosure and goes to join some other children at a worktable, looking calmer and more confident. Meanwhile three girls who have written a story featuring Peanut Butter and Jelly decide to read it aloud near the guinea pigs. "I love it when they run around and make noise when we read to them," one girl says. "They're so happy."

Time for a video — and as the lights go off, it's Robert again, squirming and pushing from side to side, interrupting the concentration of those around him. Espley calls him away from the circle. "I want you to hold Peanut Butter for a while — he hasn't been getting as much attention as Jelly, and I think he may be feeling bad. Can you do it, and stay still?" Robert nods silently and sits down right away, engrossed in his new charge.

"The guinea pigs have had a very positive effect on some of the boys," Espley says. "Sometimes I think it would be nice not to have to worry about the animals, but we all become very attached to them. Just when I get discouraged about them, I see something that reminds me of how important they are."

Tom Harder, *from an interview with Grade 4 teacher Aaron Espley at Queen Alexander School in Vancouver, British Columbia.*

- Ensure that the care of the classroom animal will be well integrated into the classroom curriculum.

- Plan and construct a suitable home for your pet. Classroom pets are most content when they are allowed to live as naturally as possible. This requires providing the best and largest possible habitat to meet their needs

- Discuss the idea with the principal before you get the animal. In many cases, schools and school districts do not have a formal policy on classroom animals, but some do. (Sample policies can be downloaded at <www.spca.bc.ca/educators>.)

- Evaluate your classroom to find out if there is a quiet space for the animal, out of direct sunlight and away from drafts.

- Find out if the temperature in the building at night remains within the range of comfort for your animal.

- Discuss the animal's presence with custodians, and negotiate the question of who cleans up should there be undue mess because of the animal.

- Plan how to include your classroom animal into fire drill procedures.

Choosing the Right Pet

Animals who make the best pets, such as cats and dogs, do not easily lend themselves to most classroom environments; and some animals often kept in classrooms do not make the best classroom pets. Some common pets are briefly profiled below with an eye to their suitability in a classroom.

Guinea pigs
Life span: 5 to 7 years.
Size: Grow to approximately 1 kg (2.2 lbs.); about 20-30 cm (8-12") in length.
Origin: Peru.
Status: Domesticated over 5,000 years ago.
Diet: Herbivore. Fresh fruits, vegetables, hay, and special commercial pellets fortified with vitamin C.
Pros: Sociable. Seldom bite. Unique personalities. Diurnal (awake during the day). Quiet, but have a repertoire of discernable calls.
Cons: Some are skittish. Require calm environment. Require a habitat that allows for ample daily exercise and a small house to retreat to.
Comments: Best kept in pairs of the same sex. Adapt best when raised in a social environment. Must have items to chew to wear down constantly growing teeth. Do not climb and are content in a large habitat.
Suitability in a classroom: Perhaps the most suitable classroom pet.

Rabbits
Life span: 7 to 12 years (depending on breed).
Size: Dwarf species from 1.5 kg to 5.5 kg (3.5 to 12 lbs.).
Origin: Tame rabbits were bred from the wild European cottontail.
Status: Domesticated. Bred as pets, food, and laboratory animals in North America. Many breeds and sizes available.
Diet: Fresh fruits, vegetables, hay, and commercial pellets.
Pros: Sociable. Seldom bite. Unique personalities. Diurnal (awake during the day). Quiet, rarely make a sound. Can be easily trained to use a litter box.
Cons: Some are skittish. Require calm environment. Require a habitat allowing for ample daily exercise, a small house to retreat to, and several hours of exercise outside of habitat. A large animal for a classroom. Can be difficult for young children to handle. Will chew outside of habitat; must rabbit-proof classroom, especially electrical and computer cords.
Comments: Some varieties of rabbits grow to be very large. Teachers may prefer the dwarf breeds. Adapt best when raised in a social environment. Must have items to chew to wear down constantly growing teeth. Require a large habitat or exercise area.
Suitability in a classroom: Suitable classroom pet for higher grade levels; requires a large habitat in classroom.

Domestic rats and mice
Life span: 2 to 3.5 years
Size: Mouse ~ 10 cm (4") body with 8 cm (3") tail; rat ~ 20 cm (8") body with 25 cm (10") tail.
Origin: Asia, although several strains of domestic rats and mice now exist.
Status: Tame, through thousands of generations of selective breeding.
Diet: Omnivore. Commercial gerbil or hamster mix containing seeds, nuts, and pellets. Supplement with hay, fresh fruits, and vegetables.
Pros: Sociable, if handled regularly. Seldom bite. Intelligent, curious, and adventuresome both day and night. Very clean.
Cons: Require a habitat that allows for ample daily exercise. Small, fast moving animals can be difficult for young children to handle. Tend to nibble on fingers. Can be easily hurt if squeezed. Easy to lose if they escape from habitat. Negative stereotypes may cause some adults to react negatively to the animals.

continued next page

● Send a note home to parents discussing the type of animal in the classroom. Ask if their child has known allergies to animals and, if so, determine the severity and work to find a solution.

● Find out the possible diseases of the animal you are considering. Turtles and other reptiles, for example, are vectors for salmonella bacteria even if their habitat is well cleaned. This makes them a poor choice for the classroom.

● Consider whether you will be able to take the animal home on weekends and during holidays.

● Determine who will be financially responsible for the care and habitat requirements of the animal.

● Have your pet examined by a veterinarian before bringing him into the classroom, and budget for regular visits to your vet throughout your pet's lifetime. Guinea pigs and rabbits must have their nails clipped bi-monthly. Have your veterinarian instruct you.

● Establish who will supervise the animal during non-instructional times (before school, recess, lunch, and after school). Handling of the animal should be restricted during these times.

---

continued from previous page

Comments: Best kept in pairs of same sex from birth. Adapt best when raised in a social environment. Must have items to chew to wear down constantly growing teeth. Habitat requires plenty of room and nest building material. Require warm, dry environment of 20-23ºC (68-73ºF).
Suitability in a classroom: Fairly good.

Hamsters
Life span: 2 to 3 years.
Size: Larger than a mouse and smaller than a guinea pig.
Origin: Northern China, Siberia, and Mongolia.
Status: Captive bred since the 1930s.
Diet: Omnivore. Commercial hamster mix containing seeds, nuts, and pellets, fresh fruits, vegetables, hay, and, on occasion, small pieces of raw meat or mealworms.
Pros: Exceptionally clean. Can be tamed to accept handling.
Cons: As nocturnal animals they should not be disturbed or handled during the daytime. Shy, solitary creatures. Require calm, exceptionally quiet environment. Require a habitat that allows for ample nightly exercise. Prone to nip. Can be easily hurt if squeezed.
Comments: Enjoy solitary living, although two females could be kept in the same habitat if born and raised together. Must have items to chew to wear down constantly growing teeth.
Suitability in a classroom: Not recommended.

Gerbils
Life span: 2 to 3.5 years.
Size: Mouse-sized.
Origin: North African and central Asian deserts.
Status: Captive bred since the 1960s.
Diet: Omnivore. Commercial gerbil mix containing seeds, nuts, and pellets, fresh fruits, vegetables, hay, and, on

occasion, small pieces of raw meat or mealworms.
Pros: Sociable. Seldom bite. Very active, curious and adventurous both day and night. Very clean.
Cons: Require a habitat that allows for ample daily exercise. Small, fast moving animals can be difficult for young children to handle. Tend to nibble on fingers. Can be easily hurt if squeezed. Easy to lose if they escape from habitat.
Comments: Best kept in pairs of the same sex from birth. Adapt best in a social environment. Need items to chew to wear down constantly growing teeth. Habitat requires plenty of room, nest-building material, and a medium for burrowing. Require warm, dry environment of 20-23ºC (68-73ºF).
Suitability in a classroom: Fairly good.

Red-eared slider turtles
Life span: 15 to 20 years.
Size: Shells grow from the size of a quarter to over 30 cm (12") in diameter.
Origin: Wild habitat of Eastern United States and south into Mexico.
Status: Wild animal; farmed commercially as well as taken from the wild: approximately 100,000 per year go to the pet store trade.
Diet: Omnivore. Varied diet including earthworms, tubifex worms, meat, raw fish, shrimp, lettuce, spinach and other greens, reptile food.
Pros: Could be brought in for a day to discuss why turtles don't make good pets or for discussion of the pet trade.
Cons: A wild animal. Although popular as pets because they are inexpensive, these creatures are best left in their native habitat. Special requirements: heated tank, filtered water, large environment, full spectrum lighting. Turtles can spread salmonellosis. Hands should be washed after handling or gloves used. Habitat must be kept very clean.
Suitability in a classroom: Not recommended.

◐ Consider who will care for the animal should you be ill and miss one or more days of school. You cannot rely on a substitute teacher to know how to care for your animal. One solution is to start an animal care club from which older students can be recruited to help in these situations and to teach responsible pet care to others. For suggestions on starting and running a kids' club, visit <www.spca.bc.ca/educators>.

◐ Be prepared to deal with students' grief should your pet die, as well as with practical matters such as disposal of the body. Many humane societies and all veterinary clinics offer cremation services. If there are no municipal bylaws restricting animal burials for small animals, you could consider a grave and marker somewhere on the school grounds. Be aware that the students' grief is real and must be acknowledged. Discussing feelings and paying tribute to the animal are vital to the healing process. There are many resources to help with the grieving process (see, for example, the list of books on-line at <www.spca.bc.ca/educators>).

Classroom strategies

◐ Explain all the facets of responsible pet care to students.

◐ Discuss why the animal needs to be kept in the quietest place in the classroom. Discuss stress factors in animals, and establish a rule of "no running or shouting" near the animal.

◐ Establish a feeding and cleaning routine. Create a care schedule designating which student will care for the animal for the day.

◐ Demonstrate the correct way to handle your animal. Animals can sustain life-threatening injuries if dropped. Children should never be allowed to walk around while holding animals. Students should be sitting down when they handle the animal, and the animal placed with them by the teacher. Having a special area for the animal in the classroom helps to create a controlled setting.

◐ Instruct students to wash their hands before and after handling the animal. Do not allow children with colds or other illnesses to handle the classroom animal.

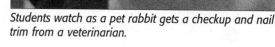
Students watch as a pet rabbit gets a checkup and nail trim from a veterinarian.

◐ Allow children time with the animal in a one-on-one situation or, at most, in pairs.

◐ Set a limit on the amount of time children can interact with the animal during a normal school day. Structure quiet periods when the animal is to be left alone. Be sure the animal has a place within its habitat to which he can retreat from children.

◐ If you suspect a student is deliberately being cruel to the animal, deal with the incident immediately. If you determine it to be accidental and no real harm is done, then, after a private discussion with the student(s), address the inappropriateness of harming animals in a general way with the class. A deliberate act of cruelty, especially where no remorse is expressed, is cause for concern and should be addressed with the principal, counsellors, and parents.

◐ Emphasize close observation techniques — a naturalistic approach to learning about the animal by observing normal living functions (eating, sleeping, and activity cycles).

◐ Never perform negative-reinforcement experiments on any animal in the classroom. Do not subject the animal to activities that can cause pain or discomfort or interfere with the health of the animal.

◐ Do not breed animals in the classroom. There are many unwanted animals in animal shelters, and finding good homes for offspring is not as easy as you might think. It quickly becomes difficult and burdensome to care adequately for large numbers of animals. This situation can convey negative messages about responsible care of animals.

◐ Hatching fertilized chicken or duck eggs in the classroom is not recommended. Chicks grow quickly and must be placed in a proper environment such as a farm in order to thrive. Most commercial farms will not take the offspring because of disease considerations.

◐ Beware of the classroom animal "honeymoon syndrome." Conscientious care of the classroom animal sometimes wanes after the first month or two as the focus of classroom activities changes. ๕

Plants and Animals

Stephen Huddart, now with the McConnell Foundation in Montréal, is the former Director of Education of the British Columbia Society for the Prevention of Cruelty to Animals. Craig Naherniak is the General Manager of Humane Education of the British Columbia Society for the Prevention of Cruelty to Animals in Vancouver.

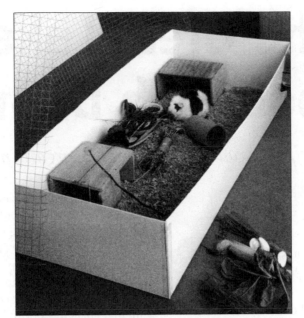

The calm and sociable guinea pig makes a good classroom pet.

Notes

1 Peter M. Senge, *The Fifth Discipline*, Doubleday, 1994, p. 64.

2 E.O. Wilson, *Biophilia*, Harvard University Press, 1984.

3 Several empirical studies are cited in E.S. Paul and J.R. Serpell, "Why Children Keep Pets: The Influence of Child and Family Characteristics," *Anthrozos* 5, p. 231.

4 C.C. Wilson, "The Pet as an Anxiolytic Intervention," *The Journal of Nervous and Mental Disease* 179, 1991, pp. 482-489.

5 Eileen B. Folse et al, "Animal-Assisted Therapy and Depression in Adult College Students," *Anthrozos* 7, pp. 188-201.

6 G. Guttman et al, "The Influence of Pet Ownership on Non-verbal Communication and Social Competence in Children," *The Human-Pet Relationship*, Institute for Interdisciplinary Research on the Human–Pet Relationship, 1985, pp. 58-62.

7 Several studies on development of empathy are cited in F.R. Ascione, "Enhancing Children's Attitudes About the Humane Treatment of Animals: Generalization to Human-directed Empathy," *Anthrozos* 5, 1992, pp. 176-191.

8 Discussed in A. Katcher, and G. Wilkins, "Dialogue with Animals: Its Nature and Culture," chapter 5 in Kellert and Wilson, eds., *The Biophilia Hypothesis*, Shearwater, 1993.

9,10 Drawn from responses by teachers and students to Humans Acting With Kindness, the classroom animal adoption program of the British Columbia Society for the Prevention of Cruelty to Animals.

11 Katcher and Wilkins, 1993.

12 Guttman et al, 1985.

13 Katcher and G. Wilkins, 1993.

14 F.R. Ascione, "Children Who are Cruel to Animals: A Review of Research and Implications for Developmental Psychopathology," *Anthrozos* 6, 1993, pp. 226-247.

15 S. Huddart, "This is the First Dog That's Ever Loved Me," *Humane Leader*, Spring 1995, p. 4.

16 See, for example, Chuck Heath, "The Refuge — The Creation of a Nature Sanctuary," *Humane Leader*, Spring 1995, pp. 2-3.

17 "Exposure to Dogs and Cats in the First Year of Life and Risk of Allergic Sensitization at 6 to 7 Years of Age," *Journal of the American Medical Association* 288:8, August 28, 2002, pp. 963-972.

Resources

Books

Delta Society. *Animals in the Classroom*. Delta Society, 1999. A compendium of articles, curricula, animal care guidelines, and other resources for keeping animals in the classroom. See <deltasociety.org>.

Robinson, I., ed., *The Waltham Book of Human-Animal Interaction*. Pergamon, 1995. Articles and studies focusing on the benefits of animals in the lives of children and adults.

Selby, David. *EarthKind: A Teachers' Handbook on Humane Education*. Trentham Books, 1995. Practical K-12 cross-curricular activities to assist in creating a humane and convivial classroom environment.

Websites

<www.aspca.org> American Society for the Prevention of Cruelty to Animals. Animal care books and other humane education materials.

<www.spca.bc.ca educators> British Columbia Society for the Prevention of Cruelty to Animals. Animal care information, classroom animal guidelines, pet loss support information, curriculum-linked classroom units and other resources for teachers.

The Great Lakes Food Web Drama

A read-aloud script introducing freshwater organisms and food webs

by Marjane L. Baker

Grade levels: 4-5

Subject areas: science, language arts, drama

Key concepts: freshwater food webs, trophic levels, invasive species

Skills: researching, identifying and drawing freshwater aquatic species, dramatic reading, voice projection, problem solving

Location: indoors

Time: 1 to 2 hours class time; 30 minutes homework

Materials: script (1 per student), drawing paper, construction paper, poster board, vocabulary list (optional)

Forming the largest basin of fresh water in the world, the Great Lakes are home to a vast array of organisms. From the intricately twisted spyrogyra algae to the pop-eyed sculpin or the gaggling gull, this community of plants and animals is sustained by interactions that form a dynamic web of interdependency. As everywhere, the great game of survival in this underwater world is to eat, reproduce, and avoid being eaten. During the past 200 years, the health of the Great Lakes ecosystem has been dramatically affected by humans — nearly 32 million of whom now live on and around the lakes' watersheds and 16,000 kilometers (10,000 miles) of shoreline. Overfishing, habitat destruction, pollution, and the introduction of such exotic species as the abundant zebra mussel and predacious sea lamprey have all taken their toll on the natural balance of organisms and trophic levels in the lakes.

Introducing students to this complex system can be difficult without a fetching teaching device. The Great Lakes Food Web Television Special provides such a hook. It is a read-aloud drama that introduces students to some of the major organisms of the Great Lakes and to the

five trophic levels they occupy in the food web. For students, the play provides a fun way to be introduced to the scientific names, physical characteristics, and feeding habits of these creatures, as well as to the many ways in which they depend on and interact with one another. The drama can serve as a springboard for discussing the concept of food webs and the environmental challenges posed by human interference with natural systems such as the Great Lakes. Those who do not live near the Great Lakes may wish to have their students research the food chain in a different ecosystem and create a similar drama based on local organisms.

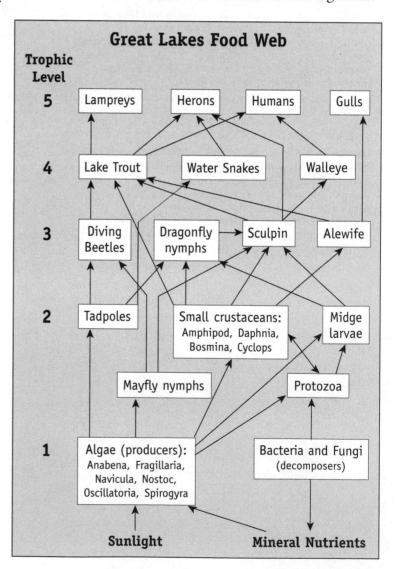

Great Lakes Food Web

Plants and Animals

Introducing the Great Lakes food web

Some prior research will help students understand the concepts of trophic levels and food webs, and the roles of the specific organisms within the Great Lakes food web (or other ecosystem you are dramatizing). As a motivator, bring some fresh water from a nearby lake or stream so that students can begin to identify some of the organisms in the drama. (My students' level of enthusiasm increased 100 percent after they observed a daphnia in motion!) Each student could research the organism he/she will play in the drama and answer such basic questions as: What does this organism eat? What eats this organism? What does this organism look like? In what part of the watershed would you be most likely to find this organism? How does this organism move? What is the role of this organism in the food web? From this information, students may wish to revise or add more details to their scripted speeches in the drama.

As an introduction to different groups of organisms, students could look up the definitions of "algae," "bacterium," "fungi," "crustacean," and "protozoan," so that they are familiar with these terms from the beginning. Other vocabulary words that students will encounter in the play are "trophic," "organism," "chlorophyll," "diatom," "microscopic," "omnivorous," "producers," "consumers," "decomposers," "parasites," and "exotic species." Students could make a chart with the terms and definitions, or small groups of students could present terms as commercials at regular intervals during the play.

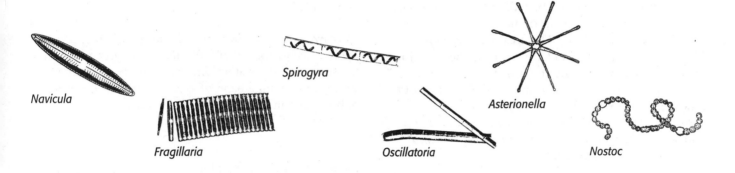

Navicula

Spirogyra

Fragillaria

Oscillatoria

Asterionella

Nostoc

Great Lakes Food Web Television Special

Preparation:

1. Hand out copies of the script (see pages 110-114) and assign a role to each student. There are 30 roles in all, including the Announcer. The roles of several of the organisms, such as the nostoc, mussels, and midge larvae, could be assigned to any number of players, allowing adaptation to any class size.

2. Explain to students that they are to read their speeches aloud but need not memorize them. Allow them to take the scripts home for an evening to practice reading their parts. Some may need help with the pronunciation of names or other terms, but encourage students not to worry if they make a mistake — even adults have trouble pronouncing scientific terms.

3. Have students mount an illustration of their organisms, along with a short description, on construction paper. The illustrations can be enlarged on a photocopier, or students can make their own drawings. These illustrations are carried during the play and used to complete the food web chart afterward.

CAST OF CHARACTERS

Announcer

Trophic Level 1
Anabena
Asterionella
Fragillaria
Navicula
Nostoc
Oscillatoria
Spirogyra

Trophic Level 2
Amphipod
Bosmina
Cyclops
Daphnia
Mayfly Nymph
Midge Larvae
Protozoa
Tadpole

Trophic Level 3
Alewife
Crayfish
Diving Beetle
Dragonfly Nymph
Mussels
Sculpin
Zebra Mussel

Trophic Level 4
Lake Trout
Walleye
Water Snake

Trophic Level 5
Heron
Herring Gull
Human
Sea Lamprey

Illustrations courtesy of Ohio Sea Grant College Program

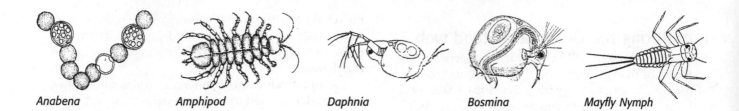

Anabena   Amphipod   Daphnia   Bosmina   Mayfly Nymph

Scene: A television studio in an interview setting. The announcer is dressed casually. Each organism enters carrying an enlarged picture of itself with a short description.

Announcer: Ladies and gentlemen, tonight we will be meeting Great Lakes organisms. Some people say that these Great Lakes organisms are having trouble, and we thought that, if we met them, we might be able to help solve some of their problems.

    The first group we will be talking to are the smallest organisms but the largest in number. They are referred to as Trophic Level One. The creatures live in the Great Lakes watershed and are eaten by the organisms in Trophic Level Two. By the way, the word "trophic" refers to what we eat. Organisms in Trophic Level One are eaten by those in Trophic Level Two, and organisms in Level Two are eaten by those in Level Three, and so on. [*pauses, as Navicula enters out of breath*] And who do we have here?

Navicula: I'm Navicula, a one-celled organism from Trophic Level One. I heard you announce my trophic level, so I thought I had better hurry into the studio. Notice my shape. Some people say that I'm shaped like a boat. Actually, I'm an alga, which is like seaweed. I live on the surface of mud and objects in water. [*proudly*] Did you notice my beautiful green color?

Announcer: Yes, I did. That's a fabulous green. Please tell us more about yourself.

Navicula: I have a hard outer shell that is made of silica, which is a hard glossy mineral. In my one cell, I use green pigments to collect and change sunlight into nutrients. I'll bet you've heard of chlorophyll.

Announcer: Yes, chlorophyll is the green part of plants. Now, you say that you're a member of Trophic Level One, but are you a part of any other group?

Navicula: I'm proud to announce that I'm a member of the diatom group. We are all algae, tiny one-celled plants. I'd like you to meet my friends. We're pretty small, so look carefully. [*The rest of Trophic Level One enters*] Hi, Fragillaria. [*to the announcer*] She's my friend.

Fragillaria: [*announcing herself*] I'm Fragillaria and also a member of Navicula's diatom group. The difference between us and Navicula is that we live in colonies. In other words, we're always hooked up in groups of more than one. In fact, if you look at us through a microscope, you'll see that we look like movie film cut up. Actually, we're rectangular cells that form flat chains.

Announcer: It's good to meet you Fragillaria. Now, our next Trophic Level One group is called Spirogyra. Tell us a little about yourself.

Spirogyra: You'll know you've found us when you come upon a stringy mass that looks like slimy green hair on the surface of the water. Under a magnifying glass, we appear to contain a band of green that looks like water bubbling up in a spring. Sugar is made in each of these spiral bands. In fact, my name comes from my spiral look.

Announcer: I get it. You look like a spiral and you're pretty sweet, Spirogyra. Oh, here is Oscillatoria. Please tell us about yourself. I really like your name.

Oscillatoria: You like my name and others like my color. I'm blue-green and I grow as slimy tangled hairlike bacteria on water surfaces or on wet soil. I look like a worm and some say that I'm like a hula dancer because I move back and forth in a regular swinging motion.

Announcer: Show us a bit of your dance. [*Oscillatoria dances a hula.*]

Asterionella: [*interrupting*] Hey, Announcer, look my way. I thought you'd never get to me. I'm the star here; actually that's my shape. I'm a very slender, star-shaped diatom and I float around. You know how, when you come near a lake, you smell a fishy odor? Well, it's likely that the odor is not caused by fish but by us, the Asterionella. Just remember us as the star-shaped diatoms that smell up the place!

Announcer: I did notice a funny odor. Look, here comes another blue-green group.

Tadpole

Cyclops

Midge Larvae

Protozoa

Mussel

Nostoc: Yessirree! We're the Nostoc, blue-green bacteria. Look for us in colonies or groups enclosed in a covering that's like jelly.

Anabena: Hey, don't forget me. I'm Anabena. Our group is another hairlike blue-green bacterium — that's another name for blue-green algae. We look like a string of beads and we make sugar while floating with the rest of our group.

Announcer: I guess it must be sweet to be around you, too. Now is that all from Trophic Level One?

Anabena: I guess we're it. Don't forget: we may be small in Trophic Level One, but we're really important.

Announcer: I think you Trophic Level One organisms had better duck out, because here comes Trophic Level Two. And you know what they would like to do when they see the likes of you.

All Trophic Level One Organisms: Yikes, let's get out of here. Trophic Level Two organisms like to feast on us. See you later. [*They hurry away.*]

Announcer: [*calling after them as they leave*] Yes, but you all need each other. Without Level Two, you'd become overpopulated and you'd probably all die. Oh well. Let's say hello to Trophic Level Two organisms of the Great Lakes food web.

Amphipod: [*with a lean hungry look*] I'm sorry they left in such a hurry. Hello, I'm Amphipod and I'd like to introduce you to my friends from Trophic Level Two. I'm a shrimplike crustacean, which means that I have a hard outer shell. I walk and swim among the lake algae, which I love to eat. I was really getting hungry coming in here. Something smelled awfully good. [*rubs stomach*] There are a huge number of us even though we are such small critters. In one square meter of lake water, there might be more than 10,000 amphipods. I never get lonely.

Announcer: Wow! I had no idea there could be 10,000 of you in a square meter of water: awesome! Don't you worry about overpopulation? [*suddenly notices Daphnia*] You're an interesting looking organism. You're transparent and I can see inside your stomach. Who are you?

Daphnia: I'm Daphnia, a water flea, and I'm proud to announce it. We're the most common crustaceans — you know, hard-shelled creatures — in fresh waters. We eat planktonic algae, bacteria, and protozoa. Of course, they're all microscopic so you'd hardly notice they're there. But when you get them in a bunch, my, do they taste good! Of course, we have our enemies to look out for — insects, fish, protozoa, and even carnivorous plants. I hope you understand that carnivorous plants are meat-eaters. Did you catch the idea that protozoa eat us and we eat them? Interesting little detail, eh?

Announcer: You are interesting creatures. Instead of dog-eat-dog, it's daphnia-eats-protozoa and vice versa. How do you get around?

Daphnia: We swim by moving our large second pair of antennae. Be sure to watch for us. Now, I'd like to introduce my cousin, Bosmina.

Bosmina: Hello, I'm Bosmina. I'm another water flea closely related to Daphnia. Notice how we're different and how we're the same. My body shape is quite like Daphnia's and we eat the same things.

Announcer: [*turning to Mayfly Nymph*] Say, I'm curious about you.

Mayfly Nymph: I'm proud to introduce myself as Mayfly Nymph. We walk and swim among the algae, on which we feed. On our abdomens, we have seven pairs of leaflike gills that end in the form of a three-tailed filament. Don't you think we look neat?

Tadpole: [*interrupting*] Hey, I'm Tadpole, which is a beginning form of a frog. A tadpole is a frog's larval stage. How many of you have caught one of my brothers or sisters and tried to raise them? When we hatch from our eggs, we have gills and a tail, but no legs. As we grow, our diet changes from algae to meat, our gills disappear, our legs develop, and we start to look like a frog.

Announcer: Heh, heh. I remember catching many tadpoles in my day. That wasn't such a smart thing to do, was it? Humans are part of the food web, but catching you just for fun when we aren't going to eat you is different. [*looking at Cyclops*] Hey, who are you?

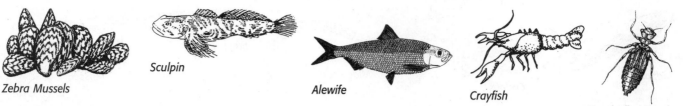

Zebra Mussels   Sculpin   Alewife   Crayfish   Dragonfly Nymph

Cyclops: Well, I thought you'd never ask. I'm Cyclops, and the reason I'm called this is because I have one red eye located at the top of my shell. My shell looks like a helmet, and two bristly antennae come out of my head. Notice how my body becomes thinner down to my slender abdomen, which ends in stiff bristles. The females in our group carry eggs in sacs at the sides of the abdomen. When you find us you'll be impressed. Now, let me introduce the Midge Larvae. You'll notice them because of their bright red color.

Midge Larvae: Oh yes, aren't we beautiful? We have a substance like hemoglobin in our blood, which make us bright red. We are quite important, because we eat waste material at the bottom of the lake. We spend the first part of our lives in the water, but after our larval stage we become the flying midges that you see around your porch lights at night. You must have seen many of us flying around!

Announcer: Yeah, people think you're a bit of a nuisance, but I guess we should remember the important things you're doing, too. Now, what do we have here? You're tiny: you must be the lake leprechauns!

Protozoa: I guess you could say that. We're Protozoa, those single-celled creatures that biology teachers like to look at under microscopes. We eat bacteria and other organisms tinier than we are. We move about using our beating hairs, our whipping tails, and our false feet. I'd like to introduce you to two other very interesting members of Trophic Level Two. The first are the mussels.

Mussels: You could say we're happy as clams because we enjoy life at the bottom of the Great Lakes. There are plenty of us and we're always busy. One group of us are newcomers that are always getting their name in the media: the zebra mussels. Here they are.

Zebra Mussel: I guess you could say that we're exotic creatures. You see, we didn't start here in the Great Lakes. We came from a far-off land and got here because we attached ourselves to the bottoms of ships that eventually came through the St. Lawrence Seaway. Those media reports say that we've caused a huge amount of trouble, because we love to attach ourselves to rocks, boats, sewer pipes, and lots of other handy

things. There are a lot of us around here because there's lots for us to eat and no creature here wants to eat us. Some people like me because I make the water look cleaner. But these days there are just too many of us. We're becoming overpopulated.

Announcer: Yes, you certainly are a problem to humans. Well, it looks as though that's all the organisms here from Trophic Level Two. Remember that they're only some of the many creatures in that group. [*Trophic Level Two organisms leave hurriedly.*] Now, here comes Trophic Level Three: I see there are only five species here from your group. Let's start with the smallest and go up to the largest. Hello, Sculpin, you look a bit like something from a creature feature.

Sculpin: I've been told that. It's probably because of my large mouth and eyes near the top of my spiny head. One thing that's lucky about being a sculpin is that, because of my ugly looks, most people don't consider me edible. That often saves my life. Really, I'm just a tiny fish. Speaking of fish, let me introduce you to Alewife. Now, don't get me wrong, she's not a wife, she's not sick, and she's not something you drink.

Announcer: We understand that, thanks.

Alewife: Hi, I'm Alewife, a small fish with a blue or blue-green luster on my back. I have an upturned mouth, which is really useful for surface feeding. Sometimes people call me a mulhaden, gray herring, golden shad, or skipjack. Have you ever heard those names?

Announcer: I can't say that I have. [*notices the crayfish*] Hey, I recognize you: you're a crayfish. When I was in New Orleans, we had plates and plates of you for dinner.

Crayfish: Please don't be so crude! People in Louisiana may like to eat us, but we're very helpful creatures in the Great Lakes. I live on the bottom of the lake and make sure that certain creatures don't become overpopulated. And you understand how I do that, eh? They're a tasty bunch.

Dragonfly Nymph: Hey, don't forget me. I'm Dragonfly Nymph. I walk among hairlike ropes of algae in search of prey, which I catch with a large scoop on the under-

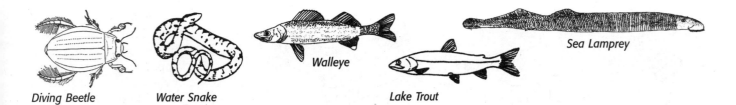

Diving Beetle   Water Snake   Walleye   Lake Trout   Sea Lamprey

side of my head. Don't you wish that you had a scoop like mine? My gills are located inside my rectum, so I can breathe under water. Isn't that strange but useful?

Announcer: Now, let's not forget to introduce the last creature in Trophic Level Three. What is your name?

Diving Beetle: I'm Diving Beetle. They call me that because I'm a fierce predator who can dive very rapidly and swim quickly. Scary, eh? You know how predators are. We like to plunder and loot, so I guess we're not very popular. We eat tiny fish, tadpoles, and other small organisms.

Announcer: You truly are an interesting group. [*Tropic Level Three creatures leave.*] Next, we'll meet three species representing Trophic Level Four: Walleye, Lake Trout, and Water Snake. I've never met a snake before, so let's start with Water Snake. How do you say hello to a snake? Let's try "hello."

Water Snake: Hello, I'm Water Snake. I'm a harmless reptile who's semi-aquatic, which means that I spend part of my time in the water and part of my time on land. Because we can swim and slither in both environments, we can eat tadpoles, frogs, salamanders, and some fish. You know, we can get to be quite large. We can grow up to 2 meters (6½ feet) long. But we have to be alert, because we can be eaten by birds of prey and by certain mammals such as badgers. To eat or be eaten, that is the question.

Announcer: You've changed my idea about snakes. I didn't know you could be so poetic. Now, here's Walleye.

Walleye: I have large glassy eyes on the sides of my head and a spiny fin on my back. I'm a brassy yellow color, except for my milky white belly. Walleye females can grow to 1.3 meters (50 inches) in length. That's quite large.

Lake Trout: Hello, I'm Lake Trout, the one with the deeply forked tail. I have dark spots on a dark background, but my body is brightly colored. We can grow to be 45 to 50 centimeters (17 to 20 inches) long. Humans think that we're mighty tasty fried in butter, so we have be constantly on guard for those hooks in the water.

Announcer: Well thanks for that. [*Tropic Level Four creatures leave.*] Moving along, we're going to bring in Trophic Level Five, to which humans belong. But let's begin with the Sea Lamprey.

Sea Lamprey: Hi, I'm Sea Lamprey. We're jawless fish that suck life juices from other fish. Our color is blotchy brown, which is good for camouflage. We can grow up to 60 centimeters (2 feet) long. We have round sucking mouths with long teeth that we use to attach to whatever fish we want to eat. Sometimes a fish is caught that has one of us stuck right to the side of it. They call us parasites. Just like the zebra mussels, we're not from the Great Lakes; we also came on big ships from far away. We've heard that people are trying to get rid of us, but we're thriving here.

Heron: I'm Heron, a gray-blue bird. You might have observed me standing motionless in shallow water? I'm waiting for prey to swim by. I have long skinny legs that allow me to stand with my body above the water. The plume on top of my head makes me look as if I have a crown. You don't usually see us in a group, because we like to work alone. In fact, we herons aren't very sociable except at mating season when we can be quite noisy nesting together in trees.

Herring Gull: Unlike the herons, we herring gulls get together a lot. We're noisy white birds, 60 centimeters (2 feet) long, with black-tipped gray wings, a yellow beak with a red spot in the lower jaw, and pink legs. We eat just about any food, so I guess you could say that we're not choosy. We often search beaches or follow fishing boats for scraps. Out in the fields, we even follow plows looking for insects. You've probably fed us at one of your picnics. But life for us has been getting difficult. Pollutants in the lakes are causing some of our females to lay soft-shelled eggs and sometimes the birds that hatch have deformed beaks.

Announcer: How did the pollutants get there? We need to think about this problem. If it is harming this organism, it is probably harming others as well.

Human: I think you'll find that we humans are responsible for those pollutants. We humans are bipedal, so we have two feet for moving about, but we haven't been satisfied with that! We don't hatch from eggs and

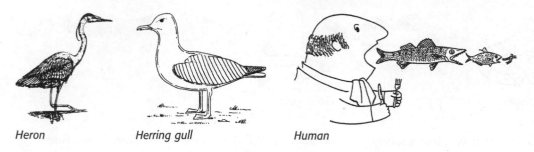

Heron   Herring gull   Human

we don't have feathers or fur or scales. Since humans are mammals, we have our babies live and have hair on our bodies. We humans are omnivorous, which means we can eat both plants and animals. We have a huge impact on other creatures because our behavior affects the world we all share. But we have a large brain relative to our body size; we can use it to think more about what we are doing that is harming our environment and try to figure out ways to make things better.

Announcer: You're right. Today, we have had a rare chance to hear from organisms in all five trophic levels. They all need to survive in the Great Lakes watershed. Can I ask all of them to return to the studio? [*Everyone returns, some reluctantly, holding up the pictures of themselves.*]

Thank you. Let's try an arrangement that can help us to understand what's going on. Trophic Level One creatures, please stand in a straight line. Organisms in Trophic Level Two, please step up behind them and touch an organism that you eat. Just touch now, no sampling! Now, creatures from Trophic Level Three, please step up and touch one organism that you eat. Next, organisms from Trophic Level Four, please touch one organism that you eat, and Trophic Level Five, please do the same.

Now, any creature who does not have anyone touching him/her, please wave. [*Sea Lamprey, Zebra*

Mussel, and Human wave] That's right, no one here eats the sea lamprey, the zebra mussel or the human. Now, we already know that these three creatures have been causing some problems in the Great Lakes watershed. I'll invite everyone to sit down and discuss these and other problems. Maybe we can find some ways to solve these problems.

Wrap-up: In the discussion, students should conclude that overpopulation of the sea lamprey and zebra mussel is a problem. When asked to come up with solutions to this problem, students may raise many interesting suggestions, such as using chemicals or introducing another species that eats the sea lamprey. Talk about the problems connected with each of these solutions, and discuss the potential effects and possible implications for the future of the Great Lakes.

Students could also complete a "Great Lakes Food Web" chart (see example on page 108) by taping or pinning the name and picture of their organism in the appropriate trophic level.

Assessment activity (optional): Have students use the information from the play and from associated lessons to explain the meaning of the following statements:

1. What we do today affects tomorrow.

2. It is important to learn about the Great Lakes food web. ✐

Marjane L. Baker teaches at Tonda Elementary School in Plymouth-Canton School District, Michigan, and is a consultant for the Michigan Geographical Alliance.

Plants and Animals

Marine Food Web Simulation

A simulation of the dynamics of food webs and predator/prey relationships in the marine environment

by John Ogletree

Grade levels: 4-6

Subject areas: art, science

Key concepts: primary producers, predators, prey, food chain, marine food web

Skills: listening, observing, cooperating as a group

Location: indoors or outdoors

Time: 5-8 minutes per round

Materials: flipchart paper, index cards, drawings or photographs of marine organisms, glue, 2 metal cans, 2 small stones, 2 wooden sticks, stopwatch or watch with a second hand

 lants, with their ability to transform the sun's energy into food through photosynthesis, are called the primary producers of our global ecosystems; and microscopic plants called phytoplankton that drift near the surface of the oceans account for more productivity than all the plants on land. The transfer of food energy from a plant source through a succession of animals eating and being eaten is called a food chain. Food chains are in turn linked together in a complex interlocking pattern called a food web.

In this activity, students play the roles of marine organisms in a food web, and must find food while avoiding being eaten by their predators. For the purposes of the game, the web example is greatly simplified, with no reference to decomposers, zooplankton, or many other groups of marine organisms. As the students learn more about the marine environment they may wish to play the game using different species.

Outcomes:
It is expected that students will:

- recognize the importance of marine food producers

- recognize seven to eight individual marine organisms

- identify three or four food chains in the marine food web

Preparation:
1. Prepare a set of food web I.D. cards according to the numbers of organisms shown on the "Food Web Organisms" chart (see next page). The organisms listed correspond to those in the food web example given, and the numbers are for a group of 22 students. Add organisms (and cards) as needed to ensure that each student will have one card. In addition, make extra phytoplankton cards for use as described in Step 6 below.

To make the cards, glue photos or drawings of the organisms on card stock. (Wall calendars having a marine theme are an excellent source of photos.) Alternatively, have students research the marine organisms and make drawings of them on cards as a means of learning the characteristics of these organisms. If possible, laminate the cards.

2. On a large sheet of paper or chalkboard, draw the food web (see "Marine Food Web," next page).

3. On a large sheet of paper or chalkboard, list the organisms and their identifying sounds, as shown on the "Food Web Organisms" chart.

Procedure:
1. Introduce the "Marine Food Web" chart and discuss the concepts of food chains and food webs. Ask students to identify the various food chains in the web (e.g., algae → periwinkle → dogwinkle → crab → human). As each food chain is discussed, show the cards depicting those organisms so that students become familiar with all of the members of the web.

2. Outline an area with boundaries to represent an area of the ocean. Assign a marine organism to each student by handing out the food web cards.

3. Explain to the group that together they represent the ten different marine organisms in the food web, and they must catch food for themselves while avoiding being eaten by a predator. Allow a few seconds for students to find their position in a food chain and review which organisms are their prey and predators.

4. To begin the game, ask students to move slowly around the "ocean," holding their cards in front of them

so that they are visible. Explain that, to catch their prey, predators must touch the card of the prey organism. If a prey organism is caught, it has been eaten and must leave the game (go outside the boundary). Begin timing the round.

5. Continue the round until all of the prey have been consumed. Record the time.

6. Discuss the round and how quickly prey organisms were eaten. Ask students how the simulation might be changed so that more prey are available and the food web can be sustained for a longer period of time. Then incorporate some of their ideas in ensuing rounds of the game. Variations might include the following:

☙ Simulate reproduction and/or the migration of animals into that area of the ocean by allowing some of the captured prey organisms to return to the game following a "death interval."

☙ Change the composition of the food web so that as many as four-fifths of the prey organisms return as phytoplankton (additional phytoplankton cards are needed for this variation).

Collect and redistribute the cards between each round so that students have the opportunity to play the roles of different organisms. Continue timing the rounds.

7. After several rounds, introduce a twist: explain that the object of the game will remain the same, but the only way the players will be able to identify their predators and/or prey is by the unique sounds they make. Introduce the "Food Web Organisms" chart and, as a group, practice making the sounds described. Alternatively, invite students to suggest sounds for each organism, and record these on a chart. The important thing is that each organism has a unique sound and that the group agrees on how these sounds are produced so that everyone will be able to recognize them.

Marine Food Web

Note: In lower grades, the simulation is easier to run using only visual identification of animals. For older students, the sound identification is a good representation of the importance, for some marine animals, of having a highly developed sense of hearing.

8. After handing out the food web cards, give students a few seconds to review which organisms are their prey and predators and the sounds these organisms make. Then ask them to keep their cards out of view as they move slowly around the ocean, making their identifying sounds and listening for the sounds of the organisms they feed on. To catch their prey, predators must touch the prey organism and show their own card as "predator I.D."

9. Graph the times of all of the rounds and conclude by discussing the factors that helped to sustain the food web the longest (e.g., migration, reproduction, increasing the number of primary producers or of other organisms at the lower ends of food chains).

Extensions:
☙ Discuss how an oil spill, toxic chemical, or other human interference might affect the food web.

☙ Adapt the activity to another ecosystem under investigation. ↝

*This activity was designed by Cheryl Rowatt and modified by **John Ogletree**, professor of Education at the University of Western Ontario in London, Ontario.*

Food Web Organisms		
Organism	**Number**	**Identifying sound**
Phytoplankton	4	Say "photosynthesis" or "making food"
Periwinkle	3	Say "graze, graze"
Sea urchin	3	Say "spiny-spiny"
Scallop	3	Say "squirt, squirt"
Dogwinkle	2	Rotate stones in can (drilling sound)
Starfish	2	Say "yum-yum"
Fish	2	Hum
Bird	1	Whistle
Crab	1	Snap fingers (claws) or strike sticks
Human	1	Remain quiet

Plants and Animals

Megan McNairn

Environmental Issues

Population Pressure

Studying the impact of the human population on the natural world begins with understanding of ecological concepts

by Marci Mowery and Lindsay Aun

Grade levels: 3-5

Subject areas: science, math, language arts, social studies

Key concepts: carrying capacity, environmental change, exponential growth

Skills: discussion, interviewing, math, writing, research

Location: indoors

Time: 1 week

igratory birds are excellent indicators of the health of the environment. Like a giant hemispheric barometer, the number of birds returning to North America each spring reveals much about environmental conditions in Latin America, just as the number migrating back to wintering grounds in the autumn gives an indication of health of northern breeding habitats. In recent years, the U.S. Fish and Wildlife Service estimates that the populations of at least 26 percent of migratory species have significantly declined, although this number varies by habitat type and migration distance. Habitat loss takes most of the blame for the declining numbers of birds and mammals worldwide — a loss caused primarily by human population growth and resource depletion.

In Argentina, population growth has created a drive to convert native pampas grassland into high-yield crops. One result is the decline of the bobolink that used to serenade the midwest prairies of the United States after wintering in Argentine grasslands. According the National Audubon Society's 2004 report "State of the Birds," bobolink populations have declined by nearly half. In northeastern United States and Canada, much of the nesting habitat of the Bicknell's thrush has been lost to ski area development and acid rain. The thrush's wintering grounds in the forests of Haiti and the Dominican Republic have also been devastated, by too many people burning down too many trees for fuel and farmland.

It is not only wildlife that is affected by the loss of natural areas — humans also suffer. In 1994 an estimated 1.1 billion people were without access to clean drinking water and 2.8 billion lacked sanitation services. Water scarcity affected more than 20 countries in 1995. Clearly, the connection between environmental degradation and human population cannot be ignored.

According to a 1999 United Nations report, 78 million people are added to the planet annually, down from the highest annual increase of 86 million, which occurred in the 1980s. From 1960 to 2000 our population doubled, reaching 6 billion in 1999; and in the next 50 years, if current trends continue, we will add more humans to the face of the Earth than in all the previous 500,000 years of human history. In an effort to support this rapid population growth, we have destroyed one-fifth of the world's topsoil and cut down one-third of all the forests that existed in 1950. Each day, between 100 and 300 plant and animal species become extinct due to human activity.

Gail Littlejohn

The United Nations reports that 95 percent of the projected population growth in the coming decades will occur in the developing world, where economic growth and natural resources cannot hope to meet the needs for food, water, and shelter. Caught in a seemingly hopeless cycle of swelling population and crushing debt, nations with high birth rates are understandably driven to exploit their natural wealth, even though they are jeopardizing their future. Simply trying to meet basic needs has already led to massive destruction of forests, wetlands, and grasslands in many developing countries. The combination of increased population and destruction of natural resources often results in economic and social problems such as food shortages, poverty, and inadequate education and health services.

In the developed world it is not a high birth rate so much as unrestrained consumption of natural resources that threatens to rock the balance of nature. The U.S. Department of Energy estimates the global emissions of the greenhouse gas carbon dioxide to be more than 3.2 billion metric tons annually, nearly three times the

amount scientists consider to be consistent with a stable atmosphere. According to Paul Harrison, an international consultant on population, the average European leaves, at the end of a lifetime, a monument of waste almost 1,000 times his body weight. The average North American's waste mausoleum is 3,900 times body weight. As the highest per capita consumers of the world's natural resources, North Americans are the greatest polluters in the world.

Whether by human numbers or human consumption, the changes we make to the natural world affect not only wildlife, but all life, including humans. Education and awareness can slow down, and even reverse, some of these trends. For some, studying of the impact of the human population on the natural world appears to be too depressing, but it does not need to be, for balancing stories of loss are stories of hope and success. The foundation of these success stories is an understanding of ecological concepts and a movement towards action. From having students monitor stream quality to encouraging the adoption of an endangered species, teachers can make a difference.

Activities for population studies

The following activities will acquaint students with some of the key concepts in population dynamics and provide opportunities for discussing some of the environmental issues facing our increasingly populated world.

Population Squeeze!

Carrying capacity, or the maximum population that can be supported by the resources of a specific area, is a very important concept when discussing population and habitat. In order to have enough food, water, and shelter, a population must be in balance with the natural resources found in its habitat. For example, if too many deer are in an area with insufficient resources, competition for food and water will force some to move to another area or die of starvation. Likewise, when too many people live in a place where there is a limited resource such as water, problems of scarcity arise.

Materials: Meter stick or yardstick, masking tape, colored blocks, books, paper

Time: One hour, not including preparation time

Procedure:

1. Draw a circle about two meters (six feet) in diameter on the floor of the classroom or outside on the ground. Place 8 to 10 colored blocks inside the circle to represent food; place 10 to 12 books (or blocks of another color) in the circle to represent water; and place 12 to 14 sheets of paper to represent shelter.

2. Have two students go into the circle and divide up the resources.

3. Send in two more students and have them divide the resources again. Continue to add students to the circle, two at a time, until everyone is in, further dividing up the resources as fairly as possible until they are gone (no breaking or tearing them in half!).

4. Discuss what happened as more people were added to the circle. How did students feel as the resources were being divided and the space was becoming more crowded? Who had enough resources and who was left out? What might happen to people or wildlife if they do not have enough resources? What are some solutions to these problems?

Making Connections

Materials: colored markers, one large sheet of paper

Time: 30 minutes

Procedure:

1. Create the beginning of a concept map by writing the words "more people" in a circle in the middle of a large sheet of paper.

2. Ask students to suggest some of the benefits and some of the negative consequences of an increase in the number of people on the Earth (e.g., more houses, fewer trees, more friends).

3. Draw lines outward from the circle, and use one color of marker to list the benefits and another color to list the negative consequence. Compare and discuss.

Extension: Have students create their own web map around the words "less wildlife habitat." Share and compare the maps. Challenge the class to come up with solutions to some of the issues.

Gail Littlejohn

How Populations Grow and Change

Populations of people and wildlife are always changing. Whether a population will grow or decline depends on many factors, such as the availability of land, food, and clean water; weather conditions; disease; accidents; and habitat destruction.

Have students interview adults who have lived in their neighborhood for many years to find out how the area has grown and changed, and if the number and diversity of trees, birds, and other wildlife have changed as well. Students can share the information they gather with the class or write stories for a class or school newspaper based on the interviews. The following are suggested interview questions.

⚅ How long have you lived in this neighborhood?

⚅ Are there more people here than before? If so, how has this changed life in the town?

⚅ How has population growth changed the landscape of the town?

⚅ What changes have there been in the number and variety of birds and other wildlife?

⚅ Do you like the changes you have witnessed? Why or why not?

⚅ What can we do to make things better for people who live here?

⚅ What can we do to bring more birds and other wildlife back to this area?

Seeing Double

Populations often grow exponentially, doubling over and over until a very small number becomes a very large number. The following brain-teasers illustrate the "power of two."

1. A father complained that his son's allowance of five dollars per week was too much. The son replied, "Okay, Dad. How about this? Let's change my weekly allowance for one month using this rule: You give me a penny on the first day of the month, two cents on the next day, four cents on the next, eight cents on the next, and so on for every day of the month." The father readily agreed. Who was more clever? What would the son's allowance be on day 31?

120

Answer: The son was more clever. His allowance on day 31 alone is $10,737,418.24. This does not count what he received on all previous days. This is a good example of how doubling even a small amount over time can really add up.

Day 1—$.01
Day 2—$.02
Day 3—$.04
Day 4—$.08
Day 5—$.16
Day 6—$.32
Day 7—$.64
Day 8—$1.28
Day 9—$2.56
Day 10—$5.12
Day 11—$10.24
Day 12—$20.48
Day 13—$40.96
Day 14—$81.92
Day 15—$163.84
Day 16—$327.68

Day 17—$655.36
Day 18—$1,310.72
Day 19—$2,621.44
Day 20—$5,242.88
Day 21—$10,485.76
Day 22—$20,971.52
Day 23—$41,943.04
Day 24—$83,886.08
Day 25—$167,772.16
Day 26—$335,544.32
Day 27—$671,088.64
Day 28—$1,342,177.28
Day 29—$2,684,354.56
Day 30—$5,368,709.12
Day 31—$10,737,418.24

2. You are a lily pad on a pond. Today there is only one fellow lily pad on the pond with you. But your population is growing, and every day your population will be twice as large as the day before. Tomorrow there will be four of you. It will take exactly 20 days for your pond to be completely full of lily pads. On what day will the pond be half full? *(Day 19)* When your pond is half full of lily pads, do you think that you and your fellow lily pads will be worried about running out of space? *(Discuss students' responses. Ask, Is this similar to our present situation? Why or why not?)*

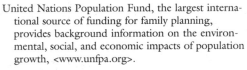
Bob Johnson

Marci Mowery *provides professional development workshops for educators on the human/environment connection. She is the former Director of Education for Audubon Pennsylvania and a former high school educator.*
Lindsay Aun *teaches elementary school in Montana and is the former Population Coordinator for the National Audubon Society's Population Campaign.*

The "Making Connections" activity and the "Seeing Double" riddles are adapted from *Counting on People: Elementary Population and Environment Activities,* Zero Population Growth, 1994.

Resources

Population Connection (formerly Zero Population Growth) offers education resources. Population Connection, 1400 16th Street NW, Suite 329, Washington, DC 20036, 202-332-2200, <www.populationconnection.org>.

The Population Reference Bureau provides timely and objective information on international population trends. Population data sheets, fact sheets, and education materials are available. Population Reference Bureau, 1875 Connecticut Avenue NW, Washington, DC 20009, 202-483-1100, <www.prb.org>.

United Nations Department of Economic and Social Affairs Division, Population Division offers on-line reports and an annual newsletter on various issues related to population and environment, <www.un.org/esa/population/unpop.htm>.

United Nations Population Fund, the largest international source of funding for family planning, provides background information on the environmental, social, and economic impacts of population growth, <www.unfpa.org>.

U.S. Agency for International Development provides funding for family planning worldwide. US AID, Information Unit, Center for Population, Health, and Nutrition, 1300 Pennsylvania Avenue NW, Washington, DC 20523, 202-712-0540, <www.usaid.gov>.

Mathematics and Garbage

Collecting and measuring their families' garbage can lead to lessons in mathematics and a new respect for the valuable materials we call trash

Illustrations by Tom Goldsmith

by Sylvia Helmer and Shirley Parker-Creasy

Grade levels: 4-6

Subject areas: mathematics

Key concepts: reduction and recycling, waste management

Skills: problem solving, using weigh scales, recording, creating and completing tables, generating and solving math problems, producing graphs, making presentations

Location: indoors (outdoor field trip optional)

Time: 1 week (collecting and measuring)

Materials: spring scales (ideally, 1 for every 4 students), paper and pencils, labels and tape, large plastic garbage bags

arbage! Students tend not give it a second thought as they discard things into the garbage can. However, when prodded, they can become quite engaged in investigating the growing issue of trash: Where does it all go? Why is there so much? What happens to it? What about the stuff that does not break down? What happens when our landfill is full? What can you recycle and what has to happen to it to make it useful again? How do we reduce the amount of garbage we create? To answer some of these questions, a group of Grades 4 and 5 learners were encouraged to spend some time considering the sheer volume of garbage produced in their own homes. After estimating how much garbage their families produce, students collected it for three days, brought it to class, and practiced their math skills to sort, tally, and report it. The process served to give learners a new understanding of this stuff called garbage. Perhaps more importantly, the active engagement and opportunity to use mathematics in a relevant and challenging way — that could be demonstrated to peers and parents — served to motivate and enhance learning.

Focus questions

The project began with a discussion during math class about items that had "accidentally" been put into the garbage can instead of into the class's recycling container. As we talked, questions emerged and were written on the board — and the math and garbage project was born. Our focus questions were:

๑ How much (non-organic) garbage does each family produce in three school days?

๑ What kinds of (non-organic) garbage does each family produce in three school days?

Making predictions

Students were asked to estimate how much garbage they thought was generated in their homes in one day as well as in three days. Immediately, they began to talk about different types of garbage, how much it might weigh, and such practical questions as "How much is a kilogram or pound anyway?" This led to an instant lesson in estimating what a kilogram or pound looks like. Some students estimated that their families would generate close to their own body weight in garbage in three days — showing that they really had no conception of what such a basic unit of measurement as a kilogram or pound really meant. Some demonstrations of weighing classroom items on a spring scale provided some needed input for helping students make realistic estimates. How many erasers in one kilogram or pound? How many exercise books? How many textbooks?

After discussion and some revisions of their personal "garbage estimates," students recorded their projections in their Math Learning Logs (a journal of daily

learning). They were then asked to collect their families' non-organic garbage and to bring it to class each day for three days. Students were sent home with a letter explaining the project and its intent. Detailed guidelines were included about washing, compacting, and bagging garbage, and taking care not to get cut on cans or sharp objects.

Preparing for the garbage audit

In preparation for our "garbage days," we had a class demonstration of how to wash and compact garbage

so that it could be brought into the classroom. There was also much discussion of how best to keep track of the garbage. It was decided that sorting it into types and weighing it by categories was probably the best idea. A chart was created that could be used both to tabulate individual students' results and to create a class total by category as well as a grand total. (See chart below.)

Readying the classroom for an onslaught of garbage was the last preparatory task. A section of the room was dedicated for this purpose. The school custodian supplied large plastic bags for sorting materials and agreed to remove from the classroom — but keep in storage — any bags filled at the end of each day. The bags were labeled, one for each category of garbage. Students were asked to bring their clean, dry garbage in plastic or paper shopping bags that could be hung on their cloakroom coat hooks until the weighing and sorting had been completed. For this week only, coats could be hung on desks and chairs.

Day one
Sorting and weighing

Students worked in pairs following a sequence of tasks set to make sorting and weighing the garbage as efficient as possible. It took quite some time that first day as there was much to monitor, and we needed to revise our parameters in response to evolving

My Family's Garbage for Three Days			
Garbage Type	Day One	Day Two	Day Three
cardboard			
textiles			
glass			
newsprint			
magazines, fine paper			
metal			
plastic (soft)			
plastic (hard)			
Styrofoam			
wood			
other (specify)			

problems. The partners sorted their garbage into categories, working on one family's garbage and one bag of garbage at a time. They then weighed the waste in each category using the spring scale, recorded their results, and placed the sorted garbage into the large labeled bags supplied by the custodian. Students assisted one another by holding the scales steady or conferring on how to complete the various tasks and their data charts.

Days two and three
Representing the data

With the sorting and weighing now a fairly efficient task, students had time to concentrate on other elements of data gathering. We discussed how to represent the various types of garbage as well as the sheer volume. It was decided that large charts, tables, and tabulations could be used to demonstrate how much and which types of garbage were being generated, both by individual families and by the class as a whole. Pie charts — which we had recently encountered in a social studies textbook — were considered a great way to show visually what the whole class collected in the three days (see example). There was also discussion of extrapolating from the class results to arrive at an estimate of the garbage generated by the entire school community, both daily and over time. Such charts would be part of our effort to demonstrate our learning for the benefit of parents and the rest of the school.

Sample math problems

Students were encouraged to come up with real and hypothetical problems using the data collected. The following are some of the math problems they generated.

  ☙ If the amount of garbage collected each day is 5 kilograms (or 11 pounds) per family, then how much garbage will be collected by each individual student at the end of three days? How much will be collected by the whole class daily and at the end of three days? (31 students in the class.)

  ☙ If John has collected 5 kilograms (11 pounds) of garbage and it includes glass bottles weighing 3.5 kilograms (7.7 pounds), how much does the rest of his garbage weigh?

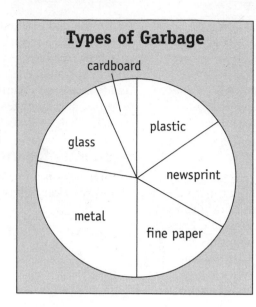

Types of Garbage

cardboard
plastic
glass
newsprint
metal
fine paper

  ☙ Jessica's family has daily newspaper delivery. The newsprint, magazines, and flyers she collects over three days weigh twice as much as all the other materials she collects. If the total weight of the garbage is 16 kilograms (35.2 pounds), how much does the paper weigh?

  ☙ What is the average collection by weight over three days for this class? Who has collected more, the boys or the girls? How much more?

    The following teacher-generated questions and problems were given to the students to answer.

  ☙ Which type of crushed garbage takes up the most room? Try weighing all categories of garbage and placing the same weight of each type of garbage into the same type of container. Is this a fair way to decide?

  ☙ Which material is easiest to get into the container? Which is hardest? How does what you have learned relate to running out of room in landfill sites?

  ☙ Which type of crushed garbage is heaviest? What criteria can you use to decide this?

  ☙ Which category of garbage is the largest in weight for the class overall? Which is the largest in volume?

  ☙ How much garbage might the whole school generate if every student collected the family garbage for three days?

Day four
Examining the results

Once the collecting and weighing were completed, and charts had been filled in and totals calculated, it was time to examine the results visually. All the garbage we had collected — now bagged for distribution to recycling plants — was brought back into the classroom. Even neatly organized by category and bagged, it was an intimidating heap.

    This generated a discussion of overpackaging and the identification of some items that could be avoided entirely, such as drink boxes and wrappings. Students expressed interest in the weight-to-volume ratio: some groups of objects that took up a lot of space did not actually weigh very much, and vice versa. Students were then asked to use their recently honed estimating

124

skills to estimate what portion of the total weight the various categories of materials represented. The use of fractional estimates was encouraged (e.g., one-third the total weight is newsprint). Accurate figures were later generated using the raw data in the tables, and became part of the presentation of our findings to parents and the school community.

Day five
To the recycling plant

With much parental and staff support, all of the sorted and bagged garbage was taken to the recycling plant — along with the class. Students had been surprised at the amount of garbage we had collected, but they were in awe when they saw the mounds at the district solid waste plant. We toured the facility and watched a demonstration of how larger items of mixed materials, such as sofas and box-spring mattresses, are crushed in a large pit. Needless to say, there was much conjecture about what would happen when the pit became full.

Extensions and conclusions

In this project, doing math became a game and creating problems related to "our" garbage became a friendly competition. However, there are many directions in which to take a project on recycling beyond this mathematical focus. For example, younger students might investigate what is recyclable in their community and create posters to inform others of the categories of recyclable materials. Older students could research how recycled products are made and where they are used. (A useful reference is the Recycled Content Product Directory by the California Integrated Waste Management Board at <www.ciwmb.ca.gov/RCP/>.)

A simple question can lead to profound learning. The teachable moment may lead you away from your pre-set lesson, but the learning that can take place — and you will find that invariably it *does* fit into pre-scribed learning outcomes — is worth the additional effort required. Our math-and-garbage week provided opportunities for the students to sort and classify, make predictions, record data, perform calculations, work with weights, learn about averages, practice the use of fractions, create and solve problems, and communicate their learning to others. At the same time, the experience opened students' eyes to the impact of the choices they make in purchasing and using resources. The lessons will not be quickly forgotten by the students, and neither they (nor I) will ever again look at garbage with the nonchalant indifference that set this project in motion. ✿

Sylvia Helmer is the English as a Second Language Consultant for the Vancouver School District. She has taught at most grade levels and enjoys infusing a "green" perspective into all aspects of her work with learners. Shirley Parker-Creasy teaches Grade 2 at Cecil Rhodes Elementary School in Winnipeg, Manitoba.

Resources

Annenberg/CFB. "Garbage: How Can My Community Reduce Waste?" on-line at <http://www.learner.org/exhibits/garbage/intro.html>. Information and activities on waste and waste management.

Gross, F. *The Power of Numbers: A Teacher's Guide to Mathematics in a Social Science Context*. Educators for Social Responsibility, 1993.

Public Broadcasting System. "Mathline: Earth Day," on-line at <www.pbs.org/teachersource/>. Math activities and lessons on recycling and other environment-related themes.

Schwartz, Richard H. *Mathematics and Global Survival* (4th edition). Ginn Press, 1998.

Animals in Jeopardy

A schoolwide theme on endangered animals

Photographs by Annette Payne

Animal riddles draw morning crowds around the "Hall of Fame" bulletin board.

by Annette Payne

Grade levels: K-5

Subject areas: science, visual arts, music, language arts

Key concepts: endangered species

Skills: research, awareness, understanding, empathy

Location: indoors and outdoors

Time: teacher preparation, schoolwide, 2 months; related classroom activities/preparation, 1 month; theme week activities, 1 week

As children begin to develop a personal connection with the natural world, they may become deeply committed to sharing their environmental concerns with others. As teachers, one of the best ways we can help students to do this is to organize a series of special activities and events focused on a theme of particular interest. This article describes a project in which a school community cooperated in planning and carrying out a week of schoolwide and classroom activities focused on the theme of endangered species. Most of the planning guidelines and many of the activities are readily adaptable to other themes.

Getting organized

No matter what the topic, a schoolwide theme requires organization and cooperation. Here are a few tips for getting started:

๑ Begin by sending flyers around inviting staff to join an organizing committee, and talk to people informally about what you are proposing. The more staff on board, the less work for everyone in the long run. This should be done early: about one or two months before schoolwide activities begin.

๑ The initial meeting should be a brief brainstorming session. At subsequent meetings you can make concrete decisions and set definite dates.

๑ Plan on having several committee meetings. Let committee members decide what needs to be discussed, when meetings will be, and how long they should be. Make up an agenda for each and stick to it, leaving time at the end for new business. Pass out a copy of the minutes to every staff member — even those who are not on the committee, as they appreciate knowing what is going on.

๑ People often find working with others makes a task more enjoyable, and the job is shared more evenly. Consider working within the committee in grade-level groups or with "reading buddy" classes.

☙ Act as consultants, not directors. The organizing committee should work on planning schoolwide activities and leave classroom activities related to the theme up to individual teachers.

☙ As schoolwide events are planned and scheduled, post a calendar in a prominent place in the staff room to help keep everyone organized.

Announcing the theme

Include your plans and activities in the school's daily announcements during the weeks leading up to the theme week. This not only increases interest and participation among students and staff but also serves as an educational tool. In our school, pairs of reading buddies took turns making the announcements every day for four weeks before the final bash. Everyone learned a great deal about endangered species from these announcements. Students gave facts about their class's adopted animal as well as general information about endangered species. They read poetry and played songs. Grade 4 students, along with

Making mobiles and sculptures of endangered animals.

their senior-kindergarten reading buddies, played a question-and-answer game called "Animals in Jeopardy." The game was so popular that "Animals in Jeopardy" became the name of our school theme.

Classroom animal research

Every class chose an endangered animal as their symbol, and students became experts on that particular species. The methods of research used to gather information about their animal were decided by individual teachers. Some classes read stories and others did group research projects. While the organizing committee encouraged the selection of endangered animals native to North America, individual classes had autonomy in choosing their species and thus we had elephants along with humpbacks.

After sea turtles made from painted paper plates appeared outside the Grade 1-2 room, imaginatively crafted animals began to show up outside other rooms all over the school. Polar bears were clothed in soft white cotton balls, elephants were sponge-painted to highlight the texture of their wrinkled skin, paper repli-

cas of tole loggerhead shrikes — one of our local endangered species — sat on real hawthorn branches, and wolves watched warily from masks. Each class was given a box to decorate to look like its adopted animal. All of the boxes were then stacked into a totem pole and placed in the entrance of the school to greet visitors.

Time-is-running-out murals

Because we are losing species so quickly — at a rate of one to three each hour — a Grade 4 class decided to give us a concrete illustration. The students made three murals representing the three main biospheres of sky, land, and water. The murals were put up on a wall in the hallway, and every student in the school was invited to contribute a small drawing of an endangered animal. Accompanying the mural was a clock, and, each hour, a student from the class moved the clock forward and took off one of the animals. It took very little time for all the species to disappear. The empty murals communicated a sense of loss, and a banner reading "We Are Gone" was placed across them.

Animal riddles

Each day, students in each grade-level division were given an endangered species riddle to solve. These were made up by the teachers on the committee. Students put their answers in a box and, if they correctly answered the riddle, their name would go up on a chart in our "Hall of Fame." The riddles for the primary grades were quite easy to solve, and after a day their "Hall of Fame" chart was almost full. The Grades 4-6 riddles were a little more difficult and it took about three days before their chart was full. The Grades 7-8 students' riddles were a real challenge for staff as well as students and no one solved the first one! This activity was a great success. After the first day, students formed crowds every morning around the Hall of Fame bulletin board to read the daily riddles and the previous day's results.

Elective days

Grades 1-4: Teachers organized a full day of activities, and their six classes rotated through them. The half-hour activities included:

- playing bird bingo from the book *Introducing Birds* by Pamela Hickman[1]

- playing Project Wild's "Quick Frozen Critters" game,[2] adapted to suit students at each grade level and followed by a discussion of predator/prey relationships and food webs

- learning a song and dance called "Food Chain in the Sea"

- making animal mobiles using cardboard pizza plates, scrap paper, yarn, and stencils

- viewing videos on wolves, bears, and other animals

- reading and discussing the book *Wolf Island* by Celia Godkin.[3] This story describes how the balance of nature is disrupted when one species is removed. Even Grade 1 students, upon hearing the story, were easily able to understand the concept

Students' displays of their research on "adopted" animals.

Grades 5-8: Students chose two of the following presentations and activities that were arranged for an afternoon:

- A local world issues center made a presentation called "The Chocolate Bar in the Classroom," which informed students of the link between chocolate and endangered species (in many tropical countries rainforests have been destroyed to make way for cocoa plantations).

- Representatives of the regional conservation authority facilitated games designed to help students understand why animals become endangered.

- A skillful parent guided students in making bird feeders and nesting boxes from pre-cut pieces of wood.

- An entomologist from a nearby college introduced students to an amazing insect collection and presented a slide show that stimulated interest in endangered invertebrates.

- Representatives of The Body Shop gave an informative slide presentation as part of the company's campaign to raise awareness about endangered species.

Endangered species zoo trip

Students in Grades 5 and 6 discussed zoo issues and then visited a large zoo for a guided tour of endangered species and a presentation on the topic of species interdependence. In the afternoon, the students were given a zoo checklist and, working in groups, were required to observe and assess the condition of a specific animal and its habitat in the zoo. The experience increased students' awareness of zoos and led to some interesting discussions and debates.

Taking action

One way for students to increase their awareness and become actively involved in protecting endangered species is to "adopt" an animal. Although adoption of native endangered species was encouraged, students at our school chose to adopt an elephant and a black rhino, along with a humpback whale. They raised funds for this effort in the following ways.

Elephant Bake Sale: The Grade 7 and 8 students had a bake sale and raised enough money to adopt an orphaned African elephant. Although rumors were flying that they were going to adopt an elephant and put it in the zoo, the money really went to the Kenya Wildlife Fund, where 100 percent of it was used to buy food for orphaned elephants. The students were very proud when they received their adoption certificate and pictures of "Imenti" the elephant.

Humpback Adoption Agency: Grades 2, 3, and 5 students got together to open an adoption agency for humpback whales. They chose candidates for adoption from several whale portfolios. Students who donated 25 cents could vote on the whale they wanted to adopt and their name went into a draw for one of eight wildlife bookmarks. Enough money was raised to adopt three whales.

Animal Coin Walk: We laid down animal footprints to mark off each meter along the lines on the gym floor. Students placed their change on the line and at the end of the day had collected 44 meters of coins. Combined with the money raised from a cupcake sale, they had enough to sponsor a black rhino named "Scud" through the Kenya Wildlife Fund and become guardians of 0.4 hectare (1 acre) of Canadian wilderness through the World Wildlife Fund.

Closing ceremony

On the last day of our "Animals in Jeopardy" week, we brought things to a close with environmental readings, music, and a slide presentation of our activities throughout the theme. By the end of the week, there was new awareness among the students that, because of human activities, we are in danger of losing something very precious. But the students also became aware that they can be part of the worldwide effort to educate others about and find solutions. ✎

Annette Payne teaches at Pope John Paul II School in Lindsay, Ontario.

Notes

1 Pamela Hickman, *Hands-on Nature: Introducing Birds,* Federation of Ontario Naturalists.

2 see "Quick Frozen Critters" in *Project WILD K-12 Curriculum and Activity Guide,* available to participants in Project WILD workshops. In the U.S., contact Project WILD National Office, 5555 Morningside Drive, Suite 212, Houston, TX 77005 <www.projectwild.org>. In Canada contact WILD Education, Canadian Wildlife Federation, 350 Michael Cowpland Drive, Kanata, ON K2M 2W1, <www.wildeducation.org>.

3 Celia Godkin, *Wolf Island,* Fitzhenry and Whiteside, 1993.

Going to great lengths to raise funds for protecting endangered species, students contributed 44 meters of coins to the Animal Coin Walk.

Resources

Wildlife adoption

Many organizations have wildlife adoption programs that support their work in protecting endangered and threatened species. Check for programs administered by local conservation agencies or contact the following national and international organizations:

African Wildlife Foundation (adoption of elephants, gorillas, and lions): <www.awf.org>.

Defenders of Wildlife (adoption of endangered animals native to North America): Defenders of Wildlife, 1130 17th Street NW, Washington, DC 20036, <www.defenders.org>.

International Wildlife Coalition, Whale Adoption Project (humpback whales): <www.whales.org>, 1-888-MYWHALE (699-4253).

World Wildlife Fund (symbolic adoptions of several endangered animals): see U.S. website at <www.worldwildlife.org> or Canadian website at <www.wwf.ca>.

Zoo checklists

The following organizations have free checklists that students may use to assess the living conditions of zoo animals:

Humane Society of the United States <www.hsus.org>.

People for the Ethical Treatment of Animals <www.peta.org>.

Zoocheck Canada <www.zoocheck.com>.

Information on endangered species

Canadian Nature Federation: kit available at 1-800-267-4088 or at <www.cnf.ca/species/>.

Committee on the Status of Endangered Wildlife in Canada: list of endangered species at <www.cosewic.gc.ca>.

Friends of the Earth <www.foe.org>.

Species Survival Commission of the World Conservation Union: <www.iucn.org/themes/ssc/>.

U.S. Fish and Wildlife Service: list of endangered species available at <http://endangered.fws.gov>.

World Wildlife Fund <www.worldwildlife.org> or <www.wwf.ca>.

Investigating Air Quality

Activities for acquainting children with the properties of air and air quality

by Esther Railton Rice and Janice Gardner-Loster

Grade levels: 3-5

Subject areas: science, social studies, language skills, mathematics, health

Key concepts: properties of air, air pollution, personal health, changes in environments

Skills: observation, investigation, comparison, analysis, communication, decision making

Location: classroom, outdoors, or at home

Time: about 20 minutes per activity

 Quick! Do you know where your next breath of air is coming from? We are becoming increasingly conscious of the need for clean air. Yet in recent decades population growth, urbanization, industrialization, and automobile use have dramatically increased air pollution, not only in cities and suburbs but also in rural areas. Once regarded as Earth's invisible life-giving ether, air is becoming more and more visible, and sometimes life-threatening, as a result of pollutants such as smog, small particles of dust stirred up by wind, and smoke from wildfires, factory stacks, and fireplaces. In many cities around the world, air pollution alerts have become nearly daily occurrences. We cannot escape air pollution indoors, either. Vapors and particles from cigarettes, aerosol sprays, gas appliances, and cleaning products permeate the air. Even perfume releases volatile compounds that can trigger allergies in some people, as can particles of dust, and dander from the coats of pets.

Children need to be aware of the quality of the air they breathe: to know where and when it is safe to ride a bicycle or rollerblade, activities that involve inhaling big breaths of air, often near busy streets and highways. If they have allergies or asthma, children need to know when to expect and how to avoid pollen, molds, and dust in the air.

The following lessons acquaint children with the properties of air and some causes and consequences of poor air quality. They are organized in a sequential order from the simplest concepts to the most difficult. Children begin by building a foundation of knowledge about air — that it is invisible but takes up space, has weight, exerts pressure, and contains particulate matter — through observation, communication, and comparison of characteristics inherent in objects. They are then prepared to investigate the quality of air, look for signs of polluted air, and think about ways to take action to improve the air quality in their environment.

Air is all around us

What does air look like? Where is it? How do you know? The following activities show children that air is present almost everywhere and that it is essential to life.

Illustrations by Tom Goldsmith

130

Living things need air

All living things need air to live and grow. We cannot see air or how plants use it to flourish, but we can feel its substance as we breathe in and out. This activity helps children to become conscious of the presence of air in their bodies.

Materials: a facial tissue for each child

Procedure:

1. Have the children take a deep breath, shut their lips tightly, and pinch their noses shut as long as they can. Try it a second time. Ask, Why did you let go? What does your body need?

2. Give each of the children an unfolded tissue and ask them to hold it near their nose and mouth. Now ask them to take another deep breath and to push that air out. Ask, What happened to the tissue?

3. How does your body take in air? Have the children try breathing in and out, first through their noses only and then through their mouths. Ask, Where do you think the air is going?

4. Have the children lie down on the floor and put their hands on their chests. Once again, have them take deep breaths and let the air out slowly. Ask, What did you feel?

Air has no definite shape but fills its container

Just as we can feel our chests expand and contract as we breathe, we can see the same effect when we compress a paper bag. This activity shows that air fills empty containers even though it cannot be seen.

Materials: several small paper bags, some made of heavy paper and some of thin paper

Procedure:

1. Ask, Can the bags be full of something you cannot see? Have the children open the bags, look inside, and put a hand inside. Ask, What do you see? What do you feel?

2. Ask the children to close the bags, leaving a small opening at the top. Ask, What do you feel if you push on the outside of the bags? If you push on the bags quickly, does the air feel different from when you push on them slowly?

3. Ask the children to blow into the thin bags. Ask, How can you keep the air inside? What happens if you pop the bag? What made the hole?

Air is almost everywhere

We can again demonstrate the presence of air by having children "capture" air in a bag just as their lungs do when they breathe.

Materials: a small plastic bag and a twist tie for each child

Procedure:

1. Give each child a plastic bag. Ask, Where do you think air does not exist?

2. Have the children try to collect air in those places by swishing their bags and then closing them with plastic twist ties. Ask, How does your bag feel when you press on it? Were there any places where air could not be found? Can you think of other places where air might be but cannot be collected, such as in water?

Air has volume and weight

Children learned the importance of air in the first activities. They now have an opportunity to investigate some properties of air in the following activities.

Air has substance

Even though air cannot be seen, children learned from the previous activities that they *could* collect it in a container. This activity will show how air moves about.

Materials: a large, deep glass bowl; 2 small glasses; water

Procedure:

1. Fill the bowl three-fourths full with water.

2. Hold a glass with the open end down. Push it straight down into the water.

3. Put a second glass in the water sideways so that it fills with water.

4. Tip the first glass. Try to "pour" the air up from the first glass into the second glass. What happens to the water in the higher glass? the lower glass? How can you get the air back into the first glass?

Air occupies space

Children observed air moving from one glass to the other. Can air also contain solid materials? Try this activity!

Materials: large, deep glass bowl, 2 small glasses, water; a piece of paper

Procedure:

1. Fill the bowl three-fourths full with water.

2. Crush a dry piece of paper and push it into the bottom of a glass so that it will not fall out when the glass is held upside down.

3. Hold the glass upside down and push it straight down to the bottom of the bowl of water. What happens? (The space in the glass is occupied by air.)

4. Tilt the glass slightly and watch the air escape from the glass in the form of bubbles.

5. Now lift the glass straight out of the water and remove the paper. Is it still dry? Why?

Air collects in unlikely places

Every day we use air to breathe, but we also use it to help us with activities in our everyday lives. We blow up inflatable swimming pools with it. We fill our bicycle tires with it. We blow up balloons for celebrations with it. Children will understand that air can be collected in many places.

Materials: bicycle air pump, deflated inner tube

Procedure:

1. Let the children play with the air pump and feel the air coming out of the hose.

2. Then have them fill a deflated inner tube. Ask, Why did the inner tube change size?

3. Deflate the inner tube by having someone sit on it. Ask, What happened?

4. Ask the children to find other places that air is hidden and to prove it by putting that object in water to see the bubbles. Examples might be a brick, a piece of lava, a cloth handkerchief, or a sponge.

Air has weight

In the previous activities children learned they could collect air. But how can we weigh something we cannot see? The paper bag didn't seem heavy, but this activity will show children that air does have weight.

Materials: 2 matching balloons, meter stick or yardstick, string, scissors, tape

Procedure:

1. Tie a string around the center of a meter stick and hang it on a horizontal plane from a doorway using tape.

2. Attach a string loosely to each of the two deflated balloons and tape each string to an end of the stick. Be sure the stick is level after the

balloons are hung. If not, place a paper clip on the stick where needed to balance it.

3. Blow up one balloon and re-hang it. Ask, What happens? How can you make the stick level again? (The strings must stay at the ends of the stick.)

Air presses on everything on all sides

Can we feel air pressing on our bodies or see it pressing on objects around us? No. So how do we know whether it does? This activity will show children that air has pressure.

Materials: plastic lid from margarine container, small drinking glass, sink or plastic dishpan

Procedure:

1. Fill a drinking glass with water. Press a plastic lid over the top of the glass and hold it firmly against the rim of the glass with the palm of one hand.

2. Grasp the base of the glass with the other hand and quickly turn the glass upside down over the dishpan or sink. Ask, What will happen if you let go of the lid? (The plastic lid and the water will remain in place because the pressure of the air on the plastic lid is greater than the pressure of the water against it.) What will happen if you tip the glass sideways? (The water will still stay in the glass because air exerts pressure in all directions.)

Air pollution

Now that some distinct properties of air have been identified, the children have a background for studying air quality and the effects of pollution.

Air carries odors and other gases

Take a deep breath. What do you smell? cookies baking? smoke from the fireplace? flowers in bloom? exhaust from cars? Our noses are always sniffing smells — pleasant and unpleasant — that are in the air. In this activity children measure the time and distance over which odors travel. They also discover that their sense of smell might not detect polluted air.

Materials: a large onion, kitchen knife, portable fan, oil of peppermint, jar with a lid, clock or watch with a second hand, pencils and paper for each child or chalk and a chalkboard

Procedure:
1. Name five or six children to be "air monitors" and ask them to stand in various places around the classroom. Instruct them to raise their hands as soon as they smell the odor of onion. Ask the other children to be timekeepers, counting the seconds on a clock or watch.

2. Place the fan near one wall of the classroom and turn it on. Peel an onion in front of the air current. Ask, Who smelled the odor first? How long did it take the odor to travel from one side of the room to the other? How long does it take the odor to mix with the air in the room so that it cannot be detected any longer?

3. Pour a few drops of oil of peppermint into the jar. Have the children place the jar near their noses and record how much time it takes before they no longer smell the odor. Then put the lid on the jar. After five minutes, remove the lid and smell the odor again. Ask, Can you still smell it? If you can "get used to" the smell of the peppermint, can you also get used to the odor of polluted air? Does it stop harming you when you become accustomed to it? What might you do if there is a harmful or unpleasant odor in the room?

Air contains solid particles

We can smell odors and gases in the air, but does air contain any solid matter? What makes you sneeze when flowers are in bloom? Where does a cigarette go as it is being smoked? This activity enables children to see that air contains particulate matter and to compare the number of particles found in different places.

Materials: 5 index cards, 5 pieces of white graph paper cut to fit the file cards, petroleum jelly, glue, 5 rocks (or masking tape), hand lenses for each child, pencils for each child

Procedure:
1. Glue one piece of graph paper to each index card. Coat the paper with petroleum jelly, leaving a margin to tape and one line to write on.

2. Have the children suggest various places where they might collect particles, such as near a chalkboard, an air duct, a bus stop, a garden or farm field with freshly tilled soil, an incinerator, a smoking area or fireplace, or where trees or grasses are shedding pollen. Write the locations on the index cards and put them in the selected places. Weight the index cards with a rock or tape them in place.

3. Pick up the cards after one day. Use a hand lens to examine the particles that collected on the paper. Count the particles in three different squares of the graph. Average the numbers. Use that number to estimate how many particles might have fallen on the entire paper, in the classroom, in the schoolyard.

4. Ask, What different kinds of particles did you see? Where do you think they came from? Where could you collect more samples? Which place would have the most particles of that kind? the least? Does height, time, or wind affect the number of particles collected? How do particles in indoor air compare with those collected outdoors?

5. Talk about what is causing the particles. Discuss how the pollution might be controlled and how we might avoid being exposed to it, such as by wearing a mask while working with something dusty like plaster or clay, or closing a door or window.

Humans can change air quality
Cigarette smoke pollutes the air

The smoke from cigarettes is a problem for both the smoker and those who breathe the smoke secondhand. Children can observe the effects of tobacco smoke on air quality by watching as the teacher performs the following experiment. As the experiment requires the use of lighted cigarettes, it may not be allowable or advisable in some school settings.

Materials: 2 wads of slightly dampened cotton; 2 clear plastic detergent bottles, one with the lid on but with the plug removed; 2 cigarettes that just fit into the plug hole of the detergent bottle (and masking tape, if the fit is not exact); matches

Safety note: This activity should be demonstrated by the teacher outdoors, with the children standing upwind.

Procedure:
1. Put a piece of slightly dampened cotton into each clear plastic bottle.

2. Light a cigarette and insert the unlit end into the neck of one bottle. If the cigarette fits loosely, use masking tape to seal the gap around it.

3. Have the children watch as you squeeze and release the bottle gently, simulating how a person might breathe and puff tobacco. Put out the cigarette and let the children observe the bottle closely. Ask, What has happened to the inside of the bottle and the cotton?

Could this happen to the inside of a smoker's lungs?

4. Relight the cigarette (or, if necessary, light a new one) and place it in the opening of the first bottle. Have the bottle "puff" on the cigarette while the open neck of the second bottle is held close by. Then carefully put out the cigarette. What happens to the second bottle? Ask, How might secondhand smoke be a problem for nonsmokers? What can you do about it?

5. Have the children tell about how they were able to get someone who lives with them or near them to stop smoking.

6. Have the children role play effective ways to refuse a cigarette and polite ways to respond to someone who is smoking near you.

Emissions of chemicals and particles pollute the air

Is the air in your community healthy? How do you know? Children can try this activity to see whether they can observe signs of pollution.

Procedure:

1. Take a neighborhood or schoolyard walk to observe signs of pollution. Ask, What do you see? hear? smell? feel?

2. Have the children list the ways that air is being polluted in their community (e.g., by vehicles, factories, farm machinery). Ask, How does air pollution affect the landscape? Are trees on busy roads as healthy as those on streets with less traffic? Are leaves green or are they coated with dirt? Do you see signs of pollution around buildings? Do you feel gritty from soot or blowing dust? Do you smell mold or musty odors? disinfectants?

3. Discuss the causes of each pollutant, its effects on the environment, and methods of reducing or eliminating it.

We can improve air quality in our homes

Can one person make a difference? Yes! Children will find that they can make changes in their own homes to improve the air quality.

Materials: pencils and paper for each child

Procedure:

1. Have children take an inventory of their homes and make a list of things that can be done to improve the air quality (e.g., cleaning to remove mold, using non-aerosol sprays, cleaning furnace air ducts and burners, using biological controls in the garden, using eco-friendly disinfectants).

2. Have children share their inventories with their families and encourage them to make changes.

We can improve air quality in our community

Now that the children have encouraged changes to improve the air quality in their homes, what can they do on a community scale? After working together to brainstorm ideas, children can make an impact in their communities by becoming involved.

Materials: pencils and paper for each child, local telephone book, telephone

Procedure:

1. Have children think of ways that they can make a difference in their communities. Some suggestions are the following:

◊ Write letters to your city works department asking them to coordinate the timing of stoplights and the placement of stop signs in order to shorten idling time and reduce emissions of car exhaust.

◊ Ask the school principal to send letters to parents, asking them not to idle their cars on or near the school property when picking up or dropping off students.

◊ Call the hotline in your area to report cars with faulty exhaust systems to help prevent smog.

◊ Ask people around you to cover their mouths when they cough or sneeze to avoid spreading germs to others.

Write letters to people who are causing pollution to explain how harmful it is and to ask them to find a way to reduce it.

2. If your community has a warning siren that blows when there is a health hazard, invite a speaker from the fire department to tell children about it and what they should do to protect themselves if they hear it.

Children often cannot prevent air pollution, but they can understand its causes and effects and learn ways to protect themselves from it. An increased awareness of this serious environmental problem will enable them to make informed personal decisions, to take action to improve air quality in their homes, and to recognize that individual actions can accumulate into societal change.

Esther Railton Rice is a Professor of Education Emerita at California State University, Hayward, and a consultant on environmental education. She is the co-author, with Phyllis Gross, of Teaching Science in an Outdoor Environment *(University of California Press, 1972) and has contributed to numerous books and journals on outdoor and environmental education.* **Janice Gardner-Loster** *has a Master of Science degree in Environmental Education Curriculum and experience in curriculum development at the Lawrence Hall of Science, University of California, Berkeley.*

References

Carin, Arthur A., Joel E. Bass, and Terry L. Contant. *Teaching Science as Inquiry* (10th edition). Pearson Education/Prentice Hall, 2004.

Harlan, Jean D., and Mary S. Rivkin. *Science Experiences for the Early Childhood Years: An Integrated Affective Approach* (8th edition). Pearson Education/Prentice Hall, 2003.

Jacobson, Willard J., and Abby Barry Bergman. "Science Experiences for Young Children." Chapter 5 in *Science for Children: A Book for Teachers* (2nd edition). Prentice Hall, 1987.

Peters, Joseph M., and Peter C. Gega. *Science in Elementary Education* (9th edition). Prentice Hall, 2001.

Victor, Edward, and Richard D. Kellough. *Science K-8: An Integrated Approach* (10th edition). Pearson Education/Prentice Hall, 2003.

Ziemer, M. "Science and the Early Childhood Curriculum: One Thing Leads to Another." *Young Children*: 44-51, September 1987.

The Water Game

Photographs by Jennifer Baron

by Jennifer Baron

Grade levels: 2-3

Subject area: science

Key concepts: water has three states, but many forms; clean water is an increasingly scarce resource; water conservation and protection are everyone's responsibility

Skills: water conservation and protection habits

Location: outdoors

Time: 90-120 minutes

Materials: class set of water-form game cards (see instructions below); 12 10-centimeter-square (4-inch-square) pieces of plywood, acrylic board, or sturdy cardboard for making placards; 2 wooden craft sticks per student; 2 brightly colored sports vests; 14 orienteering punches or a class set of pencils.

hildren universally know that water is important. If asked what all living things need to survive, even the youngest school-aged child would include water. Yet as the science curriculum becomes more demanding across North America, young children are expected to understand more complex concepts about water. They are expected to be able to identify water's three states and many forms. They are expected to know that the same amount of water

has existed on the planet for billions of years; and that while close to three-quarters of the Earth's surface is covered by water, the world's supply of clean fresh water is diminishing. They are expected to gain an awareness of the need to use water wisely, which means to conserve it and not pollute it. While all of these concepts are important, they are abstract to most young children. Some children, especially those who live near large bodies of fresh water such as the Great Lakes, may find it difficult to understand that fresh water is scarce.

The Water Game described here is a fun, interactive means of teaching and reinforcing these concepts about water. Through playing the game, students become familiar with different forms that water can take and gain an understanding of how water pollution reduces the amount of fresh water available for human use. The Water Game is ideally suited for students in Grade 2, but I have played it with students up to Grade 8.

Game overview

Players are each given a game card with 16 squares on it (see page 138). Twelve water-form placards, each with a word and symbol denoting a form of water (e.g., rain, snow, vapor), are hidden at eye level on trees, bushes, and posts around the playing area. Attached to each placard is an orienteering paper punch on a rope (see note below). Players must find each hidden placard and punch the corresponding square on their game card (or, if punches are not used, draw the symbol of the water form in the square).

Note: Orienteering punches are sets of paper punches that have different pin configurations so that each punch makes a different mark on the game card. Using these ensures that students go to each placard and eliminates the danger of carrying sharp pencils. The punches can perforate even laminated game cards. (See the Resource list for suppliers.)

Earning points

⚬ For each water-form square that is correctly punched, players earn two points.

⚬ At any time during the game, players can earn one point by telling the leader, or "Conservation Officer," a fact about water. This fact may come from players' prior knowledge of water or it may be something new they have learned from the lesson, but it cannot be a simple statement of the obvious, such as "water is wet." An appropriate fact would be: "Water exists in three states: solid, liquid, and gas." (See also "Quick Water Facts" sidebar.) To record the point, the Conservation Officer writes "+1" in the Conservation Officer box on the player's game card.

Losing points

⚬ If students go out of bounds ("down the drain") and are caught by a boundary patroller, or "Drainpipe," they lose one point. To record this, the Drainpipe writes "–1" in the Drainpipe square on the game card.

⚬ If a player is not playing safely or fairly, the Conservation Officer may deduct a point by writing "–1" in the Conservation Officer square.

⚬ If a player is caught by a Toxic Substance (oil spill and pollution, introduced in the second half of the game), the player loses one point. The Toxic Substance records this by writing "–1" in the appropriate Toxic Substance square on the game card. (Alternatively, Toxic Substances can use orienteering punches.)

Orienteering punches can be attached to water placards with a short piece of rope.

Preparation:

Making game cards: To make the water-form game card, begin with a piece of paper 8½ by 5½ inches. Leave space at the top of the card for entering the student's name and the number of points earned. Divide the rest of the card into 16 rectangles of equal size. Label the 12 rectangles around the outside of the card with the names of water forms, such as Rain, Dew, Snow, Frost, Vapor, Sleet, Hail, Fog, Ice, Slush, Mist and Steam. If orienteering punches are to be used, include a symbol for each water form on the game card (e.g., a snowflake for snow, a raindrop for rain, as in the example shown); otherwise, put only the words on the card and have the players draw the symbols as they find the placards. Label the four inner rectangles as follows: Conservation Officer, Drainpipe, Oil Spill, and Pollution. Make a photocopy of the card for each student.

Making and setting up placards: On each of the 12 placards, write the name of one of the 12 water forms that appear on the game card. Next to the word, draw the symbol for the water form (the same symbol that is used on the game card). Placards should be about 10 centimeters (4 inches) square — small enough that students must look for them, but large enough to be visible from several meters away.

Marking boundaries: Mark off a playing area in the schoolyard. The area must be large enough for the class to run around in, and must have hiding spots for the 12 placards. You may wish to use pre-existing and obvious boundaries on your site, such as fences or sidewalks. Alternatively, mark boundaries using pylons or brightly colored flagging tape. Choose a site in the middle of the playing area as the home base or "Hydroelectric Dam." If there is no natural landmark for this, designate the home base by placing a hoola hoop on the ground.

Setting up placards: Hide the placards on trees, bushes, posts, or other structures within the playing area. Place them at the students' eye level so that when they find the placards they will be able

---

Quick Water Facts

⚬ Water exists in three states: solid, liquid, and gas.

⚬ Water appears in many forms in the environment (e.g., dew, snow, fog, frost, rain).

⚬ Approximately three-quarters of the surface of the Earth is covered by water.

⚬ Approximately three-quarters of the human body is water.

⚬ Less than 1 percent of the Earth's water is fresh, accessible, and clean enough for human consumption: approximately 97 percent is salt water and 2 percent is in the polar ice caps.

⚬ Water is essential for the health of all living things.

⚬ Fresh water is not evenly distributed on the planet.

---

to see clearly the words and symbols written on them. This is possible to do even in the most urban and asphalt-covered schoolyard, as duct tape will stick to just about any surface, even concrete walls and metal posts. If you have a set of orienteering punches, attach a punch to each placard with a short piece of strong rope or wire. If you are not using orienteering punches, the students will need to carry pencils to draw the symbols onto their game cards.

Note: To adapt this game for older students, hide the placards in more difficult places, or change the height of the hiding spot from eye level to below the knees or just above the head. (Students must still be able to read the placards.)

Prior knowledge

Before playing, introduce the concepts of the game by reading aloud a book that explains the water cycle. (See the children's books listed in the Resources section for recommendations.)

Procedure:

1. Before the game begins, walk the boundaries with the students so that they know exactly where they can and cannot play.

2. Assign a few students or parent volunteers to be the boundary patrol, and explain that the boundary patrollers play the role of Drainpipes. If players go out of bounds, they go down the drain and lose one point.

3. Gather students at the Hydroelectric Dam. Introduce yourself as the Conservation Officer, and explain the following rules of the game (detailed in Game Overview, above):

⑥ They must find as many of the 12 water-form placards as they can and punch the matching squares on their game cards.

⑥ They can win extra points for telling a fact about water to the Conservation Officer.

⑥ They can lose points for going out of bounds or playing unsafely or unfairly.

Explain that during the game, students can come back to the Hydroelectric Dam if they are hurt or need help, and that they must return whenever the teacher (Conservation Officer) blows the whistle.

4. Begin the game. Allow enough time in the first round for students to find several, but not all, of the water-form placards.

The Water Game		Name:	Points:
Rain	Mist	Sleet	Hail
Snow	Pollution	Drainpipe	Vapor
Fog	Oil Spill	Conservation Officer	Slush
Frost	Dew	Steam	Ice

Note: A player who finds a placard may draw the attention of other students to that hiding spot. With young children, this is often more of a help than a hindrance in the game. When playing the game with older children, swear them to secrecy when they find a placard. Older students enjoy this competitive element.

5. Before any student finds all of the game placards (usually after 10 to 20 minutes), blow the whistle and bring all of the students back to the home base. Check to make sure that everyone is safe and accounted for before beginning the next round of the game.

6. Choose two students to represent oil spills and pollution, two Toxic Substances in the water supply. Have these two students don colorful sports vests so that they will stand out.

7. Give each of the players two wooden sticks and explain that each stick represents a raindrop. Together, all of the raindrops represent the world's total fresh water supply. Tell the students (or have them calculate) the total number of raindrops that have been handed out. This number will be needed in the follow-up at the end of the game.

A player is tagged by a Toxic Substance and must hand over one of her raindrops (wooden sticks).

8. Explain that in the second round of play, the task of the players is twofold: to continue finding the water-form placards and punching or drawing the symbols on their game cards, and to avoid being tagged by a Toxic Substance. Should a Toxic Substance tag a player, the player must give the Toxic Substance one raindrop (wooden stick) and lose one point (the Toxic Substance writes "–1" in the appropriate Toxic Substance square or punches the square with an orienteering punch). A student who loses a raindrop by accident can get a replacement by going to the Hydroelectric Dam and telling the Conservation Officer a water fact.

Note: It is important to wait to introduce the Toxic Substances until part way through the game, as students may otherwise become so preoccupied with avoiding being tagged that they neglect to collect water-form symbols.

9. At the end of the game, check the punches or symbols and tally the points on the students' game cards (a pre-punched answer card makes this faster). Then make an analogy between the number of points and the water cycle. For example,

❀ 0 to 9 points: you got stuck in a glacier for thousands of years as ice

❀ 10 to 20 points: you have gone through the water cycle a few times

❀ 20 or more points: you have traveled very quickly through the water cycle many times

10. Collect the raindrops (wooden sticks) from the players, noting how many of the sticks were captured by the Toxic Substances. The total number of sticks at the end of the game should equal that at the beginning. This represents the fact that water never disappears, but just changes form as it goes through the water cycle.

11. Do some quick mental math to determine the percentage of the total water supply that has been polluted with toxic substances during the game. Discuss the fact that water usage and water pollution are increasing, and these factors reduce the amount of fresh water available to humans and other organisms. You may wish to debrief these concepts with a read-aloud story, such as *The Water Hole* by Graeme Base (see Resources, next page).

12. Follow up the game with activities that reinforce the message that it is everyone's job to conserve fresh water and not to pollute it. Some examples are:

❀ Create a fictional story of a raindrop as it goes through the water cycle and changes form.

❀ Make a list of many different ways to conserve water and keep it clean.

❀ Organize a cleanup of a section of the local watershed.

❀ Create a pictorial journal entry to illustrate the following poem. Put two or more lines of the poem on each page and draw a picture to represent the meaning of those lines. (The poem can be copied on the back of the water-form cards in advance.)

Air and Water in the Environment

There are two things that we all must get:
Air that's pure and water that's wet.
They help us to live every day,
But there's a problem in the way.
Pollution gives me quite a scare,
If it gets in the water and the air.
Smog, oil spills, garbage, too,
But there are things that you can do.
Change your habits; use your wit,
And our environment will benefit.
So make a plan and stick to it
Because every step helps a little bit. ✍

Jennifer Baron teaches at the Sibbald Point Outdoor Education Centre of the York Region District School Board in Sutton, Ontario.

Resources

Water activities and experiments

Lambert, Sue, and Sandi Rickerby. *Water: Grades 2-4*. Solski Group, S&S Learning Materials, 1999.

Murphy, Bryan. *Experiment With Water*. Scholastic Press, 1991.

Project WET <www.projectwet.org>. Excellent resources on water education for teachers.

Wick, Walter. *Drop of Water: A Book of Science and Wonder*. Scholastic Press, 1997.

Children's literature

Base, Graeme. *The Water Hole*. Doubleday Canada, 2001.

Greenaway, Theresa. *The Water Cycle*. Raintree, Steck-Vaughn Publishers, 2001.

Jeunesse, Gallimard, and P.M. Valat. *Water*. Moonlight Publishing, 1991.

Locker, Thomas. *Water Dance*. Harcourt Brace & Company, 1997.

Orienteering punches

Go Orienteering – Orienteering Supplies, 1920 Schiller Avenue, Wilmette, IL 60091, 866-424-8377 / 847-293-4253, <http://my.core.com/~gdt/Catalog.htm> (or search the Internet for "orienteering supplies").

A Working Model of a Stream

*This simple, easy-to-create model helps children understand
stream dynamics and the impact of human activities on water quality*

by William F. Hammond

Grade levels: 2-5

Subject areas: science, ecology

Key concepts: watershed, riparian zone, runoff, erosion, point-source pollution

Skills: experimenting, observing, predicting, manipulating materials

Location: outdoors or indoors

Megan McNairn

Is there anything more captivating to children of any age than a stream of running water? Children will mess about for hours building and breaking dams, changing the direction of the water, making pools, and racing floating-leaf boats or sticks. A stream, it seems, tempts the "beaverness" deep in our human spirit. Yet in urban neighborhoods, streams are often converted into conveyances hardened with cement or rock riprap, or even sent underground into systems of culverts that are out of sight and mind of children. With these changes, children lose powerful learning opportunities that come from exploring a local stream in a joyful, experimental manner.

We want students to learn about watersheds and stream riparian conservation. We want to enhance their appreciation of the subtle relationship of streams to the landscapes through which they flow. We want them to recognize the complex interaction between aquatic and terrestrial life that is intimately woven into the seasonal rhythms of the water. Yet when children lack a founda-

tion of personal experience, it can be difficult to interest them in learning about streams and water issues In an ever more urbanized environment we must find new ways to create the "Velcro for the mind" — experiences that stimulate children to want to learn about streams, rivers, lakes, and estuaries.

Schoolyard explorations

One way to begin to engage children in stream studies is to go on a mini field trip to investigate how water flows on the school grounds and in the local neighborhood (this may also be a homework assignment). During or after a heavy rain, students can follow the flow of water as it is pulled by gravity off the school roof, across sidewalks and parking lots, through pipes and gutters and along curbs, forming puddles (mini ponds and lakes) in low spots until it finds a storm drain or a stream. Have students visualize where it goes from there: on to a bigger river, possibly to a lake, and eventually to the ocean or back to the atmosphere as vapor that will condense as clouds. Tracing the flow of water locally in this way is a first step toward understanding the concept of a watershed.

An interactive stream model

A very successful yet simple model for learning more about watershed and stream dynamics has been implemented at the Kingfisher Environmental Interpretive Centre in Enderby, British Columbia. The model originated when director Neil Brookes and his staff of volunteers were faced with the arrival of an unexpectedly large group of schoolchildren. Under pressure to create an additional learning station, the staff had the idea of creating a small model stream in the woods adjacent to the center. Using a pump and a fire hose, they brought water from a nearby river and let it run off the bank of the parking lot into the woods. One of the volunteers paddled home and brought back a children's toy village made of wooden blocks, along with a set of toy farm animals and fences.

Spillway

Cement block dam

Village water intake

William Hammond

A model dam creates a reservoir that supplies the town's water through a PVC pipe.

The visiting students were instructed to build a village with a bridge, a dam, a farm, a factory, and anything else they would like, along the banks of the model stream. When they had completed their work, after about 30 minutes, the flow was increased so that the miniature stream flooded the toy dams. As the village's bridges, homes, farms, and factories were washed out, the amazed and dismayed students were told, "Floods happen! Now, rebuild the village so that if a flood comes again things won't get washed out."

After being rebuilt, most of the structures in the students' new village withstood the next flood. A lesson in biology was then added as Brookes walked up the little stream with a plastic salmon on the end of a wire. As he walked, he told the story of "Salmon Ella" coming home to lay her eggs, and described the kind of stream bottom and conditions she was searching for after her three-year journey in the Pacific Ocean.

Model enhancements

Over the past ten years the model stream at the Kingfisher Centre has become far more sophisticated. A water intake pipe now flows through a dam to provide water to the toy village. It then runs underground into

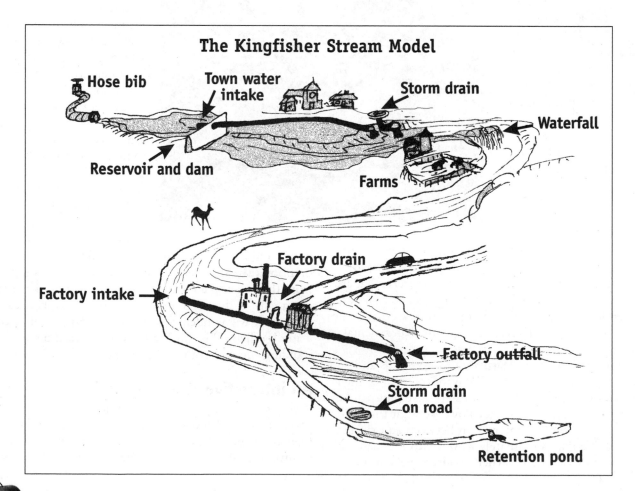

The Kingfisher Stream Model

Hose bib

Town water intake

Storm drain

Waterfall

Reservoir and dam

Farms

Factory drain

Factory intake

Factory outfall

Storm drain on road

Retention pond

the stream to simulate the village's sewer outfall. Other additions to the site include storm drains, a factory with an intake and outfall pipe, a variable-level dam system, and models of wildlife along the stream's wooded edges. A "good farm" has protective fencing to keep livestock out of the stream, while a "bad farm" has pigs and cattle roaming freely. Bags of pebbles are used for riprap, and twigs or Lincoln logs with strings or small chains simulate stream erosion diverters. Baskets made of hardware cloth and filled with gravel serve as gabions for erosion control, stones are used as check dams, and there are trowels for digging ponds near the town and on the farm.

Food coloring is used so that children can trace the flow of contaminants introduced to the system. It can be put into the village's water intake and traced to the sewer outfall. It can be used to trace runoff from roads as it enters storm drains on roadways and goes into the village's storm sewers. And poured down the factory drain, it can be seen coming out of a downstream outflow, forming a plume that is eventually diluted in the stream.

Children are encouraged to discuss and compare the real creeks and streams they have observed and the model stream. They begin to understand that a native stream is a very complex set of communities and wildlife habitats sensitive to water quality, flow rates, and temperature, and that when humans reconfigure a stream, many of these natural values are lost.

Top: Students constructing a town, farm, and factory.
Bottom: At a "bad farm" that has no riparian buffer or protective fencing, livestock wander freely into the stream and old cars rust on the bank.

Explorations and experiments

The Kingfisher Model has terrific potential for helping students refine their concepts of streams and of land use in riparian zones along stream floodplains. Students can experiment to discover the best management practices for maintaining or improving water quality and for controlling erosion, flooding, and other watershed problems. They can try to implement management ideas such as detention and retention facilities without destroying the natural functions of the stream or turning it into an urban water conveyance. They can have fun while manipulating the stream with dams and diversions. In doing so, students can also learn about the formation and operation of cut and depositional banks, of deltas, gravel beds, rapids, waterfalls, oxbows, riffles, and pools. They can simulate ponds and examine the connection between the water table and the level of the stream or reservoir above the dam. They can bring in their own toys and objects to use in creating new model stream projects.

Making a model

Models similar to the one at the Kingfisher Centre can be built on school grounds, and even in classrooms. Outdoors, an optimal size for a stream model is about 5 to 7 meters long (15 to 20 feet) and about 1 meter (3 feet) wide, with a slope or drop in elevation of about 1 to 1.5 meters (3 to 4 feet). A basic model can be built by simply running a garden hose down an embankment, or by making a large sloping sandbox bordered by logs, cement parking-lot car stops, or donated lumber. Grow cloth or weed fabric placed under the sand stops the sand from migrating and the weeds from growing in the sandbox. For the water supply, use an ordinary garden hose with a hose bib to control the flow. Indoors, a model can be built by laying construction-grade plastic sheeting over a frame of boards and filling the area with sand on a 20-degree pitch. Use your imagination and innovation to adapt building materials, and invite parents to give advice and assistance in constructing the model stream.

The Kingfisher Model has many possibilities for making learning authentic and experiential. It has been used as an interactive stream model with participants ranging from pre-schoolers who just need exploratory time to graduate students in environmental education who found that the model helped them to conceptualize the workings of larger stream watersheds that they were studying.

Megan McNairn

A "good farm" has protective fencing to keep livestock out of the stream.

Excited by the Kingfisher Model, many teachers who have attended summer institutes in environmental education at Simon Fraser University in Vancouver are now building model streams on their school grounds using garden hoses and sandboxes. Some have proposed that their towns install a similar model at a local water park so that students can experiment before engaging in studies of actual streams around their communities. At Florida Gulf Coast University in Fort Myers, the Family Resource Center is building an expanded Kingfisher-type model where children ranging in age from six months to five years can "mess about" in a learning mode. The model will include two miniature stream systems and a boardwalk through a forest.

Exploratory play with a model stream cannot replace idle hours spent beside natural local creeks. However, in urban areas where this childhood experience is now nearly extinct, a model can stimulate thinking and nurture the generation of questions and experiments while building children's sense of "streamness." ❧

William F. Hammond teaches ecology, interdisciplinary studies, and marine systems at Florida Gulf Coast University in Fort Myers, Florida.

The author thanks Neil Brookes and the volunteer staff of the Kingfisher Interpretive Centre Society whose work on the model stream was the inspiration for this article. They can be contacted at: Kingfisher Interpretive Centre Society, 2550 Mabel Lake Road, Enderby, BC V0E 1V5.

Resources

British Columbia Ministry of Environment, Lands, and Parks. *Stewardship of the Water of British Columbia.* Water Management Branch, 1993.

Fisheries and Oceans Canada, Salmon Enhancement Program. *The Stream Keepers' Handbook: A Practical Guide to Stream Care.* Salmonid Enhancement Program, 1994.

Friends of Environmental Education Society of Alberta (FEESA). *Adopt A Stream.* FEESA, 1993.

Leopold, Aldo. *A Sand County Almanac, With Essays on Conservation from Round River.* Random House, 1966.

Mitchell, M.K., and W.B. Stapp, *Field Manual for Water Quality Monitoring.* Thomson-Shore Printers, 1991.

Oregon Department of Fish and Wildlife. *The Stream Scene: Watersheds, Wildlife and People.* Department of Fish and Wildlife, 1990.

Project WILD. *Project WILD K-12 Curriculum and Activity Guide,* available to participants in Project WILD workshops. In the U.S., contact Project WILD National Office, 5555 Morningside Drive, Suite 212, Houston, TX 77005 <www.projectwild.org>. In Canada, contact WILD Education, Canadian Wildlife Federation, 350 Michael Cowpland Drive, Kanata, ON K2M 2W1, <www.wildeducation.org>.

One Fish, Two Fish

An activity that builds analytical skills while introducing young children to basic concepts of population and resource management

by Michele Hoffman-Trotter

Grade levels: 1-4

Subject areas: mathematics, science

Key concepts: conservation, resource management, offspring, species, reproduction, survival, population, distribution

Skills: deductive reasoning, analysis, problem solving, data gathering

Location: indoors

Time: 30 minutes

Materials: For a class of 25 students, 50 small containers or plastic bags (2 per student), 25 red and 25 blue gummy fish candies, 375 white jellybeans; 3 buckets, 3 "fishing poles" with magnets at the end of the lines, 50 fish shapes cut from card stock (25 red and 25 blue), 50 paper clips

How do you explain fisheries resource management to young children? The easy answer is that you don't, but that is not to say that you can't try. Resource management guidelines, while often complex, are based on relatively simple principles, none of which is beyond the grasp of a young eager mind. For instance, even seven-year-old students comprehend that not all animals live for the same length of time, that most produce different numbers of offspring, and that certain animals are found in more places around the world than others. These simple concepts provide an approach to teaching about projected life expectancy, offspring viability, and distribution of species.

I have used the following activity to show students as young as Grade 1 how these three factors help to determine when, where, and how we fish, and why we must fish responsibly to ensure a future for the fish we like to eat.

Science begins with childlike curiosity and questions for which there may not be simple answers. Making the effort to help young students learn to think analytically is to nurture that curiosity, encourage the questions, and teach the keepers of our future the way to find answers.

Preparation:

1. For each child, place 1 red gummy fish and 5 white jellybeans into one container (or plastic bag), and place 1 blue gummy fish and 10 white jellybeans into another container.

2. Using red and blue card stock, cut 50 fish shapes, 25 red and 25 blue. Attach paper clips to the mouths of the fish.

Illustrations by Tom Goldsmith

3. Label the three buckets "Atlantic Ocean," "Pacific Ocean," and "Indian Ocean." Into the "Atlantic Ocean," place 13 red fish and 8 blue fish. Into the "Pacific Ocean," place 12 red fish and 7 blue fish. Into the "Indian Ocean," place 10 blue fish.

4. Make three fishing poles by tying strings to the ends of meter sticks or yardsticks (or find sticks outdoors). Attach magnets to the ends of the strings to represent hooks.

Procedure:

Introducing red fish and blue fish

1. Give each child one container with the red fish and one container with the blue fish. Make it clear *before* you begin handing them out that the children are not to eat them or to mix up the contents of the two containers.

2. Ask the children to look at what is inside each container and tell you what they find. Explain that the jellybeans are the red and blue fish's eggs, or offspring.

3. Ask the students which fish they would prefer to fish for if they had to fish for a living. Count the votes, write the counts on the board, and ask students why they prefer one fish over the other. Answers will vary, but at least one student is likely to point out that there are more blue fish than red fish. Use this opportunity to explain that when there are large numbers of a certain species, people often want to use it as a food source simply because it is plentiful.

Learning about offspring viability

4. Explain that not all the offspring will survive to become adult fish capable of reproducing. Ask the class if they can think of reasons that an egg might not survive to adulthood. You may need to coach young children for answers, such as by asking why they sometimes do not come to school on a school day ("I get sick."). Other answers to coach for are that a fish's home gets dirty with pollution, that fish get eaten, and that storms can kill fish.

Note: With older students, you might add concepts such as global warming, harvesting of certain species for producing pharmaceuticals, and so on. The reasons for fish stock declines are fairly limitless and could be a whole lesson on their own.

5. Explain that, although the blue fish lay 10 eggs each year, only 6 offspring on average survive to adulthood; and of the 5 red fish eggs, 4 are likely to become adults. At this point, tell the children that they can eat the number of "fish eggs" that are not likely to survive: from the blue fish container, they can eat 4 jellybeans, and from the red fish container, they can eat 1 jellybean.

6. Ask the students again which fish they would prefer to fish for and mark these results on the board (as in Step 3 above).

Learning about life expectancy

Note: This topic will be more difficult conceptually for young students because not all of them will understand what death is. Therefore, this section has to be treated carefully. Warm-up questions could include:

☺ Were all of you born on the same day. No? So are you all exactly the same age?

☺ Are you the same age as your parents? as your brothers and sisters?

7. Explain that, unless they are caught or die in some other way, red fish can live for 12 years, while blue fish can live for only 8 years.

8. Ask the students if they think it makes a difference that one fish lives longer than the other, and why. You may want to explain that, when fish live longer, they have more time to produce offspring.

9. Following this discussion, ask the students which fish they would prefer to fish for and mark the results on the board. Explain that fish that live longer often have a larger population (but there are no guarantees).

Learning about distribution of species

10. Divide the class into three groups and assign each group to an ocean bucket.

11. Give each group one fishing pole and ask them to take turns fishing until their bucket (ocean) is empty.

12. Ask the groups to count how many blue fish and how many red fish they caught. Mark the numbers on the board. (They should correspond to the numbers you put in each bucket: Atlantic Ocean, 13 red fish and 8 blue fish; Pacific Ocean, 12 red fish and 7 blue fish; Indian Ocean, 10 blue fish.)

13. Ask the students which fish they would want to fish for and mark the votes on the board.

14. Now ask a volunteer to count all of the red fish found in all three oceans and another volunteer to count all the blue fish caught in all three oceans. (The total number of each should be 25.)

15. Ask the class by a show of hands who is surprised that the number of red fish is the same as the number blue fish and, if so, why. Explain that, because of the way the fish are distributed, it might seem that one fish is more abundant than another when it is not. The blue fish lives in all three oceans and the red fish lives in only two, but their worldwide populations are the same.

16. Ask students why they think all types of fish are not found in all places.

Discussion:

Now take a closer look at the data. Even though 6 blue fish survive to adulthood but only 4 red fish survive, their population numbers are equal. If each red fish lives for 12 years and has the maximum 4 offspring each year of its life, 48 red fish will be added to the population. Likewise, if each blue fish lives for 8 years and each year produces 6 offspring, then 48 blue fish will be added to its population. This simplification of population dynamics does not take into account exponential growth in populations, which would be a difficult concept for young students. However, it serves to introduce one of the major factors (population numbers) that resource managers must consider when setting fishing quotas.

Again review the distribution of fish in the three oceans. There were blue fish in all three oceans but red fish in only two, so that it appeared that there were more blue fish to catch. However, the totals were the same across the three oceans, 25 of each species.

Conclude the activity by asking how many students voted to fish for the same fish every time, and ask those who changed their minds why they did so. One reason for designing an activity that seems so tricky is to show that even scientists can make mistakes by assuming certain things about nature. You could explain that some things warrant very careful analysis before any conclusion can be reached, no matter how simple the data may seem.

Extensions and adaptations:

⚅ As an extension, tell students this true story of the impacts of overfishing:

The gemfish, which lives off the coast of Australia, is a beautiful deep-sea fish approximately 1.2 meters (4 feet) long. For a long time people did not have the ability to fish at extreme depths. But once commercial deep-sea fishing was possible, species such as gemfish became available in markets. When people discovered that gemfish are very delicious, they began demanding more of them, and more and more gemfish were caught. At first gemfish were readily caught, but there was a problem. Nobody knew very much about their reproductive processes because their bodies were biologically different from those of fish living in shallower water. People had been catching and eating gemfish for 10 years before scientists finally learned anything of significance about their biology. By then, almost all the gemfish were gone. In 1993, all fishing of gemfish was stopped and remained so until 1996. By then, scientists had gathered information to help the fishing community develop a plan to sustain the gemfish populations. There is hope that, because of careful management, gemfish populations may be restored.

⚅ Adapt the activity for older students by applying it to a real species and preparing a worksheet that includes the following information: the animal's average life span, the average number of offspring produced each year, and its geographic distribution. A good place to gather such information is at the website of the National Marine Fisheries Service, <www.nmfs.noaa.gov/>. ✻

Michele Hoffman-Trotter teaches oceanography and other sciences at Columbia College in Chicago, teaches scuba diving at Scuba Systems in Skokie, Illinois, and is a recent graduate of DePaul University College of Law.

Resources

Ashworth, William. *The Late, Great Lakes: An Environmental History.* Wayne State University Press, 1987. This book is a wonderful resource on environmental threats to Great Lakes species and efforts to avert them. It may inspire lesson planning ideas.

Habitat Mediacan. *Empty Oceans Empty Nets* (video). This film provides a brutally truthful view of the current status of fisheries, best used as a reference for teachers. Available at <www.habitatmedia.org> under Projects.

Marine Fish Conservation Network <www.conservefish.org>. A coalition of national and regional environmental organizations, commercial and recreational fishing groups, aquaria, and marine science groups dedicated to conserving marine fish and promoting their long-term sustainability. The website provides information on current issues and how to get involved.

Pacific Fishery Management Council <www.pcouncil.org/>. The website has excellent fact sheets about species of fish, identifies legal matters, and provides a good example of how a protection agency manages its business.

Western Australia Fisheries <www.sifh.wa.gov.au>. The website has a special section for children that includes virtual dives to identify fish species (click on Fishtales in right margin).

Investigating Ocean Pollution

Experiments demonstrating why plastics and petroleum are two of the worst pollutants of the world's oceans

by Sue LeBeau

Grade levels: 3-5

Subject areas: science, social students, reading, writing

Key concepts: ocean pollution, recyclable plastics, non-biodegradable materials, harmful effects of oil spills, animal protection

Skills: reading, writing, research, observation, critical thinking, drawing conclusions

Location: indoors or outdoors

Time: 2 to 3 weeks

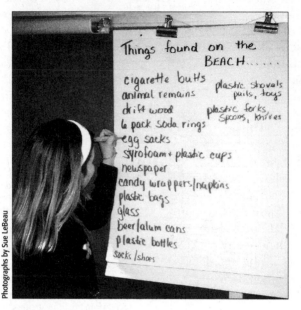

Photographs by Sue LeBeau

Seen from space, Earth's continents are islands completely surrounded by ocean. From that vantage point, it is clear to see that we live not so much on an earth planet as on a water planet. Covering 71 percent of the Earth's surface, the oceans and are the life force of the planet, and, without a doubt, the future of all living things is linked to their fate.

Living in a seaside community on the Atlantic Ocean, my Grade 5 students are keenly aware of some of the pollution problems that plague not only the Atlantic, but all oceans and waterways. In an effort to increase our awareness of the causes and effects of these problems, we embarked on a study of two major forms of ocean pollution: plastics and oil. These are just a few of the many activities that a teacher can use to help students recognize our all-important role in ensuring the future well-being of the world's oceans.

Plastic: A floating menace

Our readings informed us that plastic pollution of the ocean has serious and sometimes fatal consequences for marine animals, and so we began our study by learning more about this ubiquitous material. Working in groups, the students listed the types of trash they had seen wash up on the ocean shore. They then speculated on where it had come from and its effects on marine

wildlife and habitat. Most students listed plastic, in one form or another, as the number one material found at the shoreline... and right they were!

More than half of the trash that washes up on beaches is plastic, according to the Center for Marine Conservation. Many of these plastics will not break down for hundreds of years. Scientists estimate that plastics are killing as many as a million seabirds and more than 100,000 sea mammals each year. Plastics have been found in the stomachs of manatees, fish, birds, dolphins, and whales. Leatherback turtles frequently mistake plastic bags floating in the sea for one of their favorite foods, jellyfish. As plastic accumulates in their intestines, the animals slowly starve.

Keeping plastics journals

Students started to keep a "plastics journal" in which they recorded all the plastic they threw away daily, both at home and at school. After several days, they were shocked to realize just how much of it they discard each day.

Separating plastics

To become aware of which plastic items are easier to recycle than others, we separated plastics according to the code numbers inside the "recycle" triangle stamped on the containers. Students learned that codes 1 through 6 stand for six different plastic resins, while containers marked 7 are made of a mixture of plastics. The lower the number, the more easily the plastic can be recycled. Students were very interested in these codes and we soon had a separated and coded collection of various types of plastic.

Testing buoyancy and biodegradability

Throughout our discussions, I reminded students that plastics are designed to last and do not break down readily. Even so-called biodegradable plastics do not

148

Environmental Issues

necessarily break down completely, but instead disintegrate into plastic particles.

To test the ocean-going behavior and degradability of plastics and other materials commonly found in beach trash, students gathered aluminum cans, cardboard boxes, and numerous plastics such as wrappers, bottles, yogurt containers, six-pack rings, and shopping bags. They first predicted whether or not their items would sink or float, and then put the items to the test by dropping them into a large container of ocean water. Predictions and results were recorded, compared, and discussed. (In doing this experiment, keep in mind that salt water is denser than fresh water, making floating objects more buoyant. If ocean water is unavailable, mix one tablespoon of salt per liter of tap water to simulate ocean conditions. It may be necessary to cut up some of the larger pieces of trash.)

Next, students tested the items for their ability to decay by burying them in large coffee cans filled with salt water or sand. After two weeks, students checked the items and observed and recorded any changes. Upon their request, we continued to bury and check the items every two weeks. We had previously done this activity with organic waste such as fruit peels and coffee grounds, which broke down relatively quickly. It was an interesting comparison for the students to see that the plastics didn't break down at all.

As a final activity, we drew up a class list of ways to reduce the amount of plastic we use, as well as some alternatives to plastic containers and products.

Oil: A slick killer

Another topic that continually emerged during our study of the ocean is the harmful effect of oil spills on ocean life. We discussed how people all over the world depend on oil for heating homes, fueling vehicles, and making plastics, to name only a few uses. The more oil we use, the more wells we need to drill, both on land and under the ocean, and the more frequently we transport oil. Both ocean drilling and ocean transport increase the likelihood that oil will be leaked, spilled, or dumped into the ocean.

We read two very thought-provoking and informative books as we began our study of oil spills. In *Spill! The Story of the Exxon Valdez*, author Terry Carr recounts how the Exxon Valdez ran aground in 1989 off Prince William Sound in Alaska and lost 245,000 barrels of oil. *Prince William* by Gloria Rand tells the story of a young girl who witnesses volunteers working to wash beaches, contain the oil slick, and rescue wildlife, and who helps a baby seal after it has been rescued from the oil spill. Both books were stepping stones to the following simulation, which demonstrates that oil spills are almost impossible to clean up.

Oil spill simulation

In this activity, students create and then try to clean up an oil spill near a simulated ocean shore.

Materials: For each simulation (one per group of students), one large aluminum cooking pan, 500 ml (2 cups) vegetable oil, 3-4 teaspoons of black powdered tempera paint, glass jar, approximately 750 ml (3 cups) sand, 3 straws, string, paper towels, spoons, cups, water

Preparation: Prepare a quantity of imitation "crude oil" by mixing in a glass jar 6 to 8 teaspoons of black tempera paint powder per liter of vegetable oil. Shake well to mix. You will need 500 ml (2 cups) of this mixture for each simulation.

Procedure:
1. Have students form a slope of sand at one end of a large aluminum cooking pan to simulate an ocean shore.

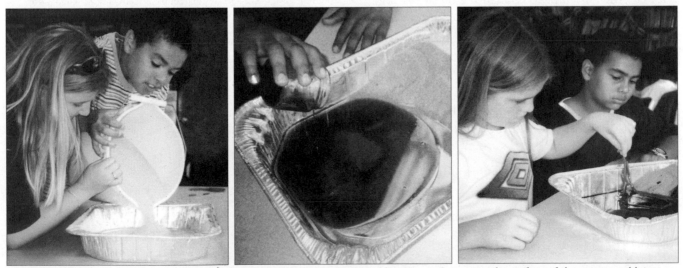

This simulation of an oil spill at sea demonstrates how quickly oil is distributed by wave action across the surface of the ocean and how difficult it is to clean up. L to R: Building a sandy shore; pouring in pigmented vegetable oil; containing the spill with a boom.

2. Partially fill the pans with water, to a level of about 2.5 centimeters (1 inch) up the sandy "beach."

3. Have students pour approximately 500 ml (2 cups) of imitation crude oil into the water near the sandy beach.

4. Ask students to rock the pans back and forth gently to produce waves and observe the behavior of the oil. Students should quickly realize that the oil forms slicks that travel on the surface of the water.

5. Discuss the ways by which oil that is spilled at sea can be carried to beaches (e.g., by currents, tides, and waves). Explain that, eventually, much of the oil spilled far out at sea congeals to forms tar balls, and that these often wash ashore, ruining shorelines and destroying plant and animal life.

6. Ask students to experiment with different tools to try to find the best way to clean up the oil, such as by sponging it with paper towels or skimming it from the surface of the water using spoons or cups. Introduce the concept of an oil boom, which is a tool used to contain an oil spill by creating a physical barrier around the oil on the surface of the water. Have students make their own booms by cutting three plastic straws in half, inserting a string through the straw halves, and tying the ends of the string together to close the boom. They can then attempt to contain the oil by placing the boom on the water so that it encircles the oil slick.

7. After students have experimented with a variety of tools and techniques, discuss which methods, if any, were successful in removing the oil.

In performing this activity, it did not take long for my students to discover that none of the tools used to scoop out or absorb the spilled oil was very useful.

Students learn to distinguish different types of plastic by sorting materials according to their recycling codes.

The oil booms did a good job of containing the oil, but removing it was still a complex, time-consuming, and messy procedure. We discussed how such oil slicks threaten fish, waterfowl, and other animals that live or breathe at the water's surface. The students soon realized that it would be much better to prevent oil spills in the first place than to clean up after oil spills!

Sue LeBeau teaches fifth grade at West End School in Long Branch, New Jersey, and is a regional editor of Green Teacher *magazine.*

References

Carr, Terry. *Spill! The Story of the Exxon Valdez.* Franklin Watts, 1991.

Center for Marine Conservation (now Ocean Conservancy). "Plastics in the Ocean: More Than a Litter Problem." Report prepared for the Environmental Protection Agency, 1987.

Dalferes, Katie, Brittany Schilling, and Clare Tupper. "Saving Polluterville: An Ocean Pollution Investigation." WebQuest for students, on-line at <http://oncampus.richmond.edu/academics/education/projects/webquests/oceans/>.

Dunphe, Mary Beth, Marian Ferrick, and Kathleen Markt. "Oceans in Peril." WebQuest for Grade 5 students, on-line at <http://www.sandwich.k12.ma.us/webquest/oceans5/>.

Feldman, Gene Carl. "Oil Pollution" (script of "Ocean Planet," a 1995 Smithsonian Institution exhibition). On-line January 24, 2005 at <http://seawifs.gsfc.nasa.gov/OCEAN_PLANET/HTML/peril_oil_pollution.html>.

Ford, Brent A., and P. Sean Smith. *Project Earth Science: Physical Oceanography.* National Science Teachers' Association, 1995.

Ingrum, Peyri. "The Ocean's in Trouble." WebQuest for Grades 4-6, on-line at <http://projects.edtech.sandi.net/grant/oceanpollution/>.

Oceana <http://www.oceana.org/>. This website has useful information pertaining to ocean pollution.

Oceanlink, "Ask-a-Scientist: Marine Pollution." On-line at <http://oceanlink.island.net/ask/pollution.html>.

Oceanlink. "World Oil Pollution: Causes, Prevention, and Clean Up." On-line at <http://oceanlink.island.net/oceanmatters/oil%20pollution.html>

Rand, Gloria. *Prince William.* Henry Holt and Company, 1992.

Michael Castagnaro

Building Community

Questing: Discovering Community Treasures

Questing in Beaver Meadows, Norwich, Vermont.

by Steven Glazer

Grade levels: 3-8

Subject areas: social studies, language arts, visual arts

Key concepts: interrelationship between local environment and community heritage; community continuity and change

Skills: observation, research, drawing, using and making maps, using primary and secondary resources, gathering oral history, writing

Location: indoors and outdoors

Time: 10 to 12 lessons, undertaken intensively over a 2-week period or spread over 4 to 8 weeks

asking in brilliant autumn sunshine, two people meander along a country road in Norwich, Vermont. They are reading and following verse clues on a hand-drawn map:

Walk southeast away from the chapel.
Where a house once stood now find trees of apple.
There was a mill here where cider was pressed.
Walk up to the corner, then take a rest.

A few towns northwest, in Chelsea, children race ahead of their parents, following a rhyming clue in their hunt for a letter of the alphabet that can be seen on a public building:

On the South Common look up and you will see
A golden dome shining like the sun,
Making us the Shiretown, a special one.
Judicial sessions keep us so safe and free.

Look below the dome and find a letter that appears in
all three words: Write it here: ___

What are all these people doing? They're out Questing!

Questing began 150 years ago when an Englishman named James Perrot hid a jar containing his calling card at Cranmere Pool in Dartmoor. Other walkers completing the trek out to the pool — and lingering long enough to find his hidden "treasure box" — were rewarded with an invitation to visit and exchange pleasantries with Mr. Perrot. Over the ensuing century and a half, hidden treasure boxes began popping up all over

Dartmoor. The tradition became known as "letterboxing" and evolved to include riddle-like verse clues, hand-drawn maps, sign-in books, and unique, site-specific hand-carved rubber stamps. Today, thousands of boxes are hidden in and around Dartmoor, and thousands of people hunt for them, following rhyming clues and discovering many stories about this fascinating place.

Educator David Sobel witnessed this unique Dartmoor phenomenon while visiting southern England in 1987. He brought the letterboxing idea back to New England, where he helped to transform it into Questing, a community-based, sense-of-place education program. Student and community groups across Vermont and New Hampshire's Upper Valley region have created more than 175 distinct Quests. They lead to favorite trees, hilltop overlooks, forgotten cemeteries, historic villages, old mill sites, forests, wetlands, and more.[1]

For each Quest, students create verse clues and hand-drawn maps to guide Questers, and hidden "treasure" boxes that contain scrapbooks, sign-in books, and rubber stamps. Children, families, and adults alike search for the hidden boxes as they explore the community's landscape and heritage. Families head out Questing on holiday outings and for children's birthday parties; homeschoolers, daycare programs, and public schools use Quests as educational field trips; local adults and visiting tourists enjoy Questing as well. All of these people benefit — and learn — from the work of the students.

James E. Sheridan

Fourth grade class working on The Beal Cemetery Quest in Lyme, New Hampshire.

How Questing works

"Wisdom sits in places," writes anthropologist Keith Basso, quoting an Apache elder. But what does this mean? Places, it seems to me, are physical spaces — experiential environments — where specific elements are gathered, where particular things have happened and traces linger.

No matter where you live, your community is full of interesting places. As you begin to investigate, you will discover that each place itself consists of smaller elements that nest together into larger discernable patterns, and that these patterns reveal processes: the stories of your community. The stories might be geological or geographical — stories of human movement and settlement, of distinctive neighborhoods or industries, of native flora and fauna. For example, here is a natural depression where rainwater and snowmelt collect and amphibians lay their eggs ... a *vernal pool*. Another example: All the buildings in this village are made of brick and date from the 1830s and 1840s; pick up a handful of earth from that hillside; what does it feel like? This is clay ... and this was our community's *brickyard*.

Every place contains such clues to its the natural and human history, and, as you discover them, they begin to fit together. Through fieldwork and community research, the stories of our places can be mapped and shared. For example, while they were conducting fieldwork, fourth-grade students in Lyme, New Hampshire, found the gravestones of Abigail and Samuel Hovey in the cemetery. Researching these names in *Patterns and Pieces*, a history of the town, the students learned that the Hoveys moved to Lyme in 1772. In examining a variety of community maps spanning two centuries, the students found that there was once a Hovey Island, and they were able to track the changes in both the name and size of the island over time. They transformed what they learned into the following verse and shared it through a Quest:

Abigail and Samuel Hovey came here, too.
They moved to Lyme in 1772.
There was a "Hovey Island" in the Connecticut River,
It's now known as "Grant's" but is smaller, just a sliver. *

*When it was built, the Wilder Dam raised the Connecticut River 14 feet and Hovey Island shrank.

Studying and building community

On the surface, a Quest seems fairly straightforward: rhyming clues, a hand-drawn map, and a hidden treasure box. But that's just the tip of the iceberg. Beneath the fun is a program that teaches community history and fosters a sense of place. Quests focus on three things: (1) mapping the cultural and/or natural assets of our communities — our special places; (2) teaching local history in an integrated, multi-sensory, and experiential way; and (3) deepening community interrelationships: between children and adults, schools and communities, newcomers and old-timers, and among the various members of the community.

In northern New England, exploring our villages opens doorways for studying local history and community heritage, and the relationship between local stories and larger, national ones of immigration, movement and settlement, technology, and transportation. Other groups have used Quests to study trees, forests, wetlands, beaver ponds, and vernal pools. Almost any place — and any story — can be studied, mapped, and shared using the Questing process.

Vital Communities

Maps and verse clues lead Questers on tours of discovery.

While Quests can be designed and adapted to explore a wide variety of places, what follows is a brief overview of a neighborhood or Village Quest.

1. Preparing for a Quest

Before you begin working with your students, try to pay a bit more attention to *your* surroundings. Look at a contemporary topographical map of your community. Follow a few indirect routes to school. As you travel, look for clues about the past: older buildings, agricultural buildings, buildings set close to the roads, cemeteries, schoolhouses, mill buildings or factories, and the like. See if you can discover patterns, in building materials, for example, or in architectural style.

Next, try to find at least one historical map of your town, city, or village. In examining the old map alongside a recent one, you will inevitably make comparisons between what once *was* (or seemed so) and what now *is* (or appears to be). An older town map, for example, may feature up to three dozen one-room schoolhouses instead of the single public school complex that is in the town today. Looking at maps of the same place from two different time periods raises many questions and launches further inquiry: Just what is the "Poor Farm" or a "Tannery?" Is "Cole Hill" named for the Cole family? Who were the Coles? When did they live? When did the railroad first come to town? What effect did it have?

Look for a history of your community in your local library. My tendency is to open such a book at random and meander until I discover a story that capti-

Laminated section of an historical map.

vates me. Then, eager to learn more, I start back at the beginning, while simultaneously plowing through as many parallel sources as I can find. This "grazing" process will help you begin to link specific locations with significant community events or stories.

Finally, if your community has a village museum or historical society, arrange to visit it. Ask for a guided tour focusing on the different primary and secondary sources available. If possible, walk through one or more of your neighborhoods with a long-time resident.

What you are doing at this stage is beginning to Quest for yourself; you are learning what resources are available to help you with your project — potential partners, field trips, source materials — and you are becoming inspired, breathing in the spirit of *your* place.

2. Learning to see villages

Make a ledger-sized (11-by-17-inch) photocopy of an old map of your community or town. (F.W. Beers & Company mapped most of our region's towns during the period from 1865 to 1875.) Laminate the photocopy, and then cut it into as many pieces as you have students (see example). Give one map piece to each and ask the students to examine their piece and consider what it is they are looking at. Then, stimulate discovery by asking and answering questions together, as in the following example:

What are we looking at? *A map.*
Of what? *Of our town.*
How do you know? *I recognize ….*
Does anyone else see that? What are some things that you notice on your piece? *I see a ….*
Can anyone else find this? How many of you have a school on your piece? *(Count the raised hands.)*

Keep on asking questions, helping students learn how to read maps, decipher symbols, work with map keys, and recognize what their community used to look like. Encourage the students to teach each other how to identify the different features. What does a brook look like on the map? *A brook is a single line.* So how does a road appear on the map? *A road is a double line.* And the flattened sea urchin? *Oh, that's a hill!*

When you feel that you have exhausted the possibilities, invite the students to put the map together … in silence. Then, hand each student a ledger-sized copy of the map of the community — the same map they have just assembled from their pieces. After having them consider the map — the "big picture" — in silence for a few minutes, brainstorm together a list of key features (e.g., rivers, schoolhouses, roads, bridges) that they would like to hunt for. Then have them hunt for the key natural and cultural features of the community and color code them using colored pencils or highlighters.

3. Investigating your village

Use a photocopier to enlarge one section of your community map. Focus on a single village or neighborhood so that part of the map fills one side of a legal-sized (8½-by-14-inch) or ledger-sized sheet of paper. In Vermont and New Hampshire, many of our villages are more like intersections, featuring, perhaps, a church, an old school house, a general store and/or post office, a cemetery, a bridge or two, and a cluster of houses. For your Quest, a neighborhood or an area of a couple of blocks (or a few hundred square meters) should provide more than enough information.

The next step is to consider closely one part of town and discover how it has changed over time. Take a field trip out to that section of town and go for a walk. As you begin your exploration, help the students orient themselves both to their surroundings and to their maps. Which direction is north? Who can find the river on the map? Some students will struggle more than others, but each one, in turn, will have a moment of realization as he or she becomes oriented and begins to make connections. Be sure to ask students to color code and annotate their map as you explore, noting what is still there, what has disappeared, and what seems to be new. Ask them to make concrete observations ("This house has four columns.") and record field notes ("The 1877 map shows a house labeled 'Cook' on the corner, but today there is no building on the corner — only poplar trees.") Challenge them to think about *what* has changed, and then discuss *why* things might have changed.

The Cornish Flat Baptist Church and Meeting House, drawn by students in Ros Seidel's third grade class, Cornish, New Hampshire.

4. Drawing your village

Now that you have conducted an initial site exploration, you can begin to "adopt" your place. Break the class into smaller groups of two to three students. Each group can focus on a single element of the village, a house or shop, for example. Have the students make elevation drawings (e.g., of store fronts) or detailed drawings (e.g., of a sign, a doorway, or other architectural element) and write prose descriptions of their site. Provide the students with pencils (with erasers) and five-by-seven-inch index cards to work with so that all drawings will end up being similar in size. This consistency will be important when these drawings are incorporated into the Quest map. Students might also take digital photographs of their site so that they can continue to refine their drawings back in the classroom or at home.

Time spent drawing allows students to let their attention linger, patterns to emerge, and personal experiences to manifest. Drawing also encourages students to develop a bond with the site and a much deeper level of investment in the research phase. When students look back and forth, again and again, from hand to paper to place, a certain level of intimacy and attachment begins to arise.

5. Mapping your village

Once the preliminary sketches are complete, invite students to refine their drawings and then draw over them in ink (doing so will help darken the drawings to improve photocopy reproduction). When the drawings are complete, sit together in a circle, and create a map of your village in the open space on the floor. Ask students to place "landmark" elements first, to define the space. You might use construction paper for hills, masking tape to mark roads, yarn or tape for brooks. After the setting is roughed out, begin adding the buildings — the students' drawings — one at a time. As they work and learn together, the students might need to move elements of the map.

When all of the buildings are on the floor, ask the students these important questions: Is this map complete? What else might we need to add so that this map *really* represents our place? Brainstorm a list, which might include trees, plantings, stop signs, fire hydrants, benches, people, cars, mountains, rivers, and color.

If you have time, you may choose to go back into the field and make additional drawings, or have students draw from memory.

Re-size the polished drawings using a photocopier or scanner, and then create a "final" map by gluing the reduced images onto a large sheet of paper. Typically, students' drawings will be reduced to perhaps 4 by 5 centimeters (1½ by 2 inches) and then glued onto a ledger-sized sheet of paper. The reduced drawings can also be used to create a decorative border around the edge of the map.

Quests deepen relationships between school and community and provide meaningful ways for children and elders to interact.

Providing a few leading questions helps the students begin to use the source materials without being overwhelmed by their sheer size (or unfamiliar typefaces). Later, when the students visit the historical society or other resource, place the source materials at different stations and have small groups rotate through them. They will be learning to use a variety of source materials at the same time they are finding out more about the village in general and their chosen element in particular.

6. Researching your village

Now that your students have an overall familiarity with the setting and are more curious, particularly about a specific site element, the next step is to take them on a visit to your local library, town office, museum, or historical society to look through source materials that will help them learn more about their chosen village. Before taking the whole class, go with a student volunteer or two. In an hour or less, you'll discover many wonderful things: town charters and maps, county gazetteers and atlases, tax assessment books, cemetery records, old letters, ledgers, newspaper articles, and photographs.

Once you've found sufficient source materials, focus on the best four to six. For each one, develop a few leading questions that will encourage students to explore. For example: Using the account ledger from Thorton's Store, find the name of one person who shopped at the store in November 1920. What were three things that person bought, and how much did each item cost? Is Thorton's Store still open? If not, where do folks in town shop today? What might *you* want to buy at a store in November? Is that item (the thing you want today) in the 1920 ledger? If it is, what did that item cost in 1920? What does it cost today? If the item is not in the 1920 ledger, why isn't it?

Students' drawings of buildings and landmarks are arranged to create an illustrated map of the entire community.

7. Gathering oral history

Now that they have combined field experience and geo-spatial awareness with some research into primary and secondary sources, students can benefit from collecting oral history from community elders.

The importance of oral history — of connecting with living members of your community — cannot be overstated. It is a key ingredient in the creation of a Village Quest, for a number of reasons. First of all, people in the community know many stories and would love to share them. Every village is home to people who went to the one-room school, who shopped at the general store, who helped rebuild the bridge after the flood, and who foraged the brookside for fiddleheads. Equally important, bringing different groups of people together to do real work builds a sense of community. Unfortunately, fewer and fewer activities unite people of diverse age groups in our communities. Children gather in schools, adults gather in the workplace, and elders are perhaps alone — or gathered in an assisted living facility. Often, these groups do not have meaningful contact with each other. The oral history aspect of the Quest provides significant opportunities for different generations to interact in a new way — as allies and resources for each other. The elders' stories are

156

Quest Assessment

Quantitatively, the Quest unit allows teachers to meet curriculum standards while exploring local places and stories. Qualitatively, however, each Village Quest is a unique doorway and journey into another world. Sixth-grade students in Norwich, Vermont, for example, discovered a village that had been demolished to make way for an interstate highway. While most of these students pass over the Ledyard Bridge every day, not one of them had recognized that beneath the four-lane divided thoroughfare lay the rubble and cinders of a ghost town. But then they read in an editorial from the *Hanover Gazette* of April 20, 1967: "More than two hundred years of history was brought low this week when the village of old Lewiston was leveled by bulldozer and flame." Students subsequently watched a slide show of images of Lewiston: a covered bridge, Sargent's Coal, Raycroft's Grocery, H.P. Hood and Son's Creamery. Using an old fire insurance map and measuring tape, they staked out the "footprints" of buildings in this ghost town. Once oriented to the site, they were equipped to meet with community elders, ask questions about Lewiston's history, and take good notes. They used what they had learned to create clues, which their teacher assessed, as shown below:

Students' Clues

Face the Ledyard Bridge and to the left you will see
A grassy place where the Lewiston general store used to be.

Now this is a place for metal road signs

But there was a village store here once-upon-a-time.

Inside, the Raycrofts sold gum for one cent
It was here most of the local kids' money was spent!
There was also the post office with stamps on sale
Twice a day they delivered the US mail.
— *The Lewiston Quest*

This work might be assessed using a rubric as follows:

Teacher's Commentary

Evidence of source: 1913 fire insurance map

Evidence of field observation

Evidence of awareness of continuity and change

Evidence of oral history from community elders

Task-specific Rubric — Clues

Unacceptable	Weak	Adequate	Commendable	Exemplary
Writing lacks clarity, does not include a teaching or movement component, and neglects standard writing conventions and mechanics	Writing does not include a teaching or movement component *or* lacks proper use of grammar and mechanics	Writing is understandable, includes a teaching or movement component, *and* shows correct use of grammar and mechanics	Writing also includes vivid description or good historical information or vocabulary, *or* has excellent meter and flow	Writing features vivid description, good historical vocabulary, *and* has excellent meter and flow

passed on to the students, and the students pass on this knowledge to the community through the published Quest.

8. Writing the Quest

Now that students have completed their investigations, they can begin writing their Quest. First, ask the class questions like these: What is a natural starting point for our Quest? A good starting point will feature a place to park, a well-known or easily recognizable landmark. What is a natural ending point? The best place to end your Quest is at the site that best ends your story. It should be both a pleasant place to linger and a place where you can hide the treasure box so that it is safe from vandalism. If necessary, treasure boxes can be hosted in public locations, such as behind the front desk of an inn or in a coffee shop or store. Once you have determined the beginning and ending points of your Quest, the ideal route (or sequence of movements) leading to the most interesting sites will quickly emerge.

Now have the students — continuing to work in small groups — draft two sets of clues. The movement clues move or guide visitors from one spot to another. The teaching clues provide content knowledge.

Movement clue:
With your back to the porch walk past four trees.
When you reach the rock, stop if you please.
Look both ways before you cross.
Make a right turn so you don't get lost.

Teaching clue:

Leavitt's Inn opened in January of 1794.
Original stenciling is hidden behind the front door.
This once was the place for the stagecoach drop.
Between Boston and Montréal, people would stop.

Movement clues are, essentially, procedures — instructions for how to get from here to there. They can incorporate, in verse, the cardinal directions, body orientation (right and left), or observations (the four trees). The teaching clues synthesize students' field observations, their primary source research, and their oral history notes.

Group 1 will draft a movement clue that leads the Questers from point A to point B and a teaching clue about point B, Group 2 will compose a movement clue leading from point B to point C and a teaching clue about point C, and so forth. The final group determines the hiding place of the Quest box. Once groups have drafted movement and teaching clues, take the class out to test the work.

9. Completing the Quest materials

As your Quest project comes to a close, have students revise or complete all of the Quest materials. One group can type up and proofread the full set of clues; a second group can refine the map that the class created and design a compass rose to indicate north; another can determine the best layout for all of these elements on the finished Quest publication.

Handmade rubber stamps.

Other groups can compose thank-you letters to your community partners, create a sign-in guest book for the Quest treasure box, or create a project scrapbook. One student might carve a rubber stamp that symbolizes your village and will be placed (with an ink pad) in the treasure box.

10. Testing and publishing your Quest

As a penultimate step, ask someone who has *not* participated in your project to test the Quest to make sure that it works. Have students follow behind, watching the tester carefully. Ask them to note where and how the Quest does not work and, in the field or back in the classroom, revise the clues as necessary. Finally, publish your Quest: send a copy home with each student, submit it to the school newspaper, or ask your school principal to include it in the weekly letter home. Many local daily or weekly papers will be happy to publish your Quest.

The key points

When Questing, students are at the center of a web of relationships:

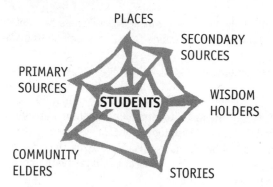

Within this context, Questing can deepen students' knowledge of the community's geography, local history, native flora and fauna, landscape, and assets. Questing can build bridges between schools and communities, youth and elders, newcomers and natives, the past and the present, strengthening the bonds between people and places. Finally, Questing helps us discover community treasures — the richness of the place we live. ☙

Steven Glazer coordinates the Valley Quest program of Vital Communities in White River Junction, Vermont. He is the co-author, with Delia Clark, of Questing: A Guide to Creating Community Treasure Hunts, *and the editor of* Valley Quest: 89 Treasure Hunts in the Upper Valley, Valley Quest II: 75 More Treasure Hunts in the Upper Valley, *and* The Heart of Learning: Spirituality in Education.

A fuller presentation of the Village Quest model appears in *Questing:A Guide to Creating Community Treasure Hunts* by Delia Clark and Steven Glazer (University Press of New England, 2004). The Village Quest model was developed by Valley Quest staff in partnership with Marguerite Ames of the Marion Cross School in Norwich, Vermont. Learn more about Valley Quest by visiting the Vital Communities website at <www.vitalcommunities.org>.

Note

[1] These Quests have been collected and published in Steven Glazer's books *Valley Quest: 89 Treasure Hunts in the Upper Valley* (Valley Quest Publications, 2001) and *Valley Quest II: 75 More Treasure Hunts in the Upper Valley* (Valley Quest Publications, 2004).

Asphalt Artisans:
Creating a Community Eco-map

Students inventoried the special features of their neighborhood and transformed their school environment with a colorful playground map

Grade 6 students transferring their eco-count art to the street template.

by Paul Fieldhouse and Lisa Bunkowsky

Grade levels: K-8

Subject areas: social studies, science

Key concepts: understanding community, mapping

Skills: observation, map making, counting, painting

Location: outdoors

Time: eco-count throughout the year; map painting in spring

indsor School is a small community school located in Winnipeg, Manitoba. For some years the school has run a project known as "Windsor Green" that is designed to enhance the environment surrounding the school as well as provide a resource for taking the curriculum outdoors. In 1998 Windsor School embraced the principles and goals of the inter-national Healthy Schools movement,[1] including a commitment to student-led decision-making. These twin initiatives provided the foundation and guiding principles for a community mapping project that became known as the eco-count.

The eco-count was conceived of as a simple, innovative, and enjoyable way for students to learn more about the place where they live by looking closely at their local environment. We wanted to create a tangible connection to the urban ecology through a dynamic and participatory process. We did this by having students explore and create representations of their neighborhood in a two-phase process carried out over a school year. In the first phase, students worked together to develop inventories and maps of environmental features of the local neighborhood. The students then used this data as a basis for creating a large community map and educational game that they painted directly onto the school playground. The project involved the entire student body, as well as teachers, parents, and other volunteers, and incorporated curriculum topics from math, language arts, social studies, and art.

Project goals

The main goals of the project were to promote learning about the local environment and urban ecology and to engage students and teachers in outdoor curriculum-related activities. In designing the project we also wanted to accomplish several other objectives. First, we wanted to involve the whole school community. Often students at different grade levels have limited opportunities to interact within the school setting. Having all students working together on a project is a way of enhancing the feeling of unity and connectedness within the school. Second, we wanted to enhance local community interest in school activities. Building strong school/community linkages has many positive implications for the school. Both the eco-count and map-paint-

The artist and parent volunteers creating a template of the community's streets.

ing phases of the project were highly visible and provided opportunities for talking to community residents. Third, we felt it was important to have a tangible product at the end of the project that would demonstrate students' accomplishments visually and serve as an ongoing reminder of their work. The nature and form of this product — a durable "green map" of the neighborhood — emerged as the project evolved.

Phase 1: The eco-count

Student participation and student-led decision making were key principles of the eco-count project. Windsor School has an ad hoc Healthy School Action Group comprising student representatives of Grades 1 to 6, teachers, and parent volunteers who help plan and implement projects. The concept of the eco-count was discussed in this group and then taken to each class. Classroom discussions generated further suggestions that student representatives brought back to the action group. Through this process, decisions were made to

use small-scale maps of the neighborhood to develop a series of eco-inventories. These eco-inventories would focus on the following five categories, which the students chose and defined:

- green environment: parks, trees, bush, riverbank, gardens, playgrounds
- built environment: dwellings, businesses, churches
- transportation environment: cars, buses, and other vehicles
- living environment: wildlife and pets
- litter and recycling

We obtained neighborhood maps from the municipal planning department. Choosing as small a scale as possible, we cut and pasted so that each city block fit onto a legal-sized (8½-by-14-inch) sheet of paper. Although a variety of features could have been preprinted on the maps, our maps showed simply the streets and lot outlines. To provide some consistency in mapping techniques we looked to the international Green Map System (GMS),[2] which was developed in 1995 as a flexible approach to creating local community maps with an environmental focus. GMS has designed an internationally standardized set of 125 ecological and cultural symbols, or map icons, that represent a wide range of environmental features such as recycling sites, special trees, and marine habitats. Our students selected a subset of map icons relevant to their neighborhood and purpose. These were printed from the GMS website, and a student and teacher reproduced them as small peel-off stickers that the students could use in mapping features of the neighborhood.

Approximately 150 students from Grades 1 through 6 participated in the eco-count. Students were assigned to mixed-grade groups to encourage class interaction, and went out twice into the community to collect information "on the ground." A teacher or parent volunteer led each group. On the first outing, the leader gave each student a legal-sized clipboard, a pencil, and a small-scale map of a designated area of the neighborhood, which showed main streets, back alleys, and parks. As the students moved through the neighborhood they filled in their maps with appropriate map icons and other written and graphic notations. On the second outing, the students had eco-inventory checklists for recording systematic counts of features such as trees, animals, and cars. Each group had an official student photographer who was to document the group's activities. Some groups chose to share this function among members. One group made a video recording of the outing. The sight of students busy in the community aroused the curiosity and interest of many local residents, creating spontaneous opportunities for conversations and explanations. Most residents were pleased and impressed to hear what the children were doing.

Once the inventories were complete, junior high students got involved in the project. As part of their social studies class, they sifted through and collated the wealth of information collected in the eco-count to produce a wall map of the community to be displayed in the school. However, the major use of the data came in the second phase of the project.

Phase 2: The playground map

Students were keen to present the information they had discovered in a visual and innovative way that would have some degree of permanence. Once again students brainstormed possibilities, taking into account criteria of location, availability of materials, and

Top: Younger students filling in sections of the streets in primary colors to create a game board. Bottom: Teachers Lisa Bunkowsky (left) and Val Mowez at the paint table.

Paul Fieldhouse

ease of implementation. The option they chose was to paint a community map on the asphalt surface of the playground. The map was also to function as a game giant board, with a pathway that players would follow as they responded to quiz questions. (See "Using the map as a game," next page).

We were fortunate in recruiting a local professional artist, Cameron Cross, to oversee this ambitious project. Cameron was experienced in working with large canvasses and, as a former schoolteacher, could relate well to students. He spent one week in the school, working with each class in turn to develop a map design and helping individual students produce draft artwork derived from their own eco-count data. This artwork took the form of drawings or paintings, done on large sheets of white paper, of community features such as specific animals, flowers, vehicles, and trees, as well as more abstract symbols such as a stylized sun. Later in the term, the artist returned for a second week to coordinate the playground painting.

Preparing the base map

The 9-by-11-meter (30-by-36-foot) playground area where the map was to be created was prepared by sweeping it clean. Then a base color wash of regular commercial oil paint was laid down. The next step was to mark an outline on the painted asphalt using a tape measure and chalk line. The map represented the actual street plan of the neighborhood, with the streets joined at the ends with loops so as to form a continuous track that could later be used as the pathway in the board game. The track was divided into a series of rectangles (also for use in the board game), and features such as the school and community club were outlined. Next, with the chalk lines as a guide, the street and building outlines were re-marked using black oil paint applied with long-handled paint rollers. The artist and some parent volunteers carried out these preliminary steps.

The finished map, measuring 9 by 11 meters (30 by 36 feet).

Painting the map

All 300 students from kindergarten to Grade 9 participated in the painting. Each class was assigned a particular area of the map to work on, and no more than two classes were painting at any one time. Younger children had the job of filling in the rectangles along the track in alternating primary colors, while older students painted the areas between the streets. Students taped their drawing paper to the asphalt and copied their designs on to the playground map.

Paint tables were set up to the side of the map area. Classroom teachers and parent volunteers were kept busy taping blueprints to the asphalt, mixing paints, replenishing supplies, coping with spills, and cleaning brushes — and students! For paint holders we used six-cup muffin tins, which worked reasonably well and were relatively cheap. A high school student came up with the useful technique of anchoring the tins by filling two or three of the muffin cups with small pebbles (an experiment using egg trays ended in disaster when the wind came up!). Keeping the paint supplies flowing and avoiding stepping on wet paint were two of the major challenges. We needed a lot more supplies than anticipated, and someone was always dashing off to obtain more of something that had run out. As the map progressed, we encountered another logistical problem: waiting for paint to dry meant that we had to extend the schedule and that fewer students could paint at one time. In four days the map was complete. The artist, together with a few high school volunteers, spent another half day painting over spills, redefining lines, and generally tidying up. Later the map was covered with a transparent anti-graffiti spray.

Using the map as a game

Because many students had expressed interest in using the eco-count data to create a game, we decided to incorporate this element into the map by making it function as a giant game board (recall that the streets were divided into rectangular sections painted in the primary colors). Quiz questions aimed at the Grade 2 and Grade 3 levels were devised in three categories: the school, the community, and the environment. To play, a class divides into teams, each team selecting one member to be its "game piece." The players start at one edge of the map and move along the streets on the roll of an oversized die. As they land on a rectangle, their team must answer a question from one of the three categories, depending on the color of the rectangle. A correct answer is rewarded with a further move along the track. While the game mechanism remains to be refined and game variations will be developed over time, the children have been using the map for their own impromptu games at recess.

Involvement in the project

As the project evolved, people chose different ways of participating in it. One teacher took overall responsibility for coordinating the project, including planning with the artist. Other teachers accompanied their students on the eco-count exercise and supervised them during map painting. In addition, they spent class time in preparing for the fieldwork and in follow-up activities. The parent project co-coordinator took responsibility for writing grant applications, producing the maps and icons used in the eco-count, and making publicity and media contacts. Another parent volunteer obtained maps and aerial photographs of the neighborhood and documented the project in photographs. Other parents volunteered to accompany classes on the eco-count and to assist with the map painting. The school principal supported the project and ensured that all parents were informed via newsletter announcements. He also provided bridging funds until external grants were received. The school caretaker was kept busy conducting the press and visitors to the school roof for photo opportunities! While older students approached the project with mixed attitudes, some became very involved — volunteering to help with tasks such as brush cleaning and with the final touch-up of the map. We realized afterward that it would have been useful to recruit some of these students earlier and to involve them in the planning as artist-aides.

The project succeeded on a number of levels. Through the eco-count, teachers became more aware of the possibilities for taking the curriculum outdoors and for using local resources. Involving all students in hands-on mixed-grade activities contributed to a sense of school identity and school spirit. The playground map, in visually enhancing the school grounds, has been a showcase for students' creativity and has attracted considerable community interest. Over the two years since its completion, it has held up fairly well despite some cracking of the asphalt from frost heave and some fading of the colors from the impact of thousands of feet. It has created a pride of ownership among the students, who have learned that they can make a difference in transforming their school environment.

Extending project opportunities

The eco-count concept could be modified or extended in many ways. For example, school/community links could be emphasized by following the school eco-count week with a weekend community eco-count and barbecue, held perhaps in association with a local community club. The local historical society could be invited to work with students to place historic markers throughout the neighborhood during the eco-count week. Older students might be challenged to produce audio maps of the neighborhood, documenting on tape the sounds of various community locations. ✐

Paul Fieldhouse is a health promotion specialist with Manitoba Health and Healthy Living and a parent volunteer at Windsor School in Winnipeg, Manitoba. Lisa Bunkowsky taught Grades 2 to 3 at Windsor School at the time of the project and is currently teaching at Dr. D.W. Penner School in Winnipeg.

Notes

[1] Healthy Schools is part of an international movement to promote health in school curricula and to ensure that schools are safe and healthy environments in which to learn and work. The movement is known variously as Health Schools, Health Promoting Schools, and Comprehensive School Health. Information and resources can be found at the Health Promoting Schools website <www.sofweb.vic.edu.au/hps/index.htm>, the Safe and Healthy Schools website <www.schoolfile.com/safehealthyschools>, or the Healthy Schools Network website <www.healthyschools.org/>.

[2] Green Map System is a nonprofit organization that promotes the creation of community maps featuring local culture and ecology. Tips on getting started, along with many examples of completed green maps, can be found at the Green Map System website <www.greenmap.com>.

Resources

Sobel, David. *Mapmaking with Children: Sense of Place Education for the Elementary Years.* Heinemann, 1998.

Thomson, Gareth, and Sue Arlidge. *Five Minute Field Trips: Teaching About Nature in Your Schoolyard.* Alberta Teachers Association, 2000. Available in PDF format at <www.cpawscalgary.org/education/pdf/5min-fieldtrips.pdf>.

Educating the Community: A Watershed Model Project

by C.S. Perryess

Grade levels: 3-5

Subject areas: science, social studies

Key concepts: watershed science, geology, geography

Skills: topography, framing, cement work, public speaking

Location: indoors and outdoors

Time: 3-4 weeks

It's a Friday evening at Monarch Grove Elementary on California's central coast. A few dozen parents and community members mill around in the third grade courtyard. With a bit of bravado, a young man stands before the crowd. "Hi. I'm Shane. I'm in sixth grade here at Monarch, and I'd like to thank you all for coming out to see our watershed model." He is poised and comfortable in front of the crowd. "We made it out of cement, so I'll just stand here on it." He steps up onto two conical green mountains on the far end of the model and addresses the adults.

Shane explains that he is standing on a scale model of the 19,600-hectare (48,400-acre) Morro Bay watershed, built by local kids and their parents. The base of the cement structure is roughly 4 by 4 meters (12 by 12 feet). Its highest peaks rise nearly one meter (three feet).

"How many of you know what a watershed is?" Shane pauses. The adults look to one another. They raise eyebrows. A man in the back shrugs. A half dozen squirming kids raise their hands to answer. "That's right," he says to a second grader up front, "a watershed sheds, just like a duck's feathers shed water. It also works like a shed in your backyard: it stores things. So, a watershed does two things. It stores water and it sheds it off. What you're looking at is a model of our watershed — all the land that drains through creeks to the Morro Bay estuary and out to the Pacific Ocean."

Shane then helps the crowd identify local landmarks. People point out Hollister Peak and Cuesta Ridge. They locate their favorite hiking spots: Bishop's Peak, the sand spit, and the Irish Hills. Shane points

out the Morros, or Seven Sisters, ancient volcanic plugs that march between the two valleys of the watershed. He names each of them, ending with the area's most photographed landmark, Morro Rock. Next, he steps off the model. "Let's say I spray some rain right here." A few people back up as he unrolls a garden hose and carefully sprays onto the green, cement hillside. "Notice. The rain goes down the hills into San Bernardo Creek, then flows into Chorro Creek, and out into...." Shane looks up hopefully. A few kids up front join him, saying, "the estuary."

He turns off the hose and moves near the highest mountains. "Now, if I spray some rain here at the very top of Cuesta Ridge some of the water flows into the headwaters of Chorro Creek, past the prison and the college, then out to the estuary. But what happens to the rain that falls on the other side of the ridge?"

He points to the water flowing over a painted blue stream, and then off the backside, onto the gravel path that surrounds the model. "See, that's the edge of our watershed, because right at the top of Cuesta Ridge, one raindrop can flow into the Morro Bay watershed, while one that falls right next to it could go down the other side and into Atascadero. From there it joins the Salinas River, and guess where that flows into the ocean?"

"Monterey?" somebody asks.

"Yes, over a hundred miles away!" Shane lugs the hose around the model, identifying all the streams by "raining" on them. He points out sub-watersheds and the southern and eastern boundaries of the watershed. He then introduces Maura, a third grader who also helped build the model.

Maura explains how important topsoil is to the local farmers and then sifts dirt onto their fields. She asks how many people in the crowd wash their cars. Hands go up.

"Great," she says. "Here's your car, and here's yours." She points out two adults and skips across the model to place two toy cars in the most populated areas. "You use soap on your cars, don't you?" She looks out at the group. "On your dishes you use soap to get rid of germs, 'cause you eat off 'em, right? So, do you eat off your cars?" Maura pauses and smiles.

Top: Fertilizing the fields with bright red drink crystals. Bottom: Rainfall on Los Osos Valley.

"Well, we'll put some soap on anyway." She squirts some soap on top of each car.

"Do you all like nice green lawns?" she asks. "We'll need some fertilizer." She shakes some powdered drink mix through the suburbs. "Oh, and let's not forget the golf courses — they need lots of fertilizer." She hops across the model. "And the farmers need fertilizer to grow the food we eat." She shakes a bit more on the farmlands. "And," she continues, "do any of you have dogs? Do you walk your dogs? And what do your dogs do on their walks?" There are a few throat-clearings, but no real response. Maura holds up a plastic bottle of cake sprinkles. "When dogs take walks, they poop!" She unscrews the lid of the bottle. "They poop over here, and they poop over there." She shakes sprinkles through the suburbs. "I bet you walk your dogs on the beach! I bet you walk them out on the sandspit, too, and out by Morro Rock." She bounds over the model, generously sprinkling as she goes.

She uses an eyedropper to squirt a little motor oil on the roads, and in an imagined empty lot where somebody pours his used oil instead of using the county's curbside oil recycling program. Next, she grabs the garden hose. "So," Maura asks, "where will that topsoil and the fertilizer go? Where will the motor oil and dog poop go when it rains?"

"The estuary," a few members of the audience say.

"The estuary!" she repeats. She smiles and showers her garden-hose rainstorm onto the hills. The creeks run red from the fertilizer, transporting suds, soil, and cake-sprinkle dog poops. Maura stops the storm and an ugly swirl of oil rises to the bay's surface. Topsoil settles, filling in the estuary, and a dirty stream of sudsy water flows out past Morro Rock to the sea.

"So," she says, putting down the hose. "Isn't that the bay where you like to kayak? Isn't that beach by the rock where you like to surf?" Heads nod. A little girl in the front row kneels to point out the dog poop lining the edges of the bay.

Maura looks very serious now. "What can we do to keep that from happening?" She leads the group in a discussion that starts with leaving the detergent in the kitchen and keeping our cars in good mechanical shape. She explains how washing our cars on the lawn will allow the runoff to percolate into the soil instead of draining down the driveway, out to the street, and down-hill to the estuary. The discussion moves to the possibility of driving our cars less, to fertilizing sparingly, and taking plastic bags along while walking the family dog. She even demonstrates the use of the plastic bags. Maura bows, accepts her applause, and yields the lumpy cement floor to a thin, intense boy.

"I'm Will. I'm in fourth grade, and I bet you think those farmers will be out of business soon if they keep losing their topsoil." Will launches into a lively discussion of riparian buffer zones, illustrated with soil-catching strips of fleece laid along the creek banks.

"See how the farmers keep their soil, now that I planted that buffer zone?" he asks, "And notice how only a little of the dirt gets into the stream. If I hadn't planted that buffer zone, where would all that soil end up?"

"The estuary!" the audience says.

He then walks over the Morros to point to a low-lying piece of land near the bay. "Anyone know what's here?" Will is pointing to Chorro Flats, farmland rife with flooding problems for years. Recently, local agencies have worked together to restore a portion of the farmland to flood plain. "When they broke the levee and let Chorro Creek meander through this field," he explains, "the water slowed down and all these willows grew in." He slaps the soggy fleece down. "Now," he says, sprinkling soil upriver, "the topsoil has time to stop and settle in Chorro Flats." He digs through his pocket to find a crumpled piece of paper. "Over 160,000 cubic yards in the last five years."

The crowd watches as Will sprays a light rain on the hills and the model works its magic. "And," Will says, "just like the soap and the oil and the dog poop, where would all that topsoil end up if the river didn't slow down on Chorro Flats?"

Wire mesh holds the cement on the vertical edges of the model.

The crowd chants out, "The estuary!" Will takes a bow.

Last, a woman who has watched from the sidelines steps out front. "Hi," she says, "I'm Judy Neuhauser, 4H Watershed Project Coordinator. How about a round of applause for our presenters, Shane, Maura, and Will?" The crowd applauds. Judy breaks in, "Now don't think you've seen it all tonight. The model will help the kindergartners study the water cycle. Third graders will get a more complex look at the water cycle and will study where the Chumash villages were. They may even build some temporary villages right here where the Chumash lived, comparing lifestyle, resource use, and population density now and then. Fourth graders will bring their geology study out here, mapping soil types and taking a look at substrates; and fifth graders will demonstrate the model, as you've seen tonight, during their land-forms and watershed unit.

"It took about thirty volunteers just over three weeks to build it." She lists all the volunteers and asks for another round of applause. As the audience leaves for home and the sun sets, Judy is wresting the hose from Will and Maura, who are performing a second show for no audience at all. ✒

C.S. Perryess, formerly at Monarch Grove Elementary School, teaches English, dramatic arts, and home economics at Los Osos Middle School in Los Osos, California.

The Morro Bay watershed model at Monarch Grove Elementary School was coordinated by Judy Neuhauser of the 4H Watershed Project in San Luis Obispo, California. Judy worked with at-risk high school students to construct a similar model of the Arroyo Grande watershed south of Morro Bay. An eight-minute video of their experience, *The Watershed Project*, is available from Davidson Films, 735 Tank Farm Road, Suite 210, San Luis Obispo, CA 93401, <www.davidsonfilms.com>. *The Watershed Model Construction Manual*, which includes detailed building plans and curriculum notes, is available at the San Luis Obispo County 4-H Office website at <http://clubs.ca4h.org/sanluisobispo/r2rwe/!conman.html>.

Building a Watershed Model

by C.S. Perryess

A project such as the Morro Bay watershed model requires administrative approval and sufficient open space on the school grounds. If your school ground space is limited, consider building the model in partnership with a local park. Alternatively, a smaller model can be constructed using architectural foam board covered in papier mâché and finished with a few coats of polyurethane. The prototype for the Morro Bay model was a nearly-portable model built on a 4-by-4-foot piece of ¾-inch plywood. Such a model can provide a similar educational function. We found, however, that finding storage space for our smaller model was actually more challenging than adding the larger model as a permanent feature on the school grounds.

The cost of materials for a large model can mount up, but we found local contractors and hardware stores who were excited to support the project — including a contractor who loaned us his cement mixer. The cost of the Morro Bay model was just under $1,500. Such an expense would have been out of the question for an isolated one-time project for one class, but because the model is permanent and available for various curricular ties, we considered it money well spent. As time passes, we imagine the model will inspire previously unthought-of applications. Might it help in the study of slope, gravity, physics, local vegetation patterns, measurement? Time — and engaged students and teachers — will tell.

The following outlines the basic materials and procedure used in constructing the 4-by-4-meter (12-by-12-foot) Morro Bay watershed model.

Materials: 20 rigid 2-inch foam boards with plastic or foil backing, 2-by-6-inch framing boards for the perimeter; sand and gravel or decomposed granite; rebar; chicken wire; 1 cubic meter (30 cubic feet) of cement; 7.5 liters (2 gallons) concrete glue; cement dye

Procedure:

1. Identify the boundaries of your watershed and mark them on a topographical map.

2. Determine a scale that will work for the topography and area of your watershed and the size of the site you have available for the model (the 48,400-acre/19,600-hectare Morro Bay watershed translated well into a 12-by-12-foot/4-by-4-meter model). It is wise to accentuate hills and mountains to ensure that landmarks are recognizable and that water will run off. Do this

continued next page

The 12-by-12-foot schoolyard model of the Morro Bay watershed in California was constructed from layers of Styrofoam insulation assembled on a foundation of crushed granite and covered in cement and stucco. The vertical scale was exaggerated by a factor of three to ensure functional runoff and make landmarks easier to identify. Volunteers as young as three donned rubber gloves to smooth and color the mountains and valleys with dyed stucco.

continued from previous page

by working on a larger scale vertically than horizontally. For example, the Morro Bay model represents landforms ranging from an elevation of 730 meters (2,400 feet) down to sea level. Its vertical scale is three times its horizontal scale. Landmarks are easy to identify and it functions better as a runoff model than it would without the vertical exaggeration. We used one 2-inch layer to represent every 60 meters (200 feet) of elevation, but this ratio should be adjusted to the topography of your watershed. For example, in a fairly flat watershed the features will be more recognizable and the drainage improved by using one layer of foam for every 30 meters (100 feet) of elevation.

Topographical lines traced onto transparencies are then projected onto foam boards.

3. Stake your site and lay 2-by-6-inch boards as cement forms along its perimeter. Inside the perimeter, dig an area for a footing approximately 30 centimeters (1 foot) wide and 10-13 centimeters (4-5 inches) deep, reinforce with rebar, and pour cement. Check for level, and scree (scratch) the surface of the cement before it dries (if your watershed is relatively flat, consider "level" to be a slope that is 10-15 centimeters/4-6 inches higher at the top of the watershed than at the outflow). Inside the footing, lay down crushed granite or construction-grade sand as a base for the model, again grading from the top of the watershed to the outflow to accentuate the vertical dimension.

4. Transfer a topographical map of your watershed to a transparency. Project the transparency onto 2-inch foam insulation boards and use a marker to trace each contour line onto the foam, beginning with the lowest elevation. Cut along the lines with a jigsaw. It will be easier to position the layers after they have been cut if you trace the next-highest elevation line on each piece of foam. For example, when tracing and cutting out the 60-meter layer of a 240-meter hill, trace the next highest contour (90-meter or 120-meter, depending on your interval) on the same piece of foam as a guideline for placing the next

layer. Pin the insulation pieces to one another by pushing nails from one level into the next.

5. Place the assembled foam pieces on the site, pinning the bottom piece into the sand with nails. If your watershed has landforms so flat that they do not appear on your lowest contour lines, use thinner foam or shape the sand itself to represent these finer points.

6. Cover the model with cement, filling in the stair steps of the foam layers to create smooth hills. To ensure that water will flow where it is supposed to, make sure that exuberant volunteers do not fill in gullies, near-flat valleys, and any other subtle water flow areas. These areas must be shaped carefully to create slightly accentuated divets where the streams will flow. Run chicken wire around the vertical edges of the model, pinning it to the foam with nails. Spread cement onto the mesh.

7. When the first coat of cement is dry, check the model for runoff and identify areas that need special care. Then add a thin second coat of cement, being certain to cover any still-exposed foam and taking special care with the problems, if any, identified during the runoff test. Cement any landmark rocks into the appropriate landforms. Conduct another runoff test after the second coat of cement has dried, again identifying areas for special care.

8. Add a stucco coat (no gravel in the mix). Again, smooth it on by hand, being sure not to cover landmark rocks. Check runoff once the stucco has dried.

9. Finish with a thin coat of stucco that is mixed with cement dye to approximate local colors. We used an orangey tan for grasslands and a green for scrub areas and riparian corridors. Apply the color just as you did the first coat of stucco. To obtain a mottled, more natural effect, mix a wet slurry of slightly darker and/or lighter color to sponge randomly over the original color coat. Finally, paint in the riverways, streams, bays and such with blue-dyed stucco.

Monument to a River:
An Interactive Playground Sculpture

Celebrating the history and ecology of a local river

by Bruce Robert Dean

Grade levels: K-3

Subject areas: science, geography, history, design and sculpture

Key concepts: renewable energy, river geology, stream dynamics, community history

Skills: inquiry and research of local history

Location: indoors and outdoors

You rolling old river,
You changing old river,
Let's you and me river,
Run down to the sea.
— Bill Staines

Conquering the challenge of traveling upstream, two boys lower locks into a river channel to raise the water level for their boats. A few feet away, many small hands are submerged in an estuary, pushing aside silt, picking out pebbles, and discovering what creatures live in the ocean bay. Another child is tracing a time-line, from the first amoeba to the modern airplane. Pre-schoolers stare skyward at a passing cloud and then cheer as the spray rises in the solar-powered fountain and the river starts to flow again.

Welcome to the interactive river sculpture located behind an early childhood center in Uxbridge, Massachusetts. Designed by local artists and built in 1994 with the assistance of school and community volunteers, the Blackstone River Monument has become the focal point of our outdoor classroom, providing lessons in the cultural and natural history of our local river. The monument is an operational model of the nearby Blackstone River, and its canal is a living laboratory demonstrating principles of technology and science. Simulating the river's source, a vertical fountain of water "springs" from an upper basin and flows down a curved "riverbed" to an "estuary," represented by a lower basin. Embedded in a steel-reinforced, concrete wall 70 centimeters (28 inches) high and 90 centimeters (36 inches) thick, the river meanders more than 6 meters (20 feet) from fountain to estuary. It serves as a place for river studies, play, exploration, and discovery.

A working model of canal technology

Along the riverbed are a number of features that demonstrate river and canal technology. Miniature boats navigate a ladder of locks made of Plexiglas squares that slip into aluminum slots to raise the water level. Near the upper basin is a mill dam where spinning waterwheels show how power is generated and invite experimentation. Young children assemble waterwheels in class with pre-cut parts (paddles cut from milk cartons and attached to Styrofoam circles rotating on dowels), while older students measure, cut, and test their own models. By varying the length and number of the paddles, and the materials they are made of, students learn how these design features affect the rotation of the wheels. By pressing their fingers against the cement

Photographs by Michael Castagnaro, Worcester Telegram & Gazette

riverbed, they can observe that when the channel is narrowed the rate of flow increases and more potential energy becomes available to turn the wheels.

A story of river geology and history

Sand and stones placed in the basins and the riverbed demonstrate the power of water to move soil, sand, and gravel, helping students to understand how melting glaciers and spring floods create, carve, and reshape riverbeds. Colorful freeform tiles on the riverbanks point out events and artifacts, and mosaics covering the top and sides of the monument show the natural and human history of the river. The images include animals and plants of the region and pictures of the ways in which people have used the river. A series of nine clay plaques around the sculpture summarize the history illustrated in the mosaics. One plaque explains:

Students assemble and experiment with water wheels of different designs.

> *For thousands of years, Native Americans fished, hunted, farmed, and gathered berries, nuts, and wild rice along the river. Then white settlers forced them away from their valley, and white people's factories and cities polluted the river. Now we are learning that people of all races can live here, and we are learning to make the river clean again.*

Another reveals:

> *In the 1820s, people built the Blackstone Canal so boats could carry goods 45 miles between the inland city of Worcester and the ocean port of Providence. Canal locks lifted the canal boats to get past waterfalls and shallow places. Horses pulled the canal boats.*

All around the top play surface is a poem, written in two-inch blue ceramic tile letters, which tells the river's story:

> *Glaciers dug me a million years ago! I drink from streams that drink from rain and snow. The Ocean drinks from me. Nipmuc people named me Pawtucket a thousand years ago. I carried their canoes; I'll carry yours! I welcomed Reverend Blackstone. I powered Slater's mills two hundred years ago. I lifted boats to Worcester. My animals and plants need me! Please take good care of me!*

On the sides of the monument a geologic timeline of terra cotta tiles in tessellating patterns resembles a series of petroglyphs, emphasizing the river's ancient significance to people who have lived along it. The underside is celestial, with planets, stars, and suns contrasting a black stained background.

A demonstration of solar power

At the same time children are learning about canal technology and river history, the fountain at the river's spring gives them a chance to observe the workings of a more modern technology. The fountain is powered by an inexpensive solar pump and demonstrates photovoltaics in action. A 43-by-100-centimeter (17-by-40-inch) 50-watt photovoltaic panel is mounted atop a 5.5-meter (18-foot) aluminum pole. Children can turn a wheel to maneuver the panel toward or away from the sun. The solar-powered pump circulates the "river" from a 225-liter (60-gallon) drum buried underground, up to the fountain, downriver to the estuary, and back through a filter to the drum. Underground pipe laid from the school to the monument provides a backup to the solar-powered recirculating system.

Making an interactive river monument

The creation of a river monument is a project worth consideration at any school. It can help to instill appreciation of a local river's essential role in our lives. Equally important, it can become the focal point of learning about responsible stewardship of a watershed. The Blackstone River Monument has done just that.

River history mural

While our solar-powered sculpture is one of a kind and involved the work of professional artists, planning and creating a river monument need not be daunting or difficult. A relatively simple starting point is to create a mosaic mural for an outdoor play area or garden. Students can research their local river, sketch ideas, put them on an idea board, and move them around into a workable sequence. Start with line drawings and then add color. A group outdoor mural on river history is rich with potential.

Portable river exhibit

If a permanent structure is not feasible, a portable river exhibit for a school courtyard is easily created using a plastic playground slide or a commercially available water table and a pump. Place a bucket at the base of the slide and pump the water from the bucket back to the high end of the slide (experiment with the incline). A series

Children can maneuver a solar panel toward the sun to power the fountain.

of funnels placed upside down will create obstacles. A solution of liquid soap, water, and food coloring will make the water currents visible, enabling you to simulate ocean currents, aerodynamics, turbulence, convection, and coastal erosion. Commercially available rheoscopic fluid produces similar striking visual images of currents within a liquid.

Outdoor sculpture

The next level is to plan a permanent outdoor sculpture. The following are some pointers.

◔ Get everyone in the community involved, including a landscape architect and a building contractor. Check out local colleges, science centers, and environmental groups for project partners. These people will have practical suggestions to shortcut many potential problems.

◔ Consider partnering with a local middle school or high school technology education class. Your project may tie in with several of their curriculum areas, such as renewable energy, mechanical engineering, and construction.

◔ Begin with a small-scale project that promises a high probability of success, and design it in phases to ensure a sense of achievement at steps along the way.

◔ From the start, inform and involve key administrators, teachers, and community leaders. Emphasize that the project will always need some degree of care. Write down who is responsible for what in a maintenance plan. Establish a maintenance fund before construction begins.

m Document the entire process with slides and video, and display pictures of the "doers" in action. Get newspaper coverage. Make all decision makers and funders aware of your progress and celebrate your accomplish-

ment with a dedication ceremony.

In our case, local environmental groups provided interesting facts and photographs of the river. The garden club provided information on regional flora. Local businesses gave us discounts on materials and donated their time to dig the foundation. Parents and students worked together to construct the form for pouring the foundation, and to set, grout, and polish the tiles. A local pole and line company lifted the 5.5-meter (18-foot) aluminum pole into place to support the photovoltaic panel that powers the solar pump. A community metal worker engineered an aluminum frame and rotational support for the panel. Local high school technical education teachers and students worked with a designer of museum exhibits to build a working water wheel exhibit. The Blackstone River Valley Heritage Corridor Commission, part of the National Parks Service, sponsored the dedication ceremony, and the rangers spoke of the importance of the monument as an interpretive site.

Once you have established working relationships and learned who you can count on for what, you will have developed a project team that can take on other projects. Our play yard became a community project in 1982, and each year for the next 20 years something new was added. We invited community artists to get involved and partnered with an outstanding regional science museum. With our Blackstone River Monument, we transformed a school playground into a place where interactive learning happens everywhere and environmental education is part of the culture. ✎

Bruce Robert Dean teaches art at Leominster High School in Massachusetts. The Blackstone River Monument was designed and created by artists Lance McKee and Bill Greenlaw.

Recommended Resources

Boyer, Edward. *River and Canal.* Holiday House 1986.

Cherry, Lynne. *A River Ran Wild.* Harcourt Brace 1992.

Sneider, Cary I., Katharine Barrett, et al. *River Cutters.* (Grades 6-8 teacher's guide.) Great Explorations in Math and Science series. Lawrence Hall of Science, 1995.

Waste-Free Lunches: A Lesson in Environmental Stewardship

Tips and suggestions for starting a waste-free lunch program at your school

Photographs by Amy Hemmert

by Amy Hemmert

Grade levels: K-5

Subject areas: science, social studies, mathematics

Key concepts: reduce, reuse, recycle, decomposition, environmental stewardship

Skills: research, observation, analysis, writing

Location: indoors and/or outdoors

Time: year long, or dependent on how many activities are undertaken.

A typical lunch brought to school by a North American child today contains far more packaging than ever before. With families relying on the convenience of prepackaged lunch items and single-use wrappings such as baggies, aluminum foil, and plastic wrap, it is no surprise that lunchtime trash is second only to office paper as the leading source of

school waste. The New York State Department of Environmental Conservation estimates that the average child taking a disposable lunch to school generates 30 kilograms of garbage per school year. Annually, that adds up to more than half a billion kilograms of lunch waste for the 64,000 public U.S. elementary schools alone. And where does all this lunch trash go? It is hauled off to incinerators and landfills, of course, where it is burned or buried. As landfills across North America reach capacity, communities must find new landfill sites, and these new sites are usually farther away from where the waste is generated. This greater distance results in longer transit times, higher waste-hauling fees, increased pollution from fossil fuel emissions, more truck traffic, and greater wear and tear on public roads.

The good news is that lunch habits have started to change. In some school districts, environment-conscious parents, teachers, school administrators, and environmental organizations are reducing school lunch waste by implementing waste-free lunch programs. Their aim is not only to reduce campus waste, but also to teach students that small changes in their daily routines can have a very large impact on the environment and on their personal health. These programs help schools to save money and increase the likelihood that families will choose fresh fruits, vegetables, and whole grains over highly processed, prepackaged meats and salty or sugary snacks.

What is a waste-free lunch program?

A waste-free lunch contains no throwaway packaging and produces little or no food waste. The typical homemade waste-free lunch is packed in a lunch box or backpack. The food is put in reusable containers rather than wrapped in disposable packaging. A drink is packed in a refillable bottle. Cloth napkins and stainless steel utensils replace disposables. All containers are resealable, so that leftover food and drink can be saved for later.

Enjoying a waste-free picnic.

Hot lunch programs that are waste free provide reusable tableware — plates, cups, utensils, and napkins — which may be washed in the school kitchen, sent home with students for washing, or washed by a third party such as a caterer or restaurant that provides meals to the school. Food waste is minimized through education and training and by implementing low-waste serving procedures. Some schools, for instance, allow students to take only what they know they will eat. Some offer self-serve salad bars.

Waste-free school lunch programs vary tremendously. Some focus on hot lunches only and some on lunches brought from home, while many tackle both. Some schools encourage students to pack waste-free lunches every day, while others hold waste-free lunch days once a week, once a month, or once a year for Earth Day. Many programs develop gradually, starting with a one-week waste-free lunch program the first year, then expanding to once a week or once a month the second year, and then launching a more comprehensive program the following year. Some schools fully integrate their waste-free lunch program with their curriculum or school gardening program. Some rely on intrinsic motivation, while others offer incentives such as prizes.

The components of a waste-free lunch program vary from school to school, but may include:

⊚ Performing an initial trash audit to determine the type, amount, and sources of school waste, and additional audits at regular intervals to assess the effect of any changes that have been implemented. (See trash audit guidelines, page 177.)

⊚ Sending letters or newsletters to students' families to enlist their support and to keep them up to date. They'll need to know what a waste-free lunch is, why a waste-free lunch program is important, and what they can do to pack waste-free lunches quickly and conveniently. After the program is launched, providing families with the results of your ongoing trash audits is a great way to let them know how they're doing.

⊚ Sending memos to teachers about your goals, activities, and plans, so that they can support the program.

⊚ Holding contests to motivate students.

⊚ Making presentations or holding workshops to educate students about environmental problems and solutions related to school lunch waste.

⊚ Implementing or expanding school recycling programs to prevent recyclable materials from going to the landfill or incinerator.

⊚ Instituting or expanding an on-site composting program to divert food waste for use in a school garden or in planter boxes.

⊚ Hanging signs or posters about waste-free lunches in classrooms, the lunchroom, and other common areas.

⊚ Assembling a display or bulletin board to provide lunch-making ideas and examples of waste-free lunch dos and don'ts. (See sidebar, page 175.)

⊚ Organizing student recycling teams or training students as waste managers so that students are involved and take responsibility for their actions. In addition to monitoring and emptying recycling bins, students can help to educate their peers by presenting workshops and creating informational posters.

No matter what activities you choose, starting a waste-free lunch program requires cooperation, patience, and communication. Trying to change human behavior is always challenging, but in the many communities where waste-free lunch programs are being implemented, families and schools are meeting that challenge with enthusiasm and pride.

Implementing a program

The first step in implementing a waste-free lunch program is to organize a waste-free lunch committee, ideally made up of parents, students, teachers, administrators, custodial staff, and lunch program staff. Post announcements for your first meeting, include an announcement in the school newsletter, and send e-mails to staff. Speak with parents and teachers personally to encourage them to attend, and ask parents and teachers to recruit students who might be interested. At your first meeting, ask for a volunteer who will take the names and contact information of all committee members and then type up the list and distribute it.

Work together to define the scope of the waste-free lunch program and to establish manageable goals. Then decide what activities you might sponsor to reach your goals. Once you have the support of the staff (see

A third grader takes food scraps to the garden composter.

"School staff" below) and a list of the activities agreed on by the committee, create a calendar of waste-free events so that everyone knows what's happening and when. Ask for volunteers to work on each of the activities needed to prepare for the events. Break down each event into manageable tasks and set up a timeline listing the deadline for each task and the names of the people responsible. For example, if you plan to implement a waste-free lunch program during Earth Week, you might decide to undertake the following activities:

1. Provide waste-free lunch information to families and school staff the week before Earth Week, encouraging everyone on campus to pack waste-free lunches for the entire week.

2. Conduct a trash audit one week before Earth Week.

3. Conduct a second trash audit on the last day of Earth Week.

4. Compare the results of the two trash audits.

5. Post the audit results in the school, on the school website, and in the school newsletter

A timeline for these activities might look like the example shown.

Pre-Earth Day Trash Audit Timeline

Task	Deadline	People in charge
Determine trash audit procedure	3/15	Committee
Write a letter to families	Submit to committee for review by 3/25; submit to newsletter editor by 4/4	Anne, Toni, Lillian
Write a letter to staff	Submit to committee for review by 3/25; submit to web master by 4/4	Mark, Susan
Recruit volunteers for trash audits	4/10	Alicia, Tamara
Send letter to families	4/12	Newsletter editor
Send letter to school staff	4/11	Cliff, web master
Obtain audit supplies	4/10	Lori
Compile audit results	4/21	Sam
Post results in school, give results to web master and newsletter editor	4/23	Sam

Example of a planning timeline: each waste-free lunch event is broken down into a series of manageable tasks with clear deadlines.

Educating the school community

The biggest challenge that most waste-free lunch committees face is to convince families and school staff that such a program is worthwhile. When parents and teachers feel overworked, or that they have already established successful routines, they may resist change. The committee must be able to demonstrate that a waste-free lunch program can benefit the school, the students, and the environment: the school will reduce its waste-hauling fees, students will likely have more nutritious lunches, and the entire school community will learn more about the environmental benefits — healthier bodies, cleaner air, and cleaner water — associated with their food and packaging choices.

School staff

Before any changes are made, present your ideas to school staff — preferably in person. If you believe the staff will be receptive to your ideas, presenting a plan already developed by the waste-free lunch committee may help to speed implementation of the program. If, on the other hand, you believe the staff might be resistant or feel overwhelmed, you could present your ideas over several meetings. Allow time for the staff to adjust to the idea and invite them to participate, perhaps by presenting the lunch-waste problem to them and giving them a chance to come up with possible solutions.

For example, at an initial meeting, you may want to mention that you have noticed a great deal of trash

Waste-Free Lunch Tips for Parents

🍃 Include items that can be purchased in bulk, such as dried fruit and nuts.

🍃 Include items that come in their own natural wrappings, such as bananas, oranges, and hard-boiled eggs.

🍃 Pack water in a refillable bottle instead of prepackaged sugary drinks. It's healthier, less expensive, and easier to wipe clean if it spills or leaks.

🍃 To avoid food waste, cut fruits and vegetables into pieces so that your child can eat some at lunchtime and save the rest for a later snack.

🍃 Use a thermos or other reusable bottle for drinks, reusable plastic containers for foods, and utensils that can be washed and reused.

🍃 Label all containers and water bottles to ensure they will make it back home.

🍃 Purchase (or make) cloth napkins that your child can decorate with fabric paint, being sure to include his or her name in case a napkin gets left behind at school.

🍃 Avoid throwaway bags, plastic wrap, foil, polystyrene, single-use cans and cartons, and paper napkins.

🍃 Pack lunches in lunch boxes, small packs, or cloth bags.

🍃 Invite children to help plan, prepare, and pack their own lunches.

🍃 Prepare extra food at dinnertime and use leftovers for lunches.

🍃 Minimize the morning rush by packing lunches the night before and storing them in the refrigerator overnight.

at lunch time and ask if anyone knows how much the school pays in waste-hauling fees; if no one knows, volunteer to find out. At the next meeting, discuss your findings and mention that, as a concerned member of the community, you have done some preliminary research to see how other schools are dealing with this issue. You might present a few statistics about how much waste on average is generated in schools at lunchtime (e.g., refer to the statistics above or at the Global Stewards' "Pack a Waste-Free Lunch" web page, listed on page 178). Mention that many schools throughout North America are implementing waste-free lunch programs and volunteer to do more research. To follow up, let the staff know what other schools are doing by presenting some success stories (visit the website of wastefreelunches.org, listed on page 178, for ideas). Offer to conduct a lunch room trash audit and then report your findings on how much waste is being generated, whether it is brought from home or generated through the school lunch program, whether it is primarily packaging or food waste, and what type of packaging waste and food waste is found. Elicit ideas for change, including changes that staff members themselves would be willing to make.

Working with ideas that the staff proposes, come up with a waste-free lunch plan. Consider starting with a one-week plan and performing a second trash audit at the end of the week. Look at the data, compare the results, and calculate how much money the school would save over the entire year if a comprehensive waste-free program were implemented. Report to the staff with a recommendation on whether to focus on school lunches, on lunches brought from home, or on both.

Parents

Since parents usually make the lunch decisions, it is essential to get their support as soon as possible. You can communicate with them through the school newsletter, by phone, or by email. Listed below are some opportunities for communicating with parents.

⚙ After your initial trash audit, send a letter home to parents describing what you found. Explain that the amount of waste generated at lunchtime has a negative impact on both the environment and the school budget. Encourage them to use less disposable packaging.

⚙ Send home a detailed letter explaining what parents can do to reduce lunchtime waste.

⚙ Congratulate families for packing lunches in reusable containers and remind them to label containers, lunch boxes, thermoses, and reusable drink bottles so that these can be returned if they are lost or forgotten.

⚙ Post waste-free lunch reminders in the lunch area, in classrooms, and in common areas where all members of the school community can see them. (As an example, see the waste-free lunch flyer at The Environmental Forum of Marin website <www.marinefm.org/waste-free-month-2002.html>.)

Students

Educating students about the impact of their food choices on the environment is a key component of any waste-free lunch program. The aim, of course, is to influence not only the choices they make at lunchtime, but also those they make all day, every day. Here are some suggested activities. (Detailed lesson plans on these and other topics can be found at some of the websites listed on page 178.)

⚙ Conduct trash audits with students and use the information to teach math (i.e., arithmetic, graphs, tables, word problems).

⚙ Facilitate group discussions about reducing lunch trash and other ways that students can conserve resources.

⚙ Find out where your school's trash ends up. If it goes into a landfill, have students find out where the landfill is, when it is estimated to reach capacity, and what the community plans to do once it is full. If possible, take students on a field trip to the landfill or to a recycling facility.

At Gateway School in Santa Cruz, California, the waste-free lunch program is integrated with the school composting program and vegetable garden. A student covers the day's food scraps with straw.

⚙ Involve students in art projects using salvaged materials, and have them estimate how much new material they have avoided using. Put the artwork on display in the lunchroom.

⚙ Involve students in on-campus recycling and composting.

⚙ Start a worm composting program to eliminate lunchtime food waste and to show students how soil is enriched naturally.

⚙ Conduct food choice workshops in which students learn about the ingredients of processed foods. For example, have students find out how much sugar and food coloring is in soft drinks and juice-flavored drinks. Ask them to decide what constitutes a healthful school snack, and discuss why it is important to provide the body with essential nutrients. Talk about the benefits of drinking water. If appropriate, discuss the causes and symptoms of obesity, heart disease, high blood pressure, sleep apnea, and type 2 diabetes.

⚙ Integrate your waste-free lunch program with a school gardening program so that students connect their lunch with life cycles.

⚙ Have students research a particular issue related to food or the environment and present their findings to the class.

A word of caution: No child should ever be singled out for not packing a waste-free lunch, as young children are rarely responsible for their lunch choices. Families make decisions based, in part, on their lifestyle, values, and socio-economic background. Avoid activities that single out individual students.

Measuring success

Before implementing the waste-free lunch program, decide how to measure its success. You may want to analyze and graph your trash audit results and, perhaps, collect anecdotal evidence from teachers, parents, custodians, and students. If you succeed in reducing waste-hauling fees — either by reducing the size or the number of dumpsters — make sure that everyone in your school community knows about it. Contact your local newspapers and solid waste agency, too, to share with your community what your school is doing for \the local environment.

Making it last

To keep your program alive, your committee must continue to communicate with families and staff. Have students create new and inventive reminder posters, and replace any that are not in good condition. Continually send out reminders, notes of praise, and tips for packing waste-free lunches. As new families enter the school, make sure they are made aware of the school's efforts to reduce waste. Share with families and staff what other schools are doing to reduce waste, and ask the committee if some of these ideas could be added to your program. Involve students in trash audits throughout the year. Consider purchasing or making a school trophy that can be awarded each week to the

---

A Lunch Trash Audit

Conducting a trash audit is a great way to find out what's in your school's lunch trash. Once you know what's being thrown out, you can institute changes to reduce the waste and measure the results over time. Trash audits can be conducted by a class of students or by a waste-free lunch committee. Ideally, the trash generated by each class or grade is audited separately so that students can monitor their own group's waste reduction and, possibly, compete for prizes.

Materials: 1 trash bag per class/grade, 1 bucket for each waste category you choose to monitor, 1 large tarp, a scale, a pair of rubber gloves for each participant, a permanent marker, paper and tape for labels, a Trash Audit Tally chart, and a clipboard.

Procedure:

1. Make a chart with the classes/grades along the x-axis and the waste categories you choose along the y-axis. Include a column to record the weight of each empty bucket. Place the chart on the clipboard.

2. Label one garbage bag for each class or grade. Instruct students to throw their lunch trash into their group's garbage bag instead of dumping it into the trashcan. If they

normally recycle, let them do so; if they don't, have them put their recyclable items into the garbage bag (you can remove them later).

3. Once all the trash has been collected for one class or grade, dump it on to the large tarp.

4. Label each bucket for one of the waste categories on your chart. Then weigh each empty bucket and record the weights on the chart. Place the buckets along one edge of the tarp.

5. Give participants gloves and instruct them to sort the trash by placing each item in the appropriate bucket.

6. When there is no waste left on the tarp, weigh each bucket and record the weight less the weight of the bucket for each category on the chart.

7. Empty the buckets by transferring their contents into appropriate containers (e.g., recycling boxes, school composter, garbage bin). Then repeat steps 3 to 6 for each class or grade participating in the trash audit.

Note: If you wish, you can also sort the non-recyclable trash into categories, such as prepackaged items, plastic bags, paper, Styrofoam, other plastic items. Count or weigh the items in each category for future reference.

Trash Audit Tally: Record the weights for each category in the column for your grade level.								
	empty bucket	K	Grade 1	Grade 2	Grade 3	Grade 4	Grade 5
non-recyclable trash							
non-compostable food waste							
compostable food waste							
unopened food and drink							
aluminum cans and foil							
plastic bottles							

class that produces the least waste by weight or brings the highest number of waste-free lunches. Make sure that worm boxes and recycling bins are conveniently and prominently placed where students can use them. And enlist the ongoing help of parents and staff to ensure that lunch cleanup procedures are properly adhered to.

Waste-free lunch programs help schools reduce waste and save money. If every child attending elementary school packed a waste-free lunch, billions of pounds of lunch waste could be diverted from the waste stream. That's a lot of trash, and that translates into potentially huge savings for our families, our schools, and our environment. ✒

Amy Hemmert is a teacher, small business owner, and mother of two school-age children in Santa Cruz, California. She is the author of several books, including The Laptop Lunch User's Guide: Fresh Ideas for Packing Wholesome, Earth-friendly Lunches Your Kids Will Love.

A second grader waters her class's garden plot.

Websites

<www.wastefreelunches.org> Wastefreelunches.org. Sample letters to families, information on trash audits, classroom activities, and success stories from around the world. You can also share your own waste-free lunch story at this site.

<www.virtualrecycling.com> Virtual Recycling, Manitoba Product Stewardship Corporation.Tips on organizing waste-free lunches, including contest suggestions.

<cwmi.css.cornell.edu/TrashGoesToSchool/TrashIntro.html> Trash Goes to School, Cornell Waste Management Institute. Classroom activities for Grades K-12, sample letter to teachers, and background information on solid waste management, reducing, reusing, and recycling.

<www.globalstewards.org/lunch.htm> Global Stewards. The "Pack a Waste-Free Lunch" page provides lunch waste statistics and tips on packing waste-free lunches.

<www.rco.on.ca/intro/upcoming/awards/forms.html> Recycling Council of Ontario. A "3Rs Waste Reduction Survey" that can be adapted.

<www.deq.state.or.us/wmc/solwaste/rethinkrecyc/rethinkrecyc.html> Rethinking Recycling, Oregon Department of Environmental Quality. This site offers an adaptable waste reduction curriculum for Grades K-5. Click on "Extension: Creating a No-Waste Lunch Display" for a downloadable flyer that may be helpful in designing a waste-free lunch information sheet for parents and students.

<www.recycleworks.org/schools/index.html> San Mateo County California Recycleworks. Information on packing a no-waste lunch, conducting waste audits, worm composting, and starting a composting program.

<www.resourcefulschools.org/teachers.html> Saint Louis County Resourceful Schools Project. Guidelines for waste-free lunch programs and school waste audits.

The Warriors of the Rainbow

*An extracurricular environment club inspired by
a Cree prophecy of the restoration of the Earth*

by Roberta Oswald and Carmel Preyra

Grade levels: 3-6

Subject areas: science, social studies

Key concepts: stewardship of the Earth, respect for life, personal responsibility

Skills: communication, inquiry, decision making, problem solving

As teachers, we want our students to appreciate the natural world and, more importantly, to have a deep understanding of the sacredness of life on Earth. We hope that this understanding will instill in them empathy for living things and a lifelong desire to protect our environment. Working with students from a diversity of cultures and backgrounds, we have found the Cree legend of the Warriors of the Rainbow to be a perfect vehicle for the message that we all need to work as one. The word "warrior" in this context is not associated with aggression or war, but is closer to the Tibetan word *pawo*, which means "one who is brave." It refers to an honorable warrior tradition among North American aboriginal peoples that encompasses personal strength, courage, and tenacity.

The following is a synopsis of the Warriors of the Rainbow legend.

The old woman Eyes of Fire sat dozing under the shade of the cottonwood tree by the creek when a youth of 12 summers wandered down beside her, looked into her eyes, and said, "I want to ask a question. Why did our grandfather in the sky allow others to come to this place, take our land, and cause such sad things to happen to our people?"

Eyes of Fire became as still as a desert fox crouched at the hole of a kangaroo rat. "You are the first to ask that question," she whispered. "The Heart of all Beings said that it was necessary for others to come to this place because here they would one day learn to live in harmony with all people."

Eyes of Fire told how, in their dreams, the old ones saw their great nation split apart; they saw their people lose their spirit; they saw the Earth grow sick. But they also saw that one day a great awakening will occur. Those who chase after material wealth will see that they have left behind the truly important things. They will seek the knowledge of the ancestors to restore the Earth and learn to live in harmony with the great circle of life.

As she stopped talking, Eyes of Fire and the youth saw a brilliant rainbow arc across the sky. Seeing it, she said, "The rainbow is a sign from the spirit who is in all things. It is a sign of the union of all peoples like one family. Go to the mountain, child, and learn to be a Warrior of the Rainbow, for it is only by spreading love and joy to others that hate can be changed to understanding and kindness, and war and destruction shall end!"

In our class, this legend sparked much discussion: parallels were drawn between the colors of the rainbow and the many nations on Earth, and we discussed the rainbow as a symbol of hope appearing after a storm or period of great turmoil. These ideas culminated in the formation of an environmental club called Warriors of the Rainbow for students from Grades 4 to 6. The students chose the rainbow as their symbol and designed a club logo. They developed a coat of arms; wrote a pledge to be read at meetings; planned an initiation ceremony; decided what actions the group would take at school, at home, and in the community; and produced a newsletter on environmental issues.

How to Earn Your Warrior of the Rainbow Beads

Color	Symbolic Meaning	Requirements
Purple	Courage — becoming a leader and role model	Start a club focused on a particular cause; teach others, including family members, to respect nature; write a poem or a speech expressing how you feel about a problem and share it in a public forum; organize a school initiative to improve the environment.
Blue	Appreciation — becoming one with other living things	Spend at least six hours in parks, backyards, zoos, or natural areas to deepen your understanding of other living things; this can include cross-country skiing, bicycling, and hiking in natural areas, gardening, or volunteering at an animal shelter. Share your experience and insights with others by developing a slide or multimedia presentation, a visual display such as a poster, or a dramatic portrayal.
Green	Planet change — taking action as a group and making a lasting difference	Take actions such as starting a butterfly garden; raising seedlings and planting trees; educating others (including school staff) about energy conservation and environment-friendly approaches to cleaning; overseeing recycling and composting programs at home and school; raising funds for an environmental organization.
Yellow	Action — making lasting personal changes	Make at least three personal changes and maintain the new behavior. These changes might include eating healthier foods; packing waste-free lunches; reducing your use of non-renewable energy by walking or riding a bike; picking up litter in your neighborhood; turning off lights and conserving water at home and school.
Orange	Peace/humanity — helping other people and nations	Organize a collection of clothes or food for distribution to people in need; visit the elderly on a regular basis; initiate an anti-bullying campaign; raise funds for the homeless and awareness of their plight; become a buddy to a new student from another country.
Red	Passion — taking on an activity with all your heart	Decide what your passion is and pursue it, either by yourself or with a group. Examples are nature photography or art, bird watching, and tai chi or another physical activity.
Black	Knowledge — deepening your understanding of Earth issues	Research and make a detailed report on an environmental or global issue such as acid rain, global warming, depletion of the ozone layer, nuclear power, habitat destruction, endangered species, hunger, waste management, pollution, or over-population. The report can be an essay, a comic book, a photo journal, a story, or a poem, and will be displayed.
White	Sharing — empowering others	Visit other classes or schools to encourage students to join the Warriors of the Rainbow. Address an assembly to promote solutions to environmental problems. Create a newsletter to promote your ideas. Create a display for your school or a library that many people can enjoy.

Like the warriors in legends, the children take on challenges, with each member working toward earning a string of colored beads that proffers the right to be called a Warrior of the Rainbow. Each bead symbolizes a personal attribute or value and requires the completion of certain tasks. The fulfillment of these requirements is demonstrated by a report or project, or verified by a letter from a teacher or parent. The beads are presented ceremoniously as they are earned, until each student has a necklace of eight beads and becomes a full-fledged Warrior of the Rainbow. (See "How to Earn Your Warrior of the Rainbow Beads.") The group's promotion of a gentler way of living on the planet has won over many students and teachers to their cause and become part of the culture of our school community. ✤

Roberta Oswald and *Carmel Preyra* *are educators in Toronto, Ontario.*

The synopsis of the Warriors of the Rainbow prophecy is abridged and adapted from William Willoya and Vinson Brown, *Warriors of the Rainbow: Strange and Prophetic Dreams of the Indian Peoples*, Naturegraph Publishers, 1962, pp.1-15. Other versions of this legend can be found on-line by searching on "Warriors of the Rainbow."

Cool Schools: A Schoolwide Conflict Resolution Program

The skills of conflict resolution are the skills of the negotiator and problem solver — critical to the development of leadership and environmental citizenship

Photographs by Fran Jovick

by Fran Jovick

Grade levels: K-5

Subject areas: social literacy

Key concepts: mediation, social skills

Skills: communication, listening, anger management, problem solving

Cutting old-growth forests, draining wetlands for new housing developments, overfishing the oceans — these are environmental issues that we often ask students to consider through debate, discussion, and role play. Such deliberations on real-world problems are intended to help students develop skills of problem solving and informed decision making that will enable them to become responsible environmental citizens. But because environmental issues usually feature conflicts between groups of people with very different interests, in the real world they become controversies that elicit strong emotions and can even result in extreme behavior. Classroom approaches to these issues usually encourage students to try to understand differing points of view. However, they often stop short of helping students develop the specific skills needed to resolve disputes.

The skills of conflict resolution — empathy, assertiveness, anger management, non-judgmental listening, non-violent communication — are critical to the ability to interact positively with the world at large. Learning and practicing these skills early can empower children to deal creatively with family, classroom, and schoolyard conflicts. Later, such "social literacy" skills will enable them to make positive contributions and assume leadership roles in resolving problems and conflicts in broader spheres. The following describes a schoolwide peer mediation and social literacy program which, for over ten years, has been teaching children — and teachers, principals, and parents — to collaborate to work out their differences.

Cools schools — the background

The idea of "cool schools" was sparked more than a decade ago at an elementary school on the Sunshine Coast in British Columbia. Noticing an increase in aggressive behavior on the playground and not wanting to be the sole arbitrators in students' personal disputes, the staff envisioned having a process that would enable students to resolve their own conflicts. Their first step was to set up a peer mediation program in which children from Grades 4 to 7 who volunteered as peer counselors were trained to mediate playground disputes. Teachers soon realized that, for the program to be most effective, everyone had to be trained in the skills and process of negotiation and mediation — not just the student mediators. Within a year, the teaching of these skills became the core of a schoolwide social literacy program. The program teaches children specific skills as well as a general problem solving process and encourages them to take direct responsibility for their actions.

The peer mediation program

Each year, between 20 and 30 students volunteer to be peer counselors. For one hour a week, they receive training in communication skills (particularly listening), anger management, building empathy (that is, staying curious and not being judgmental), assertiveness, negotiation, and mediation. The 25-week training period also includes a one-day team-building retreat. During their training, the peer counselors work on:

⑥ communication skills such as deep listening; asking open, not closed, questions; giving "I" rather than "you" messages (e.g., "I am angry," not "You make me angry.")

⑥ understanding reasons for behavior (e.g., attention, revenge, control, discouragement, anxiety)

⑥ understanding the dynamics of anger, and managing and diffusing anger

The Eight-Step Problem-Solving Model

1. Set guidelines:
⑥ agree to solve the problem
⑥ use no blaming, name calling, or rude gestures
⑥ tell the truth
⑥ listen without interrupting

2. Each person tells the problem as he/she sees it.

3. Each person has to repeat back what he/she heard the other person say.

4. Each person gets to include anything he/she left out or wants to clarify.

5. Each person gets to tell his/her ideal solution.

6. Each person gets to say what solution he or she thinks is attainable and will work.

7. Agree to a solution that both parties will try.

8. Check up: agree to and set a time for a follow-up meeting to see how things are going or, if necessary, to look at another solution.

⑥ practicing mediation through role playing that uses an eight-step problem-solving process (see sidebar).

Peer counselors work in teams at recess and lunch, along with an adult on duty. They help in resolving a variety of problems, such as disputes over a ball or skateboard or someone not playing by the rules, name calling, spreading gossip, or not letting someone join in. Skillful peer counselors tend to offer help as soon as a conflict presents itself, or will take preventative action by asking a student if he or she wishes to talk or walk around. To gain the trust of fellow students, peer counselors have to be aware of how to use the power they have as mediators. They must, for example, always use the mediation process to settle disputes rather than simply making a judgment or taking direct action (such as taking a ball from one student and giving it to another). The skills of the peer counselors vary, and students get very good at selecting the best ones so that some peer counselors get more "business" than others.

Trained peer counselors meet once a week to discuss issues and to practice specific skills. These weekly meetings usually focus on successes as well as conflicts that the peer counselors feel were not resolved. An unresolved conflict is discussed by the group and then usually referred to the school counselor or a classroom teacher. In some cases, peer counselors, with the assistance of the school counselor, will address the problem again as a group — particularly in the case of a student who continually causes problems. Both training and meetings are scheduled during school time as a clear message to students that teachers believe it is worthwhile.

The conflict resolution process has led to the formation of support groups for students who are being bullied. The school counselor initiates these support groups, often with peer counselors or students identified as having a "good heart" and status with their peers. The support group invites — one by one — those students who are using "bully power" in order to ask for their help. Most of these students end up join-ing the group and using their status to help stop the bullying behavior. These groups have been powerful tools in making and maintaining change, and in helping bullied students strengthen their own voices and feel cared for. Some of the anti-bullying groups have evolved into permanent problem-solving groups who help students who are not being treated well and are in need of some coaching to turn things around.

Schoolwide social literacy program

During the past few years, the school-wide social literacy component of the program has grown through the sys-tematic teaching of skills that are critical to positive social interaction. These include:

Peer mediation counselors meet weekly to discuss issues and practice skills.

- ௴ communication skills such as listening with-out interruption

- ௴ anger manage-ment

- ௴ assertiveness, such as standing up verbally for one-self

- ௴ empathy, the ability to see things from someone else's perspective, to walk in another's shoes

- ௴ positive self-talk, the ability to count to ten before responding or to say to oneself, "Slow down" or "I can manage this"

- ௴ expanding feelings vocabulary to express a wider and more complex range of emotion than is con-veyed by such terms as "mad," "sad," or "happy"

- ௴ handling criticism

- ௴ recognizing unhelpful thoughts and changing to helpful thoughts (e.g., from "I'll get him back!" to "I can handle this.")

- ௴ managing stress through relaxation techniques involving music, drawing, and breathing or visual-ization exercises

- ௴ using the eight-step model to solve problems (see opposite)

These skills are not mutually exclusive, nor is the list hierarchical. As teachers are encouraged to tailor the training to meet the needs of their own students, the focus varies from class to class.

Critical to the social literacy program is setting aside class time every week to introduce a specific social skill. During the session, the teacher introduces a scenario in which a problem must be solved using the particular skill being taught. Scenarios are frequently constructed to reflect conflicts happening in the school community, such as one student pushing another out of line for the school bus. In this example, the skill might be anger management. The class discussion would focus on understanding the anger-arousal cycle and slowing it down with positive self-talk such as "Stop and think before you react." The teacher dem-onstrates positive self-talk and then role-plays with students. Each role play is debriefed to reinforce the specific skill, and students are en-couraged to com-mend one another when they use the skill in daily activities.

As children gain skills in social literacy, a school-wide model for conflict resolution produces a forum in which they can practice these skills. Skills cannot be taught in the abstract. Playground disputes, interper-sonal conflicts, and misuse of personal power in rela-tionships provide real material to work on.

The peer mediation process and social literacy pro-gram are now entrenched in the school culture, so that students, teachers, principals, and many parents use the eight-step problem solving process in their daily inter-actions. Teachers and principals still make "rulings" when safety is an issue, but they use the problem solv-ing process for the personal aspects of the conflict. Students use the process for solving their own conflicts with friends and, in some cases, with parents and teach-ers. If these avenues fail, both students and teachers can book mediation with the school counselor. Teachers and parents support problem solving by allowing stu-dents time for such mediation.

Cool schools work

Peer mediation and social literacy programs are not quick-fix solutions to conflict. Rather, they make use of conflict as a context for learning social skills. As these skills increase, so does children's ability to recognize and create options for themselves. New students arriv-ing at a school that practices mediation comment on how different it is from their last school — noting that they are not used to the "problem-solving business." This is not surprising. It sometimes takes them a while to realize that they will be held accountable for their actions. Without such accountability, students may say to a teacher or principal "You decide." Then, if they do not like the ruling, they feel free to engage in revenge or passive resistance. Under a mediation program, students move away from the "revenge mode" to look for a solution to which they are willing to commit themselves. It is a radical shift from the traditional process whereby adults make and hand down decisions. It takes time for the teachers and students to get used to collaborative problem solving and to move toward a "power with" rather than a "power over" concept. But the results are worth it.

The most difficult challenge facing schools committed to schoolwide conflict resolution programs is to keep the energy for the program at a high level. Students are enthusiastic but need continual support, encouragement, and expertise, as do new teachers and students just entering the school community. It helps when everyone is philosophically committed to the program and knows its benefits first hand.

With the escalation of physical and verbal violence in our communities — and the violence being waged on the Earth itself — there is a growing need for these programs. While conflicts are an inevitable part of living, children, as well as adults, can learn positive ways of handling them. Learning to listen, to empathize, to be nonjudgmental, to negotiate with people who hold different views — these are the skills that children need in order to develop relationships, to function as members of communities, and to advocate and take action in the wider world. We ask children at an early age to consider the extent of the global problems we face. We must also give them to the tools they will need to work together to solve them. ✒

Fran Jovick is an elementary school consultant with the Sunshine School District in Gibsons, British Columbia.

Resources

Bodine, Richard J., Donna K. Crawford, and Fred Schrumpf. *Peer Mediation: Conflict Resolution in Schools — Student Manual* and *Program Guide*. Research Press, 1997.

British Columbia Ministry of Education. *Focus on Bullying: A Prevention Program for Elementary School Communities*. BC Safe School Centre, 1997. Available in PDF format at <www.bced.gov.bc.ca/specialed/bullying.pdf>.

Committee for Children. *Second Step: A Violence Prevention Program*. Committee for Children, 1997. This program includes curriculum for teaching social and emotional skills for violence prevention. See <www.cfchildren.org>.

Committee for Children. *Steps to Respect: Bullying Prevention Program*. Committee for Children, 1998. A schoolwide curriculum that uses literature units to focus on decreasing bullying and teaching children the skills to build respectful peer relationships.

van Gurp, Hetty. *The Peaceful School: Models that Work*. Portage & Main Press, 2002.

van Gurp, Hetty. *Peer Mediation: The Complete Guide to Resolving Conflict in Our Schools*. Portage & Main Press, 2002.

Karen Green

Global Awareness

Global Education in Kindergarten

Some starting points for introducing young children to environmental issues and the global community

Reusing "found" materials to make models of family members.

by Karen Green

Grade level: K

Subject areas: mathematics, language, social studies, science, art, physical education

Key concepts: interdependence, local and global community

Skills: sorting objects, collecting, recording and comparing data, developing a persuasive argument, asking questions, problem solving, working cooperatively, fine motor skills

Location: indoors and outdoors

There are many wonderful ideas and projects for teaching students about global issues — *if* they can read and write. Have you said that too? But even kindergarten teachers can become global educators. A global educator tries to promote responsible decision making and the critical thinking skills necessary to address global issues. If you invite your students to choose and organize some of their own learning activities each day, and if you emphasize a problem-solving approach to dealing with interpersonal conflict, then you are already a budding global educator.

I have found a couple of other starting points for global education in kindergarten. These are concepts that I introduce while working on the learner expectations stated in our provincial kindergarten program. Even if "global awareness" and "the environment" are not specifically mentioned in your curriculum, these themes can touch on many mandated learner expectations.

Connecting to our environment

First, students can be introduced to the ideas that humans are part of the environment and that what we consume affects the environment. During an Animals theme, my class creates a list of statements that are true for all animals. Then we go down the list to see whether the statements hold true for people. If you want to set up a situation where five-year-olds are challenged to develop a persuasive argument, opening a debate on whether people are animals will do it!

When we get to our Farms and Food theme, I stress the connection between the foods we eat and their original plant or animal sources. That information becomes the basis for sorting objects according to their attributes. One year we were fortunate to have a father come in to show his fishing gear and fillet a fish, as well as a grandmother visit to pluck a chicken. A series of photos of such processes can lend themselves to lessons on sequencing events.

Reduce, reuse, recycle

We tackle environmental concerns more directly in a two-week theme on the environment emphasizing the need to reduce, reuse, and recycle. After viewing a film about water conservation, small groups brainstorm suggestions for not wasting water. I list their ideas on large chart paper — a wonderful opportunity for modeled and shared writing — and then transcribe the list onto ordinary paper and copy it. The children sign their lists and then take them home to share their water conservation ideas with their families. We also talk about reducing garbage. The children make bar graphs

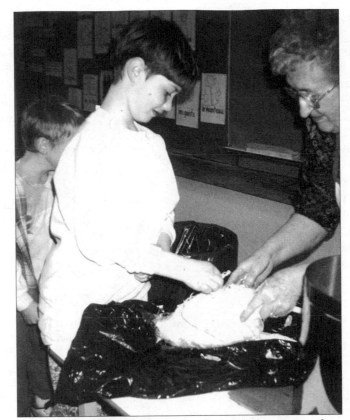

A grandmother demonstrating how to pluck a chicken as part of a Farms and Food theme.

to show the types of materials we find in our classroom garbage cans. We discuss which items could be reused or replaced by reusable things. Thereafter, we designate one of the classroom the garbage cans to be used for compostable materials only.

We practice reusing by making crafts from paper that has been printed on one side. Parents are pleased to send in such items as broken jewelry, toilet paper rolls, and egg cartons for creative crafts. Craft books are full of ideas for crafts from "found" materials — and so are five-year-olds!

A film on the fabrication of cardboard boxes introduces children to recycling. That same day we open a classroom paper recycling center. Making recycled paper is so simple that, if a parent supervises the first day, students can subsequently complete most steps on their own. They tear scrap paper into tiny bits and put them in a blender with an equal amount of water. The blended pulp is poured onto a rectangular piece of window screening that has been taped around the edges. Another screen is then laid on top of the wet pulp and pressed, in order to squeeze the water out of it. Students engage in problem solving by trying to come up with ways to remove more water (pile heavy things on the screen? stand on it?). Once it is pressed, the recycled paper is tapped off the screen onto newspapers to dry.

The environment theme culminates with a walk to our local bottle depot. We collect litter on the way back to the school.

The global community

As another starting point for global education in kindergarten, I build on the general learner expectation that says that each child should "demonstrate ... a willingness to learn about the environment and community." If the children are well prepared, it is painless to move beyond the local community to the global community.

Years ago, as a novice to teaching kindergarten, I showed a globe to my students and explained what it was. After one of my students asked "You mean people live in there?" I put it away and didn't bring it out again for a long time. Now I use the globe to introduce the world map, and to introduce the globe I use a space trip. The space travelers settle in a cleared corner of the kindergarten room and fasten their seat belts. They close their eyes and we take off to the tape-recorded sound of a whistling kettle screaming louder and louder. When the children open their eyes, the room is dark and glow-in-the-dark star stickers are shining on the walls. A light shines on the globe in front of them. I inform the space travelers that the globe is Earth, the planet from which we've just taken off. I explain that a world map is a picture of Earth's crust flattened out — as the peel of an orange can be removed and flattened out.

The world map I use in my classroom is two meters (six feet) wide, made with the help of an overhead projector. A globe and atlas are kept near the map. Throughout the year, we tack pictures or other items on the map to mark the places of origin of things: show-and-tell items from other countries, folk tales read to the class, foreign stamps used in our writing center-cum-post office, fruits brought in as snacks. When a grandparent comes to visit from afar or a parent vacations to some exotic

Taking a closer look at the world by the "Where Does It Come From?" bulletin board.

place, we mark those places, too. One of our specific learner expectations is to "Describe some ways people and goods are transported," and so we post drawings of different modes of transportation on one side of the map and discuss how things get to us from other parts of the world.

I have just made a start at global education but am discovering that, once you get the ball rolling, it gathers momentum on its own. A parent who was about to leave for Holland asked me if I would like to partner with a pen pal class there. That sounds a little too ambitious. Although … if we used class-dictated letters or paired students with older reading buddies, it might work. Just by exchanging information on schoolyard games, we could "Ask questions," "Give directions," and "Dictate to a scribe" — all learner expectations. Maybe … ✒

Karen Green taught kindergarten for 13 years and currently teaches Grade 1 French immersion in Westlock, Alberta.

Resources

Levine, Shar. *The Paper Book and Paper Maker.* Somerville House Books Limited, 1993.

Morris, Ann. *Bread, Bread, Bread.* Viking, 1989.

The World in a Cake

*A tasty focal point for exploring how our food links us
to people and places around the world*

by Jackie Kirk and Mary Gale Smith

Grade levels: K-7

Subject areas: social studies, health, family studies, math, science

Key concepts: food interconnections, food production

Skills: mapping, food preparation, measuring

Location: classroom

Time: 2 hours

Materials: class copies of a world map (or one large world map for display); cake ingredients; pictures of ingredients, their production, and their processing; cake-making equipment (measuring spoons and cups, mixing bowl, wooden spoon, grater, rubber spatula, 9-by-13-inch rectangular cake pan or muffin pans and paper liners)

Jackie Kirk

By the time you have eaten breakfast in the morning, you have already depended on half the world.
— Martin Luther King

 ood is a basic human need. Yet many of us, and especially young children, are distanced from the sources of what we eat. Most of us buy our food rather than grow it ourselves, and in families where food is bought packaged and pre-prepared, children have few opportunities to help in the kitchen or even to see the process of food preparation. When meals are presented ready to eat, little thought may be given to where the ingredients came from, who grew them, how they were processed, or what impact our choice of food has on our health and the health of the planet.

Cooking and preparing foods in the classroom can give children the opportunity to reclaim at least some of their food. It is a wonderful confidence- and team-building activity that can fit into all areas of the curriculum and make important links between home and school. Just as important, classroom cooking affords opportunities to explore our connections to other people, cultures, and environments. In *Filters Against Folly*, Garrett Hardin talks of the need for citizens to develop not only literacy and numeracy, but also "ecolacy." To be "ecolate" is to understand that the world is a complex of interconnected systems; it is to ask "And then what?" in order to perceive these connections and understand the consequences of our actions. As children are the consumers and decision makers of the future, we need to help them become aware of the ramifications of their decisions, even in the supermarket, on the lives of other people and on the state of the Earth.

Baking a world cake

In the elementary classroom, baking a cake or other dish that contains ingredients from around the world is an excellent way of raising many different issues and ideas, in addition to covering many areas of the curriculum. I used the preparation of a cake as part of our school's One World Week celebration, but it could be part of exploring a variety of other topics. At its most basic, it is a cookery lesson. When developed and extended, it can become the starting point for an investigation into the food we eat, where it comes from, the people who produce it, and the distances it travels.

The recipe presented here (see sidebar) is very simple and adaptable. You can adjust the fruit and nut ingredients to focus on one particular country or issue or, in a pre-school class, on one letter of the alphabet. You can also modify ingredients in order to make use of what is available locally (e.g., choose either zucchini or carrots), to avoid nuts (use coconut instead), or to replace all-purpose flour with whole wheat flour for a focus on nutrition. If you do not have access to a stove, the cake can easily be prepared in the classroom and then taken elsewhere for baking. You could even bake the cake at home and then have students sample it and speculate on its ingredients. If the cake is made as a class project, the measuring of various ingredients could be assigned to groups of students.

If possible, try to obtain some fair trade products to use in your cake, or use some organic ingredients or free-range eggs, and discuss with the children the decisions you made when buying these products. Even better, take the children shopping for the ingredients and present them directly with the decisions.

As each of the ingredients is added to the mixing bowl, share information about where the ingredient may have been produced. (See "About the Ingredients," page 192, and ask students to check the package to see if the source is identified on the label.) Have students find and mark these locations on a large classroom map. Discuss how each ingredient was grown and how it has been processed to arrive here in its present form. (Upper elementary students may research the production and processing of each ingredient in advance of making the cake.) If possible, show pictures of the raw ingredients being harvested around the world and being processed by real people (you might develop a PowerPoint presentation from Internet sources). Encourage the children to think about the lives of the pickers, factory workers, and shippers who have all contributed to their cake.

Follow-up and extension activities:
⑥ After making the cake, have students create a display table with the raw ingredients, pictures of the harvesting of raw materials, and maps with the routes each ingredient might have taken to arrive here. Include the children's written comments about the cake, as well as comments by other people in the school.

⑥ If fair trade products have been used in the cake, discuss the advantages of fair trade (i.e., people get a living wage, child labor may be reduced so that children can go to school) and the disadvantages (e.g., the products usually cost more). You could use a similar approach to discussing organic foods.

⑥ Once students have located the origins of the ingredients on a map, have them estimate the distance each product has traveled. You could also guide students to identify aspects of food production and distribution that use energy (e.g., farm machinery, fertilizer and pesticide production, transportation, processing machinery, packaging production, refrigeration).

⑥ Have students identify which ingredients in the cake are local and which come from afar. For the non-local ingredients, have students suggest local substitutes (e.g., instead of pineapple, try apple sauce; instead of walnuts, try hazelnuts; instead of raisins, try dried cranberries or blueberries). Encourage students to suggest other class cookery projects that would use locally produced ingredients. Discuss the advantages for the environment in choosing local foods.

⑥ Ask students to think of ways to reduce the amount of packaging when purchasing ingredients (e.g., buying in bulk from bulk containers, buying loose fruits and vegetables, taking cloth shopping bags).

⑥ Discuss the nutritional benefits of adding nuts, fruits, and vegetables to the cake.

⑥ Have students investigate the process of sugar refining and find out which sugar source — beets or sugar cane — is more environmentally friendly. Both require large amounts of energy, but the by-product of sugar cane extraction can be burned as a source of energy, whereas the refining of sugar beets uses fossil fuels. Children could also investigate the milling of wheat or the process of turning cacao beans into chocolate.

⑥ Discuss the possibility of putting "the world" in a lunch box or of making muesli that is "The World in a Bowl."

World Cake Recipe

1 cup	vegetable oil	250 mL
1 cup	sugar	250 mL
1 cup	brown sugar	250 mL
3	eggs	3
1⅓ cups	whole wheat flour	330 mL
2 cups	all purpose flour	500 mL
1¼ tsp	baking soda	6 mL
1¼ tsp	baking powder	6 mL
2½ tsp	cinnamon	12 mL
1 tsp	salt	5 mL
2½ cups	grated carrots *or* zucchini	625 mL
1 14-oz. can	crushed pineapple with juice	400 mL
1⅓ cups	chopped walnuts (*or* shredded coconut)	330 mL
1⅓ cups	sultanas (*or* raisins, chopped dried apricots, or other dried fruit)	330 mL

Jackie Kirk

Procedure:

1. Preheat oven to 350°F (180°C).

2. Grease and lightly flour a 9-by-13-inch cake pan. (To make cupcakes instead of a cake, use muffin pans with paper liners. The recipe will make 25-30 cupcakes.)

3. Combine all the ingredients in a large mixing bowl and mix until well blended.

4. Pour into cake pan (or spoon into muffin cups, filling two-thirds full).

5. Bake cake 60 to 70 minutes (cupcakes 25 to 30 minutes), or until a toothpick inserted in the center comes out clean.

6. Cool. Dust with icing (powdered) sugar and grated chocolate for serving, if desired.

⚅ Have students collect a variety of food labels and add these to the map to reinforce the connections they have with the rest of the world through food.

⚅ Enhance the lesson with a field trip to a market garden or community garden so that students can see how such vegetables as carrots and zucchini are grown (or visit another food-producing facility to learn about the processing of other ingredients). Another possible field trip is a supermarket tour where students can investigate the sources of various foods.

⚅ Invite local farmers or gardeners to talk about their produce, and, if it is autumn, ask them to bring some samples so that the children can taste freshly harvested natural foods.

⚅ Introduce author Candace Savage's idea of assessing food choices based on the criteria of the 5 Ns: nutritious, now, near, natural, and naked. Ask these questions:

Is it *nutritious*?
Is it fresh or in season *now*?
Does it come from *nearby*?
Is it *natural* or processed as little as possible?
Is it *naked* or packaged as little as possible?

⚅ Have students choose a favorite food item and develop a poster to inform others of the ways in which the food connects us to the rest of the world.

⚅ Have students conduct a community food audit by mapping the area around the school and noting all of the places where food is grown, refined, packaged, or sold.

⚅ Connect the cake baking with science lessons on the chemical reactions of leavening agents or on plant growth.

⚅ Read stories and books that focus on foods, such as "Stone Soup" (there are many variations of this children's favorite) or books by Ann Morris, such as *Bread, Bread, Bread* (Viking, 1989).

⚅ Have students research the ways in which plants and animals raised for food have been distributed around the world through history (e.g., by explorers, sailors, and immigrants).

⚅ With older students, do concept clarification exercises so that students learn to distinguish between farming (small agricultural holdings run by families) and agribusiness (large tracts of land given over to production of single crops run by large corporations);

Teaching Green: The Elementary Years

About the Ingredients

Vegetable oil: Of the wide variety of edible vegetable and nut oils, those most commonly used for cooking in North America are canola oil and soybean oil. Canola, a member of the mustard family, is mostly grown on the Canadian prairies and in the northern United States. Soybeans originated in Asia and now grow in many parts of the world, including Canada and the United States. The seeds of these plants are crushed to obtain the oil and the remainder is fed as a high-protein supplement to pigs, cattle, and chickens.

Did you know? Vegetable oil — even used cooking oil — can easily be turned into biodiesel, a diesel-engine fuel that is renewable and cleaner burning than fossil fuels.

Sugar: Sugar is obtained from either sugar cane or beets. Sugar cane, a very tall grass with big stems, is grown mostly in the Caribbean, South and Central America, and Australia. The sugar beet is a root resembling a large parsnip that is grown in temperate North America.

Did you know? When sugar has been extracted from the juice of the cane plant, a strong-tasting black syrup known as molasses remains. When white sugar is made, the molasses is entirely removed, whereas brown sugars retain varying amounts of this natural syrup. The more molasses in brown sugar, the stickier the crystals, the darker the color, and the stronger the flavor. However, the presence of molasses does not change sugar's nutritional value.

Eggs: Eggs are produced nearly everywhere that people live, so there is a good chance that the eggs you eat come from a nearby farm. Eggs labeled "free range" are from hens that are allowed to move around outdoors in the fresh air and are not confined in small cages; eggs labeled "organic" are from animals that are not fed antibiotics and growth hormones.

Did you know? The difference between brown eggs and white eggs has to do with the breed of the chicken and not the nutritional value of the eggs.

Flour: Flour, which is made by grinding wheat, is the staple food of millions of people. In North America, wheat production is concentrated in the prairie regions.

Did you know? The wheat grain consists of the outer layer (or bran), the part that would grow into a new plant if the grain (or germ) were planted, and the part that supplies the energy for the new plant (or endosperm). Whole wheat flour contains all parts of the grain and is more nutritious than white flour. White flour is wheat that has been processed to remove the bran and germ, leaving only the endosperm, which is primarily starch. In general, the more a food is processed or refined, the less nutritious it becomes.

Baking soda and baking powder: Baking soda and baking powder are chemical leaveners. They produce the gas carbon dioxide that bubbles through the baked product to lift it and make it rise. They are produced in Canada, the United States, and many other countries.

Did you know? To produce carbon dioxide, baking soda must come into contact with an acidic liquid ingredient (e.g., lemon juice, vinegar, sour cream, buttermilk, or yogurt). Baking powder contains baking soda and an acid salt, so it requires only moisture to produce carbon dioxide.

Cinnamon: Cinnamon is the dried bark of trees in the genus *Cinnamomum*. The main producers of cinnamon are Sri Lanka, Seychelles, Madagascar, Indonesia, China, Vietnam, and India.

Did you know? Flavorings made from the bark and seeds of plants are called spices, whereas those from leaves are called herbs.

Salt: Salt is a mineral that is added to recipes to enhance the flavor of other ingredients. Salt is produced by evaporating sea water and by mining halite, or rock salt that formed through the evaporation of sea water millions of years ago. More than three-quarters of the salt that is used worldwide is produced in North America.

continued next page

between subsistence crops (crops grown to feed a family) and cash crops (crops grown to sell and bring money into the family or corporation). Students could research sustainable agriculture (where practices are used that ensure the land will continue to produce food for future generations). They could discuss what happens when farmers are forced to rely on one export crop instead of growing food that is more suitable for their land and which could, in a less processed form, feed their own people.

*Jackie Kirk has baked many "world" cakes with children in different countries. Formerly an elementary school teacher, she is now a research associate at the McGill Centre for Research and Teaching on Women in Montréal, where she works particularly on teacher training in emergency and post-conflict settings. **Mary Gale Smith** teaches home economics education in the Faculty of Education at the University of British Columbia in Vancouver, British Columbia. This article was originally written by Jackie Kirk; it was expanded and updated in 2005 by Mary Gale Smith.*

continued from previous page

Did you know? Table salt appears to be white, but actually consists of clear cubes. Salt lowers the melting point of water and is often used to melt ice on highways in winter.

Carrots and zucchini: Carrots and zucchini are vegetables that are very easy to grow and are often cultivated in home gardens. Both are grown in Canada and the United States and many other countries.

Did you know? Vegetables that are "certified organic" are grown on farms that are regularly inspected and approved as following practices that do not deplete the soil or pollute the land, such as avoiding the use of agricultural toxins (pesticides, herbicides, fungicides, and chemical fertilizers). Most organic farmers keep fossil-fuel use to a minimum and emphasize producing foods of high nutritional quality.

Pineapple: Most pineapples eaten in North America come from Hawaii or Central America, although the top four producers of pineapples are Thailand, Philippines, Brazil, and India. Pineapples usually have labels indicating where they are from. Pineapple is often processed and canned so that it can be kept longer than fresh fruit.

Did you know? The pineapple is native to southern Brazil and Paraguay. It was spread by indigenous peoples through South and Central America to the Caribbean. In 1493, Columbus brought the fruit from Guadeloupe to Spain. The Spanish then introduced it to the Philippines and may have taken it to Hawaii and Guam early in the 16th century. The reason that the pineapple traveled so far is that it was carried on sea voyages as a source of vitamin C for protection against scurvy.

Walnuts: Most walnuts purchased for baking in North America are grown in California. Walnuts are also grown for export in China, Iran, Turkey, and Mexico.

Did you know? Archeological evidence dating back to about 7,000 BCE indicates that walnuts are one of the oldest tree foods used by humans. Black walnuts are native to North America, while "English" walnuts likely originated in Persia (Iran) and were so named because English merchant ships transported the nuts for trade around the world.

Coconut: A coconut is the seed of the coconut palm tree. The coconut originated on the Pacific islands of Melanesia and has been widely distributed, carried by water (coconut seeds float) and by humans, to all parts of the tropics and subtropics. Top producers of coconut are Indonesia, India, and the Philippines. The white "meat" inside the hard shell of the coconut is grated and dried and sold either sweetened or unsweetened as shredded coconut.

Did you know? A coconut is the largest known seed in the world. Once it falls from a palm tree, it takes about three years to take root and sprout.

Sultanas: Sultanas are a variety of seedless grape native to Turkey. When dried, sultana raisins are eaten as is or used in baking. They are similar enough to golden raisins that they can be substituted for each other in recipes. Golden raisins are produced from Thompson seedless grapes grown in California.

Did you know? The name of sultana grapes is derived from the Arabic word "sultan," which means king or prince.

Chocolate: The source of chocolate is the cacao bean, which grows in long melon-shaped seed pods attached to the cacao tree. The Ivory Coast is a major world supplier of cocoa.

Did you know? Many cocoa producers get so little money for their product that they are trapped in a life of poverty, and they often have no choice but to use children as workers. Child cocoa workers rarely have an opportunity to attend school. Some consumers purchase chocolate that is labeled "Fair Trade." This means that the producers of the chocolate receive a fair price for their product, which enables them to pay adult workers a living wage rather than relying on child labor.

— *by Mary Gale Smith*

This teaching idea is based on "The Whole World Cake," an activity in "Live Thoughtfully: An RE Curriculum for Global Citizenship," a teaching resource for ages 7 to 11 produced by the Christian Aid Society (available in PDF format on-line at <www.christianaid.org.uk/> at the "le@rn zone").

References
Books

Hardin, Garrett. *Filters against Folly: How to Survive Despite Economists, Ecologists, and the Merely Elegant.* Viking, 1985.

Savage, Candace. *Eat Up: Healthy Food for a Healthy Earth.* Douglas and McIntyre, 1992.

Savage, Candace. *Get Growing.* Douglas & McIntyre, 1991.

Fair trade products

Bridgehead markets fair trade products globally. For information, contact Bridgehead at 366 Bank Street, Ottawa, ON K2P 1Y4, 1-800-565-8563, <www.bridgehead.ca>.

The Fair Trade Federation has a listing of retail stores selling fair trade products in each state of the U.S. <www.fairtradefederation.org>.

TransFair Canada and TransFair USA websites have information on fair trade and directories of outlets for fair trade coffee, tea, cocoa, sugar, and fruit (see <www.transfair.ca/> or <www.transfairusa.org>).

Learning About Interconnectedness

Introductory activities for teaching young children relational thinking and cooperation skills

Illustrations by Tom Goldsmith

by Graham Pike and David Selby

Grade levels: K-4

Subject areas: social studies

Key concepts: interdependence

Skills: communication, cooperation, problem solving, relational thinking

Location: indoors or outdoors

Interconnectedness is the conceptual glue that binds together the ideas, fields, focuses, themes, and topics that fall within the orbit of global education. In economic, environmental, social, and political terms, global educators are concerned with the nature and effects of connections, propelled by movements of goods, people, and information that link all humanity together — albeit not always within relationships that are just and equitable. They are likewise at pains to show that any global issue is linked, to a greater or lesser degree, to all other global issues; that

issues of development, environment, peace, and social justice are interwoven. Phases of time are also seen as interconnected: past, present, and future are not discrete periods but are deeply embedded, one within another. At a personal level, global education is concerned with the synergies that can arise from helping students mindfully connect their mental, emotional, physical, and spiritual potentials and their inner well-being to the well-being of the planet.

A challenge for the global educator is how to help students think in a relational mode. The introductory activities offered here suggest some practical ways forward with younger children.

Cooperative Loops

This is a useful activity for promoting cooperative attitudes and skills and for illustrating interconnectedness. It also gives practice in communication and problem solving.

Materials: one piece of drawing paper, one pencil, two colored crayons per student

Time: 20 minutes

Procedure:

1. Give each student a piece of paper, a pencil, and two crayons of different colors. Divide the class into two groups.

2. Ask students in one group to use their pencils to draw from the top left corner of their paper to the bottom right corner, making five loops as they draw. Ask students in the second group to start at the bottom left corner and end at the top right, again making five loops.

3. Ask the students to color in the loops they have made, using a different color for each loop. However, explain that they are each allowed to use only the two crayons they were given. Therefore, they must get help from each other to complete the coloring.

4. When all have finished their coloring, ask the students to join their loops together into one continuous line, perhaps by standing in a circle holding their pieces of paper. Students must position themselves so that end loops on adjacent squiggles are of different colors.

Messagematch

In this activity, students are each given one or two words on a card and must join their words with those of other students in order to complete a message. The activity emphasizes cooperation, interdependence, and relational thinking.

Materials: index cards

Time: 30 minutes

Procedure:

1. Write several short messages on index cards, and cut the cards so that each student will have a piece of a complete message. Examples are:

Fish / swim / in deep / ponds
Birds / fly / in clear / blue / skies
Gophers / burrow / in prairie / fields
Bears / hibernate / when / winter / comes

Vary the length of the messages to accommodate the number of students, as each student's piece must fit with others to form a message that has no duplicated pieces. With a group of 18, for example, create three six-piece messages or six three-piece messages; with a group of 26, a combination of four-, five-, and six-piece messages would be needed.

2. Hand out the message pieces, one per student, and tell the students how many different messages have been distributed. For the first round, you may wish to use only one message, duplicated as many times as necessary. For the second round, circulate more than one message.

3. Ask students to move around the room and join others to make a whole message. Explain that success in the game requires that every member of the class be part of a message.

4. Divide the class into groups of four to six and have each group devise its own message on blank cards. The messages must have the same number of pieces as the number of students in the group.

5. Jumble all of the message pieces, distribute one piece to each student, and play another round as described in Step 3.

6. Conclude by asking students to share their experience. Some questions to ask are:

☙ How did students set about finding what the whole message might be?

☙ What made the task difficult? easy?

☙ At what moment did a group feel they had the right answer? Did they then have to accommodate any changes?

☙ Did students remember that success involved everybody's being part of a message?

☙ Who was easiest to find: the first, second, or last person in the message? Why?

Variation: To make the activity easier for young students, tell the students how many pieces make up a whole message, or write "Start" and "End" on the appropriate cards. ❧

Graham Pike is Dean of the Faculty of Education, University of Prince Edward Island in Charlottetown, Prince Edward Island. David Selby is Professor of the Faculty of Education at the University of Plymouth in England.

"Cooperative Loops" was suggested by Alan Simpson, West Walker Primary School, Newcastle upon Tyne, England. "Messagematch" was developed by Graham Rowland, Fenton Primary School, Devon, England; an earlier version was published in *Global Teacher, Global Learner* by Graham Pike and David Selby (Hodder and Stoughton, 1988).

Around the World in 90 Days

Students enhanced their knowledge of world geography by visiting seven continents in 90 days — without ever leaving the classroom

Photographs by Michelle Cusolito

Making cut-paper "tiles" in the fashion of Roman mosaics provided lessons in art, history, and mathematics.

by Michelle Cusolito and Bill White

Grade levels: 4-6

Subject areas: multidisciplinary

Key concepts: world geography, ecosystems, culture

Skills: map making, observing, measuring, researching, organizing ideas, writing, reading, creating, self-evaluating

Location: primarily indoors

Time: 3 months

Are your students short on world geography? If so, you are not alone. Studies have found that many children in North America are substantially less knowledgeable about world geography than their counterparts around the world. But is it possible for teachers to contribute to geography learning without neglecting the curriculum or increasing their workload? We think so. Rather than teach a geography unit out of a book, we reorganized our instruction to integrate subjects and still address the concepts we were required to teach. The result was an integrated unit called "Around the World in 90 Days" that takes students on a "tour" of the seven continents. The unit can be adapted for use at several grade levels and can include studies in physical geography, history, trade, culture, and the environment. The Around the World theme thus provides a natural springboard for integrating social studies, language arts, art, math, science, music, and physical education.

Getting organized

To focus our Around the World unit, we chose to limit the study of each continent to physical geography, ecosystems, and cultures. Physical geography would be the common thread leading students from one continent to the next. For example, the students would study rivers and rainforests in South America and then find the same physical features in Africa, as well as additional ones to learn about.

We introduced the theme to our students in September by saying, "We're going around the world. What could we do or see on our journey?" We used the

196

students' responses to create a semantic map (web), categorizing ideas by continents, oceans, and interesting sights, both natural and human-built. This enabled us to assess our students' prior knowledge and to organize their thinking for the learning experiences that would follow. We also asked the students to draw an outline map of the world on a sheet of graph paper. We decided as a class where to place the equator and compass rose, and then students worked independently to complete their maps without using atlases or any other resources. We saved these prior-knowledge maps until the end of the unit.

A young woman visiting from Uganda told how receiving a goat from the development agency Heifer Project International had changed her family's life. Afterwards, the students raised money for the project.

Setting sail

The official launch of the unit was a classroom visit by a local man who had spent two and a half years sailing around the world. He shared journal entries, artifacts he had collected, and stories about his experiences both at sea and in other lands. After listening to the visitor's tales and recording their impressions of his journey in their learning logs, the students were ready to begin their own journey. We gave each student a blank outline map of the world, and we hung large wall maps in the classroom on which we posted the image of a sailing schooner at our hometown port of Plymouth,

Massachusetts. These maps would link students' learning from continent to continent. As they learned about new landforms and other geographical features of the continents, they recorded them on their outline maps. And as we traveled around the world, we moved the ship on the wall map to each new location. We also gave students "passports" to document their travels. These were booklets with the students' names and photographs, similar to real passports. As we arrived at each new location on our journey, students wrote the date and the place in their passports and had them stamped by the teacher.

We spent our first week in North America, establishing procedures for using passports, as well as for recording information on the outline maps and in students' learning logs. We began with a study of local geography that included field trips to a woodland and to the rocky intertidal zone of the shore. For the rest of our North American study, we focused our attention on mountains and plains, as these are the dominant landforms on this continent. Students marked on their maps the mountains and plains of North America and created a key to explain their use of colors and symbols. In this way, they began to turn their basic outline maps into relief maps.

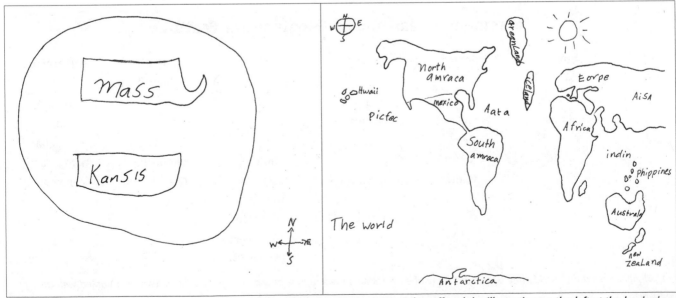

Before and after: Given the task of drawing a map of the world, one young cartographer offered the illustration on the left at the beginning of his fourth grade year. Three months later, the same student produced the map on the right.

We studied the next five continents — South America, Africa, Europe, Asia, and Australia/Oceania — in the same fashion, allotting two weeks for each. At each stop on our journey, our study began with a look at two new landforms or other physical features (see the chart "Incremental Learning of Geographical Features") and then expanded to include plants, animals, and ecosystems. Finally, we concentrated on how the physical environment has influenced human culture on each continent. Visitors were an important resource in this part of the project because they helped to make the connection between landscape and culture. A parent who had grown up in Venezuela talked about her life as a child in South America; an exchange student from Belgium talked about the different regions and cultures of that country; and students and teachers alike shared artifacts from their travels or family collections. As a way of comparing the cultures, students often asked visitors the same questions. For instance, they asked each person how to say "welcome" in their language, and this information was added to our international welcome bulletin board. One student was particularly intrigued by the word for "banana" in each visitor's language!

Integral to our studies were art projects connected to the continent being studied. These projects tapped students' different learning styles and intelligences and made the Around the World theme come alive for them. When we studied Central and South America,

Papier mâché cat mummies of ancient Egypt.

for example, students learned the process of bark painting from the art teacher, and we connected this to a study of Mexican culture. During our study of Europe, the art teacher integrated a unit on impressionist painting. While studying Australia, our classes researched the flora and fauna of the Great Barrier Reef and worked together to make a 4.5-meter (15-foot) mural of a coral reef along the corridor wall. As students worked on their projects, we played music from the continents being studied, thereby further increasing students' exposure to the culture.

Students take the helm

When we arrived in Antarctica, we decided to allow our students to take control of their own research. To do this, we created a skeleton framework and then let them choose their focus. We began by listing what our students knew about Antarctica. Some of their statements were inaccurate, but we recorded them nonetheless. We then elicited students' questions about Antarctica and listed these on chart paper. The students cut the list into separate questions and sorted them according to criteria that they determined. The three categories of inquiry that they settled on were geography, plants and animals, and people.

The students sought answers to their questions by reading books and articles about Antarctica. They also e-mailed an artist in Antarctica and a scientist who had returned from Antarctica. As their questions were

Incremental Learning of Geographical Features

North America	South America	Africa	Europe	Asia	Australia/ Oceania	Antarctica
mountains*	mountains	mountains	mountains	mountains	mountains	mountains
plains*	plains	savannah*	plains	plains	outback*	islands
	rivers*	rivers	rivers	rivers	islands	peninsula
	rainforest*	rainforest	islands*	rainforest	peninsula	permafrost
		desert*	peninsula*	desert	barrier reef*	icebergs*
				islands		
				peninsula		
				archipelago*		
				permafrost*		

As students traveled the world, they began the study of each continent with a look at two new geographical features (marked with an asterisk).

198

Global Awareness

answered, the students wrote what they learned on sticky notes and posted them under the appropriate headings on a graphic organizer that became a large KWL (What We Think We **K**now, What We **W**ant to Know, What We **L**earned) chart. All the facts were compiled and recorded so that each child would have a record of the research.

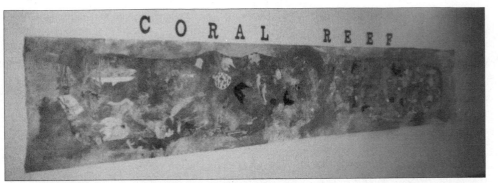

While "visiting" Australia's Great Barrier Reef, students made a hallway mural depicting the variety of creatures and habitats of a coral reef.

At the end of our Around the World tour, we returned to North America. During the rest of the year, we focused on Native Americans and the regions of the United States, which constitute the bulk of the Grade 4 curriculum.

Subject integration: The key to extending the journey

Although some of these lessons took place during social studies time, by integrating subjects we were able to increase the amount of time we spent traveling. We used science time for learning tasks and research related to ecosystems and climate. For example, while learning about the Andes Mountains, we discussed the effects of elevation and latitude on climate. We focused on animal adaptations while studying tidal pools of the North American coast, and learned about the symbiotic relationship between coral polyps and algae when exploring the Great Barrier Reef.

We also used our language arts block to the fullest. Students composed letters to e-mail to Antarctica and recorded information in their learning logs. We read books that are set in other countries, such as Beverley Naidoo's *Journey to Jo'berg* (South Africa) and Eleanor Coerr's *Sadako and the Thousand Paper Cranes* (Japan). We also used the public library extensively and kept a rack full of books concerning each continent in the classroom so that our students could read them on their own time.

Art and music were woven throughout the study: we played music from around the world almost daily and did many art projects. The physical education teacher taught our students *tinikling*, a dance from the Philippines. We integrated math by having students use measurement skills to design their graphic organizers. They also calculated the distance we traveled and determined the time changes as we went to different time zones. One of the art projects integrated math as well. While studying Rome, students created mosaic-patterned squares reminiscent of Roman mosaic tiles. These mosaics needed to have at least two lines of symmetry and an identifiable pattern. We gave students a math rubric before the project and evaluated their work on the basis of whether they demonstrated mastery of the required math elements.

Planning and assessing the unit

We found that we needed to devote two or three hours per week to planning. The time we spent overall, however, was not much greater than the amount of time we usually spent planning because we integrated all subjects, to varying degrees. Furthermore, co-planning was invigorating. We covered more ground and were able to divide tasks such as getting supplies or making copies. We also used this planning time to develop assessment tools, such as rubrics, and to decide how these assessments would be reflected on report cards.

In keeping with our methods of instruction, we used a variety of tools to assess students' progress. When reading their learning logs, we looked for clarity of thought and organization of ideas. We asked students to assess their own work on the basis of rubrics that we had given them at the beginning of the unit, although we made the final decisions regarding the scores that students earned. We also used rubrics to evaluate projects and presentations. For example, when we studied Egypt, our students constructed a 4.5-meter (15-foot) three-dimensional map of the Nile River along the floor, complete with the pyramids at Giza and irrigated farmlands. When they had finished the project, students evaluated their effort and the thoroughness of the research they had done to support their work. They also gave answers to open-response questions, explaining the importance of the Nile River to the people of ancient Egypt.

When our travels ended, students wrote letters to the school principal describing what they had learned, what they enjoyed most, and what they would change about the Around the World project. We gave the letters two marks: one for content and one for following the proper "friendly letter" format based on the rubric that we had given students before they began writing. Finally, with all the maps and globes hidden, the students again drew maps of the world from memory. The results were remarkable! Every student's knowledge had increased and nearly all students placed the continents and oceans in the proper locations.

Michelle Cusolito is the director of School Learning for the South Coast Learning Network in New Bedford, Massachusetts, and an adjunct professor at Lesley University in Cambridge, Massachusetts. She taught at Plymouth South Elementary School in Plymouth, Massachusetts, for ten years, where she and fellow educator Sandria Parsons collaborated on the Around the World project. Bill White has served as a teacher and curriculum administrator in public schools in New York and Rhode Island and in private U.S. schools in Southeast Asia and the Middle East. More recently he has been working as a resource consultant in curriculum and program development in New England. He lives in Rhode Island.

Resources
Books

Allman, Janet, and Jere Brophy. *Social Studies Excursions, K–3: Powerful Units on Food, Clothing, and Shelter.* Heinemann, 2003.

Arquilevich, Gabriel. *World Religions.* Teacher Created Resources, 2003. An interdisciplinary thematic unit for Grades 5-12. See <www.teachercreated.com>.

Bevan, Finn. *Cities of Splendor* (*Landscapes of Legend* series). Children's Press, 1998. This book highlights myths, fables, and folk tales from around the world.

Bosveld, Jane. *While a Tree Was Growing.* American Museum of Natural History & Workman Publishing, 1997. A timeline shows the historical events that occurred during the life of a 3,000-year-old sequoia tree.

Coerr, Eleanor. *Sadako and the Thousand Paper Cranes.* Dell Publishing, 1977.

Estes, Annice, ed. *Global Feast Cookbook: Recipes from Around the World.* Mystic Seaport Museum Stores, 1994. The recipes are easy to follow and have been adapted for North American cooks (no exotic, hard-to-find ingredients).

Grant, Neil, and Peter Morter. *Great Atlas of Discovery.* Knopf, 1992.

Naidoo, Beverley. *Journey to Jo'berg.* Harper Collins, 1988

O'Neill, Cynthia, Peter Casterton, and Catherine Headlam. *Goddesses, Heroes, and Shamans: The Young People's Guide to World Mythology.* Scholastic, 1994.

Roberts, Patricia L. *Literature-Based History Activities for Children, Grades 1–3.* Allyn & Bacon, 1998.

Schneck, Susan. *Multicultural Clip Art from Around the World.* Scholastic Professional Books, 1995.

Van Rose, Susanna. *Earth Atlas: The Forces That Make and Shape Our Planet.* Dorling Kindersley, 1994.

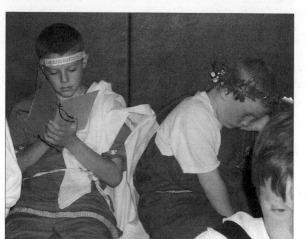

Students researched famous people they met on their travels, wrote descriptions of them, created costumes, and then posed in "wax museum" tableaus. The school community, including 400 family members, toured the exhibit.

Watt, Fiona. *The Usborne Children's World Cookbook.* Usborne, 2000. This kid-friendly cookbook is "Internet-linked," meaning that Usborne site has links to reviewed sites where students can learn more about the cultures that produced the recipes; see <www.usborne-book-store.com>.

Music

Global Celebration (*Authentic Music from Festivals and Celebrations Around the World*), Ellipsis Arts, 1993 (various artists on four music CDs).

Putamayo World Music, <www.putumayo.com>. An excellent source of world music.

Websites

<www.bfi.org/map.htm> Buckminster Fuller Institute. Here you can see the Fuller Projection map, a flat map showing the Earth without distortion of the relative shapes and sizes of the land areas.

<www.culturegrams.com> CultureGrams. Concise four-page summaries of all the world's countries, published by ProQuest, can be ordered from this site.

<www.enchantedlearning.com/geography> Enchanted Learning. Provides outline maps and geography resources and activities for elementary students.

<www.nationalgeographic.org> National Geographic Society. The main website has wealth of international information. Details about the Society's annual Geography Action program can be found at <www.nationalgeographic.com/geographyaction>.

<www.usborne-book-store.com> Usborne Books. Publisher of many great titles for world studies, such as *World Religions*, *Peoples of the World*, and *The Usborne Children's World Cookbook*.

Development Days:
A Schoolwide Theme

Photographs by Alison Flensburg

How far can a cookie stretch? Students learn about global inequalities and the importance of sharing through a simulation of the world distribution of food.

by Alison Flensburg

Grade levels: K-5

Subject areas: social studies, art, mathematics, health, science, language arts

Key concepts: development, human rights, social justice, sustainable consumption, equitable distribution of resources

Location: classroom, library (for research and presentations), gymnasium (for large simulations)

Time: 1-3 weeks

ducation must be more than the transmission of knowledge; it must also develop human beings who care deeply about others and about their world. The topics of development education — human rights, social justice, the equitable distribution and sustainable use of resources — may seem too complex for some students at the elementary level, but there are many ways of bringing these topics within the sphere of students' experience. At our school, we approached development education as part of a schoolwide emphasis on the theme of caring. Within this context, development education took on a personal meaning and a heightened emotional power. We chose the period around Valentine's Day as an especially suitable time for highlighting our theme of "caring on a global scale." At other schools, we focused on the theme as a buildup to the Unicef campaign at Halloween. The following suggestions are offered for carrying out a schoolwide Development Days theme at the elementary level.

Organizing Development Days

First, recruit an organizing committee to plan and gather resources for the theme. In addition to inviting staff members to join, consider including older students who have lived in or have an interest in the developing world.

The key to success in planning a schoolwide theme is teacher buy-in, as teachers will not be enthusiastic about a school theme that feels like an add-on to an already crowded curriculum. A first step, therefore, is to ask teachers to identify a topic in their curriculum that integrates well with development education and that they wish to focus on during the theme days. For example, a primary grade teacher who is undertaking a study of families might focus on how families around the world fulfill their basic needs. At the higher grades, the development theme could be linked to units on human rights, community service and helping others, interdependence in the global village, needs versus wants, and sustainable consumption, or the study of a particular developing country. Sometimes

Students in the Asian group of a simulation on global disparity consider their meager portions of the cookie "wealth."

a connection to the development theme can be made through one topic of a unit, such as the topic of refugees in a study of immigration or the topic of clean water in a study of natural resources. Another option is to integrate the development theme through an ongoing study of current events. Also ask teachers to indicate the kinds of resources they would find valuable, such as posters, resource people, references, audio-visual materials, and take-home materials for students. In this way, the organizing committee can provide exactly what teachers need.

The Cookie Game

In this simulation, students gain an understanding of the unequal distribution of food in the world and have the opportunity to suggest ways to correct this imbalance.

Grade levels: 2-6

Materials: Large bag of cookies or other treats

Procedure:

1. Divide a large bag of cookies into four unequal parts: 3 piles that have only a few cookies, and one pile that contains three-quarters or more of the total number.

2. Divide the class into four groups of equal number.

3. By random selection (draw numbers from a hat), distribute the four piles of cookies to the four groups.

4. Discuss the following questions:

◑ How do the three groups with few cookies feel about the distribution? If food were distributed in this way over a long period of time, what might happen?

◑ What is the relationship between the exercise and the real world?

◑ How might the global imbalance in food be redressed? List ideas and have students evaluate each.

Out-To-Lunch Game (variation)

Grade levels: 3 and up

Procedure:

1. Have each student bring one sandwich and one piece of fruit to class.

2. Divide the class into two groups, assigning one-quarter of the students to one group and three-quarters of the students to the other group.

3. Collect the sandwiches and fruit and redistribute them so that the small group receives four of every five portions. Before the students eat, they must decide how to divide the food within their groups. Students may trade and work out deals between groups, and up to one-third of the large group is allowed to migrate to the small group, but immigration criteria are decided by the small group.

4. Discuss the following questions:

◑ How is the exercise symbolic of the relationship between rich and poor?

◑ How were the students able to solve the problem of unequal distribution of lunches?

◑ What conflicts arose among the groups? How are these conflicts similar to what happens among nations?

Continental Lunch (variation for large groups)

Gathering several classes together for the simulation makes it easier to demonstrate the crowding in certain areas of the world. This activity is particularly successful when it is facilitated by someone with authority whom the students know (such as the principal or vice principal).

Grade levels: 3 and up

Materials: chairs, slips of paper, cookies or other "goodies," whistle (or microphone if the group is large)

continued next page

Gathering resources

A good place to start gathering information and contacts is non-governmental organizations that work in the field of international development. For example, we have received tremendous help from Unicef, the Red Cross, Save the Children, Amnesty International, and the Mennonite Central Committee. In addition to these large and well-known organizations, contact local organizations that support overseas development projects. Many such organizations offer excellent materials that help educators relate development issues to their particular curriculum focus. These include teachers' guides with suggested activities, as well as audio-visual resources. Most organizations will send you materials through the mail, sometimes on loan, and some may be able to provide a guest speaker. A fax or phone call describing your particular needs can be very rewarding.

Before the theme days begin, arrange to have time at a staff meeting to introduce resources and provide a schedule of activities. Print and audio-visual materials will be better used when they have been presented rather than simply left out for perusal and borrowing.

Activities and events
Simulations

A powerful tool for introducing development education is a simulation that demonstrates global disparities. As an example, during our theme days, several classes gathered in the gymnasium where the floor had been marked off into areas proportional to the sizes of the regions of the world. As the students entered, they chose a slip of paper with the name of a region and were directed to the corresponding area of the gym. The North Americans were comfortably seated on chairs, the Asians squished together. Next, goodies were distributed to the regions in proportion to the distribution of wealth in the world. The students within

---

continued from previous page

Preparation:

1. Divide a large room or gymnasium into five areas that represent the relative sizes of the following five regions: Africa, Asia, Latin America (including Mexico), Europe, and North America. (Use the percentages in the "Land Mass" column of the chart to determine how much area to allot each region.) If you are using a large gym, you may not wish to use the whole area, as it is important that certain areas be crowded. Post signs to indicate the areas.

Population, Wealth, and Land Mass by Region			
Region	**Population**	**Per Capita Wealth**	**Land Mass**
Africa	13%	2%	23%
Asia	61%	5%	37%
Latin America (including Mexico)	9%	9%	16%
Europe	12%	28%	8%
North America	5%	56%	16%

2. Place chairs in the wealthier areas of the world to accommodate all or most of the students who will be assigned to those regions. You might also wish to place one or two chairs in the other areas, to demonstrate that there are wealthy people in poor regions.

3. Prepare slips of paper, one for each student, each slip having the name of one of the regions. Use the percentages in the "Population" column on the chart to determine how many slips of paper to make for each region. You may wish to indicate on the slips one traveling negotiator

and one home-based negotiator for each group. In that case, also make a sign for each negotiator to pin on, such as "African Traveling Negotiator." Put the slips of paper in a hat or other container.

4. Divide the cookies into five portions, ready to hand out to the groups. (See the "Wealth" column in the chart for the distribution percentages.)

Procedure:

1. As students enter the room, have each one pick a slip of paper and go to the area that is marked on the slip.

2. Set basic ground rules (e.g., a whistle will be blown to get their attention or to change activities).

3. Hand out the cookies to each group and ask them to sit in a circle to discuss their situation and how they should negotiate. Explain that they may negotiate deals between groups, such as trades, donations, and immigration of some students from one group to another. To arrange deals, the traveling negotiators go to other groups and talk to the home-based negotiators there, and then return to their own areas to discuss their negotiations. Once a deal is negotiated, the arrangements are carried out by the traveling negotiators.

4. Plan for 10 or 15 minutes to debrief in the large group and encourage the teachers to continue the debriefing afterwards in their own classes. Students also benefit from writing about the experience.

— "The Cookie Game" was developed by the Canadian Red Cross Society

---

each region had to distribute their portion of the good-ies among themselves. (See the "Continental Lunch" variation of "The Cookie Game" on page 202.) It was fascinating to see the conflicts and political maneuver-ings that developed! Then students were debriefed to get their reactions to the inequality ("But that isn't fair!") and to help them understand the conflicts and issues that ensued. This powerful experience harnesses young people's natural concern for justice and fairness, and helps them to develop empathy with those who suffer the consequences of global inequity. It is an excellent opening for encouraging students to consider how global imbalances might be corrected.

There are several versions of this well-known simu-lation, a simple one being "The Cookie Game" (see page 202). Another version called "The Out to Lunch Game" is more sophisticated in that it encourages immigration and deals, such as trades and donations, be-tween groups. Ideally, every student in the school should have a simulation experience at a level appropriate to their understand-ing. Even our kinder-garten and Grade 1 classes participated in a very simple simula-tion as part of a lesson on sharing. The chil-dren were divided into groups by means of a draw of colored cards, and one group got carrot sticks and one group didn't. The group with the "wealth" was encouraged to share with the less fortu-nate — and they did!

Mother Earth enlists students' help at an assembly to launch the school's Unicef Halloween campaign.

Presenters

If you are in a city in which a number of development organizations maintain offices, you will have the option of inviting several presenters from these groups. How-ever, guest speakers do not have to be from organiza-tions. Immigrants and refugees can provide very valu-able perspectives. Teachers of English as a second lan-guage may be able to recommend former students, and staff and parents may know of people with experience on development projects.

Presenters contributed to our theme by telling stories, showing slides, and facilitating simulations.

Each was asked to make two presentations. In most cases, they spoke to individual classes, matching the content of their presentation to the teacher's curricular focus. Because we believed it was critical not to focus exclusively on global disparities, we built on multicul-tural concepts by inviting a representative of the Mennonite Central Committee to show samples of marvelous handmade items from developing nations. We grouped classes together for these presentations so that every child in the school participated.

Action projects

Most non-governmental organizations can suggest development projects that students could become involved in directly or could support through fundrais-ing. Fundraising activities might in-clude:

- having sales of items such as houseplants or vegetables that students have grown, or of used books, toys, games, records, and comic books

- organizing a school dance, or a sports challenge between students and teachers, and donating the admission fees and profits from the concession

- donating money earned doing chores at home

- asking students' families and friends to sponsor them on a "junk food fast" for a period of time

Scarce Resources Day

Consider declaring a "Scarce Resources Day" when the entire school population uses no more resources than would be typically available in a school in a developing country. Invite students to help decide what they should do without (e.g., put away computers, audio-visual equipment, calculators, pens), and how the class will adapt to scarcity (e.g., if the teacher has the only textbook, the students must copy exercises from the blackboard). To be fully effective, this exercise requires that students and all staff, including caretaking, library, and administrative staff, be carefully prepared and that the students be thoroughly debriefed.

Culminating events

As a culminating event, each class could prepare a performance piece such as a rap, a song, a skit, or a PowerPoint presentation for an assembly. Another possibility is to plan a fair and have students work in groups to prepare posters and displays on various development issues, such as the importance of clean water. This can be a multidisciplinary experience involving art, health, science, social studies, and language arts.

Once the theme and activities are planned, there is nothing more satisfying than watching the excitement grow, the awareness of development issues expand, and the seeds of caring on a global scale being nurtured in the hearts of young citizens. Helping students to believe that they can make a difference in the world is a powerful legacy. As the saying goes, "I touch the future; I teach."

Alison Flensburg has taught Grades K through 6 and English as a second language, and presently teaches kindergarten at Wildwood Elementary School in Saskatoon, Saskatchewan. The Development Days activities described in this article took place at Howard Coad School in Saskatoon.

Students add their two cents' worth to a fundraising penny trail on the gym floor.

Resources
Print and audio-visual

Bigelow, Bill, and Bob Peterson, ed. *Rethinking Globalization: Teaching for Justice in an Unjust World*. Rethinking Schools Press, 2002. This fascinating book contains background readings, lesson plans, role plays and simulations, interviews, poems, cartoons, and annotated resource lists. (Grades 4-12).

Parrish, Margaret, ed. *A Life Like Mine: How Children Live Around the World*. Dorling Kindersley Publishing in association with UNICEF, 2002. In this beautiful book about the lives of children, readers learn what is being done to protect children's rights. (Grades 1-6.)

Smith, David. *If the World Were a Village: A Book About the World's People*. Kids Can Press, 2002. Through the powerful analogy of the world as a village of 100 people, readers learn about the disparate conditions of people on Earth. A teacher's guide to the book is available at the website of A & C Black Publishing; see <www.acblack.com/globalvillage/>. (Grade 3 and up.)

Venetoulis, Jason, Dahlia Chazan, and Christopher Gaudet. *Ecological Footprint of Nations*. Redefining Progress, 2004. As background information for teachers, this report compares the ecological footprints of countries and makes connections between consumption levels and issues of environmental protection and equity. Available in PDF format at the Publications section of the Redefining Progress website <www.rprogress.org>.

World Vision Canada. *Communities Around the World, Around the Corner*. World Vision Canada, 2001. This video and teacher's guide on community studies is an excellent resource for Grades 2 to 6 teachers wanting to show relationships between environmental and global issues. It focuses on three children, one in a nomadic tribe in Tanzania, one in a mountain village in Nicaragua, and one in a slum in Delhi. Available through the World Vision Canada website at <www.curriculum.org/csc/resources/communities.shtml>.

Websites

<www.feedingminds.org> Feeding Minds, Fighting Hunger. An "international classroom" offering lessons on hunger, malnutrition, and food insecurity, as well as an excellent list of on-line resources.

<www.freethechildren.org> Free the Children. An international network of children helping children out of poverty and exploitation and empowering them to make social change.

<www.kidscanmakeadifference.org> Kids Can Make a Difference. This is a valuable website aimed at inspiring students to end hunger, both locally and globally. It includes a hunger quiz, hunger facts, and a good list of suggested books.

<www.oxfam.org.uk/coolplanet/kidsweb/index> Oxfam's Cool Planet site. This site has information and ideas for kids and a catalog of resources for schools. The teacher's section offers activities and information for classroom exploration of trade, hunger, and global citizenship. The "Water for All" section has excellent classroom activities and case studies on water-related issues for teaching 9- to 11-year-olds.

<http://readtofeed.org> Read to Feed, Heifer International. This exciting website has stories, games, and other activities for children, as well as information on the Read to Feed program which encourages students to read books while fundraising through sponsorships.

<www.thehungersite.com> The Hunger Site. The Teachers' Resources section of this site has activity ideas and an excellent resource list.

<www.worldvision.ca/home/education-and-justice> World Vision Resources. This site has an extensive list of classroom resources on global issues for Grades 2 and up.

Teaching Children about Chronic Hunger

Activities that demonstrate the connection between chronic hunger and the environment and provide ideas for taking action to help solve the problem

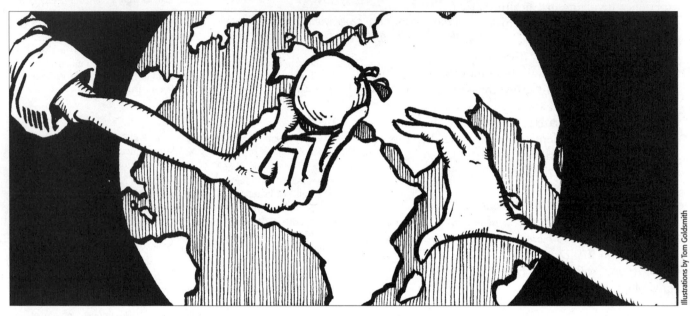

Illustrations by Tom Goldsmith

by Daniel Kriesberg

Grade levels: 4-6

Subject areas: science and social studies

Key concepts: causes of hunger, soil erosion, energy flow in food chains, cash crops, social action, food aid

Skills: modeling, map reading, experimenting, data collection, writing, speaking, problem solving

Location: mainly indoors

unger linked to environmental degradation results in a chronic cycle of misery for many people in the world. But why teach children about such huge and depressing problems? The question is a legitimate one. Yet learning about the causes of hunger can be an empowering process through which students acquire a better understanding of the world and learn skills needed to make a difference. In addition, teaching children about world hunger is an avenue to teaching them about so much else — other cultures, nutrition, government, ecology, geography, and current events. A hunger curriculum is interdisciplinary. It can involve reading newspapers and books or writing reports, stories, speeches, lessons, and letters. It fits into science through ecology and nutrition, into social studies through geography, current events, government, and culture, and into math through graphs, charts, basic operations, percentages, fractions, planning budgets, and counting calories.

The activities described here help demonstrate that the problems of hunger and environmental degradation are connected. They include suggestions for showing students how they can help solve these problems. The objective is not to make children feel guilty for what they have, but rather to empower them with knowledge and skills that allow them to help improve the lives of people around the world and around the corner.

The effects of hunger

A good way to introduce lessons on hunger and to capture the students' attention is to begin eating a favorite food, such as pizza or candy, in front of the class (hide some to share later). While eating, give the class some information related to hunger issues. For a dramatic touch, spill some food on the floor to represent waste. Before sharing the food, ask students how they felt watching you eat and waste food. Then ask them to imagine an airplane crash that killed 24,000 people. What do they think would be the world's reaction if such a crash happened every day? That is the number of people who die each day from hunger and hunger-related diseases.

A dramatic way to show the effects of hunger is to have students try to visualize the annual death toll from hunger. If 24,000 people die each day, how many die in one year? (*Almost nine million.*) Ask students to imagine nine million pencils lined up end to end and calculate how far the line would extend. Refer to statistics in an almanac or the *Guinness Book of Records* to compare the number of deaths from hunger to the number of deaths resulting from other natural and human-caused disasters.

Hunger and the environment

Poor land is a cause of hunger in many places, even in North America. Emphasize to your students that while land seems plentiful, most of it cannot be used for farming. Only 25 percent of the Earth's surface is land. Of that, one-fifth is too cold to farm, one-fifth is at too high an elevation, and one-fifth is too dry. This leaves only two-fifths of the original 25 percent (or 10 percent of the Earth's surface) available for growing crops. Subtract the land that is taken up by roads and buildings, and one can begin to imagine the value of arable soil. In areas where farmland is scarce or diminishing as the result of development or desertification, people are often forced to overuse their land, depleting it of nutrients. As the soil becomes less productive, already poor farmers need even more resources. If they can afford it, they may use chemical fertilizers, which boost production in the short term but further deplete the soil and cause water pollution. Or they may cut down trees to create new farmland, but this deforestation results in soil erosion of and loss of biodiversity. In either case, the soil becomes even less productive and the hunger cycle continues.

The following activities demonstrate the value of soil and factors related to its use.

The components of soil

Give the students hand lenses and a bucket of soil to "dissect." Have them separate the components of the soil and record what they find. Afterwards, ask them to write a recipe for making fertile soil. Their recipes should include rocks to provide minerals, organic matter to provide nutrients and texture, decomposing organisms to break down the organic material and release its nutrients, and water and air.

To demonstrate the making of soil, place a little of each of the ingredients of soil in a bucket. Then ask the students "What is missing?" The missing ingredients

are weathering and time. To form soil, rock must be broken down by climatic factors such as rainfall, temperature variation, sun, and wind. This weathering process is very slow, taking from 100 to 400 years to form a one-centimeter layer of soil. If you wish to dramatize the factor of time, drop a wristwatch into the bucket. Understanding how long it takes for soil to form naturally helps students appreciate its value, as well as the extent of the problem created when soil erodes away or is misused.

The value of soil and water

To show that soil is necessary to grow crops, challenge the students to try to grow beans in the craziest mixtures of materials they can think of. Put the mixtures in egg cartons or small cups and plant a couple of beans in each. Compare their growth to that of beans planted in soil. The beans in the crazy mixtures may sprout, but the beans in the soil will grow better. Have the students attempt to grow beans in a variety of soil types, such as sandy or rocky soil, and then observe and compare the results. Water, like the nutrients in soil, is essential for growing crops. Have the students compare the growth of plants that are given varying amounts of water.

Soil erosion

Soil erosion occurs when there is insufficient vegetation to prevent soil from washing or blowing away. It is a serious problem globally, one that threatens the livelihoods of nearly one billion people.

The effects of water and wind: Use a hose or a bucket of water to demonstrate erosion in the schoolyard or in a tray of soil in the classroom. To demonstrate wind erosion, use a fan or have the students blow on sand or soil. Look for examples of erosion around the school and classify each by its probable cause. Compare the vegetation in eroded areas and in non-eroded areas and discuss why plants would not grow well in areas subject to erosion.

The importance of plant cover: Lack of plant cover is both a result and a major cause of soil erosion. The roots of plants help to stabilize soils, and their foliage acts as a buffer against the erosive forces of rainfall and wind. When vegetation is removed, as occurs during drought or when forests are cleared for farmland, the soil begins to erode away. Where the soil is lost, new plants cannot grow, and this leads to more erosion, thus creating a deadly cycle.

To demonstrate the importance of plant cover, grow grass in a tray of soil. Fill a second tray with bare soil. Pour water over both trays or use a fan to create wind, and compare the degree of erosion in the trays. This demonstration can also be done outside in the schoolyard by comparing the effects of wind and water on a grassy spot with their effects on bare soil.

The slope of the land: Slope also affects erosion. To demonstrate this, put soil into two trays. Prop up one tray to create a steep slope. Pour water on each tray and compare the degree of erosion in each. This demonstration of erosion can also be done in the schoolyard if it has a suitable site. When trees are cut down on mountainsides to supply firewood or lumber, or to create more land for farming, the resulting erosion can be very severe.

For more information on soil, visit the GLOBE program's "Soil and Agriculture" pages at NASA's soil science website <http://ltpwww.gsfc.nasa.gov/globe/index2.htm>.

Hunger and the global economy

Much of the land in developing countries is used to grow non-essential food crops, such as coffee, cocoa, bananas, sugar cane, spices, and tea, or crops that have other uses, such as cotton, rubber, and grain for livestock. These crops are exported to wealthier countries, hence the term "cash crops." In many cases, the money earned goes to wealthy landowners or is used to pay off the country's debt. Little money reaches the average farmer. And since the best land is used for cash crops, little food is grown to feed people locally. As a result, local food prices are high and most people cannot afford to buy it.

Economies that are dependent on a single cash crop are subject to severe disruption if demand for the crop decreases or if a natural disaster destroys the crop. In addition, cash crops can severely damage the environment. Many of the crops require large amounts of chemical fertilizers and pesticides that cause water pollution. And because the most productive land is used for cash crops, subsistence farmers have little choice but to overuse and deplete the already marginal lands that are left to them.

Cash crop surveys

Have students survey their own use of imported cash crops by looking at the ingredients of various food products, such as the chocolate in a pudding. Ask them to consider whether the imported cash crops they have identified in their foods are essential to a healthy diet.

Have students research cash crop exports and imports to learn about the flow of products between countries. To help them visualize these global interconnections, put a world map on the bulletin board. As the students find connection between countries, mark them on the map using tacks and string to create a web of interrelationships. Another way to demonstrate interrelationships is to make a flag for each country and post the flags around the room. As the students discover connections, link the flags with strings, creating an overhead web.

Resource and energy budgets

In many developing countries, livestock is raised for export. Raising cattle and other livestock requires large amounts of grain, water, land, and other resources that could be used to ease chronic hunger if humans ate less meat. There is enough grain produced in the world to feed everyone, but much of it goes instead to feed livestock. Because energy is lost at each step of a food chain, eating meat is much less energy efficient than eating vegetables and grains. For example, it takes about 8 kilograms of wheat to produce 1 kilogram of beef; and while the kilogram of beef provides 174 grams of digestible protein, the wheat needed to produce it contains 800 grams of digestible protein.[1] Water, too, is used much less efficiently in meat production than in grain production. At a conservative estimate, it takes about 3,700 liters (975 U.S. gallons) of water to produce one kilogram of beef, while it takes 120 liters (32 U.S. gallons) of water to produce one kilogram of wheat.[2] For every liter of water used in production, wheat provides 36 times the calories and 18 times the protein that beef provides.[3]

Energy chains

This activity demonstrates that energy is lost at each level of a food chain and that it takes more resources to support meat eating than to support a diet based on plants.

Materials: 4 buckets, 4 paper or foam cups of equal size, water, 100 candies in a cup

Location: outdoors

Time: 15-20 minutes

Procedure:

1. Fill two buckets with water.

2. Poke one hole in the bottom of two of the cups, and poke two holes in the bottom of the other two cups. The holes must be large enough to allow water in the cups to leak out in a steady stream, but not so large that it will drain from the cups in seconds.

3. Divide the class into two relay teams and have each team line up in front of one of the two full buckets. Put the empty buckets about 20 meters (22 yards) away.

4. Explain that the full buckets represent plants, and the water in them represents energy. Plants are able to convert sunlight to energy that is usable by animals. In this game, herbivores will take energy (water) from the plants and pass it to carnivores, simulating the way in which energy is transferred in a food chain.

5. Give a cup with one hole in it to the first student in each line, and explain that they represent herbivores. Ask the herbivores to stand next to the full buckets (the plants).

6. Give a cup with two holes in it to the second student in each line. These players represent carnivores and go to stand midway between their group's full and empty buckets.

7. Explain the order of play: When you say "Go," each herbivore scoops a cupful of water from the full bucket, carries it to the carnivore, and pours it into the carnivore's cup. The herbivore then throws the herbivore cup back to the next student in line and stands in the carnivore's spot. Meanwhile, the carnivore relays the cup of water to the team's end (empty) bucket, pours the water in, and throws the carnivore cup back to the new carnivore in the middle. The next herbivore in line scoops up some water, relays it to the new carnivore, the carnivore takes it to the end bucket, and so on. Continue the cycle until the supply buckets are empty.

8. Gather the class around the two buckets of water. Ask the students to describe what happened to the water (energy). It is likely that most of it was lost.

9. Explain that in a food chain 90 percent of the energy is lost at each trophic level. To demonstrate this, show the class the cup containing 100 candies. Explain that the candies represent 100 units of energy that a plant has made from sunlight through photosynthesis.

10. Ask for a volunteer to be a herbivore. Give that student ten candies and throw the rest away. Ask "What percentage was lost?" (*90 percent*) Then ask for a volunteer to be a carnivore. Ask "If 90 percent of the energy is lost, how many of the herbivore's candies does the carnivore get?" (*1 candy*)

11. Discuss the implications: In this example, the carnivore needs a lot of plants and herbivores to support it. It took 100 units of the sun's energy to make 10 units of herbivore energy, whereas it would take 1,000 units of the sun's energy to make 10 units of carnivore energy. Humans are part of many food chains. By choosing to eat foods that are lower on these food chains we become more efficient users of resources.

Food waste

In developed countries a great deal of food and food resources (land, water, energy) are wasted. If your school has a composting program, have the students measure the volume and weight of the food waste in the lunchroom for a week and graph the results.

Another way to get children to become aware of their own practices is to examine the resources that are involved in producing the food. Pick a popular food, such as pizza, and ask "What does it take to make a pizza?" (e.g., *cheese*). Then ask "What does it take to make cheese?" (*cows, energy for transporting and processing milk*). Ask more questions, such as "What do the cows need?" and so on. Create a large chart showing all the resources needed to make a pizza, or have the students make their own charts. This activity shows that all foods require many resources, and that when we waste food we also waste the resources that were needed to produce the food.

The geography of hunger
Where in the world?
Have the students use an almanac or other reference to find countries with low per capita incomes. Then have them locate these countries on a world map. Ask the students if they notice a pattern. They should observe that most poor countries are in the Southern Hemisphere. Students could work in pairs or small groups and choose a country to "adopt." Their job is to become experts on the country's geography, history, culture, government, and economy by using atlases, newspapers, interviews, letters to the country's embassy, and so on. The students can share their learning in presentations to the class or form a model United Nations to debate and discuss the problem of hunger.

Food distribution
In many countries there is enough food for everyone, but it is difficult to get the food to all the people who need it. In times of famine and war, food sometimes sits spoiling in major cities because it cannot be distributed to the countryside. There may not be enough trucks, fuel, safe roads, or other means of transportation to move food to everyone who needs it.

Obtain road maps of various countries from tourist offices and embassies, or use an atlas that shows roads. Have students compare the road systems in various countries, including a developed and an underdeveloped country.

Have the students choose a favorite meal and find out where each of the items in that meal came from. Have them mark these locations on a world map and follow the routes that various items took to reach their local store. This activity demonstrates how dependent we are on other regions and countries and on transportation infrastructure.

The efficacy of aid
In many cases, the aid that is given to ease chronic hunger does not help the situation. Sometimes it even causes further hunger problems, as when massive shipments of donated food lower the price of locally grown food and the incentive to produce it. When aid comes in the form of such technological "fixes" as the introduction of hybrid seed stock and chemical fertilizers, traditional crops and agricultural practices that have sustained the land and the people for centuries can be lost. Long-term solutions to hunger must not only address the production of food and people's access to

it, but also help people out of poverty. Small-scale programs that enable people to become self-sufficient — rather more dependent — are the most effective.

Self-sufficiency
This activity demonstrates that the promotion of self-sufficiency is a more effective form of aid than a charitable handout. To begin, show the class a bag of candy. Tell the students that if they ask for candy, sometimes you will give them some and sometimes you will not. The decision is entirely yours. Do this for a while, occasionally giving the students candy. Then teach them a way to earn candy. For example, teach the students a new math skill and then let them earn candy every time they get a certain math problem correct. Discuss with the students which system they prefer. Discuss why it is better to help people find ways to become self-sufficient than to make them dependent on others.

Follow up the activity by having the students research and compare the work of organizations that are helping to stop world hunger. Questions they might ask are: Where does the group work? What kind of aid does it provide? Does the group work on sustainable development projects that will prevent hunger in the long run, or is it more concerned with the immediate relief of famine?

Hunger aid role play
In many cases decisions about who receives aid are based on politics, not on a determination to help those who are truly hungry. On both the local and national levels, students can have an effective voice in influencing elected officials. They can write letters, make telephone calls, and visit officials' offices. They can even work with the media to show others their concern for the hungry. This concern can translate into action to change the way governments help the hungry.

Have students research what their government is doing to aid the hungry, both at home and in other areas of the world. Which government agencies are responsible for making decisions about giving aid? What types of aid are given? How effective is the aid? Once students are familiar with the issues and the roles of government officials, they can role-play a lobbying scenario such as the following: A hearing is being held to discuss a proposed bill that would give $250 million in aid to a developing country. Have some students take the roles of staff members of various anti-hunger organizations, ambassadors of the countries seeking

210

aid, and hunger experts. The other students will be elected officials, some sympathetic to the bill and others unsympathetic. Give the students time to prepare questions, comments, and speeches for their roles. Debate can focus on questions of where the money should go and what types of projects should be funded. Establish a format in which the students ask questions, make speeches, and debate the issue, concluding with a vote on the bill. A variation would be for pairs of students to role-play a visit by a hunger activist to an elected official.

This activity does not have to be limited to a role play; students can contact their government officials themselves. The Bread for the World website <www.bread.org> has information on and suggestions for specific hunger-related issues.

Taking action on hunger

Solutions to the problems of chronic hunger fall into two categories: acts of mercy and acts of justice. Working at a soup kitchen would be an act of mercy. Providing jobs, thereby eliminating the need for a soup kitchen, would be an act of justice. Acts of justice are preventative. Preventing the problem from occurring is much more effective than dealing with it once it has happened. Hunger is such a widespread and immediate problem, however, that both acts — acts of mercy and acts of justice — are needed.

One of the most important lessons students can learn in a study of hunger issues is that they can make a difference. As hunger is a problem everywhere, student action may focus on fundraising to help people in other countries or on projects to help people right in your own community. Local projects might include collecting non-perishable food for distribution by a local service organization or planting a school garden and donating the produce to a local food bank. Contacting local hunger-aid organizations and paying attention to the news are good ways to find out where help is needed.

Fundraising

Here are a few suggestions for ways to raise money. Have your students brainstorm to come up with other creative ideas.

⚬ Students could make collection boxes covered with images and facts related to hunger, and use them to collect spare change from other students, family members, and others.

⚬ Students could hold a read-a-thon, a chore-a-thon, a car-wash-a-thon, a pick-up-litter-a-thon, or an "a-thon" of their own creation.

⚬ Students could choose to give up, for a specified period of time, a luxury they enjoy (e.g., movies, ice cream) and donate the money saved to an aid organization.

⚬ Students could put on a play, concert, or some other display of their talents, charge admission, and donate the proceeds to an aid organization.

Educating others

One of the most effective ways to create change is for students to educate others. Here are some suggestions.

⚬ Make posters, or write and present a speech or skit to inform others about hunger.

⚬ Develop interesting lessons to teach to other classes.

⚬ Organize an event such as a fair on World Food Day (October 16) and design displays to teach other students in an active manner about various aspects of the hunger problem.

⚬ Write stories or picture books related to hunger issues and share the stories with others.

⚬ Invite speakers from a hunger organization to discuss the problem of hunger and what their organization is trying to do about it.

Far from leaving students feeling depressed and powerless, a curriculum focused on hunger can be a first step in fostering their understanding of the web of interrelated environmental, economic, and political issues that contribute to complex global problems. Children want to make the world a better place. We can give them the knowledge, the hands-on experiences, and the skills that will enable them to do so. ✎

Daniel Kriesberg teaches Grade 6 science at Friends Academy in Locust Valley, New York.

Notes

[1] Nutritional data from U.S. Department of Agriculture nutritional database, cited in "The Livestock Connection," The Vegan Society, 2003, on-line February 11, 2005, at <http://www.vegansociety.com/html/environment/water/>.

[2] See J.L. Beckett and J.W. Oltjen, "Estimation of the Water Requirement for Beef Production in the United States," *Journal of Animal Science* 71, April 1993, pp. 818-26, on-line February 11, 2005, at <http://jas.fass.org/cgi/content/abstract/71/4/818>.

[3] U.S. Department of Agriculture, cited at <http://www.vegansociety.com/html/environment/water/> (see note 1).

Resources

Books

Here are a few books to read with children that touch on issues of poverty, charity, hunger, and taking action.

Ashabranner, Brett. *People Who Make a Difference*. Cobblehill Books, 1989. This is a collection of inspirational stories about people making a difference in the environment, with others and by personal example.

continued on next page ➤

Berenstain, Stan, and Jan Berenstain. *The Berenstain Bears Think of Those in Need*. Random House, 1999. The bear cubs realize that they have more toys and other things than they really need. Mother Bear has an idea that helps others and her family.

Chinn, Karen. *Sam and the Lucky Money*. Lee and Low Books, 1995. It is the Chinese New Year and Sam's grandparents give him four dollars to buy anything he wants. After meeting a homeless man, he decides what to do.

Fox, Mem. *Whoever You Are*. Harcourt Children's Books. 1997. This simple but wonderful picture book reminds us that whoever and wherever we are, we are all part of the same world.

Hoose, Philip. *It's Our World Too! Stories of Young People Who Are Making a Difference*. Little, Brown and Co., 1993. The wide variety of stories in this collection show concrete ways that young people can make a difference.

Howard, Tracy Apple with Sage Howard. *Kids Ending Hunger, What Can We Do?* Andrews and McMeel, 1992. This terrific resource for children and adults has a great deal of background information and ideas for ways to help end world hunger.

Lewis, Barbara A. *The Kids' Guide to Social Action*. Free Spirit Publishing, 1991.This helpful guide explains how children can create change and includes suggestions for letter writing, lobbying, and other tactics.

McBrier, Page. *Beatrice's Goat*. Simon & Schuster, 2001. In a village in Uganda a young girl named Beatrice is given a goat, which enables her to realize her dream — she obtains the money she needs to go to school. This is a perfect book for showing children and adults how a small investment can change a family's life.

McPhail, David. *The Teddy Bear*. Henry Holt, 2002. A homeless man finds a teddy bear lost by a little boy and grows to love it himself. When the boy finds his long lost teddy bear, instead of taking it back he acts with kindness and compassion toward the homeless man.

Meltzer, Milton. *Who Cares? Millions Do*. Walker, 1994. The stories in this book are about a wide variety of people and the ways they have helped make the world a better place.

Menzel, Faith and Peter Menzel. *Material World, A Global Family Portrait*. Sierra Club Books, 1994. Although this is not a children's book, the photographs will interest everyone. They show families from around the world surrounded by their household possessions. The contrasts are sometimes startling.

Rosen, Michael J. *The Greatest Table, A Banquet to Fight against Hunger*. Harcourt Brace & Company, 1994. This unique book folds out to look like a long table. Each page is illustrated by a different artist and invites the reader and the world to share a meal.

Shollar, Leah P. and Yehudis Cohen. *A Thread of Kindness, A Tzedaka Story*. Hachai Publishing, 2000. In this Jewish folktale, a family is given a treasure. Instead of keeping it for themselves, they share it with their whole village, making the treasure last much longer.

Smith, David J. *If the World Were a Village, A Book about the World's People*. Kids Can Press, 2002. This interesting picture book for children and adults shows that the world's resources are not divided evenly among the world's people.

Williams, Karen Lynn. *Galimoto*. Lothrop, 1990. A young boy named Kondi lives in a village in Malawi. He makes his own toy car, a *galimoto,* with the scraps of wire he finds. The story presents a wonderful snapshot of what life is like with neither toy stores nor money to buy things.

Organizations

The American Association for the Advancement of Science: Provides background information on hunger-related issues; see <http://atlas.aaas.org>.

Bread for the World: Lobbies for legislation that will help end chronic hunger. The website is a great resource for involving children in letter-writing campaigns and other actions and for background information on the issues of chronic hunger; see <www.bread.org>.

Free the Children: An organization of children helping children in need around the world. The website is a great source of ideas for taking action; see <www.freethechildren.org>.

Freedom from Hunger: Provides small business loans to women in developing countries. This process, known as micro-enterprise, is an extremely effective way of helping people out of a life of chronic hunger. The website has ideas for becoming involved and educating others; see <www.freefromhunger.org>.

Heifer Project International: Provides livestock for families in developing countries, thus helping to increase their self-sufficiency. The website has educational activities and many suggestions for ways that students can help; see <www.heifer.org>.

The Hunger Site: Provides information, suggests activities, and has a "Give Free Food" button (every time you click, the site's business sponsors donate to the effort to end chronic hunger); see <www.thehungersite.com>.

Trees for Life: Plants trees in developing countries to provide food and help improve the environment. Seeds and learning materials are available to teachers; see <www.treesforlife.org>.

United Nations Food and Agriculture Organization: A great source of information and statistics on the issues of chronic hunger; see <www.fao.org>.

Jane Hamilton

213

Creative Visualization
with Children

*An imaginary journey that became the springboard for
a year-long study of alternative futures*

All photographs by Jane Hamilton

Works of art, poetry, and prose emerge from children's creative visualization of the future of life on Earth.

by Jane Hamilton

Grade levels: 2-5

Subject areas: language arts, visual art, science, social studies

Key concepts: envisioning positive change

Skills: listening, imagining, responding to text, interpreting experience

Location: indoors or outdoors, away from disturbances

Time: 2 hours or more

few years ago during an education course, the instructor led our class in a creative visualization exercise that consisted of a journey around the sun and a return to Earth 20 years later. Most of my classmates found the world they returned to considerably degraded, but some of us found that a wonder-

ful transformation had occurred. The world I returned to was lush and green. It had clear air, clean water, dense forests, a great diversity of plants and animals, and human societies that had learned to live more sustainably. The experience was very powerful and very positive. I felt invigorated and more eager than ever to help children discover the beauty of the natural world around them. The experience also led me to wonder what creative visualization might be like for children.

Creative visualization is a teaching technique that engages the right hemisphere of the brain, the hemisphere that governs spatial, integrative thought. Our education systems traditionally favor left-hemisphere teaching techniques that emphasize verbal, analytical processes. Consider, for a moment, a prism and a kaleidoscope, both of which transform light into color and form. The left hemisphere works like the prism. As a prism separates light of different wavelengths to create a rainbow, the left hemisphere of the brain separates

214

information into its constituent parts. The right hemisphere is more like the kaleidoscope. It constructs patterns and relationships among separate parts. Creative visualization appeals to this right-hemisphere ability to synthesize.

The process of creative visualization is in many ways comparable to meditation. A soothing human voice (sometimes enhanced by music or by natural sounds, such as running water) creates pleasant images in the mind of the listener. This induces a state of heightened awareness in which mental images sometimes occur spontaneously, as they do when we are dreaming. Just as some dreams may give us insight into our waking lives, it is possible to emerge from creative visualization with a clearer understanding of a situation or a clearer sense of direction. Creative visualization, then, is meditation with a purpose. It is a versatile and powerful tool that enables the individual to envision change and to experience that change as if it were happening right now. It is frequently used by athletes, who find that visualizing a successful outcome for themselves or their teams before competition can improve their performance.

Creative visualization is particularly useful as a starting point in an exploration of environmental or social issues because it helps children to identify areas of personal significance. Once they are able to articulate what means most to them, finding ways to make a positive contribution is relatively easy.

Note: In school districts where creative visualization might be seen as a sensitive or unconventional activity, teachers are advised to consult with the school administration beforehand to be sure that they are aware of the activity and give their support.

A creative visualization project

A few months after my journey around the sun, I obtained permission to undertake a special creative visualization project at High Park Montessori School in Toronto where I was teaching. Fifty children from three classes, ranging in age from 6 to 12, volunteered to take part. I emphasized that their role as listeners was simply to be open to new experiences. My role was to ensure optimum conditions — a warm, comfortable,

quiet setting — and to create a carefully worded text with which to guide the listeners on their journey of discovery. As children — even young children — are acutely aware of the social and environmental ills that face us today, I felt that it was very important to present the notion of a positive future. I chose to tell the children that the world they returned to would be even more wonderful than the one they had left, and invited them to explore that new world through their senses and describe how it looked, smelled, felt, and sounded.

Taking the journey

I had worked with these children for a number of years and knew them well. It was therefore easy to arrange them into small workable groups of up to five children. I took each group into a quiet room and invited them to remove their shoes and sit with me in a circle. I explained the nature of the visualization and encouraged them to lie down if they wished, which most did. Then I led them through the visualization, using the text I had adapted. It took about 15 minutes. Here is the text I used:

We are going on a journey together today, an imaginary journey in time and space to a different part of the solar system. It will feel like a dream, but you will be awake. You won't feel alone on this journey. I will be with you to guide you every step of the way. I encourage you to let whatever thoughts and feelings you have simply happen. Let them rise to the surface, like bubbles. Let them float into the air and drift away. Before we begin, take a moment or two to adjust your body so that you are in a comfortable position. Take a few quiet, deep breaths. Close your eyes to help yourself concentrate.

Imagine that we are leaving this room now, rising through the roof of the school and up into the sky. Up, up we go, and soon planet Earth is far below us. We can still breathe, though, and our bodies feel comfortable, neither too warm nor too cold. Soon we see Venus, and then Mercury. Beyond us is the sun. We have nothing to fear from being so close to the sun. We are going to gain strength and wisdom from our journey. Take a few moments to travel around the sun, and I will tell you when it is time to continue. (Several

minutes elapse. Soft music improvised on a recorder or glockenspiel can enhance the introspective mood and bridge the gap of silence.)

Now we are going to continue our journey by going back to Earth. A long, long time has gone by, but we are no older than we were when we left. First we pass Mercury and then we pass Venus. Beyond us is the familiar blue planet that we call home. Down through the Earth's atmosphere we go. Soon we begin to notice what life is like on Earth now. We begin to see that a wonderful transformation has occurred during our absence. Life on Earth is more wonderful now than ever before. Take a few moments to visit different areas of your region — your neighbourhood, perhaps, or the surrounding countryside. You may prefer to visit areas that you have never seen before. You are free to visit and explore any area that you wish. I will tell you when it is time to continue. (Several minutes elapse.)

Imagine settling back into this world. What is different about it? How does it look, smell, and sound? How will you fit in, and what will you do? Take a couple of minutes to think about that. (Several minutes elapse).

We are going to come back into the school now. In a moment you will open your eyes and find yourself back in this room, and you will remember what has happened here today.

Students collaborating in an artistic expression of their vision of the future.

Recording impressions

Immediately following the visualization, I asked the children to spend about 15 minutes jotting down their experiences and impressions, including sights, sounds, smells, colors, and any other details that were particularly vivid. Most of the children focused on life back on Earth, but some found the journey in the solar system especially vivid. A few children didn't stop at Earth at all, but kept on going to Jupiter, Saturn, and beyond. Here are some examples of students' abstracts of the experience:

> "Red, blue, playful animals, flashing lights, getting dizzy, happy, stars, a feeling of freedom, a stork, two lions, thousands of miles of green grass, glowing planets, many people, hope." (Julia, age 8)

"Cars that hover and don't give out gases. A strong ozone layer. No smoke stacks. Solar energy. Green and fluorescent. No smell of gases." (Luke, age 9)

"It smelled very nice. Animals are free. No pollution. This world is clean. There's brown and lots and lots of green and bright blue and white. I love this world and when I go into space and come back I hope it will be like this." (Elizabeth, age 7)

Interpreting and sharing the experience

In the third stage, students used their abstracts to create a more detailed interpretation of their experience in the form of prose, poetry, or artwork. I allowed them all the time they needed for this, and some worked very quickly while others took up to an hour. Some children went on to use their abstracts as the basis for collaborative artwork and songwriting in preparation for a concert at the end of the school year.

A short time after this project, I attended a conference in Rio de Janeiro and took samples of the children's work with me to share with children in Brazil. On three consecutive mornings I visited the Escola Sa Pereira in Botafogo and led small groups through the visualization. (I had lived in Brazil some years before and my Portuguese, though rusty, was functional.) The format was the same as that used at High Park Montessori School: the visualization, a written abstract, and then some form of prose, poetry, or artwork. Here are some of the Brazilian children's responses:

> "A place with waterfalls, trees, animals, clean beaches, people riding bicycles. Cars and pollution don't exist. Birds flying everywhere. People as friends. The sound of birds singing, waterfalls, and the really soft voices of children playing." (Paloma, age 10)

> "When I arrived here I saw things that were green, no dirt, intact forests, no one cutting down a single tree, no one killing a single animal, and this way I found everything really beautiful as if there were no one." (Rafael, age 10)

Imagination and Celebration

"I saw strange things when I went to the sun. I saw other living things. Coming back I saw the world swallowing awful things and throwing them away. I also saw some pretty waterfalls and trees that I had never seen in my whole life. I didn't hear much, only a few things like the sound of the waterfall and my heart." (Moema, age 10)

I was surprised to see that biodiversity, pollution, quality of human life (spiritual and emotional), peace, and poverty were the top concerns raised by both groups of participants, although they came from two very different areas of the world. I was not surprised, however, at the depth of their awareness of global problems. This appears to be a constant among children growing up at this time, regardless of where they live.

Recording and sharing impressions of the journey.

Applying the learning

At High Park Montessori School, the creative visualization project was the start of a year-long look at local and global issues with a group of Grade 4 children. Using Maria Montessori's "Fundamental Needs of Humankind"[1] as a framework, I incorporated elements from the visualizations of each member of the group. Consciously or unconsciously, children gravitated to those areas that were of personal significance to them. One boy, who had written a lengthy description of the green world that he returned to on Earth, went on to examine current and future forestry practices. Another boy, whose world of the future was free of polluting gases, embarked on a detailed study of alternatives to fossil fuels. Other children examined present and future practices in transportation, farming, aquaculture, landscaping, education, childcare, and eldercare. All of these issues were directly connected to the visualizations experienced by these children, as expressed through their prose and art.

The culmination of this look at local and global issues was the building of a model of a collaborative community where all of us and our families and friends might wish to live in 20 years' time. It was an extremely rewarding finale to a process that had its beginning in creative visualization more than a year earlier. It brought me full circle, back to the question that environmental educators everywhere ask themselves: How can we help children transform their concern about the world into a deep conviction that what they do does matter and can make a difference? There are many paths to take, of course, but I am convinced that envisioning a positive future through the process of creative visualization is a very good place to begin. The future is written by the actions of each of us alive today. Envisioning a flourishing world allows a child to discover what is most important to him or her and, with the help of caring adults, find ways to make a positive contribution. After all, great changes are made up of many little changes. ✤

Jane Hamilton taught for many years at High Park Montessori School in Toronto, Ontario, and now teaches at Palmerston Avenue Public School in Toronto.

Note

1. This framework, which forms an integral part of the Montessori curriculum, aids children in classifying the physical needs of humans (shelter, nourishment, clothing, transportation, defense) and the spiritual ones (art, religion, interpersonal relationships). Maria Montessori believed that when children understand that the needs of humans are the same everywhere on Earth and at all times in history, they can begin to see humanity as a global family and to appreciate the variety of ways in which fundamental needs are met.

The Power of Stories

Stories push back the walls of the classroom, providing the experience and relationship with which effective environmental education begins

by Sue Christian Parsons

Grade levels: K-5

Subject areas: reading/language arts

Key concepts: curriculum integration, inquiry, literature selection

Skills: reading comprehension, dialogue, critical literacy, writing/storytelling

Location: indoors or outdoors

Time: all year

Photographs by Oklahoma State University

I was talking to a friend the other day. "You won't believe what I saw today," he said. You know that field of old oaks next to the grocery store? There's a new school going in there, so they're clearing the field. There was a bulldozer pushing down all the trees, and further back a crane lifting them and dropping them into a shredder. They're making mulch of them.

"I just stood there and watched, thinking about all those trees. This area's not going to be the same. Just concrete everywhere. They left one big tree standing ... off to the side. I noticed a hawk sitting up there. He was just watching those trees go down. Watching his home disappear."

My friend and I have many times lamented the toll of development in the wooded suburb in which he lives. "Such a shame," we have said over and over to each other, clucking our tongues and shaking our heads. This time, however, our talk brought tears to my eyes. The difference lay in the power of the story. Its immediacy and intimacy drew me into the scene that my friend had witnessed. The image of the trees being shredded disturbed me, seeming violent, wasteful. The hawk, seen through my human eyes and in the light of my needs, was a poignant reminder of the cost of development. Not only was I reminded that development leads to loss of habitat, I was called to care — significantly, directly, immediately — about the issue. Such caring leads to change — in attitude, in action. Such is the power of stories.

The power of stories

Stories may be fiction or nonfiction; that is, they may be constructions of reality built on general experience or, like my friend's story, they may be tellings of particular experiences. All stories, however, seek to explore and communicate a truth, some insight about what it means to live and live well. As such, stories may play a particularly powerful role in learning about the environment.

Stories provide and expand on experience

Ideally, environmental education begins with fingers in the soil, toes touching water, ears tuned to rustling leaves, and eyes alert for the subtle and magnificent. As a child, I spent hours and hours playing in the woodland behind our house. A creek ran through it, and I loved walking through moss, thrilling at the slippery sliding, examining creatures, noting how the stream claimed the soil around it and exposed the roots of trees that clung to its sides. I lay on my back and watched birds and squirrels. I followed tracks, searching for (and occasionally finding) more elusive animals.

My time in the woods helped me learn to take joy in the land. So, too, did explorations outdoors with my father, an accomplished and fervent naturalist. I cherish memories of catching a rat snake or hiking into the Davis Mountains with only a topographical map and my father's acute eye as guides. He noticed everything and could tell me about everything he noticed. He taught me to see — in detail and with an impassioned eye — just as he had been taught by others when he was a child.

Not all children — perhaps fewer and fewer in these days of closely managed schedules — have such a combination of free and guided experiences. Good teachers know the importance of experience and relationship in learning and so seek to "push back the walls" of the classroom to allow for such engagement. Stories are powerful allies in fostering engagement with the environment. While there is a wealth of informational literature that addresses the environment, and all texts provide experience, stories transport us, engage us more fully in this experience. Peterson and Eeds tell us that stories are explorations and illuminations of life.[1] We cannot help but engage in storytelling, as this is how, throughout history, we have created and maintained our sense of the world and our place in it. Stories are the very essence of the human experience. Rich stories that offer layers of thought and experience to be explored again and again have a unique power. Children come to live in such stories and, through them, to consider more deeply, to experience more richly, to be touched more profoundly. Like the informal narration of an interested and caring mentor who points out, explains, connects, and clarifies, an author's carefully crafted story can enrich our connections with the Earth.

Stories offer relationship

Stories also involve the reader in relationships. Characters summon us to enter into their settings, to share their experiences, to put ourselves in their places — to know, on both a visceral and an intellectual level, what matters here. When my friend tells his story, I, in listening to it, become his partner. I see through his eyes and learn what he has learned. The richness of his storytelling allows me to relate to the hawk in the story as well.

I think about my habitat, my home, and what the loss of it would entail.

In using this approach as a way of helping children to form relationships with the natural world, there is a danger of anthropomorphism, of making non-human creatures something other (and, therefore, less) than what they are. Yet we cannot understand except through our humanness, and we cannot see but with human eyes. Stories allow children to reach out from their natural egocentrism. In this sense, stories invite empathetic engagement with the natural world and at the same time prepare children to move beyond this very human view to examine the natural world more objectively.

Stories lead to inquiry

Again, stories are allies in teaching because they lead to inquiry. Stories provide the experiences that make children cry "Why?" and "How?" and "What can we do?" Stories have the power to instill passion, and lead us then to passionate attention to learning more. Children learn best what matters to them, and stories help them see what matters. Children seek information tirelessly when it serves their purposes, and stories help children find purposes worth serving. In this way, stories transport children to the point where they are ready to explore the rich catalog of informational literature available to them.

Stories breed stories

When children live with stories, they become storytellers, and storytelling has a deceptive significance in environmental education. While the stories we read provide experience, the stories we craft grow from our experience, requiring us to examine more fully what those experiences mean. To tell a story, one must first notice. In this manner, we might say that storytelling is a science: just as scientists observe and record, so do storytellers, structuring the results in such a way that they (and, subsequently, others) can see more clearly, feel more deeply. The power is in the constructing, which forces us to revisit and reconstruct experience. Fletcher's concept of the writer's notebook as a place for children to observe and record the world around them can play a vital role in environmental education.[2]

continued on page 222

Stories to Support Environmental Education

The following book list is not exhaustive, but it offers a good foundation of stories to support environmental inquiry. The books listed here are picture books. An abundance of children's novels dealing with environmental issues can and should be explored in classrooms. Picture books, however, are globally useful: they can be easily shared with children of all ages and abilities to spark immediate dialogue.

The categories are meant as guides for selecting reading materials, but such categorization denies the rich complexities of these texts. To say that a story "calls us to action" does not mean that it does not also impart important information or develop in us an awareness of and sensitivity to the environment. The books categorized as promoting action and awareness are filled with information, and certainly the books within each category are of wide literary appeal.

Books that call us to action

These texts have an environmental focus, inspiring us to reflect on our relationship with and responsibility to the environment and to act accordingly.

Albert, Richard. *Alejandro's Gift*. Chronicle Books, 1994. Lonely in his desert house, Alejandro builds an oasis to attract his animal neighbors.

Atkins, Jeannine, and Venantius Pinto. *Aani and the Tree Huggers*. Lee and Low Books, 2000. When a forest in northern India is threatened, the villagers seem helpless to stop the destruction of their life resources until little Aani's spontaneous response makes a difference (based on a true story).

Bang, Molly. *Common Ground: The Water, Earth, and Air We Share*. Scholastic, 1997. A parable and clear analogies help readers understand and consider the consequences of misusing natural resources.

Bunting, Eve. *Someday a Tree*. Houghton Mifflin, 1993. Alice is shocked when the old oak tree is poisoned by chemicals. Although she cannot save the tree, she finds hope in the acorns she collected when the tree was healthy.

Burton, Virginia Lee. *The Little House*. Houghton Mifflin, 1942. A country house is unhappy when the congested city grows up around her.

Cherry, Lynne. *Flute's Journey: The Life of a Wood Thrush*. Harcourt Brace, 1997. A young wood thrush struggles with diminishing habitat as he makes his first migration between his nesting ground in Maryland and his winter home in Costa Rica.

Cherry, Lynne. *The Great Kapok Tree*. Harcourt Brace, 1990. The many animals that live in a great kapok tree in the Brazilian rain forest try to convince a man with an ax not to cut down their home.

Cherry, Lynne. *A River Ran Wild: An Environmental History*. Harcourt Brace, 1996. The story of the Nashua River, from its discovery by Native Americans through the polluting years of the industrial revolution to the cleanup efforts that revitalized the river.

Cooney, Barbara. *Miss Rumphius*. Puffin Books, 1982. Great-aunt Alice Rumphius fulfills her childhood pledge to go to faraway places, live by the sea in her old age, and do something to make the world more beautiful.

Ehlert, Lois. *Red Leaf, Yellow Leaf*. Harcourt Brace, 1991. This book describes the growth of a maple tree from seed to sapling and encourages readers to grow their own tree.

George, Jean Craighead. *Everglades*. HarperCollins, 1995. This book describes the evolution of the Florida Everglades and the impact that humans have had on the abundance of life there.

Seuss, Dr. Theodore Geisel. *The Lorax*. Random House, 1971. The Once-ler describes the destruction of trees due to pollution.

Stewart, Sarah. *The Gardener*. Farrar, Strauss, Giroux, 1997. When hard times hit her family, plant-loving Lydia Grace is shipped off to stay with her somber, withdrawn uncle in the city. She uses her gift of gardening to brighten her surroundings and her uncle's life.

Van Allsburg, Chris. *Just a Dream*. Houghton Mifflin, 1990. Walter sees efforts to preserve the environment as a waste of time and energy until he has a dream about a future Earth devastated by pollution.

Books that foster wonder, appreciation, and understanding

Baker, Keith. *Who Is the Beast?* Voyager Books (Harcourt Brace), 1990. Deep in the jungle, animals are fleeing a mysterious beast, while the tiger, unaware that they are fleeing from him, sees himself as part of the threatened group.

Banks, Kate. *And If the Moon Could Talk*. Frances Foster Books, 1998. Offering a moon's-eye view of evening life, from nature scenes to a child's bedroom, this book suggests the interconnectedness of life on our planet.

Baylor, Byrd. *The Desert Is Theirs*. Charles Scribner's Sons, 1975. This book is a celebration of plant, animal, and human life and in the desert.

Baylor, Byrd. *Desert Voices*. Charles Scribner's Sons, 1981. Desert inhabitants describe the beauty of their home.

Baylor, Byrd. *Hawk, I'm Your Brother*. Macmillan, 1976. Determined to learn to fly, Rudy adopts a hawk, hoping to learn how to achieve his goal. He learns instead that wildlife needs to be free.

Baylor, Byrd. *I'm in Charge of Celebrations*. Macmillan, 1986. A desert dweller celebrates a triple rainbow, a chance encounter with a coyote, and other wonders of the wilderness.

continued next page

continued from previous page

Baylor, Byrd. *The Other Way to Listen*. Charles Scribner's Sons, 1978. The narrator tries to pay such close attention to the world around her that she will be able to hear the hills singing.

Buchanan, Ken. *This House Is Made of Mud*. Northland Publishing, 1991. This book invites the reader into a Southwestern adobe house and offers a glimpse of life in and around it.

Bunting, Eve. *Butterfly House*. Scholastic, 1999. A young girl and her grandfather rescue a caterpillar from a jay and place it in a butterfly house where they can feed and care for it.

Cherry, Lynne. *Armadillo from Amarillo*. Harcourt Brace, 1994. A wandering armadillo sees the varied landscapes of Texas, exploring cities, historic sites, geographic features, and wildlife.

Churba, Amy. *Children of the Earth*. Pleiades Publishing, 1998. Exploring the many landscapes of our planet, the book invites discovery of our own connection to all life on Earth.

Fleming, Denise. *In the Tall, Tall Grass*. Holt, 1991. This book presents a toddler's view of creatures found in the grass.

Fleming, Denise. *In the Small, Small Pond*. Holt, 1993. This book describes the activities of animals living in and near a small pond as spring turns to fall.

Howe, James. *I Wish I Were a Butterfly*. Harcourt Brace Javanovich, 1987. A wise dragonfly helps a young cricket realize that he is special in his own way.

MacLachlan, Patricia. *All the Places to Love*. HarperCollins, 1994. A young boy describes the special places his family enjoys in and around his grandparents' farm.

Martin, Jacqueline Briggs. *Snowflake Bentley*. Houghton Mifflin, 1998. This biography tells the story of a self-taught scientist who photographed thousands of individual snowflakes in order to study their unique formations.

Muir, John, retold by Donnell Rubay. *Stickeen: John Muir and the Brave Little Dog*. Scholastic, 1998. Environmentalist John Muir makes his way across a dangerous ice bridge with an independent-minded canine friend.

Rylant, Cynthia. *Tulip Sees America*. Scholastic, 1998. A young man and his dog marvel at the changing landscape as they drive west from Ohio to Oregon.

Tresselt, Alvin. *The Gift of the Tree*. Lothrop, Lee and Shepard, 1992. An ancient oak slowly dies, providing shelter and nourishment for an abundance of plant and animal life.

Wood, Douglas. *Old Turtle*. Pfeifer-Hamilton, 1992. This gentle fable explores the interconnectedness of all nature, including human beings, as God's creation and urges care of the Earth.

Yolen, Jane. *Owl Moon*. Philomel Books, 1987. On a silent winter's night under a full moon, a father and daughter trek into the woods to see the great horned owl.

Books that provide information in story form

Arnosky, Jim. *Otters under Water*. G.P. Putnam's Sons, 1992. Two young otters frolic and feed in a pond.

Bash, Barbara. *Urban Roosts: Where the Birds Nest in the City*. Little, Brown, 1990. With rich inviting text, Bash shows how various species of birds (many whose natural habitats are being destroyed) have adapted to city life.

Bunting, Eve. *Ducky*. Houghton Mifflin, 1997. Readers encounter the power of the ocean through the experience of a bathtub toy washed overboard from a ship.

Cannon, Janelle. *Stellaluna*. Harcourt Brace, 1997. After she falls headfirst into a bird's nest, a baby bat is raised as a bird until she is reunited with her mother.

Cannon, Janelle. *Verdi*. Harcourt Brace, 1993. A young python does not want to grow to be slow and boring like the older snakes he sees in the tropical jungle where he lives.

Carle, Eric. *A House for a Hermit Crab*. Simon and Schuster, 1987. A hermit crab moves into a new shell on which he hosts various sea creatures that he meets in his travels.

Cherry, Lynne, and Mark Plotkin. *The Shaman's Apprentice*. Harcourt Brace, 1998. The medicinal value of rain forest plants is explained through the story of a tribe that comes to value its traditional knowledge.

Gill, Shelley. *Alaska's Three Bears*. Paws IV, 1990. The polar bear, the black bear, and the grizzly travel across America's last wilderness to find homes in appropriate habitats.

Lowell, Susan. *The Three Little Javelinas*. Northland, 1992. A Southwest version of *The Three Little Pigs*, this book illuminates habitat adaptation through a familiar story.

Books with a literary voice

These texts are not in traditional story form but are written in poetic language that inspires a sense of wonder and celebration.

Ada, Alma Flor. *Gathering the Sun: An Alphabet in Spanish and English*. Lothrop, Lee and Shepard, 1997. This bilingual book contains poems about working in the fields and nature's bounty.

Mora, Pat. *This Big Sky*. Scholastic, 1998. Through poetry this book celebrates the people, creatures, and landscapes of the American Southwest.

Yolen, Jane. *Bird Watch*. Philomel Books, 1990. This collection of poems describes a variety of birds and their activities.

Yolen, Jane. *Welcome to the Icehouse*. G.P. Putnam's Sons, 1998. The coming of warm weather to the Arctic brings an explosion of color from flowering plants and a thundering return of wildlife.

— *Compiled by Sue Christian Parsons*

Stories foster imagination

Stories foster imagination, the value of which seems self-evident but deserves critical examination. Imagination offers children more than fanciful enjoyment. Imagination is the force that leads us to ask "What might be?" — a question of profound significance to our future. It is a question that asks us to evaluate our priorities, examine our relationships with the world we live in. It is, at its core, a question of moral significance,[3] for imagination leads us into the future as children come to conceptualize a world that is richer for our actions within it.

Selecting stories

Not every story possesses equal potential for engaging learners. We must select stories that provide for rich and varied responses and encourage inquiry. Some important considerations in selecting environmentally themed stories for the classroom are discussed below.

Celebrate the aesthetic and the efferent

When a reader reads, he or she sets a purpose for doing so. Rosenblatt describes these purposeful engagements on a continuum ranging from efferent to aesthetic.[4] Efferent reading, in its purest sense, is reading strictly for information. Aesthetic reading, on the other hand, is reading that draws the reader into the text so fully that the conscious act of reading seems to disappear as the reader is immersed in the world of the story. Different types of texts tend to position readers nearer one end of the continuum or another: a cookbook or a textbook, for example, may tend to encourage an efferent stance by the reader — a search for information — while a novel or poem may engage the reader at the aesthetic end of the continuum. During the course of reading, the reader may move to different points along the continuum: the reader who picked up the cook-

---

Maximizing the Potential of Literature in Environmental Education

☙ Focus on good stories with engaging plots, interesting characters, rich language, high-quality artwork, and evocative themes.

☙ Select from a wide variety of genres, guiding learners to explore the connections between the genre and its effect.

☙ Use discussion as a central tool for exploring texts and the questions that arise from engaging with them. (For helpful guidelines, refer to Peterson and Eeds, *Grand Conversations: Literature Groups in Action*, Scholastic, 1990.)

☙ Start close to home, choosing texts that connect to learners' experiences. Use literature to extend experiences and promote hands-on inquiry.

☙ Address scientific and literacy content and strategies purposefully, emphasizing that science and literacy (and math and art and music ...) are tools with which we may explore and change our world.

☙ Encourage critical examination of all texts. Examine texts for relevance and accuracy.

☙ Question the author's stance and purposes. Encourage discussion that moves beyond books to explore relevant social issues. Expect students to question, investigate, and act — and do these things yourself.

Adapted from S.C. Parsons and S.S. Spradling, "Selecting, Engaging With, and Integrating Environmentally Themed Children's Literature," *Journal of Balanced Reading Instruction* 10, 2003, pp. 31-44.

---

book merely to find and follow a recipe may be drawn in by engaging prose or provocative ideas and move toward the aesthetic stance; the reader of a novel may be become intrigued to explore an informational topic more fully. In fact, the aesthetic experience of story may affect the reader so profoundly that he or she seeks out information with passion. It is important to select stories that allow us to engage with and celebrate both stances and that we encourage learners to do so.

Avoid didacticism

We want children to think critically about environmental issues. We want them to ponder and analyze and come to their own understanding. This is why stories that foster environmental learning should avoid didacticism. Heavy-handed stories that seek first and foremost to teach a lesson often lack appeal — no one wants to be lectured — but, more important, they often lack the very complexity that makes stories effective in environmental education. Such stories state the case and give children nothing to "chew on." Once the lesson is swallowed, it does not warrant a second look. Environmental educators seek to make children effective at problem solving, an act that involves critical analysis, creativity, and ongoing inquiry. Didacticism, though well intended, curtails the process.[5]

Encourage personal connections

For children to engage meaningfully with texts — especially texts with environmental themes that call for active response — they must be able to find a connection between the world presented in the book and their own experiences.[6] Stories that deal with the day-to-day environment — celebrating the beauty and importance of the tree in the front yard, pondering the problem of trash — relate easily to children's lives. In selecting books that present worlds beyond children's immediate

222

experience or deal with more abstract issues (deforestation, for example), we must look for common elements to which children can relate (such as the importance of having a home). Indeed, story structure itself is a familiar, well-worn path by which the reader may enter and come to understand the world of the text.

Offer hope

Environmental stories, like all children's literature, should offer an element of hope. The preservation and reclamation of our environment is a serious undertaking that has powerful ramifications for the future. Children have an innate optimism for the future: they want to grow up, they anticipate the life ahead. Children are not afraid to act; indeed, they feel empowered by the opportunity to act because they are in many ways constantly at the bidding of adults. Stories that call children to environmental action should do so in a way that offers them hope for the future and, if presenting future dangers, provides them with a means to act. Such stories should show, realistically and accessibly, that our actions now can change the course of the world for the better.

Engaging children in stories

Too often, the inherent power of stories is lost in pedagogical practice. Good stories evoke critical thought and, as a result, deeper insight into ourselves, our relationships, our relative places within the world. Stories inspire us to connect and respond. They urge us to tell our own stories, create our own solutions, express our own celebrations and concerns. Yet the common treatment of stories in the classroom may short-circuit these possibilities. Critical engagement through literature is best attained through meaningful dialogue and inquiry-based responses.

Allow children to be meaning makers

Children are constantly making sense of their world on the basis of the information they receive through interaction, and interpreting it through the lens of their experience and current understanding. Similarly, as readers, they never merely receive a text as meaning.

Instead, they bring meaning (grounded in their experiences, their current world views) to a text and take meaning from a text. The result of this "transaction" is a unique creation that Rosenblatt terms the "poem."[7]

One of the most dangerous — and alluring — pedagogical pitfalls is for the teacher to attempt to control meaning making. Teachers who choose to focus on environmental literature often do so out of a passion for the subject. They care deeply that children come to understand and value the world around them, and they hope fervently that this generation of Earth dwellers will care for the environment. In their zeal to impart important messages, however, teachers tend to tell children what it is they are supposed to learn from a book. Instead of allowing children to respond, teachers explain, point out, and stress the important insights. In doing so, they deny children the opportunity to make their own meanings. When children engage actively with texts, they will not all perceive messages in the same way and to the same degree. But that's okay. When children find meanings for themselves (and through discussion with others), the experience will be generative.

Use the power of dialogue

Stories with morally significant themes (such as the value of and our responsibility to the environment) tend to lead children to develop significant insights, given the appropriate pedagogical setting.[8] Dialogue is an immensely powerful tool in helping children to interpret literature and to move beyond the page to connect a story with the world.[9] When a teacher asks students "So, what do you think?" and steps back to allow for extended response, the teacher assumes the role of knowledgeable participant[10] and communicates to the learners that they are responsible for considering the ideas encountered. Through dialogue, children come to share the various connections and interpretations they bring to a text, thereby broadening the experience and deepening their understanding.

Dialogue should not be rushed. Readers responding to complex texts tend to focus first on surface features of the literature (noting the sequence of events, recognizing the characters), moving to deeper features (character motivation and development, symbols and metaphors, themes) as the dialogue progresses. In complex stories the "truth" the author is seeking to communicate is usually embedded at this deeper level. When readers engage in dialogue about a text, they build on each other's meanings to construct deeper insights. These "epiphanies"[11] usually occur late in a dialogue session.

Foster an appropriate classroom context

Discussion of the environment is most effective when it occurs in a context of environmental awareness and action. As previously suggested, stories provide a context within which children can explore these ideas and issues. The broader classroom context, however, should resonate with these values as well. A classroom that supports environmental inquiry should allow for focused experiences with the natural world, house people who express environmental values and act in accordance with them, and feature a pervading attitude of respect for all living things, including, especially, each person in that classroom. ✒

Sue Christian Parsons is a member of the literacy education faculty in the College of Education at Oklahoma State University in Stillwater, Oklahoma.

Notes

1 R. Peterson and M. Eeds, *Grand Conversations: Literature Groups in Action*, Scholastic, 1990.

2 R. Fletcher, *Breathing In, Breathing Out: Keeping a Writer's Notebook*, Heinemann, 1996.

3 R. Coles, *The Call of Stories: Teaching and the Moral Imagination*, Houghton Mifflin, 1989; and S.C. Junker, "Searching for the Moral: Moral Talk in Children's Literature Study Groups," Dissertation, Arizona State University, Tempe, 1998.

4 L. Rosenblatt, *The Reader, the Text, the Poem: The Transactional Theory of Literary Work.* Southern Illinois University Press, 1978.

5 Junker, 1998.

6 Junker, 1998.

7 Rosenblatt, 1978.

8 Junker, 1998.

9 Coles, 1989; Peterson, 1990; and Junker, 1998.

10 Peterson 1990.

11 Junker 1998.

Resources

Acorn Naturalists, <www.acornnaturalists.com>. A good source of children's books on environmental themes, as well as many other resources for environmental and outdoor educators.

Center for Children's Environmental Literature, <http://ccel.schoolsgogreen.org>. Founded by author/illustrator Lynne Cherry, the Center seeks to connect children to the natural world through literature and education. The website has lists of high-quality literature as well as a variety of resources to engage readers in working to sustain the environment.

Clymire, Olga N. *A Child's Place in the Environment.* Lake County Office of Education, 1152 South Main St., Lakeport, CA 95453. Six environmental education curriculum guides that integrate science, language arts, and selected children's literature. Summaries of the guides and the literature lists for the units are available at the publisher's website <www.acpe.lake.k12.ca.us>.

The Wilderness Society Environment Award for Children's Literature, <www.wilderness.org.au/about/bookaward>. This site lists the annual winners of the organization's Environmental Children's Literature Award, honoring both fiction and nonfiction selections on a variety of levels.

Earth Tales

Traditional stories reveal our link to the natural world and to all the people who have lived on Earth before us

by Michael J. Caduto

Grade levels: 2-5

Subject areas: environmental studies, science, social studies (indigenous peoples), ethics, literature, storytelling, art

Key concepts: interrelationships, change, adaptation, consequences of decisions, Earth stewardship, environmental wisdom of indigenous peoples, living in balance with the natural world

Skills: reading comprehension, decision making, brainstorming, creative writing, riddle solving, illustration, identification of animals, developing personal responsibility toward the natural world, empathizing with wildlife

Location: indoors or outdoors

Time: 10 minutes to read story; activities ranging from 30 minutes to 2.5 hours

From Siberia to the tip of South America, and from Africa to Polynesia, traditional stories grow from the very earth upon which they are first told. Through these tales, the natural world speaks to the people who walk upon it. But stories have wings, too, which loft them upon the winds of our imaginations.

Traditional Earth tales contain the wisdom that countless generations harvested by living close to the land, growing their own food, and making the things they needed with their own hands. In order to live, they had to take care of the soil, the water, the plants, and the animals. As the stories show, people eventually learned that the harm they caused the world around them would one day come knocking on their own door. The care they showed would be returned in kind with food, clean air and water, and materials with which to fashion tools and other necessities. In this way, stories are a kind of medicine, a way of healing our relationship with nature.

In many stories it is clear that traditional cultures believe that all of nature — both the things that move and those that do not — is alive. There is a breath of life in the tree, the hawk, and the long wind that blows across open places and gently bends blades of grass. A spirit lives in the shadow that grows between the hills as the sun sets, in the rocks of the hills themselves, in the moon that rises into a starry sky, in the sweet smell of a flower, and in the joy of a newborn fawn. Over and over in the old tales we read of a common faith in a benevolent, unseen Creator of the wonders that surround us. Like the natural world, stories are sacred and are treated with respect and reverence.

No matter what culture, or cultures, our ancestors come from, traditional stories can help us trace our roots back to their source. We all have ancestral ties to Native peoples who lived close to the earth. Their wisdom lies deep in our memories. One common thread that runs through the stories is the belief that we are a part of nature, and that the community of people and the natural world depends upon a mutual, respectful relationship. Although we cannot help but change our environment as we live in it and use its resources to keep ourselves alive, we can do everything possible to have a positive impact and to nurture the natural world.

Besides entertaining and helping to teach moral lessons, traditional stories help to explain the natural world; they pass on our spiritual beliefs, our artistic traditions, and the particular ways we use language. The wisdom of Earth stories is both a link to our past and a lifeline to the beautiful, healthy Earth we want to leave as a legacy for future generations. The story on the next page, "The Wisdom of Nature," is a retelling of a Swahili story that comes from a part of eastern Africa now known as Kenya, Tanzania, and Zanzibar. The story is accompanied by activities designed for

225

children of ages 5 to 12. These particular activities are oriented to the plants and animals of North America, but can be adapted to suit the home environment of the intended audience.

Activities
Prey, Tell Me

"Every creature does what it must in order to survive," said the baboon in the story (see "The Wisdom of Nature" below). "That is the way of nature." Indeed, each plant and animal has specific *adaptations*, physical (genetic) traits and behaviors that better enable it to survive and reproduce in its particular environment. Among animals, many survival adaptations relate to eating or being eaten. In this activity, students solve riddles that describe the survival adaptations of prey animals by guessing the animals' identities.

Goals: Understand what a survival adaptation is and learn some defenses of certain prey animals.

Materials: Copy of riddles (see pages 227-228), picture of each animal that appears in the riddles.

Procedure:

1. Discuss the meaning of interrelationships and give examples of different kinds of animal relationships. Be sure to include examples of animals that have both positive and negative effects on each other. Ask the children to think of their own examples. For instance, coyotes will harm individual deer by eating fawns. But this also helps to control the number of deer living in an area so they do not overgraze the food supply. This benefits the deer population as well as the other animals that depend on that habitat for their survival.

2. Define and discuss the concept of survival adaptation with the children. Have them call out some examples of offensive adaptations of predators and defensive adaptations of prey animals.

3. Now tell them they are going to hear some riddles that describe some adaptations of animals that are often

The Wisdom of Nature

In the thick brush at the edge of the hill country lived a magnificent snake. Its eyes blazed and the scales that covered its skin were as hard and strong as any shield. Venom flowed from its long, curved fangs. In the moment of its hunger, this huge, powerful snake devoured any wild animal it desired.

One day, the snake sat sunning itself in a small clearing. Being close to the ground, the snake sensed a roar in the distance. Its tongue picked up a strong scent. Upwind, some young hunters were burning the brush to drive the game animals into the open. Crackling flames rushed toward the snake.

As it searched for refuge, the snake slithered out of the low brush and into the open along the border of a farmer's fields. "Please help me hide," asked the snake. "The hunters are coming. They will kill me."

When he saw the snake, the farmer was afraid.

"Do not fear me," the snake called out to the farmer. "I will not harm you."

The kindhearted farmer took pity on the snake, as he did on all animals that were in need of help.

"Quickly," said the farmer as he opened the mouth of a large, empty grain bag, "crawl into this sack. The hunters will never think to look for you here."

As soon as the tip of the snake's tail disappeared into the mouth of the bag, some hunters approached. They

were following the faint trail left by the snake's belly as it slid along the ground.

"Have you seen a large snake come this way?" they asked the farmer.

"No," he replied. "I have been working here all morning and have seen no sign of a snake. You must be reading an old trail."

"Thank you," said the hunters, and they walked on. When they were a safe distance away, the farmer opened the grain bag and whispered, "Come out, the danger has passed."

The snake crept out of the sack, threw its coils around the farmer, and held him fast.

"Let me go!" screamed the farmer. "I have just saved your life!"

"That is true," replied the snake. "But I have not eaten for many days. You will make a good meal."

"Then you will not let me go?" asked the farmer.

"No, I am starving."

"Before you eat me," said the farmer, "you could at least repay me for saving your life."

"That is only fair," said the snake. "I agree. Now what do you desire?"

"Let us have others decide whether you should eat me."

"If that is your wish, so be it," agreed the snake.

continued next page

226

Imagination and Celebration

hunted as prey. The riddles vary from easy to challenging. Have the children guess the answers to these six riddles. Once they are done, show them a picture of each animal, and discuss its adaptations.   The riddles are as follows.

☙ My home is a burrow in the ground. I come out only at night when it is cool and damp and when I am not likely to be seen. Lots of animals, especially early birds, love to eat me, but I can scoot down my burrow quickly if someone tries to grab me, and I am very sensitive to vibrations in the ground. Don't fish around too long for the answers.

(I am a worm.)

☙ I am a great swimmer from the minute I am born. I float almost as well as a cork. If something comes after me I use my webbed feet and tiny wings to skate quickly away over the water. The predators who spot me and try to attack from below see *down* when they look up. You may see me eating plants or fish.

(I am a duckling.)

☙ My long ears, keen hearing, and sensitive nose help me to detect danger from far off. I can make a fast getaway if spotted. Still, I come out from sunset to sunrise with darkness as my cover. I have a habit of twitching my nose. My tail is short and my feet are lucky.

(I am a rabbit.)

☙ I sing my song when summertime is aging and fall is on the way. I don't sing with my voice, though. Some people know I *wing* it. My long antennae help me to sense when danger is around. Still, my kind often become lunch for birds, shrews, and even tiny snakes. I might live under a rock or spend my time in a clump of grass.

(I am a cricket.)

☙ You know me well around your garden. My skin is bumpy and bad to taste. I eat ants and flies with a long,

---

continued from previous page

The snake followed the farmer to the edge of the field where a coconut palm tree had been planted. The tree listened carefully as each of them told his side of the story.

"Well," replied the coconut palm, "I know the nature of human beings. They eat my nuts and drink the sweet milk inside. Some even use my leaves to thatch their roofs. Why should I save a human being? I say the snake should have its meal."

"Let us ask the bee," said the farmer.

"As you wish," replied the snake.

"You must be joking!" replied the bee. "Human beings smoke us out of our homes and steal our honey. They never give us thanks. I have no compassion for the farmer."

"Perhaps the mango tree down by the road will understand my plight," thought the farmer. "Snake, let us go ask the mango to give us its judgment."

"Lead on," replied the snake.

Once it had listened to their stories, the mango tree spoke. "Year after year I stand here as generations of human beings pass by. They cool themselves in the shade of my branches and eat my fruit when they are hungry. Some break off my branches for firewood or to use as the shafts of spears for hunting the wild animals. Not once has a human being thanked me. Farmer, I see no reason why the snake should not eat you."

"How could this be?" exclaimed the farmer. "Why should my life be such a trifle in the eyes of nature?"

At that moment, the farmer spotted a gazelle grazing along the riverbank. To the gazelle the farmer now pleaded his case.

In response to his story, the gazelle told a tale of its own. "I am often the difference between life and death for the human beings. Without my meat, they would starve and perish. Because I am so generous, people take me for granted. Your life, farmer, belongs to the snake."

A baboon was listening from where it sat on the branch of a nearby tree.

"Every creature does what it must in order to survive," said the baboon. "That is the way of nature."

"But what of the snake?" asked the farmer.

"One cannot blame the snake for its hunger," replied the baboon. "Like you, the snake is part of the balance that exists in the world."

A snake is meant to eat its prey,
it catches as it can.
Its food will try to get away,
escape's the way of man.

"What, then, do you have to say about whether or not I should eat the farmer?" asked the snake.

"First, you must show me exactly how it happened," said the baboon. "That sack does not look big enough to hold a snake as magnificent as yourself."

The farmer then opened the bag and the snake crawled in.

"Are you able to close the bag with the snake inside?" asked the baboon.

"Yes," replied the farmer as he drew the cord tight and tied it securely.

"Now, farmer, we will see what you have learned," said the baboon. "Once again, the fate of the snake is in your hands."

Story ©1997 by Michael J. Caduto

sticky tongue. When you pick me up I release the contents of my bladder to startle you into putting me down.

(I am a toad.)

🌀 My skin of scales is a good hint. I am small and quick with a colorful tail. When a predator comes and grabs at the tip, I snap it off like the flick of a whip.

(I am a skink.)

Follow-up: As a follow-up to this activity, have the children create their own adaptation riddles and share them with others!

Coyote's Choice: Adapt and Survive

Adapting is not simply a matter of following a predetermined program of adaptations. Many times, like the human being in the story, the animal that survives is one that can learn from its environment and make the right choices in changing or threatening situations. In this activity, students play a game of choices to see if they are as adaptable as the coyote and able to survive in a changing world.

Goals: To understand that change, both natural and human-made, is a normal part of an animal's experience, and that adapting to change is necessary to survive.

Materials: Copies of "Coyote's Choice: Adapt and Survive"; other materials as needed depending upon the format you use for this activity, such as an exercise for each child to do individually (one copy for each child), or a course that children walk through while making the decisions (index cards, each with one of the numbered situations set up as a separate station).

Procedure:

1. Discuss the adaptability of coyotes, how they have expanded their range in recent years, and the many changes that are constantly occurring to threaten their existence. These changes can be natural, such as floods, fire created by lightning, drought, or food shortages; or they can be caused by human activities such as clear-cutting a forest, damming a river, or setting out traps or poisoned bait. Coyotes are experts at adapting to change, moving to a new habitat when they need to, or sensing and avoiding danger, even if it means turn-

---

Coyote's Choice: Adapt and Survive

1 You are a tiny coyote pup and your mother has gone off to hunt for food. While you wait in the burrow a strange piece of thin wire on the end of a stick is pushed toward you from the door of your den. You see it coming and are afraid of it so you:

(a) cower back against the wall of the burrow to escape.

(b) attack the wire by biting it.

If you chose (a) you survived. If you chose (b) you were snared and taken away by a hunter.

2 You are now old enough to do some hunting on your own. There, up ahead, you see a dead animal that looks as if it is more than big enough for a whole meal. When you get closer you see some strange tracks in the soil and smell an animal you have never smelled before. You are very hungry, but afraid to go closer to the dead animal. After watching for a while and looking for signs of danger you decide to:

(a) eat the meat of the animal.

(b) turn away and search for another meal.

If you chose (a) the meat was a poisoned trap set by a farmer and you are a goner. If you chose (b) you survived.

3 It has not rained for a long time, the plants are dying, and animals are becoming scarce. You are very weak, yet you feel an urge to travel to look for food. You begin to walk away from your burrow but you find it hard to walk. You decide to:

(a) push ahead and look for water and food elsewhere even though it means risking using up your last energy.

(b) return to the burrow and wait for the rain and food to return.

If you chose (a) you survived. If you chose (b) starvation set in and you became too weak to leave your burrow. You did not survive.

4 You go toward a place where people are living because you know there is usually food nearby. When you arrive, the smell of food is strong, yet danger is very near and threatening. As night slowly advances with the setting sun, you decide to:

(a) sneak in and eat as much of the food as you can under the cover of darkness.

(b) turn around and seek food elsewhere.

If you chose (a) you were able to eat safely while protected by the

continued next page

---

ing away from food that looks suspicious when they are hungry. They do not always make the right choice, however, and cannot always adapt successfully. Sometimes they survive; sometimes they do not.

2. Have the children read the story "Coyote's Choice: Adapt and Survive," making the choices along the way that they think a coyote might make. Even if they make the wrong survival choice at a certain point in the story, they are to continue to the end.

3. When all of the children have finished, have them share their choices, adaptations, and experiences. How many of them *honestly* made all of the right choices and survived each threat? Which choices were the most difficult? Which were the easiest?

Variation: This activity can be set up as a challenging series of stations in which the initial situation is described and children must choose one way or another and then turn over a card or lift up a flap to reveal the consequences of their decision. Then they can move on to the next station to test their wits there.

Living In Balance: The Circle of Giving and Receiving

In "The Wisdom of Nature," the bee and the mango tree complain that the human beings take what they need but never give thanks. The gazelle says that its meat keeps the human beings alive, but that the humans take it for granted. Many Native peoples see reciprocity — the Circle of Giving and Receiving — as essential to living in balance with nature.

In this activity, students list of all the gifts they receive from plants and animals, practice giving thanks when receiving each of these gifts, and create a special gift to return the generosity of the plants and animals.

Goals: To understand how numerous and varied are the gifts we receive from plants and animals; to realize that living in balance involves using only what is needed, not being wasteful and giving thanks to complete the circle of giving and receiving.

Materials: Chalkboard, chalk or felt-tipped markers, newsprint, masking tape, pencils, paper, crayons, construction paper, scissors, glue, tape, very large sheet of

---

continued from previous page

darkness. You survived. If you chose (b) your last strength was used in searching for food in another spot. You did not survive.

5 With your strength restored you travel a short distance seeking shelter: a place to sleep and digest your meal. There is a strange burrow above ground up ahead. It is large and the morning sun shines off the strange smooth skin into your eyes. You climb up into it and try walking through the place that looks like the entrance, but you bump into something you cannot see. Finally you find an opening in the skin on the side and walk in, only to find many strange smells meet your nostrils. You sniff a few times and suddenly feel very tired. You decide to:

(a) lie down and sleep here.

(b) move on to look for a safer place.

If you chose (a) you slept in an old abandoned car and made it your temporary shelter. You survived. If you chose (b) you found a large hollow tree to rest in and slept safely all day. You survived.

6 When you wake up the sun is setting and you are hungry again, but not starving as before. You leave your burrow and walk until you come to the edge of the woods. You see a field with some furry animals in it

eating the plants, but you are not sure that it is safe to enter the field or whether those animals are food or not. As you move closer you notice a freshly killed rabbit in front of you. There are strange tracks around it, like the ones you saw near that dead animal with the strange smell some time ago. But this meat smells good as you approach it and your hunger deepens. Then, as you move even closer, you notice something sticking out of the ground near the rabbit. It looks like it has large teeth and is made of the strange skin of that burrow with the smooth shiny skin. You look all around one more time to make sure that none of the dangerous animals who walk on two feet are around, then you:

(a) pounce on the rabbit.

(b) run off into the underbrush, sensing danger.

If you chose (a) you felt a sharp, cold pain climb up your leg from one of your feet. Your foot is in a steel trap and there is no way out. You did not survive. If you chose (b) you survived.

7 If you have successfully survived by making all of the right choices so far, you will now raise a new coyote family. On the way back to your burrow you meet a coyote and decide to take her or him as a mate. Soon, the next generation of coyotes is born and you have pups of your own to feed.

Activity ©1991 by Michael J. Caduto

paper such as brown wrapping paper, pictures or photographs of plants and animals as models for the children's drawings, other materials as needed to complete children's own original projects.

Procedure:

Opening the Circle — Receiving

1. Use the children's ideas and your own thoughts to make a list of the gifts we receive from plants and animals. Brainstorm a list of plants and animals that help to bring the gifts to us. Have the children go through an entire day by saying "Thank you" to a plant or animal, or plants and animals in general, each time one of these gifts is used, eaten, worn, etc. An example is "Thank you honeybee" for honey and beeswax (a common ingredient in lip balm). Encourage the children to be especially careful to use these gifts wisely: to take only what they need and not be wasteful.

Completing the Circle — Giving Back

2. Tell the children that the story "The Wisdom of Nature" reminds us that the plants and animals give us many wonderful gifts, and that living in balance means, in part, to return the gifts we receive by giving something of ourselves back. Ask the children to call out ways they may do this and write them down for all to see. Save them for use later.

3. Have each of the children write a poem or draw a picture to express a feeling of gratitude to the plants and animals. Very young children may need pictures or photographs of the plants and animals to help them visualize the images for their drawings.

4. Create, on a large sheet of paper, an outline of a coconut palm, mango, or other chosen tree, such as an apple tree. Have each child write or place her or his form of "thank you" inside this outline. Pictures may be cut out and glued or taped on. The tree could even be entirely filled with pictures or illustrations to form a collage.

5. Follow up by having the children add other ways of giving thanks to the plants and animals as they think of them. ✒

Michael J. Caduto is a storyteller, educator, ecologist, poet, and musician who lives in Vermont. He the co-author of the best-selling Keepers of the Earth *series of books and resources, and the creator of the accompanying musical recording* All One Earth: Songs for the Generations. *His* Earth Tales from Around the World *received the national Aesop Prize and a Skipping Stones Honor Award. His most recent book is* In the Beginning: The Story of Genesis and Earth Activities for Children *(Paulist Press, 2004).*

"The Wisdom of Nature" and the introductory text are reprinted with permission from *Earth Tales from Around the World*, © 1997 by Michael J. Caduto (Fulcrum Publishing, 1997). The activities, © 1991 by Michael J. Caduto, are adapted with permission from *Keepers of the Animals: Native American Stories and Wildlife Activities for Children* by Michael J. Caduto and Joseph Bruchac (Fulcrum Publishing, 1991). Illustrations by Adelaide Murphy Tyrol were first published in *Earth Tales from Around the World* and are used with the artist's permission. This story and these activities may be copied for individual classroom use only. Written permission from the author is required for any other uses. For information on books, music and programs by Michael Caduto, contact: PEACE, PO Box 1052, Norwich, VT 05055.

Celebrating Earth Week: Elemental Connections

A collection of ideas, activities, and resources for exploring and celebrating our connections to the Earth's elements during Earth Week

by Deanna Fry

Grades levels: K-6

Subject areas: multidisciplinary

Key concepts: identifying, exploring, and connecting with the four natural elements and the spirit of life across the curriculum during Earth Week

Location: outdoors and indoors

Time: 5 days during Earth Week

Photographs by Deanna Fry

 aking real and heartfelt connections to nature is crucial for our survival. It is especially important in this age of virtual reality when so many people — children included — have become estranged from the natural environment. This five-day unit, "Celebrate Earth Week," is a collection of ideas, activities, and resources for recognizing, exploring, honoring, and celebrating our connections to the Earth during Earth Week. The unit offers five daily themes: the four natural elements — water, fire, earth, and air — and the spirit of life. This elemental approach is based on the traditional medicine wheel teachings common to many aboriginal traditions, in which fire, earth, air, and water are recognized and celebrated as foundations of life. Each day, short thematic excursions outdoors give students opportunities to make connections with these elements in nature, while indoor activities invite exploration of the important roles these elements play in our modern world. The themes may be placed in any order. I often arrange them so that "Earth" day falls on Earth Day itself (April 22).

The activities outlined for each theme day should be considered open-ended suggestions to select from and to adapt or extend in any way you like. They are just beginnings, places to start, rather than detailed lesson plans. You may wish to augment some of the activities with additional resources. This thematic approach to Earth Week could be used with one class, one grade level, or the whole school. Consider, perhaps, a giant wall chart of the theme days, with their meanings simply stated and students' work displayed in a prominent place in the school. Daily morning announcements introducing the theme days and concepts are a way for the whole school to recognize Earth Week. In all, simplicity is the key. There is no need to travel far or to be extravagant. We need only open ourselves to the natural world around us and celebrate.

Water (Monday)

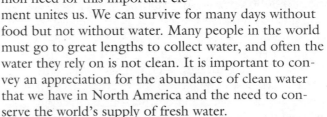

All living organisms use water in one way or another, and our common need for this important element unites us. We can survive for many days without food but not without water. Many people in the world must go to great lengths to collect water, and often the water they rely on is not clean. It is important to convey an appreciation for the abundance of clean water that we have in North America and the need to conserve the world's supply of fresh water.

A simple way to introduce the water theme by taking your class down to the fountain for a drink. Ask your students to think about where the water came from and the route it took to get to the fountain. Back in the classroom, demonstrate how much of the world's water supply is fresh and clean (that is, drinkable):

Materials: water, a small bucket, a 1-liter beaker, a 100-milliliter graduated cylinder, a small dish, and a 10-milliliter eyedropper or a glass stirring rod

Procedure:

1. On a world map or globe, direct students' attention to the amount of water as compared with the amount of land on the Earth (water covers about 75 percent of the Earth's surface).

2. Pour 1 liter (1,000 milliliters) of water into the 1-liter beaker and explain that this amount represents all the world's water.

3. Pour 30 milliliters of water from the 1-liter beaker into the 100-milliliter graduated cylinder, explaining that this represents all the world's fresh water, about 3 percent of the total amount of water on Earth.

4. Tell students that almost 80 percent of Earth's fresh water is frozen in ice caps and glaciers (point these out on a map or globe), and then pour 6 milliliters from the 100-milliliter cylinder into a small dish. Explain that this amount of water represents the non-frozen fresh water and that only about 1.5 milliliters of this is surface water; the rest is underground.

5. Use the eyedropper or glass stirring rod to put a single drop (0.003 milliliters) in the bucket, making sure students are quiet so they can hear the drop hitting the bottom of the bucket. Explain that this represents the fresh, unpolluted water available for use, about 0.00003 percent of the total!

This concrete demonstration[1] is an effective way to stress the value of clean, drinkable water. Go on to tell students that North America has about two-thirds of the world's fresh surface water and show them the Great Lakes on the map or globe. Reveal that North Americans use more water per person than people anywhere else in the world and pay the least for it!

The rapid evaporation of water paintings on the outside wall of the school is a visible demonstration of the water cycle in action.

Allow time for reflection on and discussion of these facts, and for the feelings and ideas they may invoke. Have students do this as a whole class, in small groups, or in pairs. Prompt them with the following questions:

๏ Do we value and appreciate water or do we take it for granted? Do you?

๏ How do we waste water? How do you waste water?

๏ How can we conserve water? How can you conserve water?

๏ How do people in other parts of the world get fresh water? Is it freely available?

๏ Imagine living in a place where fresh water is scarce and people have to carry it a long way. How would having to do that change your habits and your attitude toward water?

๏ Will you change the way you use water from now on?

You may want to have students complete a journal entry or draw or write about what they have just learned. Some teachers have students make a "personal water pledge" in which they outline and agree to perform water conserving behaviors and actions. Creating water collages is also a good follow-up activity. Old *National Geographic* magazines are an excellent source of photographs of water and humans using water around the world.

Switch gears by having students sing any songs they might know about water. Lead younger children in singing a round of "Down by the Bay" or "Listen to the Water" and then have them act out the basic stages of the hydrologic (water) cycle. Begin by having children pretend they are light, fluffy clouds moving across the sky. Tell them to become darker, heavier, and slower moving as they collect more water vapor from the air (condensation). Next they can be the rain falling down to the Earth (precipitation) and collecting in rivers and lakes. Finally, explain that when the sun comes out and shines on the water, they will travel back up to the clouds again (evaporation). Repeat the cycle several times, varying the types of rain (e.g., gentle rain, downpour, thunderstorm). Have children draw their own versions of the water cycle or label and color one you have prepared.

Older children can also study the water cycle. Discuss the various stages, paying attention to the changes of state that occur at each stage, such as the change from liquid to water vapor (evaporation) and the change from gas to liquid (condensation). Have students draw and label their own water cycle diagrams or create a model of the water cycle, either on their own or with a partner. For older students a discussion of watershed principles, including surface runoff, infiltration, ground water, and aquifers, is appropriate. Point out that wetlands operate as natural filters to purify water and that they are disappearing at an alarming rate due to human development. Discuss North Americans' use of potable water for all their water needs (washing, flushing, watering lawns, industry), and then look at the processes we use to purify water. Demonstrations using sand, charcoal, or other materials that function as filters help students see the process at work. Compare the taste of tap water, spring water, and distilled water, vote for a favorite, and graph the results.

Students of all ages can go outdoors for a water walk to a nearby creek, stream, lake, or puddle. Help students place this body of water in the larger context of the water cycle discussed earlier. Today is your lucky day if it happens to be raining! If a water walk is not suitable, take some clean paint brushes and a few buckets of tap water outside. Use them to paint masterpieces on the school wall and observe the water evaporate from its surface. Experiment with waterpainting in both sun and shade and compare rates of evaporation.

Finally, play some relaxing water music, such as recordings of waves, waterfalls, rain, or a babbling brook. Have students relax, close their eyes, and think of a special or fun time they had near water, perhaps at a cottage, in a pool, or on a beach. Distribute paper and have students draw to the music or share their stories orally before recording them in written, pictorial, or poetic form. An excellent finale is to create a class water book or decorate a bulletin board or hallway with the water stories, poems, and illustrations.

Variations: There are many avenues for exploring water with your class. Other topics that could be used as entry points are:

- the role of water in weather and climate

- the three states of water: solid, liquid, and gas

- aquatic life in salt and fresh water

- economic and environmental issues related to fishing and water sports

- human uses of water, such as for drinking, transportation, recreation, industry, and hydroelectric power

Fire (Tuesday)

The sun and the energy it provides are essential to life on the planet. "Fire" energy from the sun is our basic fuel. It is at the root of the food chain and is the initial source of all our energy resources.

Begin by reading a story, legend, or myth about how the sun came to be, or about the cycle of day and night or the seasons. Some examples might be the Greek myth of Demeter and Persephone, or stories such as "How Spider Stole the Sun" (Caduto and Brushac, *Keepers of the Earth*) and "Why Birds Sing in the Morning" (Terry Jones, *Fairy Tales*). Discuss the importance of sunshine in our lives. Brainstorm ideas for new and different versions of creation stories that explain the sun or day and night, and have students make up their own creation stories. Younger students could illustrate and tell or act out their stories informally, while older students could write and publish their stories. Creating an illustrated class collection of sun stories is an enjoyable activity.

Demonstrate the scientific explanation for day and night and the seasons by having one student hold a flashlight (sun) and having another student slowly rotate a ball (Earth) between his or her two hands while walking in a circle (orbit) around the sun. Encourage older students to compare the scientific explanation with the mythological ones.

Songs or other works of art related to the sun are age-old and seem to come quite naturally to children. To begin, primary students could sing "You Are My Sunshine" or Raffi's "Mr. Sun," while older students could be introduced to the Beatles by listening to "Here Comes the Sun." Invite all students to create their own artistic interpretations of the sun. Provide a wide variety of materials, such as paint, paper, yarn, fabric scraps, and wallpaper. It is very effective to display all the suns together as a "quilt" on a bulletin board or hallway wall.

Introduce the theme of fire in science class with a study of ecosystems and the food chain. Begin by showing students an orange and then sharing orange sections or slices (other fruits could be used but do not represent the sun as concretely as an orange does). Tell students that they are eating energy from the sun, and discuss how this is true: the sun's energy is made into food for the plant through photosynthesis and stored in the fruit for the purpose of self-propagation. People then pick the fruit and eat it, digesting it and using it as energy for their own growth and activity. This leads naturally to the concept of food chains and food webs in ecosystems: the sun's energy enables plants to grow, herbivores eat plants, carnivores eat herbivores, and so on. Examine a local food chain to see this energy flow at work.

Take your students outdoors to make a personal connection with the concept of food chains. Go for a walk around your school community to identify various life forms and discuss how they depend on the sun and one another. (Although the walk may be only on pavement and patches of dirt, and you may see only weeds, ants, birds, and snack leftovers from recess, the walk will still create a sense of personal relevance.) As a follow-up to your walk, students can create a pictorial presentation of a local food chain. This can vary from a drawing of what they just saw to researching information to map out a food chain.

Variations: Many other approaches to the theme of fire may be found in topics related to the role of fire and the use of energy in human society. Some examples are:

๑ fire for warmth/cooking/survival: stories of how humans got fire in the first place, the necessity of fire for human survival, life without modern energy technology (e.g., in developing countries or during pioneer days in pre-industrial North America); solar cooking experiments

๑ the sun as the basis of the energy chain: the role of the sun in producing fuels such as wood and fossil fuels for fire/energy production; nonrenewable energy sources and their environmental impact (e.g., air pollution, greenhouse effect); renewable energy and conservation

Earth (Wednesday)

The earth element is perhaps the easiest for students to connect with because it surrounds us in such a concrete way. We see, smell, and feel it, and whether indoors or out, natural or human-made, everything we come into contact with is of the Earth.

Begin Earth Day with a creation story that explains how the Earth came to be. Such stories, told all over the world, both shape and reflect a culture's values, attitudes, and relationship to nature, often suggesting the stewardship role to be played by humans. Read or tell the creation story of North American aboriginal peoples "The Earth on Turtle's Back," or "Turtle Island" as it is sometimes known (Caduto and Bruchac's *Keepers of the Earth* presents one variation of this story). The many animal roles and the repetitive pattern of this story make it ideal for dramatic re-enactment, and primary students love to make masks and costumes to use in the play. Older students may read creation myths from different cultures to compare and

contrast their explanations of nature and the guidelines they provide for human conduct. Explore with older students the scientific theories of how the Earth came to be.

Bring the Earth focus to the present by going outdoors to explore the school and neighborhood terrain. Have students notice what covers the ground and what grows out of it. Try to find a place where the cycle of birth, growth, death, and decomposition is apparent. This may be a wooded area that has rotting logs or patches of last year's leaves on the ground. Point out how your chosen example illustrates the circle of life: for example, seed, sapling, mature tree, dead tree, fallen trunk, decaying log, soil. Explain that animal remains also go through the process of decomposition and that this is how death renews life in nature. Point out the various components of the soil — humus from decomposed plant material, and stones, pebbles, and sand, the results of rock erosion. You may want to have students carefully collect fallen treasures for an art lesson or pick up a rock to use later for the "Dancing Rock Song." Back in the classroom have students follow up these activities by writing about or drawing, labeling, and coloring a picture showing the cycle of birth, growth, death, and decomposition.

Another important Earth topic is the use of natural resources by humans. Have younger students list or draw some everyday items and then discuss where their components came from (e.g., paper from trees, wool from animals) and point out the basic steps in their manufacture. Older students can look in more detail at the specific natural resources used, as well as the energy consumed at various stages in the production process. Transportation, packaging, and waste management can also be explored in relation to their impact on the Earth. Encourage students to compare their material standard of living with that of children from other parts of the world. (*National Geographic* magazines are useful resources again here.)

Planting seeds is a terrific way to extend this theme and make a lasting impression on students. Chart or keep a log of plant growth over time, or experiment with different seeds or soil types. April is a great time for planting, and the seedlings started in the classroom on Earth Day can be transplanted to a school garden or taken home later in the season.

End the day with the "Dancing Rock Song," a favorite with children of all ages (see sidebar).

Variations: Other approaches to the Earth theme could be made through:

๑ exploring the geological and human history of the local landscape: soil and rock composition, the formation of landforms, archeological finds, the history of land use and farming techniques

234

- studying native plants and animals of your region
- considering the negative effects of some human activities on the Earth (e.g., soil and groundwater contamination from industrial processes, mining, and landfills; habitat loss due to development), and ways to reduce our impact on the Earth (e.g., starting a recycling or composting program, creating habitat for wildlife)

Air (Thursday)

Air is somewhat of a mystery for students because it is far less concrete than the other elements. Made up of invisible gases, air is elusive even though it surrounds us. To introduce the theme of air to younger children, have them sing this simple song to the tune of "Frère Jacques":

> *You can't see it, you can't see it,*
> *But it's there, everywhere.*
> *It fills up balloons,*
> *It takes up space,*
> *It is air, it is air.*
>
> *You can't see it, you can't see it,*
> *But it's there, everywhere*
> *It makes things move,*
> *When it blows*
> *It is air, it is air.[2]*

New examples of what air is like and what it does can be substituted for the third and fourth lines as the song

The Dancing Rock Song

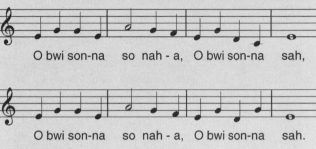

O bwi son-na   so nah - a, O bwi son-na   sah,

O bwi son-na   so nah - a, O bwi son-na   sah.

Instructions:
Ask the students to select a medium-sized rock and sit in a circle on the ground with their rocks in front of them. Teach the song, and then add a clap of the hands on the "O" in the phrase "O bwi sonna." Then have the singers tap the ground on the "O" and their left knee on the syllables "so" and "sah." Then have them tap the ground in front of them on the "O" and the ground in front of their neighbor to the left on "so" and "sah." Finally, have students pick up the rock in front of them on "O" and set it down in front of their neighbor to the left on the syllables "so" and "sah." The rocks will dance around the circle.

is repeated. To introduce the topic of air to older students, you could use the classic riddle "What is everywhere, yet nowhere to be seen?" Have them make up and exchange their own riddles about air.

Investigate air as a medium of transport. Leaves, insects, pollen, seeds, airplanes, birds, and even human voices travel through the air. Have students make scrap-paper airplanes, kites, grocery bag parachutes, or pipe cleaner bubble-blowing wands. Take everything and everyone outside (or on rainy days to a large indoor space) and allow time for flying and blowing bubbles. Encourage students to notice how air moves other things when it blows as wind.

Circumstances permitting, have students sit or lie back to watch clouds or treetops move with the air currents, and to feel the wind playing on their own skin. Remind them that air is as much a part of our inner world as it is of our outer world, that air is at work within them every moment of their lives. Have them take long, deep breaths of fresh air. Explain how all animals and plants are connected through the oxygen/carbon dioxide cycle: animals, including humans, inhale oxygen and exhale carbon dioxide, while plants take in carbon dioxide and release oxygen. Even young children are fascinated by this example of interdependence in nature if it is explained in simple terms, such as "Animals breathe in what plants breathe out and plants breathe in what animals breathe out."

Back indoors, older students might undertake a more in-depth study of science topics such as local and global wind currents, the oxygen/carbon dioxide cycle, air as a transportation medium, or the role of wind in weather and climate. Younger students might draw pictures of or discuss things that travel in air. All students could write stories, poems, songs, or raps about air and present them either individually, with a partner, or as a small group. Follow up with a story about the wind, such as *Millicent and the Wind* (Robert Munsch) or "The Wind Ghost" (Terry Jones, *Fairy Tales*).

End the day by playing soft, relaxing music and leading students in relaxation or breathing exercises so that they can feel the air flowing inside them. Draw attention to the calming effect of deep breathing, and encourage children to breathe deeply whenever they think of it. Awareness of one's breath promotes self-knowledge and self-control and helps to bring home the message that air is part of us.

Variations: Other approaches to the theme of air could include explorations of:

⚭ air in relation to weather (atmospheric pressure, the jet stream, tornados and hurricanes)

⚭ human uses of air (e.g., transportation, pneumatics, music, wind power) and the impact of some of these uses (e.g., air pollution)

Spirit of Life (Friday)

Defining and getting in touch with the spirit of life can also be challenging and elusive. Like air, the spirit of life is invisible. It is something one feels deep inside. Think of a time when you were out in nature and saw something that made you stop dead in your tracks, spellbound by the force of its uniqueness, strength, or beauty. This is an experience of the spirit of life, when part of you connects with and recognizes a similar part of someone or something else, whether it be a chickadee landing on your hand for a seed or a mountain glimpsed for the first time.

Begin celebrating this final theme by having students sit together in a large circle knee to knee. Explain that the focus for this last theme day, the spirit of life, is not so much something you think about with your brain as it is something you feel in your heart. Give examples of times when people might feel a special connection with nature, such as when they are watching a beautiful sunset, encountering a wild animal up close, seeing the morning mist rising in a field, noticing the frost patterns on an icy window, jumping into cold water on a hot summer's day, smelling the fresh air, finding a special rock on the beach, or even loving a family pet. Encourage students to think about and remember their own experiences of feeling the spirit of life. Conduct a "community circle" in which students relate their experiences as they pass a talking stick or other item from person to person, each saying, "I felt the spirit of life when ...."[3] Once everyone has spoken, ask students whether they have any questions for one another. Once they have asked and answered the questions, have students consider and discuss what was similar about all the responses during the community circle. Then ask students to consider what was different. Follow up the community circle with a drama activity in which individuals or small groups re-enact in mime or tableau one of the experiences shared earlier while the rest of the class guesses what is being portrayed. Drawing or writing about personal experiences of the spirit of life is another good follow-up activity.

End the lesson with a quiet time during which students sit or lie comfortably with the lights dimmed and soft relaxation music playing. Encourage them to breathe deeply and relax their entire bodies, using gentle reminders and positive reinforcement every few moments. Ask these questions, pausing between each one, to extend the exercise into a creative visualization:

Imagine you are in a beautiful, natural place right now. What is it like? What is the land like — flat, hilly, mountainous? How does the air feel — is it hot or cold, dry or damp? What colors do you see there? What sounds do you hear — the wind blowing, water flowing? Are you alone? Are there animals, trees, plants, or flowers? How does it feel to be there?

Allow time for students to explore the inner world they have created. Then slowly guide them back to their immediate surroundings by having them wiggle their fingers and toes, hands and feet, arms and legs, and, finally, stretch their entire bodies. Depending on how the session went, you may want to give students time to express their visions orally or through drawing or writing.

Investigating air as a medium of transportation.

Make the last outdoor excursion a celebration of all that your students have learned during the week. Point out the interconnectedness of water, fire, earth, and air: all living things on the planet are united in their need for these elements. Share highlights of the week and reinforce the elemental nature of water, fire, earth, and air; all these components are necessary for life to exist on Earth. Encourage students to use all their senses and to look high and low as well as at eye level while they are walking. Have them notice and appreciate whatever nature provides in your surroundings. Breathe deeply, and remind students that we breathe the same air expired by plants and exhaled by animals. Hug a tree, watch the clouds, count some birds or ants, smell the grass and the soil beneath it. Take a micro-walk by kneeling down and following a meter-long piece of string finger by finger, perhaps with a magnifying glass. Take out a piece of white fabric about one meter square, scoop some dirt or leaves onto the middle, and spread them out. Have students observe closely to see the tiny organisms that begin to move about. Use your imagination on this final walk outside, and let the spirit of life move you and your students!

Back indoors, conclude by brainstorming or webbing all the life forms noticed on the walk or by having students express their experience of the spirit of life through creative dance, poetry, songs, or story writing.

Finally, have students consider the roles that water, fire, earth, and air play in life on this planet. Allow time for students to reflect on all that they have explored and discovered during their celebration of Earth Week. Provide chart paper, markers, and pencil crayons to partners or small groups and have students brainstorm or create a mind map of their week of experiences and learning. End with one final community circle in which students share what they feel thankful for. Remind them of how important nature is and how important it is for us to make real and heartfelt connections with the natural world around us. Urge your students to continue to make these important connections to nature for the rest of the year — and for the rest of their lives. ↵

Deanna Fry teaches Grade 5 and directs the Lakeside Public School Green Group in Ajax, Ontario. She also works as an environmental education consultant through her business, Elemental Connections.

Notes

1 This demonstration of the distribution of water is adapted from the activity "A Drop in the Bucket" in Alan S. Kesselheim et al, *WOW! The Wonders of Wetlands,* Environmental Concern and The Watercourse, 1995, pp. 158-9.

2 From Gail Bittinger and Jean Warren, *Environmental Songbook,* Warren Publishing, 1990.

3 This activity is adapted from Jeanne Gibbs, *Tribes: A New Way of Learning and Being Together,* Center Source Publishing, 1987.

Resources

Earth Week resources

Bittinger, Gail, and Jean Warren. *Environmental Songbook.* Warren Publishing, 1990.

Caduto, Michael J., and Joseph Bruchac. *Keepers of the Earth.* Fifth House Publishers, 1989.

Horn, Gabriel (White Deer of Autumn). *Ceremony — In the Circle of Life.* Beyond Words Publishing, 1991.

Jones, Terry. *Fairy Tales.* Pavilion Books, 1991.

Kiil, Susan. *My Earth Book.* EB Publications, 1990.

Mything Links — The Four Elements <www.mythinglinks.org/ct~FourElements.html>.

Sheehan, Kathryn, and Mary Waidner. *Earth Child — Games, Stories, Activities, Experiments and Ideas about Living Lightly on Planet Earth,* Council Oak Books, 1994.

Air theme

Munsch, Robert. *Millicent and the Wind.* Annick Press, 1989.

Soutter-Perrot, Andrienne. *Air.* American Education Publishing, 1993.

Earth theme

Baylor, Byrd. *Everybody Needs a Rock.* Charles Scribner's Sons, 1974.

Soutter-Perrot, Andrienne. *The Earth.* American Education Publishing, 1993.

Fire theme

Baylor, Byrd. *The Way to Start a Day.* Charles Scribner's Sons, 1978.

Soutter-Perrot, Andrienne. *Fire.* American Education Publishing, 1993.

Spirit of Life theme

Caduto, Michael J., and Joseph Bruchac. *Keepers of the Animals,* Fifth House Publishers, 1991.

Caduto, Michael J., and Joseph Bruchac. *Keepers of Life,* Fifth House Publishers, 1994.

Gibbs, Jeanne. *Tribes,* Centre Source Publishing, 1987.

Glew, Frank. *That Chickadee Feeling.* Pmara Kutata Enterprises, 2001.

Morgan, Allen. *Brendon and the Wolves.* Oasis Press, 1991.

Silverstein, Shel. *The Giving Tree.* Harper & Row, 1964.

Water theme

Kesselheim, Alan S., et al. *WOW! Wonders of Wetlands.* Environmental Concern and The Watercourse, 1995.

Soutter-Perrot, Adrienne. *Water.* American Education Publishing, 1993.

Wick, Walter. *A Drop of Water — A Book of Science and Wonder.* Scholastic, 1997.

Index

A

Aboriginal stories, 225-230
Adaptation, 36, 39-40, 44-45, 53-55, 99-100, 226-229
Adopt-a-tree, 48, 76
Air and air quality, 130-135, 235-236
Animals, as classroom pets, 101-107
Aquatic organisms, observing, 43-45
Art
  playground eco-map, 159-163
  realistic nature drawing, 56-60
  creative journal activities, 67-69
Audit, trash, 122-125

B

Biodegradability, 10-11, 148-150
Biodiversity, 40
Bird studies, 18, 54
Blackstone River Monument, 169-171
Book lists, environmental literature, 8, 220-221
Bullying prevention, 101, 102, 182-183
Butterflies, monarch, 87-95

C

Cake, World, 189-193
Camouflage, 55
Campout, Grade 1, 49-52
Canal technology, 169
Carrying capacity, 119-120
Cash crops, 192, 208
Chickadee huddle, 54
Children's environmental literature, 8, 218-224

Citizenship
  democratic, 20-24
  environmental, 4-8, 20-24
  global, 186-188, 196-200, 201-205, 206-212
Classification, 35, 91
Classroom pets, 101-107
Coin walk, 128-129
Community studies
  eco-mapping, 159-163
  one-square-kilometer study, 61-65
  Questing, 152-158
Competition in nature, 100
Composting, 10-11
Computers, use in projects, 96-98
Concept mapping, 64, 120
Conflict resolution, 21, 181-184
Conservation, 79, 136-140, 145-147
Cookie Game, The, 202-204
Cooking, 189
Cooperative Loops (activity), 194-195
Coyote's Choice: Adapt and Survive (story), 228-229
Create a Pond Creature (activity), 44
Creative
  journals, 66-70
  visualization, 214-217
Cycles, see Life cycles

D

Dancing Rock Song, 235
Decomposition, 10-11
Deforestation, 83
Democratic education, 20-24
Development education, 189-193, 201-205, 206-212

Distribution of species, 146
Drama, read-aloud, 108-114
Drawing, 56-60, 67-69

E

Early childhood, 2-3
Earth Week, 231-237
Earthworms, drawing and sculpting, 57-60
Eco-count (community inventory), 159-160
Ecolacy, 189
Ecosystem studies
  forests, 74-80
  ponds, 42-45
  rainforests, 81-86
Endangered species, 118, 126-129
Energy (see also Food chains)
  budgets, 208-209
  distribution of, 40-41
  "Fire" theme, 233-234
Environment club, 179-180
Environmental citizenship, 4-8, 20-24
Environmental literacy
  definition of, 29
  fostering in young children, 4-8
  schoolwide programming for, 25-32
Environmental literature, 8, 218-224
Environmental monitoring
  monarch butterflies, 95
  on-line projects, 96-98
Environmental stewardship, 6-7
Environmental and Outdoor Education Model, 26
Erosion, 83, 143, 207-208
Evaluating journals, 70, 71-72
Exponential growth, 120-121